Lecture Notes in Computer S

Edited by G. Goos, J. Hartmanis and J. va.

Advisory Board: W. Brauer   D. Gries   J. Stoer

Springer
*Berlin
Heidelberg
New York
Barcelona
Budapest
Hong Kong
London
Milan
Paris
Santa Clara
Singapore
Tokyo*

A. Ferreira   J. Rolim
Y. Saad   T. Yang   (Eds.)

Parallel Algorithms for Irregularly Structured Problems

Third International Workshop
IRREGULAR '96
Santa Barbara, CA, USA, August 19-21, 1996
Proceedings

 Springer

Series Editors

Gerhard Goos, Karlsruhe University, Germany

Juris Hartmanis, Cornell University, NY, USA

Jan van Leeuwen, Utrecht University, The Netherlands

Volume Editors

Afonso Ferreira
CNRS - École Normale Supérieure de Lyon
46 Allée d'Italie, F-69364 Lyon Cedex 07, France

José Rolim
Centre Universitaire d'Informatique, Université de Genève
24, Rue General Dufour, CH-1211 Genève 4, Switzerland

Yousef Saad
Department of Computer Science, University of Minnesota
200 Union Street, Minneapolis, MN 55455-0159, USA

Tao Yang
Department of Computer Science, University of California
Santa Barbara, CA 93106, USA

Cataloging-in-Publication data applied for

Die Deutsche Bibliothek - CIP-Einheitsaufnahme

Parallel algorithms for irregularly structured problems : third
international workshop, IRREGULAR '96, Santa Barbara, CA,
USA, August 19 - 21, 1996 ; proceedings / A. Ferreira ... (ed.). -
Berlin ; Heidelberg ; New York ; Barcelona ; Budapest ; Hong
Kong ; London ; Milan ; Paris ; Santa Clara ; Singapore ;
Tokyo : Springer, 1996
  (Lecture notes in computer science ; Vol. 1117)
  ISBN 3-540-61549-0
NE: Ferreira, Alfonso [Hrsg.]; GT

CR Subject Classification (1991): F.1.2, D.1.3, C.1.2, B.2.6, D.4, G.1-2

ISSN 0302-9743
ISBN 3-540-61549-0 Springer-Verlag Berlin Heidelberg New York

© Springer-Verlag Berlin Heidelberg 1996
Printed in Germany

Typesetting: Camera-ready by author
SPIN 10513411   06/3142 – 5 4 3 2 1 0   Printed on acid-free paper

Foreword

The International Workshop on Parallel Algorithms for Irregularly Structured Problems *Irregular '96* is an annual workshop addressing issues related to deriving efficient parallel solutions for irregularly structured problems, with particular emphasis on the inter-cooperation between theoreticians and practitioners of the field. Irregular'96 takes place in Santa Barbara from August 19 to 21, 1996 , and is the third in this series of *Irregular* workshops. Previous workshops were held in Lyon (1995) and in Geneva (1994).

The scientific program of Irregular '96 consists of seven sessions, namely, Sparse Matrix Problems, Partitioning and Domain Decomposition, Irregular Applications (I and II), Communication and Synchronization, System Support, Mapping and Load Balancing. The number of papers submitted was 51. Only 28 were selected. This volume contains the selected papers plus papers by invited speakers. All papers published in the workshop proceedings were selected by the program committee on the basis of referee reports. Each paper was reviewed by at least three referees who judged the papers for originality, quality, and consistency with the themes of the conference.

We would like to thank all of the authors who responded to the call for papers, all of the referees, our invited speakers: T. Hagerup, H. Simon, R. Schreiber, T. Smith, K. Yelick, and the members of the program committee:

A. Ferreira, general co-chair, ENS Lyon
J. Rolim, general co-chair, University of Geneva
Y. Saad, program committee chair, U. of Minnesota
T. Yang, local chair, UC Santa Barbara
P. Banerjee, U. of Illinois
V. Barbosa, U. of Rio de Janeiro
R. Cypher, Johns Hopkins U.
J. Fitch, U. of Bath
T. Leighton, MIT
J. van Leeuwen, U. of Utrecht
E. Mayr, U. of Munich
R. Meyer, U. of Wisconsin
Y. Notay, U. of Brussels
V. Prasanna, USC, Los Angeles
Y. Robert, ENS Lyon
S. Sahni, U. of Florida
P. Widmayer, ETH Zurich

We also gratefully ackowledge support from the European Association for Theoretical Computer Science and from the Special Interest Group "Irregular" of the International Federation of Information Processing (IFIP). Finally, we would like to thank the local arrangement committee members: Sally Vito, Daniel Andresen and Cong Fu.

June 1996   Afonso Ferreira, José Rolim, Yousef Saad, and Tao Yang

Contents

Invited Talk

Allocating Independent Tasks to Parallel Processors: 1
An Experimental Study
T. Hagerup

Sparse Matrix Problems

Parallel Implementation of an Adaptive Scheme   35
for 3D Unstructured Grids on the SP2
L. Oliker, R. Biswas, R.C. Strawn

Solution of Large, Sparse, Irregular Systems   49
on a Massively Parallel Computer
W. Dearholt, S. Castillo, G. Hennigan

Parallel Implementation of a Sparse Approximate   63
Inverse Preconditioner
V. Deshpande, M.J. Grote, P. Messmer, W. Sawyer

Decomposing Irregularly Sparse Matrices   75
for Parallel Matrix-Vector Multiplication
Ü.V. Çatalyürek, C. Aykanat

Invited Talk

Dynamic Spectral Partitioning   87
H.D. Simon and *A. Sohn*

Partitioning and Domain Decomposition

Fast Distributed Genetic Algorithms for Partitioning Uniform Grids 89
I.T. Christou, R.R. Meyer

Towards Efficient Unstructured Multigrid Preprocessing   105
S.E. Dorward, L.R. Matheson, R.E. Tarjan

Domain Decomposition for Particle Methods on the Sphere   119
Ö. Eğeciouğlu, A. Srinivasan

Coordination of Distributed/Parallel Multiple-grid   131
Domain Decomposition
C.T.H. Everaars, F. Arbab

Invited Talk
Systems Support for Irregular Parallel Applications   145
K. Yelick

Irregular Applications I
Distributed Object Oriented Data Structures   147
and Algorithms for VLSI CAD
J.A. Chandy, S. Parkes, P. Banerjee

Parallel Progressive Radiosity with Adaptive Meshing   159
Y. Yu, O.H. Ibarra, T. Yang

Lineal Feature Extraction by Parallel Stick Growing   171
G.C. Hunt, R.C. Nelson

A Simple Parallel Algorithm for the   183
Single-Source Shortest Path Problem
on Planar Digraphs
J.L. Träff, C.D. Zaroliagis

A Regular VLSI Array for an Irregular Algorithm   195
F. de Dinechin, D.K. Wilde, S. Rajopadhye, R. Andonov

Invited Talk
Digital Libraries and Spatial Information Processing   201
T.R. Smith

Communication and Synchronization
Flexible Communication Mechanisms   203
for Dynamic Structured Applications
S.J. Fink, S.B.Baden, S.R. Kohn

Multi-Message Multicasting   217
T.F. Gonzalez

Synchronization as a Strategy for Designing   229
Efficient Parallel Algorithms
C.G. Diderich, M. Gengler

Systems Support
Supporting Dynamic Data and Processor Repartitioning   237
for Irregular Applications
J.E. Moreira, K. Eswar, R.B. Konuru, V.K. Naik

Simple *Quantitative* Experiments with a Sparse Compiler 249
A.J.C. Bik, H.A.G. Wijshoff

Using Algorithmic Skeletons with Dynamic Data Structures 263
G.H. Botorog, H. Kuchen

An Interface Design for General Parallel Branch-and-Bound Algorithms 277
Y. Shinano, M. Higaki, R. Hirabayashi

Invited Talk
Support for Irregular Computation in High Performance Fortran 285
R. Schreiber

Mapping and Load Balancing
Efficient Dynamic Embedding of Arbitrary Binary Trees into Hypercubes 287
V. Heun, E.W. Mayr

Practical Dynamic Load Balancing for Irregular Problems 299
J. Watts, M. Rieffel, S. Taylor

The Module Allocation Problem: An Average Case Analysis 307
M. Lamari, W.F. de la Vega

Dynamically Adapting the Degree 313
of Parallelism with Reflexive Programs
N.H. Reimer, S.U. Hänssgen, W.F. Tichy

On the Complexity of the Generalized Block Distribution 319
M. Grigni, F. Manne

Irregular Applications II
Adaptive Load Balancing of Irregular Applications 327
A Case Study: IDA* Applied to the 15-Puzzle Problem
N. Melab, N. Devesa, M.P. Lecouffe, B. Toursel

Manufacturing Progressive Addition Lenses 339
Using Distributed Parallel Processing
J.M. Cela, J.C. Dürsteler, J. Labarta

The Parallel Complexity of Randomized Fractals 351
R. Greenlaw, J. Machta

Author Index 357

Allocating Independent Tasks to Parallel Processors: An Experimental Study

Torben Hagerup

Max-Planck-Institut für Informatik, D–66123 Saarbrücken, Germany

Abstract. We study a scheduling or allocation problem with the following characteristics: The goal is to execute a number of unspecified tasks on a parallel machine in any order and as quickly as possible. The tasks are maintained by a central monitor that will hand out batches of a variable number of tasks to requesting processors. A processor works on the batch assigned to it until it has completed all tasks in the batch, at which point it returns to the monitor for another batch. The time needed to execute a task is assumed to be a random variable with known mean and variance, and the execution times of distinct tasks are assumed to be independent. Moreover, each time a processor obtains a new batch from the monitor, it suffers a fixed delay. The challenge is to allocate batches to processors in such a way as to achieve a small expected overall finishing time. We introduce a new allocation strategy, the Bold strategy, and show that it outperforms other strategies suggested in the literature in a number of simulations.

1 Introduction

Certain computational problems can be decomposed into a large number of tasks that can be executed in any order. As a simple example, the computation of the product of two $n \times n$ matrices can be decomposed into n^2 tasks, each of which computes one element of the product matrix. Further examples are furnished by other matrix computations such as each stage of Gaussian elimination and the numerical evaluation of (possibly multidimensional) integrals.

Computational problems of this kind are, of course, prime candidates for execution on parallel systems, since different tasks can be executed in parallel on different processors. For some problems of interest and on some parallel architectures, care must be taken to ensure that the computation is not slowed down to an unacceptable degree by memory contention between tasks accessing the same global variables. Here we will assume that memory-contention problems do not arise for the application at hand or can be taken care of satisfactorily, so that the tasks can be viewed as independent of each other.

Given an instance of a computational problem with the properties described above and a parallel machine with a certain number of processors, we would like to solve the instance as quickly as possible with the available processors. If, by convention, we say that the computation starts at time 0, this means that we want to minimize the *overall finishing time* or *makespan* of the computation, i.e., the finishing time of the last task to complete. If the execution time of every task on every processor is the same, this is easy to do: Simply divide the tasks as evenly as possible among the processors. We will assume that the available processors all have the same performance characteristics, a reasonable assumption for most true parallel machines, as opposed to clusters of workstations and the like. On the other hand, it is often not true that different tasks have the same execution time. There are two types of reasons for this. First, there may be *algorithmic variance*, different tasks carrying out different sequences of instructions. If the overall problem is the evaluation of the integral of some function f and a task is the evaluation of the integral of f over a small region, e.g., a task associated with a region in which f changes rapidly may take longer than a task associated with a region in which f is nearly constant. Second, even if there is no algorithmic variance, as perhaps in the matrix-multiplication example (still, the matrix could be sparse, and special provisions could have been made for avoiding multiplication by zero), there will still be *system-induced variance* caused by such factors as cache misses, varying memory latencies, clock interrupts, other processes in the system, and operating-system interference. Following previous authors (Kruskal and Weiss, 1985; Hummel, Schonberg, and Flynn, 1992; Flynn and Hummel, 1992), we model task execution times as independent, identically distributed random variables. This is not meant to imply that execution times are truly random or that tasks are necessarily all alike, but merely that it is too difficult or computationally expensive to figure out the execution time of a given task ahead of time, so that the probabilistic distribution of task execution times represents our best a priori knowledge.

When task execution times are random variables, the even division of the tasks among the processors mentioned above is no longer obviously optimal, since it may cause many processors to remain idle for a long time, waiting for the last processor to finish. A better approach might be not to assign all tasks to processors initially, but to keep some unassigned tasks around and assign these later to processors that finish early. This, however, takes us from *static scheduling*, performed before the computation proper (typically by a compiler), to *dynamic scheduling*, which is carried out, at least in part, at run-time, concurrently with the execution of the tasks. Dynamic scheduling is associated with an overhead, time spent accessing a pool of unassigned tasks and computing how many of these to assign. Again following previous authors, we will assume that a processor simply incurs a fixed delay each time it obtains a new batch of tasks; in particular, the delay is independent of the number of tasks involved and of whether other processors are simultaneously engaged in the activity of obtaining new batches. This assumption is probably not realistic. The same reasons that make task execution times variable would make allocation delays variable, and concurrent accesses to the pool of unassigned tasks would tend to slow down each other. On the other hand, it seems reasonable to expect that modeling the delay as a suitable random variable would have only a small effect on our findings, and Kruskal and Weiss (1985) and Flynn and Hummel (1992) argue the existence of "pool" data structures that allow accesses to proceed concurrently. At any rate, we will stick with the assumption of a fixed delay in order to keep our model simple and to enable a direct comparison with previous studies.

How to allocate batches to processors so as to achieve a small makespan is the subject of the present paper. In a sense, the problem is easy: As pointed out by Kruskal and Weiss (1985), mild assumptions on the distribution of task execution times imply that even very simple-minded allocation strategies achieve an expected makespan bounded by $1 + \epsilon$ times the optimal expected makespan, for any desired constant $\epsilon > 0$, provided that the number n of tasks is sufficiently large. Still, following the paper by Kruskal and Weiss, the problem has been the focus of considerable research interest, maybe because n is not always "sufficiently large", maybe because one would like to achieve a processor utilization better even than $1 - \epsilon$. Therefore we strive to minimize the wasted time, even if it is only a small fraction of the useful computation time. There is a vast literature on scheduling problems. However, as pointed out by Polychronopoulos and Kuck (1987), this literature does not appear to address our present concerns, because the overhead and/or variability in task execution times are not taken into account (instead tasks are assumed to have different execution times, release times, deadlines, etc.).

Section 2 describes a number of previous strategies for the allocation of batches. In general, there is a tradeoff between simplicity and performance. Many of the earlier strategies are extremely simple and can be realized with just a few machine instructions. Such strategies may not perform very well, in the sense of letting the processors finish nearly simultaneously after processing a small number of batches, but at least they will not introduce any large overhead. On the other hand, there are strategies, such as the Factoring strategy, that involve rather complicated formulas with significant evaluation time. The new Bold strategy, introduced in Sect. 3, goes one step further in this direction. Computing the next batch size, while taking constant time, is even more time-consuming than for the Factoring strategy. On the other hand, while we cannot prove any nontrivial properties of the Bold strategy, simulations reported in Sect. 4 demonstrate that it performs better than every previous strategy. It should be noted that the mathematical model of batch allocation outlined above, and hence also our simulations, do not take the complexity of a particular strategy into account, since the allocation delay is assumed to be independent of the strategy used; for this reason, the results of our simulations should be taken with more than the usual grain of salt. In a situation in which the allocation delay is essentially the time needed to compute the size of the next batch, using the Bold strategy is hardly advisable. On the other hand, if other contributions to the delay are large enough to hide the computation time, it may well be the best choice.

A final section of the paper, rather different in nature, discusses some of the problems that we faced when designing the simulations of batch allocation. We focus on two issues: Which data structures to use for the "event queue" of the simulations, and how to generate suitable (pseudo-)random batch execution times.

2 Previous scheduling strategies

This section sets the scene for the Bold strategy introduced in the next section by describing a number of other strategies proposed in the literature.

Based on the considerations in the introduction, we consider a system consisting of $p \geq 2$ initially idle processors and a central *monitor*. The monitor maintains a set of unassigned *tasks*, initially containing n tasks. At time 0 and whenever it becomes idle, each processor P accesses the monitor, a *batch* of previously unassigned tasks are assigned to P, if any are left, and P starts processing these. The time needed (by any processor) to process a batch of k tasks is $h + T_1 + \cdots + T_k$, where $h > 0$ is a fixed *allocation delay* and $T_1, \ldots, T_k$ are independent random variables with a common probability distribution D. We assume that D has mean $\mu > 0$ and standard deviation $\sigma > 0$, and that the processing times of distinct batches are independent.

The *size* of a batch is defined as the number of tasks in the batch. Any scheme for deciding on the sizes of the batches to be allocated to requesting processors will be called an *(allocation) strategy*. An allocation strategy can be viewed as a function mapping certain state variables, typically including p, the number of processors, and R, the number of unassigned (remaining) tasks, to a batch size. In order to avoid tedious discussion of special cases, we will use the following convention: When characterizing a strategy by a function $\mathcal{S}$ mapping state variables to real numbers, what we really mean is that the strategy is defined by the function $\min\{R, \max\{\lceil \mathcal{S} \rceil, 1\}\}$, i.e., we make sure that batch sizes are integral, no larger than the number of remaining tasks, and at least 1 (unless no tasks are left).

A particular execution of the n tasks by the system described above will be called a *run*. At each time during a run, each processor is in one of three states. Some of the time it is *computing*, working on the execution of some task. Between such periods, it is *coordinating*, while it experiences the allocation delay (the term "coordination" may cover such activities as awaiting access to the monitor and computing the next batch size). Finally, towards the end of the execution, it may be *idle*, waiting for the last processor to finish. Define the *total computation time* of a run as the sum over all processors of the time spent by the processor in the computing state, and the *(average) computation time* of the run as the ratio of the total computation time to the number of processors. The total and (average) *overhead* and *idle time* are defined analogously with respect to the coordination and idle times, respectively. We are primarily interested in the *(average) wasted time* of a run, defined as the sum of the average overhead and the average idle time of the run, and measure the quality of an allocation strategy by the expected wasted time of runs executed according to the strategy.

There is a clear tradeoff between overhead and idle time: Giving out large batches minimizes the overhead, but may incur a high idle time, whereas very small batches, while reducing the idle time to almost nothing by ensuring that the processors finish practically simultaneously, are associated with a high overhead. Correspondingly, we can classify allocation strategies roughly on a scale from *bold* to *timid*. A *bold* strategy tends to employ large batches, running the risk of severely uneven finishing times, while a timid strategy does the opposite.

2.1 Static Chunking (SC)

The *Static-Chunking* or *SC* strategy (the terminology is from (Hummel, Schonberg, and Flynn, 1992)), which we encountered already in the introduction, is the ultimate bold strategy that assigns all tasks right at the outset (one can be bolder, for instance by assigning all tasks to the first processor, but not meaningfully so). Using the symbol $\varXi$ to denote a (not completely specified) state that includes the initial number n of tasks, we can define the SC strategy simply by means of the function SC with $SC(\varXi) = n/p$.

In order to gain a deeper understanding of the workings of a particular strategy, it is instructive to study pictorial representations of runs made with that strategy, an example of which for the SC strategy is offered in Fig. 1 below. Horizontally is shown the time axis, beginning at 0 and normalized to have the overall finishing time in a fixed position. Each processor is represented by a horizontal stripe, divided into light gray segments (computation time) and dark gray segments (coordination time). Each light gray segment, besides the execution time of the corresponding batch (which is the length of the segment), also shows μ times the size of the batch as the length of a dark horizontal line within the segment. If the execution time of the batch is smaller than its expected value, the line doubles up on itself (if the execution time is smaller by more than a factor of 2, still only a double line is shown). The processors are shown sorted by their finishing times. Finally, three notches on the time axis indicate, in the order from left to right, the average computation time, the average computation time + overhead, and the overall stopping time (which is also the average computation time + overhead + idle time). As a visual aid, the middle notch is extended vertically as a dotted line. The wasted time of the run is the distance between the leftmost and the rightmost notch. All diagrams of this kind in the paper show the results of actual random simulations made with $n = 1024$, $p = 8$, and $h = 1$ and with D chosen as the exponential distribution with $\mu = \sigma = 1$.

As can be seen from the diagram, the SC strategy indeed suffers from being over-confident. The overhead is absolutely minimal, but idle times are long.

2.2 Self-Scheduling (SS)

At the other end of the spectrum we have the *Self-Scheduling* or *SS* strategy, the ultimately timid strategy with $SS(\varXi) = 1$. It performs very badly in the presence of nonnegligible allocation delays.

2.3 Fixed-Size Chunking (FSC)

The *Fixed-Size Chunking* or *FSC* strategy uses batches of only one fixed size (as do, incidentally, the SC and SS strategies). Kruskal and Weiss (1985), who

Fig. 1. A run of Static Chunking (SC).

introduced this strategy, attempt to calculate the optimal batch size and arrive at the approximation

$$\mathrm{FSC}(\Xi) = \left(\frac{\sqrt{2}nh}{\sigma p \sqrt{\ln p}} \right)^{2/3} ,$$

which we therefore take to define the FSC strategy. In contrast with the strategies described above, FSC takes both the allocation delay and the distribution of task execution times into account. A run of the FSC strategy is shown in Fig. 2.

Fig. 2. A run of Fixed-Size Chunking (FSC).

2.4 Guided Self-Scheduling (GSS)

The *Guided Self-Scheduling* or *GSS* strategy, introduced by Polychronopoulos
and Kuck (1987), is characterized by the function $\text{GSS}(\Xi) = R/p$ (recall that
R is the number of remaining tasks) and illustrated in Fig. 3. We do not show
the update of the state variable R as part of the strategy; it is clear, however,
what needs to be done: R is initialized to n, and every time a batch of size k is
assigned to some processor, the monitor subsequently decreases R by k.

The GSS strategy can be seen to use batches of exponentially decreasing
sizes. Polychronopoulos and Kuck motivate the GSS strategy as follows: At the
time when a batch is to be assigned to a processor, all the other processors might
be on the point of completing their current batches, so that it is unwise to give
out more than R/p tasks. Subject to this restriction, on the other hand, batch
sizes should be chosen as large as possible in order to minimize the overhead.

Fig. 3. A run of Guided Self-Scheduling (GSS).

In addition to their basic scheme GSS, Polychronopoulos and Kuck discuss
a generalized scheme GSS(k), parameterized by a positive integer k, which essentially works by eliminating batches of size less than k. They give no details,
however, except for $k = 2$, and provide no guidance as to the selection of the
parameter k (except noting that the best value of k depends on the machine
and the application), for which reasons in this paper we will understand GSS to
mean just the basic scheme.

2.5 Trapezoid Self-Scheduling (TSS)

The *Trapezoid Self-Scheduling* or *TSS* strategy of Tzen and Ni (1991) also uses
batches of decreasing sizes, but now the batch sizes decrease linearly from a first
size f to a last size ℓ; for given f and ℓ, the TSS strategy specializes to the

TSS(f, ℓ) strategy. In a preprocessing phase, TSS(f, ℓ) computes the quantities $N = \lceil 2n/(f + \ell) \rceil$, $\delta = (f - \ell)/(N - 1)$ and $k = f$. Each subsequent request for a batch size returns k and then reduces the value of k by δ.

Again, no guidance concerning the choice of f and ℓ is offered, but Tzen and Ni advocate the use of $f = n/(2p)$ and $\ell = 1$. We therefore take TSS to mean TSS$(n/(2p), 1)$; a run using this strategy is shown in Fig. 4.

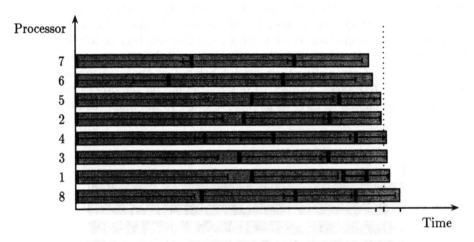

Fig. 4. A run of Trapezoid Self-Scheduling (TSS).

2.6 Factoring

Since the factoring strategy of Flynn and Hummel (1992) is closest in spirit to the new Bold strategy, as well as its closest competitor, we describe it in greater detail.

The factoring strategy operates in *rounds*. In each round, p batches of a common size are assigned (not necessarily to distinct processors), with the batch size decreasing from each round to the next. The batch size of a round is chosen according to the following principle, which attempts to ensure that no batch in the round will become the very last batch to finish: The expected maximum execution time of a batch in the round should be close to, but bounded by $1/p$ times the expected total execution time of the tasks that have not been executed when the last batch in the round is started. For the first round, since all batches in the round are started simultaneously, the latter quantity is precisely μR, where $R = n$ is the number of tasks remaining at the start of the (first) round. For later rounds, R (at the start of the round) may be too large, and Factoring uses instead as a lower bound the quantity $R - pk$, where k is the batch size of the round under consideration.

We now turn to the second key quantity for the design of Factoring, the expected maximum execution time of the batches in a round. The mean and standard deviation of the execution time of a batch consisting of k tasks are μk and $\sigma\sqrt{k}$, respectively. It is known (Gumbel, 1954; Hartley and David, 1954) that the expected value of the maximum of p random variables, each with mean μk and standard deviation $\sigma\sqrt{k}$, is at most $\mu k + \sigma\sqrt{k}\sqrt{p/2}$. This bound, coupled with the considerations in the previous paragraph, leads to the equation

$$\mu k + \sigma\sqrt{\frac{kp}{2}} = \frac{\mu(R - dpk)}{p} \ ,$$

where $d = 0$ for the first round and $d = 1$ for all subsequent rounds. Solving for k yields the formula

$$k = \frac{R}{xp} \ ,$$

where

$$x = 1 + d + b^2 + b\sqrt{b^2 + 2(1 + d)}$$

and

$$b = \frac{\sigma}{\mu}\frac{p}{2\sqrt{R}} \ .$$

The algorithm implicit in the preceding discussion is expressed below in (somewhat pedestrian) C, augmented with a few elements of standard mathematical notation such as square-root signs. The following lines describe preprocessing, to be executed once before the first batch is allocated. The C symbol '=' denotes the assignment operator.

$$c = p\sigma/(2\mu);$$
$$b = c/\sqrt{n};$$
$$x = 1 + b^2 + b\sqrt{b^2 + 2};$$
$$k = n/(xp);$$
$$count = p;$$

Each request for a batch size is implemented using the following lines. The symbol '==' denotes a test for equality, and the variable $count$ is used to ensure that a new batch size is computed once every p requests.

if $(count == 0)$ {
$\quad b = c/\sqrt{R};$
$\quad x = 2 + b^2 + b\sqrt{b^2 + 4};$
$\quad k = R/(xp);$
$\quad count = p - 1;$
}
else $count = count - 1;$
return$(k);$

Figure 5 shows an example run using the Factoring strategy, which we will denote symbolically by "Fac". Flynn and Hummel also describe a simplified version of factoring, which does away with the computation of b and simply uses $x = 2$ throughout. We denote this variant of Factoring by "Fac2". The Fac2 strategy was employed by Banicescu and Hummel (1995) as the load-balancing mechanism in N-body simulations and extended by Hummel et al. (1996) to the case of processors with different speeds.

Fig. 5. A run of Factoring (Fac).

3 The Bold Strategy

This section introduces the new Bold strategy. The Bold strategy will be seen to be decidedly bolder than its nearest relative, the Factoring strategy, which motivates its name. Most arguments in the present section are purely heuristic and make no claim at rigor. A run is a complicated random process, and analyzing it in precise terms is beyond our reach. We attempt to validate our arguments experimentally in the following section.

Open problem 1. *Justify the manipulations of the present section rigorously.*

The Bold strategy uses more elaborate state information than any of the previous strategies. In addition to R, the number of remaining unallocated tasks, it makes use of the following quantities:

- M, the number of tasks that either are unallocated or belong to batches currently under execution. M is initialized to n, and whenever a processor finishes the execution of a batch of size k, M is decremented by k.
- N, an estimate of the number of tasks that have not yet been executed. While a processor is working on a batch, the estimate assumes that it makes steady progress at the rate of exactly one task every μ time units. The computation of N uses an additional variable *total_speed*, which is initialized to 0. When a processor obtains and starts working on a batch of size k, it increments *total_speed* by $k/(k\mu + h)$, and after the execution of the batch it decrements *total_speed* by the same quantity. The value of *total_speed* indicates the expected number of tasks completed per time unit, taking the allocation delay into account, and tends to lie slightly below p/μ. The estimate N itself is initialized to n and maintained as follows: Suppose that the processing of a batch of size k begins at time t_1 and ends at time

t_2, and let t be the last point in time before t_2 at which a batch is allocated. Then, at time t_2 and before *total_speed* is updated, N is decreased by $(t_2 - t)total\_speed + k - (t_2 - t_1)k/(k\mu + h)$. The reasoning is as follows: Since time t, when N was last updated, the processors are assumed to have made a collective progress of $(t_2 - t)total\_speed$. Also, the progress associated with the batch under consideration, which is exactly k, was estimated to be $(t_2 - t_1)k/(k\mu + h)$ between t_1 and t_2, so that now a correction term of $k - (t_2 - t_1)k/(k\mu + h)$ is applied.

- Q, which is simply R/p, the number of remaining unassigned tasks per processor.

We now motivate the Bold strategy itself. Let F be the function such that $F(q)$ is the expected number of batches processed by a single processor after a situation in which Q has the value q. In actual fact, F is not well-defined, since the number in question depends both on the initial situation and on the choices made later by the strategy, but we will nonetheless allow ourselves to operate with F; moreover, we assume that F can be extended smoothly to arguments that are not multiples of $1/p$.

Suppose that it is considered to let the next batch be of size k. Increasing the size slightly to $k + \Delta k$ reduces the expected overhead for the rest of the computation from $hF(Q-k/p)$ to $hF(Q-(k+\Delta k)/p)$. We will approximate the decrease in the overhead by $(hF'(Q - k/p)/p)\Delta k$ and, in fact, by $(hF'(Q)/p)\Delta k$. This gain is offset by the risk that the batch under consideration is poised to become the very last batch to finish, in which case increasing its size by Δk will increase the expected overall finishing time by $\mu\Delta k$. If this happens with probability α, the expected increase in the overall finishing time for this reason is $\alpha\mu\Delta k$. The Bold strategy is obtained by equating the gain from reduced overhead with the loss from potential lengthening of the last batch, i.e., by setting $hF'(Q)/p = \alpha\mu$.

We need to be more explicit about $F'(Q)$ and α. Concerning α, we approximate the execution time of the batch under consideration by a random variable X with a normal distribution with mean μk and standard deviation $\sigma\sqrt{k}$. Since the execution time has the indicated mean and standard deviation and is the sum of a large number of independent, identically distributed random variables, this seems justified in light of the central limit theorem. Similarly, we approximate the time needed by the p processors to execute the remaining tasks by a random variable Y with a normal distribution with mean $\mu N/p$ and standard deviation $\sigma\sqrt{M}/p$. The choice of parameters is motivated as follows: Since N is the current estimate of the number of tasks that have not yet been executed, $\mu N/p$ is our best guess for the remaining average computation time; and since M tasks are currently "not accounted for", the standard deviation of the remaining total computation time is around $\sigma\sqrt{M}$. Assuming that the remaining computation time is divided perfectly among the processors, this translates into a standard deviation of $\sigma\sqrt{M}/p$ for the remaining average computation time.

Now $\alpha = \Pr(X > Y) = \Pr(X - Y > 0)$. The difference of two random variables with normal distributions again has a normal distribution, so $\Pr(X -$

$Y > 0) = \Pr(Z > 0)$, where Z has a normal distribution with mean $\mu k - \mu N/p$ and standard deviation $\sigma\sqrt{k + M/p^2}$. As will be seen below, we choose $k \approx N/p$, for which reason we will approximate the latter standard deviation by $\sigma\sqrt{k(1 + M/(Np))}$. Then $\alpha = 1 - \Phi(x)$, where Φ is the standard normal distribution function with mean 0 and standard deviation 1, and where

$$x = \frac{\mu N/p - \mu k}{\sigma\sqrt{k(1 + M/(Np))}} \ . \tag{1}$$

For all $x > 0$,

$$\frac{1}{x} - \frac{1}{x^3} \leq \sqrt{2\pi}e^{x^2/2}(1 - \Phi(x)) \leq \frac{1}{x}$$

(Grimmett and Stirzaker, 1992, Exercise 4.11.1). Thus $(1/\sqrt{2\pi})e^{-x^2/2}$ is an upper bound on $1 - \Phi(x)$ for all $x \geq 1$, and for large x it is a very crude upper bound. Nonetheless, we will approximate $1 - \Phi(x)$ by $(1/\sqrt{2\pi})e^{-x^2/2}$ for all x for the following reasons: For $x < 1$, our whole argument is suspect anyway, and worrying about $\Phi(x)$ is futile. And for large x, using a crude upper bound on $1 - \Phi(x)$ translates into pretending that the normal distribution has wider tails (takes on extreme values with higher probability) than it actually does. At this point recall that the normal distribution itself is only an approximation. The actual distribution may have considerably wider tails, and our approximation helps us not to rely too heavily on the sharp concentration of the normal distribution around its mean. Thus we take

$$\alpha = \frac{1}{\sqrt{2\pi}}e^{-x^2/2}$$

or

$$x^2 = -2\ln(\sqrt{2\pi}\alpha) = -2\ln(\sqrt{2\pi}hF'(Q)/(p\mu)) \ . \tag{2}$$

Putting $s = (x\sigma/\mu)^2(1 + M/(Np))$ and solving for k in (1) yields

$$k = N/p + s/2 - \sqrt{s(N/p + s/4)} \ . \tag{3}$$

As claimed above, this expression is of the form N/p minus terms that we would expect to be smaller. Among the minor terms, we expect $\sqrt{sN/p}$ to dominate. We will use this to get an idea of the function F.

Suppose that a processor obtains a batch of size k, as determined by the formula above. When it finishes the batch, N will have decreased by about pk, which means that the number of tasks left will be determined by the minor terms. Ignoring all but the term $\sqrt{sN/p}$ and roughly equating N and R, we conclude that if a processor obtains a batch at a time when $Q = q$, then when the processor returns for its next batch it will see $Q = \sqrt{sq}$. This seems to point to a doubly-logarithmic behavior of the function F. Since $(d/dQ)\ln\ln Q = 1/(Q\ln Q)$, we conclude from (2), very roughly, that for large values of Q, s is around $a\ln Q$, where $a = 2\sigma^2/\mu^2$. Let us therefore briefly investigate the sequence $\{q_i\}$ with

$q_0 = Q$ and $q_{i+1} = \sqrt{aq_i \ln q_i}$ for $i \geq 0$. Assume first that $a \geq 1$. Then $q_{i+1} \geq \sqrt{q_i}$ (unless $q_i < e$, which need not worry us here), and as a consequence

$$\frac{q_{i+1}}{4a \ln q_{i+1}} = \sqrt{\frac{aq_i \ln q_i}{(4a \ln q_{i+1})^2}} \leq \sqrt{\frac{q_i}{4a \ln q_i}} \; .$$

Thus the derived sequence $q_i' = q_i/(4a \ln q_i)$ loses at least half of its logarithm in each step, which means that after $\lceil \log_2 \ln(Q/(4a \ln Q)) \rceil \approx \log_2 \ln Q$ steps, we will have $q_i' \leq 2$ and hence $q_i \leq 8a \ln q_i$, which, to a good approximation, means that $q_i \leq b = 8a \ln(8a)$. Since q_i is clearly an increasing function of a for all i, we can conclude that after the same number of steps, q_i will have been driven below a constant if $a < 1$; we will not worry any more about this case. What happens to the sequence of successive values of Q after it has decreased below b is more difficult to analyze. Experience gleaned from many runs tell us, however, that it is not completely wrong to assume that Q decreases by a factor of about 2 between successive requests by a fixed processor. We would therefore like F to be a function that blends nicely the $\log_2 \ln Q$ behavior for large Q with a $\log_2 Q$ behavior for Q smaller than approximately b. Somewhat arbitrarily, we have chosen to set

$$F(Q) = \log_2 \left(\frac{bQ \ln Q}{b + Q} \right) \; .$$

Having settled on the form of F, we can compute x^2 from (2), form s, and finally compute k from (3). Since (1) takes only the computation time into account, whereas we anticipate an additional overhead of $hF(Q)$, we add $(h/\mu)F(Q)$ to k and return the resulting value as the size of the new batch.

$$F'(Q) = \frac{1}{\ln 2} \left(\frac{1}{Q} + \frac{1}{Q \ln Q} - \frac{1}{b + Q} \right) \; ,$$

and so the main steps of the computation are:

$s = -2(\sigma/\mu)^2 (1 + M/(Np)) \ln \left(\sqrt{2\pi} h \left(\frac{1}{Q} + \frac{1}{Q \ln Q} - \frac{1}{b+Q} \right) \middle/ (p\mu \ln 2) \right);$
$\textbf{return} \left(N/p + (h/\mu) \log_2 \left(\frac{bQ \ln Q}{b+Q} \right) + s/2 - \sqrt{s(N/p + s/4)} \right);$

Pushing as many steps as possible into the preprocessing and dealing appropriately with boundary cases, we arrive at the preprocessing

$a = 2(\sigma/\mu)^2;$
$b = 8a \ln(8a);$
$\textbf{if } (b > 0) \; \ln\_b = \ln(b);$
$p\_inv = 1.0/p;$
$c_1 = h/(\mu \ln(2));$
$c_2 = \sqrt{2\pi} c_1;$
$c_3 = \ln(c_2);$

and the following routine for subsequently determining batch sizes:

```
if (Q ≤ 1) return(1);
r = max{R, N};
t = p_inv · r;
ln_Q = ln(Q);
v = Q/(b + Q);
d = R/(1 + 1/ln_Q − v);
if (d ≤ c₂) return(t);
s = a(ln(d) − c₃)(1 + M/(rp));
if (b > 0) w = ln(v · ln_Q) + ln_b;
else w = ln(ln_Q);
return(min{t + max{0, c₁w} + s/2 − √(s(t + s/4)), t});
```

We take these program fragments as the formal definition of the Bold strategy. For the sake of comparison, Fig. 6 below shows a run of the Bold strategy with the same parameter settings as for the diagrams in the previous section.

Fig. 6. A run of the Bold strategy (Bold).

Open problem 2. *Show that the expected wasted time of the Bold strategy is $O(\log \log n)$ for n tending to infinity with all other parameters kept fixed (or perhaps p also tending to infinity in such a way that $n/p \to \infty$).*

Open problem 3. *Prove that every strategy incurs an expected wasted time of $\Omega(\log \log n)$ for n tending to infinity with all other parameters kept fixed.*

4 Simulation results

This section gives the results of simulations aimed at determining the best strategy to use under various conditions and at assessing the value of the Bold strategy. The simulations were carried out on two Sparc Ultra 1/170 computers with a simulation program written in C++ using the LEDA library (Mehlhorn and Näher, 1995). Task distribution times were generated with the aid of the standard Unix random-number generators *erand48* and *nrand48*. The transition from the uniform distribution, as furnished by these generators, to other distributions is discussed in Sect. 5.2. While not always being able to follow the admonitions of McGeoch (1996; see also the commentaries and rejoinder on subsequent pages), we tried at least to keep them in mind. In particular, since the focus of interest is the relative performances of different strategies and not the random fluctuations in task execution times, we measured the wasted time and not the finishing time; this is an instance of *variance reduction* (see, e.g., (Bratley, Fox, and Schrage, 1983)).

Our choice of parameters such as n attempted to cover what we consider reasonable operating ranges for the strategies with values about evenly spaced on a logarithmic scale, as well as to hit data points used by previous authors. Even when varying other parameters, we always kept the expected value μ of the task execution time fixed at 1. This implies no loss of generality, since all of the strategies considered are invariant under multiplication of all of h, μ, and σ by the same positive factor (this simply corresponds to picking a different unit of time). We use the following shorthand: Exponential(μ) denotes the exponential distribution with parameter $1/\mu$, i.e., with mean and standard deviation μ, Uniform(μ, σ) denotes the uniform distribution over the interval $(\mu - \sqrt{3}\sigma, \mu + \sqrt{3}\sigma)$, and Bernoulli($\mu, \sigma$) denotes the two-point distribution with $\Pr(0) = 1 - 1/r$ and $\Pr(r\mu) = 1/r$, where $r = 1 + (\sigma/\mu)^2$; the latter two distributions have mean μ and standard deviation σ.

We briefly recall a few basic concepts from statistics. Suppose that we are interested in some random quantity X associated with a run—typically, the wasted time of the run. We carry out t successive runs with the same parameter settings, for a suitable positive integer t, in order to obtain a *sample* of t values $X_1, \ldots, X_t$ for X, after which we can compute the *sample mean* $\overline{X} = (1/t)\sum_{i=1}^{t} X_i$ and the *sample deviation*

$$S = \sqrt{\frac{1}{t-1} \sum_{i=1}^{t} (X_i - \overline{X})^2}$$

(some authors divide by t rather than by $t - 1$ in the definition of S; since here t will be in the thousands, this difference is immaterial). It is usually reasonable to assume that $X_1, \ldots, X_t$ are independent random variables with a common distribution and, moreover, that this distribution is (approximately) a normal distribution with some (unknown) mean μ_1 and standard deviation σ_1. If this is so, $\overline{X}$ has a normal distribution with mean μ_1 and standard deviation $\sigma_1/\sqrt{t}$, and $E(S^2) = \sigma_1^2$. We will therefore indicate $\overline{X}$ as an estimate of μ_1 and $S/\sqrt{t}$, which we call the *sample uncertainty*, as an estimate of the accuracy of the estimate $\overline{X}$.

4.1 All Versus All

Our first simulation pitted the various strategies described in the two previous sections against each other for different numbers of tasks and processors. Each entry in Table 1 shows the sample mean of the average wasted time for 1000 runs with allocation delay $h = 0.5$ using the exponential distribution with parameter 1. The sample uncertainty (not shown) is between 0.01 and 0.05 for the SS, Fac2, and Bold strategies, and bounded by 10% of the sample mean for all entries. The entries for Fac2 for $(n, p) \in \{(2^{19}, 64), (2^{19}, 256)\}$ were also determined experimentally by Flynn and Hummel (1992, Table 4). Our figures of 10.91 and 11.37 agree well with their figures of 10.87 and 11.28, the difference being small compared to the sample uncertainty.

We make the following observations from Table 1:

(1) The extreme strategies Static Chunking (SC) and Self-Scheduling (SS) perform very poorly throughout; so poorly, indeed, that we largely exclude them from further consideration. These strategies are also easiest to analyze and therefore least in need of simulation.

(2) The Fixed-Size Chunking (FSC), Guided Self-Scheduling (GSS), and Trapezoid Self-Scheduling (TSS) strategies perform well when the number of tasks is small and the number of processors is large, and perform badly when the number of tasks is large.

(3) The Factoring strategies (Fac and Fac2) and the Bold strategy are among the best for all parameter settings, and this becomes more pronounced as n and n/p grow large.

(4) Interestingly, the performance of the full Factoring strategy Fac is almost consistently inferior to that of its quick-and-dirty variant Fac2.

(5) For fixed n, the average wasted time increases with p for the Bold, Fac2 and (less convincingly) Fac strategies, whereas for the other strategies the trend is the opposite.

(6) From this data set, the Bold strategy appears to be at least as good as any other strategy for all parameter settings.

4.2 FSC, GSS, and TSS Versus Bold

Prompted by Observation (5), we ran the GSS strategy (as a representative case) against the Bold strategy for different numbers of processors with all other parameters fixed. The result is shown in Fig. 7.

As can be seen, the overhead is small and practically the same for both strategies. It decreases with growing p, as the number of tasks per processor decreases. The idle time, in contrast, is larger and behaves differently for the two strategies. For the GSS strategy, by and large, the idle time decreases with p. We interpret this as follows: For the GSS strategy, it is quite likely that one of the batches allocated very early, possibly at time 0, becomes the last batch to finish; this carries the risk of a large idle time; as p becomes larger, the maximum batch size decreases, and its influence on the expected idle time diminishes.

n \ p	2	8	64	256	1024
1024	SC: 13.02 SS: 256.52 FSC: 11.85 GSS: 8.55 TSS: 9.58 Fac: 4.72 Fac2: 5.55 Bold: 3.51	SC: 16.97 SS: 65.76 FSC: 13.01 GSS: 7.01 TSS: 9.53 Fac: 5.87 Fac2: 5.74 Bold: 4.79	SC: 11.43 SS: 11.77 FSC: 8.38 GSS: 7.72 TSS: 7.36 Fac: 8.74 Fac2: 6.33 Bold: 6.28	SC: 8.46 SS: 7.14 FSC: 7.30 GSS: 7.43 TSS: 7.31 Fac: 7.15 Fac2: 6.66 Bold: 6.77	SC: 6.97 SS: 6.95 FSC: 7.05 GSS: 7.00 TSS: 7.01 Fac: 6.97 Fac2: 6.96 Bold: 6.99
8192	SC: 36.18 SS: 2048.55 FSC: 33.64 GSS: 20.98 TSS: 36.08 Fac: 7.31 Fac2: 7.04 Bold: 4.00	SC: 45.93 SS: 513.79 FSC: 38.58 GSS: 15.66 TSS: 35.60 Fac: 7.66 Fac2: 7.29 Bold: 5.38	SC: 28.82 SS: 67.78 FSC: 17.35 GSS: 13.24 TSS: 12.79 Fac: 11.30 Fac2: 7.85 Bold: 7.25	SC: 18.81 SS: 21.18 FSC: 12.27 GSS: 12.57 TSS: 10.75 Fac: 14.72 Fac2: 8.35 Bold: 8.12	SC: 12.89 SS: 10.47 FSC: 9.84 GSS: 10.63 TSS: 9.77 Fac: 10.56 Fac2: 8.70 Bold: 8.69
2^{16}	SC: 102.03 SS: 16384.55 FSC: 231.44 GSS: 53.23 TSS: 103.39 Fac: 15.93 Fac2: 8.53 Bold: 4.28	SC: 132.09 SS: 4097.76 FSC: 135.58 GSS: 39.61 TSS: 126.77 Fac: 10.99 Fac2: 8.81 Bold: 5.76	SC: 77.21 SS: 515.75 FSC: 43.99 GSS: 22.25 TSS: 46.06 Fac: 12.81 Fac2: 9.41 Bold: 7.81	SC: 48.47 SS: 133.12 FSC: 26.00 GSS: 24.53 TSS: 21.99 Fac: 18.14 Fac2: 9.98 Bold: 9.02	SC: 29.88 SS: 38.54 FSC: 17.32 GSS: 20.34 TSS: 14.63 Fac: 24.48 Fac2: 10.37 Bold: 10.06
2^{19}	SC: 278.33 SS: $1.3 \cdot 10^5$ FSC: 1033.57 GSS: 143.08 TSS: 293.44 Fac: 26.04 Fac2: 10.07 Bold: 4.59	SC: 359.97 SS: 32769.71 FSC: 338.05 GSS: 101.68 TSS: 369.04 Fac: 19.61 Fac2: 10.33 Bold: 6.09	SC: 212.84 SS: 4099.78 FSC: 129.26 GSS: 41.71 TSS: 145.00 Fac: 13.69 Fac2: 10.91 Bold: 8.20	SC: 130.45 SS: 1029.12 FSC: 65.67 GSS: 45.10 TSS: 73.75 Fac: 20.05 Fac2: 11.37 Bold: 9.58	SC: 77.15 SS: 262.57 FSC: 37.16 GSS: 43.72 TSS: 38.22 Fac: 30.52 Fac2: 11.92 Bold: 10.82

Table 1. Sample means of the average wasted time over 1000 runs with $h = 0.5$ and $D = \text{Exponential}(1)$ for varying numbers of tasks and processors.

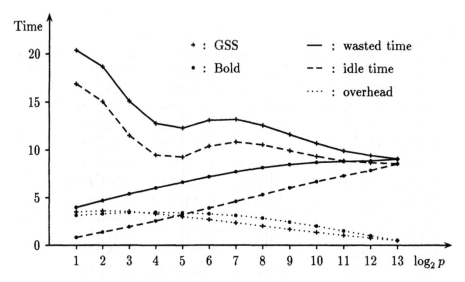

Fig. 7. Sample means of the average overhead, idle time, and wasted time over 10000 runs of the GSS and Bold strategies with $n = 8192$, $h = 0.5$, and $D = \text{Exponential}(1)$ for varying numbers of processors.

For the Bold strategy, the idle time grows very nearly linearly with $\log p$. We believe that the Bold strategy manages to eliminate the effect mentioned for the GSS strategy and, moreover, that the linear behavior is related to the fact that the expected value of the maximum of p random variables, each exponentially distributed with parameter 1, is $\sum_{i=1}^{p}(1/i)$ (Gut, 1995, Problem IV.4.13), i.e., also essentially linear in $\log p$. For $\log_2 p = 13$, there is exactly one task per processor, and the GSS and Bold strategies perform identically.

Because of Observation (2), we next exercised the FSC, GSS, and TSS strategies together with the Bold strategy for small values of n and n/p. Table 2 shows, not surprisingly, that when there are only a few tasks per processor, the strategies perform about equally well. The Bold strategy never performs worse than any other strategy, but much better than the other strategies when n/p is large. The sample uncertainties for the entries in Table 2 are bounded by 0.1, and by 1% of the corresponding sample means.

Our next experiment, the result of which is shown in Table 3, fixed $n = 128$ and $p = 8$ (corresponding to one of the boxes in Fig. 2) and instead varied the delay and the distribution of task execution times. Here and in the following, we use the following distributions: $D_1 = \text{Uniform}(1, 0.2)$, $D_2 = \text{Uniform}(1, 0.5)$, $D_3 = \text{Exponential}(1)$, $D_4 = \text{Bernoulli}(1, 3)$, and $D_5 = \text{Bernoulli}(1, 10)$. We included D_1 as an extremely "benign" distribution with very low variance, D_2, D_3, and D_4 as distributions employed by Flynn and Hummel (1992), and D_5 as an example of a distribution with a very large variance.

Not surprisingly, the wasted time increases as the allocation delay h becomes larger. For the Bold strategy, the figures given in each column eventually (as h

n/p \ p	2	8	64	256	1024
4	FSC: 1.59 GSS: 1.70 TSS: 1.83 Bold: 1.54	FSC: 3.33 GSS: 3.18 TSS: 3.37 Bold: 3.11	FSC: 5.75 GSS: 5.72 TSS: 5.72 Bold: 5.34	FSC: 7.30 GSS: 7.41 TSS: 7.30 Bold: 6.76	FSC: 8.84 GSS: 9.11 TSS: 8.84 Bold: 8.15
16	FSC: 2.76 GSS: 2.58 TSS: 2.44 Bold: 2.19	FSC: 5.44 GSS: 4.33 TSS: 4.44 Bold: 3.85	FSC: 8.35 GSS: 7.68 TSS: 7.37 Bold: 6.27	FSC: 9.97 GSS: 10.33 TSS: 9.22 Bold: 7.77	FSC: 11.63 GSS: 12.91 TSS: 10.94 Bold: 9.30
64	FSC: 4.69 GSS: 3.91 TSS: 4.04 Bold: 2.84	FSC: 9.26 GSS: 5.93 TSS: 6.45 Bold: 4.53	FSC: 13.25 GSS: 10.89 TSS: 10.16 Bold: 6.95	FSC: 15.46 GSS: 15.58 TSS: 12.46 Bold: 8.53	FSC: 17.34 GSS: 20.45 TSS: 14.66 Bold: 10.06
256	FSC: 9.95 GSS: 6.45 TSS: 5.79 Bold: 3.33	FSC: 16.95 GSS: 9.05 TSS: 14.23 Bold: 5.01	FSC: 22.96 GSS: 15.53 TSS: 18.33 Bold: 7.44	FSC: 25.95 GSS: 24.68 TSS: 21.83 Bold: 9.01	FSC: 28.24 GSS: 33.73 TSS: 25.10 Bold: 10.57

Table 2. Sample means of the average wasted time over 10000 runs with $h = 0.5$ and $D = \text{Exponential}(1)$ for varying numbers of tasks and processors.

becomes larger) approach h plus a constant characteristic of the column. The explanation for this is simple: For sufficiently large h, the Bold strategy specializes to the SC strategy. We would also expect the wasted time to grow with the variance of the task execution time; this is the case for the GSS, TSS, and Bold strategies (note that the distributions $D_1, \ldots, D_5$ are ordered by increasing variance), whereas the FSC strategy becomes degenerate in the upper right and lower left corners, due to the small size of n, and as a result exhibits a somewhat erratic behavior. The Bold strategy usually performs as well as any other strategy, but there are some exceptions for large variances, notably the pair $(h, D) = (2, D_4)$. In order to test whether these exceptions persist for larger numbers of tasks, we repeated the experiment of Table 2, but with $(h, D) = (2, D_4)$. The result, shown in Table 4, suggests that when the number of tasks per processor is around 16, TSS is the best strategy, and Bold incurs around 20% more wasted time. If n/p is smaller than 16, the difference becomes insignificant, and if it is larger, the Bold strategy is superior.

4.3 Factoring Versus Bold

We next tested the Bold strategy against the two Factoring strategies and began by extending Table 1 to larger numbers of tasks (Table 5). The Fac strategy showed an erratic behavior. While the sample uncertainties for all entries per-

h \ D	D_1	D_2	D_3	D_4	D_5
0.1	FSC: 1.54 GSS: 0.93 TSS: 1.42 Bold: 0.80	FSC: 2.10 GSS: 1.48 TSS: 1.93 Bold: 1.14	FSC: 3.09 GSS: 3.39 TSS: 3.23 Bold: 2.34	FSC: 6.24 GSS: 12.25 TSS: 9.52 Bold: 5.87	FSC: 58.30 GSS: 61.75 TSS: 60.11 Bold: 57.96
0.5	FSC: 8.65 GSS: 2.33 TSS: 2.62 Bold: 1.72	FSC: 5.31 GSS: 2.66 TSS: 3.15 Bold: 2.31	FSC: 5.45 GSS: 4.31 TSS: 4.42 Bold: 3.85	FSC: 10.34 GSS: 13.01 TSS: 10.59 Bold: 9.30	FSC: 62.89 GSS: 62.67 TSS: 60.99 Bold: 60.46
2	FSC: 17.13 GSS: 7.78 TSS: 7.12 Bold: 3.14	FSC: 4.85 GSS: 8.00 TSS: 7.71 Bold: 4.85	FSC: 9.99 GSS: 8.71 TSS: 8.94 Bold: 8.12	FSC: 15.98 GSS: 16.00 TSS: 14.73 Bold: 17.33	FSC: 66.95 GSS: 66.15 TSS: 64.48 Bold: 65.56
5	FSC: 43.83 GSS: 19.03 TSS: 16.12 Bold: 6.14	FSC: 21.82 GSS: 19.13 TSS: 16.73 Bold: 7.84	FSC: 13.86 GSS: 19.34 TSS: 18.21 Bold: 11.14	FSC: 22.17 GSS: 23.33 TSS: 23.33 Bold: 23.38	FSC: 74.94 GSS: 73.10 TSS: 71.37 Bold: 70.41
10	FSC: 80.00 GSS: 38.97 TSS: 31.12 Bold: 11.14	FSC: 42.94 GSS: 38.72 TSS: 31.73 Bold: 12.85	FSC: 29.79 GSS: 38.14 TSS: 33.40 Bold: 16.13	FSC: 28.57 GSS: 39.44 TSS: 38.40 Bold: 28.35	FSC: 82.83 GSS: 84.77 TSS: 82.71 Bold: 75.34

Table 3. Sample means of the average wasted time over 100000 runs with $n = 128$ and $p = 8$ for varying allocation delays and different distributions. $D_1 = \text{Uniform}(1, 0.2)$, $D_2 = \text{Uniform}(1, 0.5)$, $D_3 = \text{Exponential}(1)$, $D_4 = \text{Bernoulli}(1, 3)$, and $D_5 = \text{Bernoulli}(1, 10)$.

taining to the Fac2 and Bold strategies are bounded by 0.05, the sample uncertainties for the three largest entries for Fac exceed 50. Initially believing this to be evidence of a programming error, we now explain it by looking back at the formulas defining the Fac strategy (Sect. 2.6). Consider the most extreme case $n = 2^{31}$ and $p = 2$ and assume, as in our experiment, that $D = \text{Exponential}(1)$. Then the parameters of the Factoring strategy computed for the first round are $b = 1/\sqrt{n} = 2^{-15.5}$, $x = 1 + b^2 + b\sqrt{b^2 + 2} \approx 1 + \sqrt{2}b = 1 + \epsilon$, where $\epsilon = 2^{-15}$, and $k = n/(xp) \approx (n/p)(1 - \epsilon)$. Let X and Y be the execution times of the first batch allocated to Processor 1 and of all other tasks, respectively. If we approximate the distributions of X and Y by the appropriate normal distributions (this is a very close approximation), $X - Y$ will have a normal distribution with mean $-2\epsilon(n/p)$ and standard deviation (practically) $\sqrt{2}\epsilon(n/p)$, and one can show that $E(\max\{X - Y, 0\}) = (1/(2e\sqrt{\pi}) - 1 + \Phi(\sqrt{2})) \cdot 2^{16} \approx 1647$, which goes a long way towards explaining the sample mean of 1666 obtained in the simulation.

n/p \ p	2	8	64	256	1024
4	FSC: 5.77 GSS: 5.85 TSS: 5.99 Bold: 4.83	FSC: 11.18 GSS: 11.19 TSS: 11.22 Bold: 11.46	FSC: 17.45 GSS: 17.90 TSS: 17.44 Bold: 17.82	FSC: 20.57 GSS: 21.19 TSS: 20.60 Bold: 21.15	FSC: 21.71 GSS: 25.81 TSS: 21.72 Bold: 25.82
16	FSC: 8.64 GSS: 8.92 TSS: 8.65 Bold: 8.57	FSC: 16.00 GSS: 16.03 TSS: 14.69 Bold: 17.44	FSC: 24.62 GSS: 26.80 TSS: 23.12 Bold: 26.98	FSC: 29.33 GSS: 34.26 TSS: 28.18 Bold: 33.35	FSC: 33.33 GSS: 41.51 TSS: 32.38 Bold: 39.50
64	FSC: 13.74 GSS: 13.51 TSS: 11.36 Bold: 10.83	FSC: 24.97 GSS: 22.97 TSS: 20.04 Bold: 18.60	FSC: 37.76 GSS: 42.29 TSS: 31.74 Bold: 28.22	FSC: 44.65 GSS: 56.51 TSS: 38.72 Bold: 34.21	FSC: 50.47 GSS: 69.80 TSS: 45.64 Bold: 40.20
256	FSC: 21.97 GSS: 21.63 TSS: 15.93 Bold: 14.15	FSC: 42.20 GSS: 33.88 TSS: 30.49 Bold: 21.65	FSC: 60.46 GSS: 66.00 TSS: 46.95 Bold: 30.73	FSC: 70.16 GSS: 94.23 TSS: 57.58 Bold: 37.13	FSC: 78.59 GSS: 120.35 TSS: 67.77 Bold: 43.42

Table 4. Sample means of the average wasted time over 10000 runs with $h = 2$ and $D = \text{Bernoulli}(1, 3)$ for varying numbers of tasks and processors.

n \ p	2	8	64	256	1024
2^{22}	Fac: 79.49 Fac2: 11.53 Bold: 4.79	Fac: 38.66 Fac2: 11.75 Bold: 6.24	Fac: 14.77 Fac2: 12.41 Bold: 8.49	Fac: 21.21 Fac2: 12.84 Bold: 9.92	Fac: 32.58 Fac2: 13.37 Bold: 11.20
2^{25}	Fac: 188.26 Fac2: 13.04 Bold: 4.94	Fac: 110.77 Fac2: 13.30 Bold: 6.51	Fac: 15.19 Fac2: 13.87 Bold: 8.75	Fac: 22.13 Fac2: 14.38 Bold: 10.05	Fac: 33.48 Fac2: 14.93 Bold: 11.50
2^{28}	Fac: 570.51 Fac2: 14.55 Bold: 5.07	Fac: 264.74 Fac2: 14.81 Bold: 6.67	Fac: 16.28 Fac2: 15.42 Bold: 8.87	Fac: 22.63 Fac2: 15.87 Bold: 10.26	Fac: 34.50 Fac2: 16.40 Bold: 11.73
2^{31}	Fac: 1665.56 Fac2: 15.82 Bold: 5.18	Fac: 682.02 Fac2: 16.20 Bold: 6.89	Fac: 16.74 Fac2: 16.86 Bold: 9.06	Fac: 23.59 Fac2: 17.35 Bold: 10.49	Fac: 35.52 Fac2: 17.88 Bold: 11.92

Table 5. Sample means of the average wasted time over 1000 runs with $h = 0.5$ and $D = \text{Exponential}(1)$ for varying numbers of tasks and processors. "2^{31}" actually means $2^{31} - 1$.

The problem therefore is that the batches given out in the first round are so large that with nonnegligible probability, one of them will significantly outlast the collection of all other tasks, a devastating event for the run.

We omit another table, similar to Table 2 but for the Fac, Fac2, and Bold strategies, which shows all three strategies to perform similarly for $p \leq 1024$ and $n/p \leq 256$, Bold being somewhat superior to Fac2, and Fac2 being somewhat superior to Fac when p is not very small.

The experiment reported in Table 6, similar to that of Table 3, exercised the Factoring and Bold strategies for varying allocation delays and different distributions of task execution times. The entries for the Fac2 strategy for $h = 0.5$ and for the distributions D_2, D_3, and D_4 were also determined experimentally by Flynn and Hummel (1992, Table 4). Our figures of 8.29, 10.90, and 26.18 agree reasonably well with their figures of 8.30, 10.87, and 26.89, although the difference for the third pair is large relative to our sample uncertainty of 0.09.

It can be seen that the Factoring strategies cope very badly with large allocation delays. Bold is the best strategy for all parameter settings except $(h, D) = (0.1, D_5)$, although its advantage becomes insignificant for very badly behaved distributions. By what we consider to be a coincidence, the Fac and Fac2 strategies behave almost identically in the case of the distribution $D_2 = \mathrm{Uniform}(1, 0.5)$.

Figure 8 shows the behavior of the Fac2 and Bold strategies as the number of tasks varies with all other parameters kept fixed. The idle time is practically constant and the same for both strategies (indeed, the reader may have failed to notice that the bottom curve in fact consists of two curves). After an initial increase, the overhead of the Bold strategy also becomes almost constant, whereas the overhead of Fac2 follows a line with positive slope very neatly, as indeed one would expect from the definition of the Fac2 strategy.

4.4 Bold Versus Itself

In this section we compare different versions of the Bold strategy and the Bold strategy running under different conditions.

We began by investigating simpler versions of the Bold strategy, called Bold1 and Bold2, with a somewhat smaller computational overhead. Bold1 is obtained by taking $d = R$, $s = a(\ln(d) - c_3)$, and $w = \ln(\ln(Q))$ in the code defining Bold, which therefore simplifies to

```
if (Q ≤ 1) return(1);
t = p_inv · max{R, N};
if (R ≤ c₂) return(t);
s = a(ln(R) − c₃);
return(min{t + max{0, c₁ ln(ln(Q))} + s/2 − √(s(t + s/4)), t});
```

Bold2, in addition, does away with the complicated estimation of the number N of tasks that have not yet been executed and simply substitutes R, the number of remaining (unassigned) tasks (this is equivalent to taking $t = Q$ in the code

	D_1	D_2	D_3	D_4	D_5
h					
0.1	Fac: 1.75 Fac2: 2.15 Bold: 1.21	Fac: 2.50 Fac2: 2.50 Bold: 1.80	Fac: 5.75 Fac2: 5.50 Bold: 4.88	Fac: 9.48 Fac2: 22.39 Bold: 8.04	Fac: 68.53 Fac2: 250.23 Bold: 74.93
0.5	Fac: 5.95 Fac2: 7.95 Bold: 3.10	Fac: 8.29 Fac2: 8.29 Bold: 4.28	Fac: 13.76 Fac2: 10.90 Bold: 8.16	Fac: 27.58 Fac2: 26.18 Bold: 17.81	Fac: 123.46 Fac2: 256.97 Bold: 111.53
2	Fac: 21.69 Fac2: 29.69 Bold: 9.08	Fac: 30.00 Fac2: 30.03 Bold: 10.96	Fac: 43.98 Fac2: 32.00 Bold: 17.16	Fac: 92.57 Fac2: 41.49 Bold: 36.05	Fac: 310.29 Fac2: 264.03 Bold: 169.84
5	Fac: 53.19 Fac2: 73.18 Bold: 20.43	Fac: 73.51 Fac2: 73.53 Bold: 22.29	Fac: 104.91 Fac2: 74.92 Bold: 32.32	Fac: 220.37 Fac2: 80.73 Bold: 61.73	Fac: 660.39 Fac2: 284.57 Bold: 230.76
10	Fac: 105.67 Fac2: 145.68 Bold: 39.52	Fac: 146.00 Fac2: 146.02 Bold: 41.37	Fac: 206.91 Fac2: 147.08 Bold: 50.72	Fac: 432.44 Fac2: 152.39 Bold: 101.09	Fac: 1233.92 Fac2: 319.57 Bold: 297.21

Table 6. Sample means of the average wasted time over 10000 runs with $n = 2^{19} = 524288$ and $p = 64$ for varying allocation delays and different distributions. $D_1 = \text{Uniform}(1, 0.2)$, $D_2 = \text{Uniform}(1, 0.5)$, $D_3 = \text{Exponential}(1)$, $D_4 = \text{Bernoulli}(1, 3)$, and $D_5 = \text{Bernoulli}(1, 10)$.

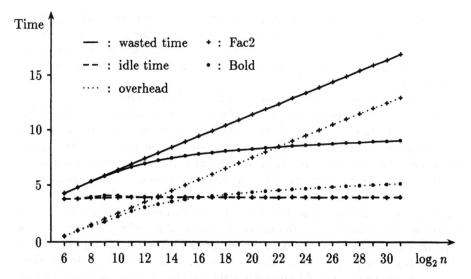

Fig. 8. Sample means of the average overhead, idle time, and wasted time over 10000 runs of the Fac2 and Bold strategies with $p = 64$, $h = 0.5$, and $D = \text{Exponential}(1)$ for varying numbers of tasks.

fragment above). Table 7 shows the sample means obtained for the Bold, Bold1, and Bold2 strategies with parameters chosen as for Table 1.

p	2	8	64	256	1024
n					
1024	Bold: 3.54 Bold1: 3.56 Bold2: 4.79	Bold: 4.76 Bold1: 5.26 Bold2: 6.30	Bold: 6.28 Bold1: 6.76 Bold2: 7.21	Bold: 6.72 Bold1: 7.04 Bold2: 7.12	Bold: 7.01 Bold1: 7.04 Bold2: 7.02
8192	Bold: 3.98 Bold1: 3.93 Bold2: 5.55	Bold: 5.38 Bold1: 5.77 Bold2: 7.49	Bold: 7.22 Bold1: 7.89 Bold2: 8.92	Bold: 8.19 Bold1: 8.89 Bold2: 9.47	Bold: 8.73 Bold1: 9.16 Bold2: 9.43
2^{16}	Bold: 4.31 Bold1: 4.51 Bold2: 6.30	Bold: 5.78 Bold1: 6.16 Bold2: 8.56	Bold: 7.81 Bold1: 8.44 Bold2: 10.23	Bold: 9.02 Bold1: 9.79 Bold2: 11.04	Bold: 10.06 Bold1: 10.89 Bold2: 11.67
2^{19}	Bold: 4.56 Bold1: 8.02 Bold2: 7.05	Bold: 6.08 Bold1: 6.71 Bold2: 9.56	Bold: 8.18 Bold1: 8.82 Bold2: 11.37	Bold: 9.52 Bold1: 10.27 Bold2: 12.31	Bold: 10.78 Bold1: 11.62 Bold2: 13.15

Table 7. Sample means of the average wasted time for the full and simplified Bold strategies over 10000 runs with $h = 0.5$ and $D = $ Exponential(1) for varying numbers of tasks and processors.

The simplified strategy Bold1 performs worse than the original strategy Bold, but not a lot worse. In particular, Bold1 is still better than Fac, and it is better than Fac2 if n is large and n/p is not too small. Bold2, on the other hand, has lost so much of the original performance that it is inferior to the simpler Fac2 strategy unless p is very small.

Recall that when a strategy asks for a batch of some nonintegral size k, the batch size actually used is $\lceil k \rceil$ (except when k is too small or too large). Other possibilities certainly exist, such as using $\lfloor k \rfloor$ or rounding in the usual way, i.e., replacing k by $\lfloor k + 1/2 \rfloor$. Our rounding convention was motivated by the following considerations: First, $\lceil k \rceil$ is clearly preferable to the other possibilities in the case of the SC strategy, and explicitly prescribed by Polychronopoulos and Kuck (1987) for the GSS strategy. And second, since certainly sizes between 0 and 1 should be rounded to 1 and not to 0, replacing k by $\lceil k \rceil$ for all k seems a natural extension. In order to explore the effects of rounding, we repeated the experiment of Table 6 for the Bold strategy, but with the rounding conventions of replacing k by (1) $\lceil k \rceil$ (as usual), (2) $\lfloor k + 1/2 \rfloor$, and (3) k itself. In the third variant, tasks were assumed to be arbitrarily divisible. A random execution time was computed for each entire task according to the relevant distribution, and then this time was split proportionally among the pieces of the task included in different batches. In all cases, batch sizes were still prevented from becoming smaller than 1.

The results obtained were inconclusive and will not be reported in detail. The best results were always achieved by one of the conventions (1) and (3), but usually the differences were small, and which parameter settings favored convention (1) over (3) did not follow any obvious pattern. No rounding convention came out a clear winner.

One might suspect that the TSS strategy would be particularly affected by rounding, since it is not "self-correcting" as many of the other strategies (it never inspects the number R of remaining tasks). In order to test this, we repeated the experiment of Table 4, but employing usual rounding (replacing k by $\lfloor k + 1/2 \rfloor$) in the case of the TSS strategy. The results (not reproduced here) show that usual rounding performs better than "ceiling rounding" for most, but not all parameter settings. The largest observed relative difference in sample means between the two rounding conventions was 8.2% of the larger value.

In order to provide some robustness against possibly imperfect random-number generators, we repeated all experiments using instead of *erand48* and *nrand48* the standard Unix random-number generator *random*, which employs an algorithm of a different type. The differences between the results obtained in the two cases, although possibly statistically significant, were quite small and not enough to upset any of the conclusions drawn from our experiments.

4.5 Dependent Task Execution Times

Our final experiment was designed to explore the consequences of relaxing one of the fundamental assumptions underlying Bold and some of the other strategies, the independence of the execution times of distinct tasks. The experiment, the result of which is shown in Table 8, in fact departs from the assumption of independence in a radical way by assuming the execution time of a batch of size k to be exponentially distributed with parameter $1/k$ (equivalently, as kX, where X is exponentially distributed with parameter 1); the execution times of distinct batches are still assumed to be independent. This alternative model makes the execution time of a large batch much harder to predict than for our standard model with $D = \text{Exponential}(1)$.

The parameter σ, while denoting the standard deviation of the execution time of a single task, is also interpreted by those of the strategies that use σ as $1/\sqrt{k}$ times the standard deviation of the execution time of a batch of size k, a correspondence that breaks down for the alternative model. This raises the question of what value to use for σ. We chose to set $\sigma = \sqrt{n/p}$, the value that lets the strategies correctly assess the variation in the execution time of the largest batches used, but lets them overestimate that of smaller batches.

The results of the experiment can be summarized as follows: In the alternative model, batch allocation is much more difficult than in the standard model. Within the parameter ranges covered by the experiment, the strategy doing best is Bold, followed by FSC and Fac.

n \ p	2	8	64	256	1024
1024 SC:	262.13	218.16	56.94	16.12	7.03
FSC:	35.77	21.32	8.69	7.12	7.03
GSS:	128.97	123.49	36.27	12.42	7.03
TSS:	62.68	63.35	19.34	7.26	6.98
Fac:	27.42	22.75	11.79	7.14	7.00
Fac2:	38.49	57.36	19.54	6.69	6.99
Bold:	27.72	13.86	7.88	6.91	7.03
8192 SC:	2048.17	1784.83	479.93	159.91	46.40
FSC:	142.48	83.26	29.14	14.30	10.56
GSS:	1056.03	1001.56	296.45	111.16	34.98
TSS:	499.06	469.62	154.91	57.44	17.03
Fac:	95.39	63.12	48.75	21.13	10.51
Fac2:	274.83	476.77	178.60	61.41	16.12
Bold:	89.55	42.11	16.57	11.45	10.16
2^{16} SC:	$1.6 \cdot 10^4$	$1.5 \cdot 10^4$	3855.08	1295.38	411.07
FSC:	577.46	335.14	117.30	53.41	23.76
GSS:	8661.74	7508.53	2432.87	898.32	297.19
TSS:	3991.30	3804.22	1257.26	458.86	151.95
Fac:	381.17	185.54	158.18	114.60	38.54
Fac2:	2087.10	3914.54	1412.73	526.09	171.49
Bold:	269.25	125.81	46.42	25.10	15.73
2^{19} SC:	$13.1 \cdot 10^4$	$11.3 \cdot 10^4$	$3.1 \cdot 10^4$	$1.0 \cdot 10^4$	3338.54
FSC:	2284.02	1303.54	443.00	196.49	83.58
GSS:	$7.0 \cdot 10^4$	$6.1 \cdot 10^4$	$1.9 \cdot 10^4$	7141.53	2376.78
TSS:	$3.0 \cdot 10^4$	$3.0 \cdot 10^4$	9847.95	3678.76	1213.59
Fac:	3028.50	596.77	467.22	419.56	262.60
Fac2:	$1.8 \cdot 10^4$	$3.0 \cdot 10^4$	$1.1 \cdot 10^4$	4280.72	1418.07
Bold:	780.79	362.59	133.82	70.37	37.60

Table 8. Sample means of the average wasted time over 1000 runs with $h = 0.5$ using the alternative model of batch execution times with $\sigma = \sqrt{n/p}$.

4.6 Discussion

In this section we attempt to draw some conclusions from the experimental results reported above.

Beginning at a salesman's pitch, we state that the Bold strategy performed well across the entire gamut of experiments; no other strategy ever achieved a significantly lower average wasted time. Since the idle times of the Fac2 and Bold strategies are practically identical (Fig. 8), it is natural to assume that they are as small as achievable. The Fac2 strategy, however, achieves this at a significantly higher price in the form of additional overhead. This is not surprising: The tradeoff between overhead and idle time, at the heart of the design of the Bold strategy, is recognized only qualitatively in the design of the Factoring strategies, neither of which takes the value of the allocation delay h into account. As shown in Table 6, they indeed perform badly when h is large. Another shortcoming of Fac (not of Fac2) was pointed out in Sect. 4.3: While generally too timid, in the first round Fac is outright foolhardy, although this does not show up unless the number of tasks is large.

The Bold strategy appears unbeatable when n and n/p are large. Again, this is what we would expect: As $n \to \infty$ with all other parameters fixed, the overhead of the SS, FSC, GSS, Fac, and Fac2 strategies eventually increases at least proportionally to $\log n$, and the expected idle time incurred by the SC and TSS strategies grows as $\sqrt{n}$, whereas we believe the expected wasted time of the Bold strategy to be $\Theta(\log \log n)$ (see Sect. 3).

There is no basis for extrapolating our experimental findings to parameter settings not investigated; on the other hand, we have tried to exercise the Bold strategy extensively, so that parameter settings forcing it to exhibit a consistently bad behavior would tend to be fairly extreme.

The Bold strategy lacks theoretical underpinnings, as does every other strategy with a good performance. It is possible to arrive at the Bold strategy through a sequence of fairly logical steps, as we attempted to demonstrate in Sect. 3. On the other hand, considerations that are at least as logical lead to different variants of the Bold strategy that just happen not to perform as well. With a better theoretical understanding, presumably one would be able to devise even better strategies, or at least ones whose performance could be safely extrapolated to new parameter values.

We stress that we have tested the Bold strategy only in simulations, not as the load-balancing mechanism in actual parallel computations. If the Bold strategy is deemed promising, it is indispensable to complement our simulations with "real" experiments; indeed, we hope to carry out such experiments in future work. We believe that there are two main reasons why the Bold strategy might not perform as well in practice as in simulations:

- *Complexity.* Computing batch sizes according to the Bold strategy is more time-consuming than for any of the other strategies. The simulations reported in Table 7 were carried out in recognition of this problem. They show that at the price of a certain performance loss, it is possible to simplify the Bold strategy. Both the original and the simplified versions of Bold call for the extraction of three logarithms per batch, which might be considered excessive. Note, however, that these logarithms are not needed with any precision, and that it is perfectly feasible to compute them via table lookup, using the first few significant bits of the argument as the index into the table. Without giving any details, we mention that this can be done particularly efficiently because the successive arguments to each occurrence of 'ln' in the code form a nonincreasing sequence.

- *Lack of independence.* One can think of many reasons why the execution times of distinct tasks would not be independent. If a processor is slowed down for some external reason, e.g., then this will affect all tasks in its batch for as long as the external influence persists. Since the design of the FSC, Factoring, and Bold strategies depends critically on the assumed independence, a violation of this assumption might have disastrous consequences. The results shown in Table 8, which came as a surprise, are encouraging in this respect. Note, however, that the strategies do not adapt automatically to a lack of independence, but need to be told a rough estimate of its extent (in the form of the parameter σ).

We end with the following tentative recommendation: If there is enough time to compute batch sizes according to the Bold strategy, use the Bold strategy. If not, use the Fac2 strategy. If there is not even enough time to follow the Fac2 strategy, our simulations are of little relevance, and a strategy should be chosen based on the available hardware and the time constraints of the problem at hand.

5 Implementation

In principle, a simulator such as the one used to gather the data presented in the previous section is a very simple program. It uses a data type *batch* with attributes *size* and *finishing_time*, with the obvious meaning, and a data structure Q, called the *event queue*, which stores the set of batches under execution at the current simulated time. The core of the simulation repeatedly determines the next event, namely the completion of a batch, and processes the event appropriately, which primarily means scheduling a new batch for later completion. Slightly more formally, we can write this as

```
while (...) {   // while simulation not over
    B = delete_min(Q);   // find next batch to finish
    now = B.finishing_time;   // update simulated time
    record_information_about(B);   // log results
    // assemble new batch B
    B.size = strategy(...);   // determine size
    B.finishing_time = now + random_time(B.size,...);
        // choose random finishing time
    insert(B, Q);   // place new batch in event queue
},
```

where *delete_min*(*Q*) returns a batch in *Q* with minimal *finishing_time* and removes this batch from *Q*, *strategy*(...) returns the size of the next batch, computed according to the chosen strategy, *random_time*(*B.size*,...) returns a random execution time for a batch of size *B.size*, picked according to the chosen probability distribution, and *insert*(*B*, *Q*) inserts *B* in *Q*. The function *strategy* was discussed in fair detail in Sects. 2 and 3. In this section we take a closer look at two remaining nontrivial issues, namely the implementation of the event queue *Q* and the generation of random batch execution times. The main issue here is speed, since higher speed, for a simulation program, translates into the possibility of executing more runs, and thus into greater accuracy.

5.1 The Event Queue

The abstract *priority queue* data structure clearly supports the two operations applied to the event queue, *insert* and *delete_min*, and a first version of our simulator used the *p_queue* data type of the LEDA library, which is implemented using Fibonacci heaps. In a quest for greater speed, the simulator was later rewritten to use a priority queue implemented as follows (see Fig. 9): For a certain positive integer *m* and for real numbers *min_time* and *max_time* with $0 \leq min\_time \leq now \leq max\_time$, where *now* is the current simulated time, the interval [*min_time*, *max_time*] is divided into *m* equal-sized subintervals. Each subinterval *I* is associated with a list containing those tasks whose finishing times belong to *I*, sorted by nondecreasing finishing time. The batches with finishing times larger than *max_time* are stored in a special list *horizon* in no particular order. The simulation proceeds in *sweeps*. During a sweep, a pointer *current* keeps track of the nonempty list associated with the subinterval with the smallest endpoints, so that the next batch to be processed can be located and deleted from its list in constant time. The processing of a batch usually causes a new batch to be inserted in some list, and the *current* pointer may subsequently have to be moved to the next nonempty list. When all *m* regular lists are empty, the minimum and maximum finishing times of the batches in the *horizon* list are computed (this can be done during the construction of the *horizon* list), these are assigned as the new values of *min_time* and *max_time*, the batches in the *horizon* list are removed from the *horizon* list and distributed appropriately among the *m* regular lists, and a new sweep starts.

The reasoning behind using the list-based event queue is that we expect the batches, possibly after a start-up phase, to be approximately evenly distributed among the regular lists. If *m* is chosen on the order of *p*, the number of batches simultaneously present in the queue, processing a batch can then be done in constant expected time, compared to $\Theta(\log p)$ for the Fibonacci-heap implementation. If the batches, for some reason, clump into just a few lists, then insertion into these lists becomes very expensive, and performance suffers. One could counter this worst-case behavior by replacing each list with a more sophisticated priority queue, such as a (usual) heap, but this is hardly worth the trouble. Although our simulation program does a lot more than maintaining

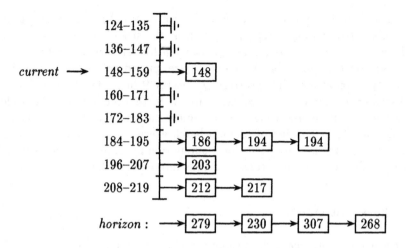

Fig. 9. A list-based event queue.

priority queues, switching from the Fibonacci-heap to the list-based event queue reduced the running time by close to 50%.

5.2 The Generation of Random Variates

A *random variate* is the value assumed by a random variable in an experiment. The simulations reported in Sect. 4 required the generation of several billion pseudo-random variates representing batch execution times. It is customary to decompose the variate-generation problem into two problems: That of generating pseudo-random variates according to the standard uniform distribution on the interval $(0, 1)$, and that of generating random variates according to the distribution of interest given a generator for the standard uniform distribution. Here we will consider only the second problem and assume, for the sake of a clean theoretical discussion, that we have a perfect random-number generator for the standard uniform distribution at our disposal. In order not to get bogged down in problems of a different sort, we also assume the availability of exact arithmetic on real numbers. A wealth of information on variate generation in this model can be found in the classic text by Devroye (1986).

Although, in principle, the variate representing the execution time of a batch of size k could be obtained as $X_1 + \cdots + X_k$, where $X_1, \ldots, X_k$ are independent random variables, each drawn from the distribution of task execution times, this would be prohibitively expensive for our simulations due to the huge number of tasks, making it imperative to generate execution times on a per-batch basis. Recall that our simulations used task execution times with three types of distributions: Exponential, uniform, and Bernoulli. We discuss these in turn.

The sum of k independent random variables, each with an exponential distribution with parameter 1, has a gamma distribution with parameter k. A number of good algorithms for variate generation according to gamma distributions are available; we used an algorithm due to Cheng (1977).

Generating a variate from the distribution of a sum of independent uniform variables is more difficult. Although we actually used a different method, the best algorithm known to us is probably one suggested by Devroye (1986, Sect. XIV.4.6). Devroye's algorithm, as well as Cheng's algorithm for the gamma distribution, guarantee an expected generation time bounded by a constant.

The sum of k independent Bernoulli variables, each taking the values 0 and 1 with probabilities $1 - p$ and p for some fixed p, has the binomial distribution $B(k, p)$ with parameters k and p. Binomial distributions, being discrete, are amenable to generation methods other than those applicable to continuous distributions. The ingenious *alias method*, due to Walker (1977), allows us to generate variates from the $B(k, p)$ distribution in constant time per variate, following $O(k)$ preprocessing time. The catch, in our context, is that we are not dealing with a fixed distribution $B(k, p)$, but with a family of distributions of the form $B(k, p)$, where p is fixed, but k (the number of tasks in a batch) varies, so that a large preprocessing time is not acceptable. Suppose that all values of k of interest are bounded by some upper limit K. We can then use the alias method to carry out the preprocessing for certain selected values of k, namely those in some set $M \subseteq \{1, \ldots, K\}$, and subsequently generate a variate for $B(k, p)$, where $k \in \{1, \ldots, K\}$, as $X_1 + \cdots + X_m$, where X_i is a variate from $B(k_i, p)$, for $i = 1, \ldots, m$, $k_1 + \cdots + k_m = k$, and $k_1, \ldots, k_m \in M$. In order to discuss this in an orderly way, let us define the *sum-size* of a set M of positive integers containing 1 as $\sum_{k \in M} k$ and the *K-decomposition number* of M, where K is a positive integer, as the smallest positive integer m such that every integer in the set $\{1, \ldots, K\}$ can be written as the sum of at most m not necessarily distinct elements of M. Provided that the decomposition of each integer in $\{1, \ldots, K\}$ into a small number of summands can be computed efficiently, it can be seen that the scheme outlined above allows us to generate variates from $B(k, p)$, for arbitrary $k \in \{1, \ldots, K\}$, with preprocessing and generation times proportional to the sum-size and the K-decomposition number, respectively, of the base set M employed. It is therefore of interest to construct sets with small sum-sizes and small K-decomposition numbers. One extreme is to take $M = \{1, \ldots, K\}$, which gives N-decomposition number K, but sum-size $\Theta(K^2)$. Another possibility is to take $M = \{1, 2, 2^2, \ldots, 2^{\lfloor \log K \rfloor}\}$, which yields sum-size $O(K)$, but K-decomposition number $\Theta(\log K)$. The latter construction is not optimal, as we will now see.

Theorem 4. *There is a constant $c > 0$ such that for all integers $K \geq 4$, there exists a set M of sum-size at most cK and K-decomposition number at most $c \log \log K$.*

Proof. Without loss of generality we will assume that K is a power of 2. It suffices to indicate a construction with sum-size $O(K \log K)$ and K-decomposition number $O(\log \log K)$. For we can apply such a construction not to K, but to $K' = K \cdot 2^{-\lceil \log \log K \rceil}$ (this allows us to compose all integers bounded by K'), and supplement its base set with the $O(\log \log K)$ numbers $K, K/2, \ldots, K'$ (this allows us to compose all multiples of K').

A sum-size of $O(K \log K)$ can be achieved as follows: We take M as the set of all integers of the form $iK \cdot 2^{-2^l}$, where $1 \le l \le \lceil \log \log K \rceil$ and $1 \le i \le 2^{2^{l-1}} - 1$ (for $l > \log \log K$ not all such numbers are integers). The sum-size of M is at most

$$\sum_{l=1}^{\lceil \log \log K \rceil} \sum_{i=1}^{2^{2^{l-1}}-1} iK \cdot 2^{-2^l} \le K \sum_{l=1}^{\lceil \log \log K \rceil} \sum_{i=1}^{2^{2^{l-1}}-1} 2^{-2^{l-1}} = O(K \log \log K) \ .$$

To see that the K-decomposition number of M is $O(\log \log K)$, identify an integer in the set $\{0, \ldots, K-1\}$ with a bit vector of length $\log K$, number the bit positions $1, \ldots, \log K$ from left (most significant) to right (least significant) and note that M contains each positive integer whose nonzero bits are all in positions $2^{l-1} + 1, \ldots, 2^l$ for some l with $1 \le l \le \lceil \log \log K \rceil$—call this l the *level* of the number. Given an integer $k \in \{1, \ldots, K\}$, we can use at most four level-1 numbers to compose an integer that agrees with k in the leftmost bit positions, up to and including position 2, and has zeros in all other positions. Then, for $l = 2, \ldots, \lceil \log \log K \rceil$, we can add at most one level-l number to arrive at an integer that agrees with k in the leftmost positions, up to and including position $\min\{2^l, \log K\}$, and has zeros in all other positions. The final integer, which is k, is the sum of at most $4 + \log \log K$ elements of M. $\qquad\square$

The proof just given is constructive, in that it shows how to decompose any given $k \in \{1, \ldots, K\}$. If the available hardware instructions do not allow the summands to be computed online, it is easy to use $O(K)$ preprocessing time and space to construct a table that maps each $k \in \{1, \ldots, K\}$ to its largest summand. Thus the variate-generation problem for the binomial distributions $B(k, p)$ with fixed p and variable $k \in \{1, \ldots, K\}$ can be solved with $O(K)$ preprocessing time and space and $O(\log \log K)$ generation time.

Open problem 5. *Discover more about the tradeoff between sum-size and K-decomposition number. In particular, are $O(K)$ and $O(1)$ simultaneously achievable? Alternatively, find out what may already be known about the problem.*

Acknowledgments. The author thanks Ioana Banicescu for introducing him to the subject, Phil Bradford for participating in initial stages of the work, Alex Lopez-Ortiz and Prabhakar Ragde for answering questions about variate-generation in Maple, Volker Priebe for enthusiasm for this work and many useful discussions, and numerous colleagues at the MPI for their help with practical computer problems.

References

Banicescu, I., and Hummel, S. F., Balancing processor loads and exploiting data locality in N-body simulations, *in* Proc. Supercomputing 1995 (http://www.sdsc.edu/SC95/techpapers.html).

Bratley, P., Fox, B. L., and Schrage, L. E., *A Guide to Simulation*, Springer-Verlag, New York, 1983.

Cheng, R. C. H., The generation of gamma variables with non-integral shape parameter, *Appl. Statist.* **26** (1977), pp. 71–75.

Devroye, L., *Non-Uniform Random Variate Generation*, Springer-Verlag, New York, 1986.

Flynn, L. E., and Hummel, S. F., A mathematical analysis of scheduling parallel loops in decreasing-size chunks, manuscript. A preliminary version is available as IBM Research Report No. RC 18462, Oct. 1992.

Grimmett, G. R., and Stirzaker, D. R., *Probability and Random Processes* (2nd ed.), Oxford University Press, Oxford, 1992.

Gumbel, E. J., The maxima of the mean largest value and of the range, *Ann. Math. Statist.* **25** (1954), pp. 76–84.

Gut, A., *An Intermediate Course in Probability*, Springer-Verlag, New York, 1995.

Hartley, H. O., and David, H. A., Universal bounds for mean range and extreme observation, *Ann. Math. Statist.* **25** (1954), pp. 85–99.

Hummel, S. F., Schmidt, J., Uma, R. N., and Wein, J., Load-sharing in heterogeneous systems via weighted factoring, *in* Proc. 8th Annual ACM Symposium on Parallel Algorithms and Architectures (SPAA 1996), to appear.

Hummel, S. F., Schonberg, E., and Flynn, L. E., Factoring: A method for scheduling parallel loops, *Comm. Assoc. Comput. Mach.* **35**:8 (1992), pp. 90–101.

Kruskal, C. P., and Weiss, A., Allocating independent subtasks on parallel processors, *IEEE Trans. Software Eng.* **11** (1985), pp. 1001–1016.

McGeoch, C. C., Toward an Experimental Method for Algorithm Simulation, *INFORMS J. Comput.* **8** (1996), pp. 1–15.

Mehlhorn, K., and Näher, S., LEDA: A platform for combinatorial and geometric computing, *Comm. Assoc. Comput. Mach.* **38**:1 (1995), pp. 96–102.

Polychronopoulos, C. D., and Kuck, D. J., Guided self-scheduling: A practical scheduling scheme for parallel supercomputers, *IEEE Trans. Comput.* **36** (1987), pp. 1425–1439.

Tzen, T. H., and Ni, L. M., Dynamic loop scheduling for shared-memory multiprocessors, *in* Proc. International Conference on Parallel Processing (ICPP 1991), pp. II 247–II 250.

Walker, A. J., An efficient method for generating discrete random variables with general distributions, *ACM Trans. Math. Software* **3** (1977), pp. 253–256.

Parallel Implementation of an Adaptive Scheme for 3D Unstructured Grids on the SP2

Leonid Oliker[1], Rupak Biswas[1], and Roger C. Strawn[2]

[1] RIACS, NASA Ames Research Center, Moffett Field, CA 94035, USA
[2] US Army AFDD, NASA Ames Research Center, Moffett Field, CA 94035, USA

Abstract. Dynamic mesh adaption on unstructured grids is a powerful tool for computing unsteady flows that require local grid modifications to efficiently resolve solution features. For this work, we consider an edge-based adaption scheme that has shown good single-processor performance on the C90. We report on our experience parallelizing this code for the SP2. Results show a 47.0X speedup on 64 processors when 10% of the mesh is randomly refined. Performance deteriorates to 7.7X when the same number of edges are refined in a highly-localized region. This is because almost all the mesh adaption is confined to a single processor. However, this problem can be remedied by repartitioning the mesh immediately after targeting edges for refinement but before the actual adaption takes place. With this change, the speedup improves dramatically to 43.6X.

1 Introduction

Unstructured grids for solving computational problems have two major advantages over structured grids. First, unstructured meshes enable efficient grid generation around highly complex geometries. Second, appropriate unstructured-grid data structures facilitate the rapid insertion and deletion of points to allow the mesh to locally adapt to the solution.

Two solution-adaptive strategies are commonly used with unstructured-grid methods. Regeneration schemes generate a new grid with a higher or lower concentration of points in different regions depending on an error indicator. A major disadvantage of such schemes is that they are computationally expensive. This is a serious drawback for unsteady problems where the mesh must be frequently adapted. However, resulting grids are usually well-formed with smooth transitions between regions of coarse and fine mesh spacing.

Local mesh adaption, on the other hand, involves adding points to the existing grid in regions where the error indicator is high, and removing points from regions where the indicator is low. The advantage of such strategies is that relatively few mesh points need to be added or deleted at each refinement/coarsening step for unsteady problems. However, complicated logic and data structures are required to keep track of the points that are added and removed.

For problems that evolve with time, local mesh adaption procedures have proved to be robust, reliable, and efficient. By redistributing the available mesh points to capture flowfield phenomena of interest, such procedures make standard computational methods more cost effective. Highly localized regions of mesh refinement are required in order to accurately capture shock waves, contact discontinuities, vortices, and shear layers. This provides scientists the opportunity to obtain solutions on adapted meshes that are comparable to those obtained on globally-refined grids but at a much lower cost.

Advances in adaptive software and methodology notwithstanding, parallel computational strategies will be an essential ingredient in solving complex real-life problems. However, parallel computers are easily programmed with regular data structures; so the development of efficient parallel adaptive algorithms for unstructured grids poses a serious challenge.

Figure 1 depicts our framework for parallel adaptive flow computation. The mesh is first partitioned and mapped among the available processors. The initialization phase distributes the global data among the processors and generates a database for all shared objects. The flow solver then runs for several iterations, updating solution variables that are typically stored at the vertices of the mesh. If desired, local mesh adaption is then performed, generating a new computational mesh. A quick evaluation step determines if the new mesh is sufficiently unbalanced to warrant a repartitioning. If the current partitioning indicates that it is adequately load balanced, control is passed back to the flow solver. Otherwise, a mesh repartitioning procedure is invoked to divide the new grid into subgrids. If the cost of remapping the data is less than the computational gain that would be achieved with balanced partitions, all necessary data is appropriately redistributed. Otherwise, the new partitioning is discarded and the flow calculation continues on the old partitions. The finalization step combines the local grids on each processor into a single global mesh. This is usually required for some post-processing tasks, such as visualization, or to save a snapshot of the grid on secondary storage for future restart runs.

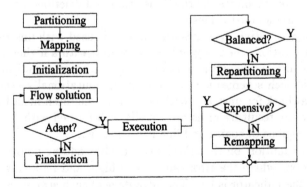

Fig. 1. Overview of our framework for parallel adaptive flow computation

Notice from the framework in Fig. 1 that the computational load is balanced and the runtime communication reduced only for the flow solver but not for the mesh adaptor. This is acceptable since the flow solver is usually several times more expensive. However, parallel performance for the mesh adaption procedure can be significantly improved if the mesh is repartitioned and remapped in a load-balanced fashion after edges are targeted for refinement and coarsening but before performing the actual adaption.

It is obvious from Fig. 1 that a quick mesh adaption procedure is a critical part of the framework. This paper presents an efficient parallel implementation of a dynamic mesh adaption code which has shown good sequential performance. The parallel version consists of an additional 3,000 lines of C++ with Message-Passing Interface (MPI), allowing portability to any system supporting these languages. This code is a wrapper around the original mesh adaption program written in C, and requires almost no changes to the serial code. Only a few lines were added to link it with the parallel constructs. An object-oriented approach allowed this to be performed in a clean and efficient manner.

2　Mesh Adaption Procedure

We give a brief description of the tetrahedral mesh adaption scheme [1] that is used in this work to better explain the modifications that were made for the distributed-memory implementation. The code, called 3D_TAG, has its data structures based on edges that connect the vertices of a tetrahedral mesh. This means that the elements and boundary faces are defined by their edges rather than by their vertices. These edge-based data structures make the mesh adaption procedure capable of performing anisotropic refinement and coarsening.

At each mesh adaption step, individual edges are marked for coarsening, refinement, or no change. Only three subdivision types are allowed for each tetrahedral element and these are shown in Fig. 2. The 1:8 isotropic subdivision is implemented by adding a new vertex at the mid-point of each of the six edges. The 1:4 and 1:2 subdivisions can result either because the edges of a parent tetrahedron are targeted anisotropically or because they are required to form a valid connectivity for the new mesh. When an edge is bisected, the solution quantities are linearly interpolated at the mid-point from its two end-points.

Mesh refinement is performed by first setting a bit flag to one for each edge that is targeted for subdivision. The edge markings for each element are then combined to form a 6-bit pattern. Elements are continuously upgraded to valid patterns corresponding to the three allowed subdivision types until none of the

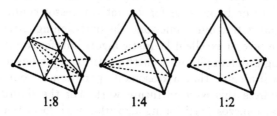

Fig. 2. Three types of subdivision are permitted for a tetrahedral element

patterns show any change. Once this edge-marking is completed, each element is independently subdivided based on its binary pattern.

Mesh coarsening also uses the edge-marking patterns. If a child element has any edge marked for coarsening, this element and its siblings are removed and their parent is reinstated. Parent edges and elements are retained at each refinement step so they do not have to be reconstructed. Reinstated parent elements have their edge-marking patterns adjusted to reflect that some edges have been coarsened. The refinement procedure is then invoked to generate a valid mesh.

Details of the data structures are given in [1]; however, a brief description of the salient features is necessary to understand the distributed-memory implementation of the mesh adaption code. For each vertex, a pointer to the first entry in the edge sublist is stored in **edges**. The edge sublist for a vertex contains pointers to all the edges that are incident upon it. Such sublists eliminate extensive searches and are crucial to the efficiency of the overall adaption scheme. For each edge, we store its two end-points in **vertex[2]**, the two boundary faces it defines in **bfac[2]**, and a pointer to the first entry in the element sublist in **elems**. The element sublist for an edge contains pointers to all the elements that share it. The tetrahedral elements have their six edges stored in **tedge[6]**, while for each boundary face, we store the three edges in **bedge[3]**.

3 Distributed-Memory Implementation

The parallel implementation of the 3D_TAG mesh adaption code consists of three phases: initialization, execution, and finalization. The initialization step consists of scattering the global data across the processors, defining a local numbering scheme for each object, and creating the mapping for objects that are shared by multiple processors. The execution step runs a copy of 3D_TAG on each processor that refines or coarsens its local region, while maintaining a globally-consistent grid along partition boundaries. Parallel performance is extremely critical during this phase since it will be executed several times during a flow computation. Finally, a gather operation is performed in the finalization step to combine the local grids into one global mesh. Locally-numbered objects and corresponding pointers are reordered to represent one single consistent mesh.

In order to perform parallel mesh adaption, the initial grid must first be partitioned among the available processors. A good partitioner should divide the grid into equal pieces for optimal load balancing, while minimizing the number of edges along partition boundaries for low interprocessor communication. It is also important that within our framework, the partitioning phase be performed rapidly. There are several excellent heuristic algorithms for solving the NP-hard graph partitioning problem [6]. Since mesh partitioning is beyond the scope of this paper, we will assume that a reasonable partition for our test meshes is available, and address this issue in future work. For the record, we used the multilevel spectral Lanczos partitioning algorithm with local Kernighan-Lin refinement from the Chaco software package [2].

3.1 Initialization

The initialization phase takes as input the global initial grid and the corresponding partitioning that maps each tetrahedral element to exactly one partition. The element data and partition information are then broadcast to all processors which, in parallel, assign a local, zero-based number to each element. Once the elements have been processed, local edge information can be computed.

In three dimensions, an individual edge may belong to an arbitrary number of elements. Since each element is assigned to only one partition, it is theoretically possible for an edge to be shared by all the processors. For each partition, a local zero-based number is assigned to every edge that belongs to at least one element. Each processor then redefines its elements in **tedge[6]** in terms of these local edge numbers. Edges that are shared by more than one processor are identified by searching for elements that lie on partition boundaries. A bit flag is set to distinguish between shared and internal edges. A list of shared processors (SPL) is also generated for each shared edge. Finally, the element sublist in **elems** for each edge is updated to contain only the local elements.

The vertices are initialized using the **vertex[2]** data structure for each edge. Every local vertex is assigned a zero-based number on each partition. Next the local edge sublist for each vertex is created from the appropriate subset of the global **edges** array. Like shared edges, each shared vertex must be assigned its SPL. A naive approach would be to thread through the data structures to the elements and their partitions to determine shared vertices. A faster approach is based on the following two properties of a shared vertex: it must be an endpoint for at least one shared edge, and its SPL is the union of its shared edges' SPLs. However, some communication is required when using this method. An example is shown in Fig. 3 where the SPL is being formed in P0 for the center vertex that is shared by three other processors. Without communication, P0 would incorrectly conclude that the vertex is shared only with P1 and P3. For each vertex containing a shared edge in its **edges** sublist, that edge's SPL is communicated to the processors in the SPLs of all other shared edges until the union of all the SPLs is formed. For the cases in this paper, this process required no more than three iterations, and all shared vertices were processed as a function of the number of shared edges plus a small communication overhead.

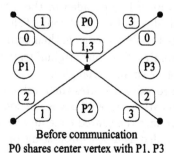
Before communication
P0 shares center vertex with P1, P3

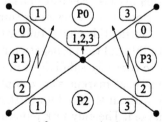
After communication
P0 shares center vertex with P1, P2, P3

Fig. 3. Example showing the communication need to form the SPL for a shared vertex

The final step in the initialization phase is the local renumbering of the external boundary faces. Since a boundary face belongs to only one element, it is never shared among processors. Each boundary face is defined by its three edges in **bedge[3]**, while each edge maintains a pair of pointers in **bfac[2]** to the boundary faces it defines. Since the global mesh is closed, an edge on the external boundary is shared by exactly two boundary faces. However, when the mesh is partitioned, this is no longer true. An affected edge creates an empty ghost boundary face in each of the two processors for the execution phase which is later eliminated during the finalization stage.

A new data structure has been added to the serial code to represent all this shared information. Each shared edge and vertex contains a two-way mapping between its local and its global numbers, and a SPL of processors where its shared copies reside. The maximum additional storage depends on the number of processors used and the fraction of shared objects. For the cases in this paper, this was less than 10% of the memory requirements of the serial version.

3.2 Execution

The first step in the actual mesh adaption phase is to target edges for refinement or coarsening. This is usually based on an error indicator for each edge that is computed from the flow solution. This strategy results in a symmetrical marking of all shared edges across partitions since shared edges have the same flow and geometry information regardless of their processor number. However, elements have to be continuously upgraded to one of the three allowed subdivision patterns shown in Fig. 2. This causes some propagation of edges being targeted that could mark local copies of shared edges inconsistently. This is because the local geometry and marking patterns affect the nature of the propagation. Communication is therefore required after each iteration of the propagation process. Every processor sends a list of all the newly-marked local copies of shared edges to all the other processors in their SPLs. This process may continue for several iterations, and edge markings could propagate back and forth across partitions.

Figure 4 shows a two-dimensional example of two iterations of the propagation process across a partition boundary. The process is similar in three dimensions. Processor P0 marks its local copy of shared edge GE1 and communicates that to P1. P1 then marks its own copy of GE1, which causes some internal propagation because element marking patterns must be upgraded to those that are valid. Note that P1 marks its third internal edge and its local copy of shared edge GE2 during this phase. Information about the shared edge is then communicated to P0, and the propagation phase terminates. The four original triangles can now be correctly subdivided into a total of 12 smaller triangles.

Once all edge markings are complete, each processor executes the mesh adaption code without the need for further communication, since all edges are consistently marked. The only task remaining is to update the shared edge and vertex information as the mesh is adapted. This is handled as a post-processing phase.

New edges and vertices that are created on partition boundaries during refinement are assigned shared processor information. If a shared edge is bisected,

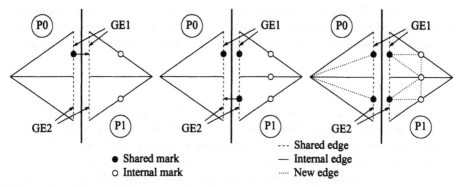

● Shared mark
○ Internal mark

--- Shared edge
— Internal edge
···· New edge

Fig. 4. Two-dimensional example showing communication during propagation of edge

its two children and the center vertex inherit its SPL. However, if a new edge is created that lies across an element face, communication is sometimes required to determine whether it is shared or internal. If it is shared, the SPL must be formed. If the intersection of the SPLs of the two end-points of the new edge is null, the edge is internal. Otherwise, communication is required with the shared processors to determine whether they have a local copy of the edge. This communication is necessary because no information is stored about the faces of the tetrahedral elements. An alternate solution would be to incorporate faces as an additional object into the data structures, and maintaining it through the adaption. However, this does not compare favorably in terms of memory or CPU time to a single communication at the end of the refinement procedure.

Figure 5 depicts the top view of a tetrahedron in processor P0 that shares two faces with P1. In P0, the intersection of the shared processor lists for the two end-points of each of the three new edges LE1, LE2, and LE3 yields P1. However, when P0 communicates this information to P1, P1 will only have local copies corresponding to LE1 and LE2. Thus, P0 will classify LE1 and LE2 as shared edges but LE3 as an internal edge.

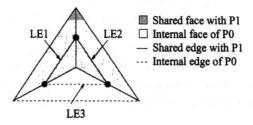

Shared face with P1
Internal face of P0
— Shared edge with P1
--- Internal edge of P0

Fig. 5. Example showing how a new edge across a face is classified as shared or internal

The coarsening phase purges the data structures of all edges that are removed, as well as their associated vertices, elements, and boundary faces. No new shared processor information is generated since no mesh objects are created during this step. However, objects are renumbered as a result of compaction and all internal and shared data are updated accordingly. The refinement routine is then invoked to generate a valid mesh from the vertices left after the coarsening.

3.3 Finalization

Under certain conditions, it is necessary to create a single global mesh after one or more adaption steps. Some post processing tasks, such as visualization, need to processes the whole grid simultaneously. Storing a snapshot of a grid for future restarts could also require a global view. Our finalization phase accomplishes this goal by connecting the subgrids into one global data structure. Individual processors are responsible for correctly arranging the data so that a host processor only collects and concatenates without further processing.

Each local object is first assigned a unique global number. Because elements are not shared, each processor can assign the final global element number by performing a scan-reduce add on the total number of elements. The global boundary face numbering is also done similarly since they too are not shared among processors. Assigning global numbers to edges and vertices is somewhat more complicated since they may be shared by several processors. Each shared edge (or vertex) is assigned an owner from its processor list which is then responsible for generating the global number. Owners are randomly selected to keep the computation and communication loads balanced. Once all processors complete numbering their edges (or vertices), a communication phase propagates the global values from owners to other processors that have local copies.

After global numbers have been assigned to every object, all data structures are updated to contain consistent global information. Since elements and boundary faces are unique in each processor, no duplicates exist. All unowned edge copies are removed from the data structures, which are then compacted. However, the element sublists in **elems** cannot be discarded for the unowned edges. Some communication is required to adjust the pointers in the local sublists so that global sublists can be formed without any serial computation. The pair of pointers in **bfac[2]** that were split during the initialization phase for shared edges are glued back by communicating the boundary face information to the owner. Vertex data structures are updated much like edges except for the manner in which their edge sublists in **edges** are handled. Since shared vertices may contain local copies of the same global edge in their sublists on different processors, the unowned edge copies are first deleted. Pointers are next adjusted as in the **elems** case with some communication among processors. A final gather operation by the host processor generates the global mesh.

4 Results

The parallel 3D_TAG procedure has been implemented on the SP2 distributed-memory multiprocessor located at NASA Ames Research Center. The code is written in C and C++, with the parallel activities in MPI for portability.

The computational mesh is the one used to simulate the acoustics experiment of Purcell [3] where a 1/7th scale model of a UH-1H helicopter rotor blade was tested over a range of subsonic and transonic hover-tip Mach numbers. Numerical results and a detailed report of the simulation are given in [5]. This paper reports only on the performance of the parallel version of the mesh adaption code.

Timings for the parallel code are presented for one refinement and one coarsening step using various marking and load-balancing strategies. Two marking strategies are used for the refinement step. The first set of experiments consists of randomly marking 5% and 10% of the edges, while the second set consists of marking the same numbers of edges in a single compact region of the mesh. In general, we expect real marking patterns to lie somewhere in between these two significantly different scenarios. Since the coarsening procedure and performance are similar to the refinement method, only one case is presented where 35% of the edges of the largest mesh obtained after refinement are randomly coarsened.

Table 1 presents the progression of grid sizes through the two adaption steps for each marking strategy. Notice that the meshes obtained after refinement for the randomly-marked cases are much larger than those for the locally-marked cases even though exactly the same number of edges are marked. This is due to the difference in the propagation of edge markings. The random cases cause significantly more propagation since refinement is scattered throughout the mesh. The local cases, on the other hand, cause propagation only at the boundary between the refined and the unrefined regions since all edges internal to the refined region are already marked.

Table 1. Progression of grid sizes through refinement and coarsening

		Vertices	Elements	Edges	Bdy Faces
Refinement	Initial mesh	13,967	60,968	74,343	16,818
	5% random marking	24,293	114,415	143,011	8,550
	5% local marking	17,920	82,259	104,178	7,999
	10% random marking	54,389	284,086	345,425	13,606
	10% local marking	21,851	103,582	129,976	8,962
Coarsening	Initial mesh	54,389	284,086	345,425	13,606
	35% random marking	25,689	122,850	152,853	8,630

4.1 Refinement Phase

Table 2 presents the timings and parallel speedup for the refinement step with the random marking of edges. The performance is excellent with efficiencies of almost 90% on 32 processors and 60% to 73% on 64 processors. Notice that the communication time is less than 10% of the total time for up to 16 processors. On 32 and 64 processors, the communication time although still quite small, becomes comparable to the computation time and begins to adversely affect the parallel speedup. This indicates that the saturation point has been reached for this example in terms of the number of processors that should be used. For example, on 64 processors, each partition contains less than 1,000 elements with 31% of the edges on partition boundaries. Since additional work and storage are necessary for shared edges, the speedup deteriorates as the percentage of such edges increases. Parallel mesh refinement when 10% of the edges are marked shows better performance than the 5%-marked case due to a bigger computation-to-communication ratio. In general, performance will improve as the problem size increases. This is because the computational time will increase while the percentage of elements along processor boundaries will decrease.

Table 2. Performance for the refinement step when edges are marked randomly

# Procs	% Shared Edges	5% Marked			10% Marked		
		Comp Time	Comm Time	Total Speedup	Comp Time	Comm Time	Total Speedup
1	0.0	12.941	0.000	1.00	39.237	0.000	1.00
2	3.2	6.652	0.090	1.92	19.698	0.045	1.99
4	12.1	3.659	0.094	3.45	10.091	0.105	3.85
8	23.2	1.927	0.107	6.36	5.245	0.281	7.10
16	23.9	0.952	0.100	12.30	2.638	0.233	13.67
32	29.2	0.323	0.129	28.63	1.098	0.287	28.33
64	31.0	0.246	0.091	38.40	0.646	0.189	46.99

Table 3 shows the timings and speedup when edges are marked in a single compact region of the global mesh. The performance is extremely poor, with speedups of only 5.1X and 7.7X on 64 processors. This is because we are simulating an almost worst case load balance behavior. This strategy primarily targets elements on one processor only. Most of the other processors remain idle, since none of their elements need to be refined. Noticeable speedup is achieved only when using at least 16 processors. This is because the refinement region remains confined to only one partition until enough processors are used. Once the refinement region straddles multiple partitions, parallelization becomes effective. However, the computation time does decrease somewhat for up to 8 processors, even though all the work is performed by a single processor. This is due to the reduction in the local mesh size for each individual partition. As a result, even though one partition is performing all the work, it has a smaller number of elements to process.

Due to the poor parallel performance when edges are marked in a single compact region of the global mesh, it is worthwhile to load balance the mesh adaption code based on the distribution of targeted edges before these edges are actually refined. The mesh is repartitioned if the markings are skewed beyond a specified tolerance. This significantly improves the performance of the mesh refinement phase. As a bonus, a more balanced mesh is generated after the refinement since the final grid is generally determined by the marking patterns.

Using this methodology, the localized-marking experiment was run again after performing a repartitioning step based on edge markings. A simple heuris-

Table 3. Performance for the refinement step when edges are marked in a single compact region of the global mesh

# Procs	% Shared Edges	5% Marked			10% Marked		
		Comp Time	Comm Time	Total Speedup	Comp Time	Comm Time	Total Speedup
1	0.0	5.581	0.000	1.00	8.806	0.000	1.00
2	3.2	4.351	0.000	1.28	7.517	0.000	1.17
4	12.1	3.828	0.006	1.46	7.036	0.008	1.25
8	23.2	3.362	0.008	1.66	6.462	0.008	1.36
16	23.9	3.230	0.012	1.72	4.232	0.012	2.07
32	29.2	0.982	0.710	3.30	1.188	0.955	4.11
64	31.0	1.083	0.021	5.06	1.104	0.044	7.67

tic of assigning an additional weight to elements containing edges that have been marked for refinement was given to the partitioner. Table 4 presents the performance results of this repartitioned local refinement phase. The communication times are not reported but are considered when calculating the total speedup. Note that the parallel speedups are now comparable to those for the random-marking case. This demonstrates that mesh adaption can deliver excellent speedups if the marked edges are equidistributed among the processors.

Table 4. Performance for the repartitioned refinement step when edges are marked in a single compact region of the global mesh

# Procs	5% Marked				10% Marked			
	# Elements in Min Set	# Elements in Max Set	Comp Time	Total Speedup	# Elements in Min Set	# Elements in Max Set	Comp Time	Total Speedup
1	60,968	60,968	5.581	1.00	60,968	60,968	8.806	1.00
2	9,069	51,899	2.486	1.72	6,867	54,101	3.977	1.80
4	5,575	28,983	1.446	3.44	3,074	42,701	2.376	3.47
8	2,120	14,498	0.824	6.62	1,272	21,358	1.244	6.89
16	389	7,249	0.287	12.19	595	10,670	0.622	12.91
32	190	3,629	0.251	21.22	281	5,340	0.352	24.26
64	95	1,812	0.132	36.24	141	2,670	0.147	43.59

4.2 Coarsening Phase

The coarsening phase consists of three major steps: marking edges to coarsen, cleaning up all the data structures by removing those edges and their associated vertices and tetrahedral elements, and finally invoking the refinement routine to generate a valid mesh from the vertices left after the coarsening.

Timings and parallel speedup when 35% of the edges of the largest mesh obtained by refinement are randomly coarsened are presented in Table 5. Note that the computation time does not include the follow-up mesh refinement time. It is, instead, only the time required to mark edges to coarsen. This was done so as to demonstrate the parallel performance of the modules that are only required during the coarsening phase. Notice that the communication time is negligible while the cleanup time is dominant. Since the cleanup time depends on the fraction of shared objects, performance deteriorates as the problem size is over-saturated by processors.

Table 5. Performance for the coarsening step when edges are marked randomly

# Procs	Comp Time	Cleanup Time	Comm Time	Total Speedup
1	3.184	6.949	0.000	1.00
2	1.648	3.564	0.005	1.94
4	0.850	1.822	0.006	3.78
8	0.439	0.962	0.011	7.18
16	0.270	0.499	0.024	12.78
32	0.144	0.271	0.020	23.29
64	0.085	0.132	0.038	39.74

4.3   Initialization and Finalization Phases

Recall from Fig. 1 that unlike the execution phase where the actual adaption is performed, it is not critical for the initialization and finalization procedures to be very efficient since they are used rarely (or only once) during a flow computation. Table 6 presents the results for these two phases. The initialization step is performed on the starting mesh consisting of 60,968 elements, while the finalization phase is for the adapted mesh consisting of 114,415 elements. It is apparent from the timings that the performance bottleneck for the two steps are the global broadcast (one-to-all) and gather (all-to-one) communication patterns, respectively. These times generally increase with the number of processors

Table 6. Performance for the initialization and finalization steps when 5% of edges are marked randomly

# Procs	Initialization			Finalization		
	Comp Time	Bcast Time	Total Speedup	Comp Time	Gather Time	Total Speedup
1	4.500	0.328	1.00	4.035	0.682	1.00
2	2.479	0.645	1.55	2.312	0.665	1.58
4	1.523	1.175	1.79	1.494	0.676	2.17
8	0.962	0.918	2.57	1.019	0.714	2.72
16	0.568	1.008	3.06	0.647	0.785	3.29
32	0.409	1.214	2.97	0.393	0.890	3.68
64	0.242	1.503	2.77	0.286	0.977	3.73

so a speedup cannot be expected. However, the computational sections of these procedures do show favorable speedups of 18.6X and 14.1X on 64 processors. In any case, the overall run times of these routines are acceptable for our purposes. Note that the broadcast and gather times are non-zero even for a single processor because the current implementation uses a host to perform the data I/O. The number of processors shown in Table 6 indicates those that are actually performing the mesh adaption.

5 Summary

Fast and efficient dynamic mesh adaption is an important feature of unstructured grids that make them especially attractive for unsteady flows. For such flows, the coarsening/refinement step must be performed frequently, so its efficiency must be comparable to that of the flow solver. For this work, the adaption scheme of Biswas and Strawn [1] is parallelized for distributed-memory architectures.

The code consists of approximately 3,000 lines of C++ with MPI which wrap around the original version written in C. The serial code was left almost completely unchanged except for the addition of 10 lines which interface to the parallel wrapper. This allowed us to design the parallel version using the serial code as a building block. The object-oriented approach allowed us to build a clean interface between the two layers of the program while maintaining efficiency. Only a slight increase in space was necessary to keep track of the global mappings and shared processor lists for objects on partition boundaries.

Parallel performance is extremely promising showing a 47-fold speedup on 64 processors compared to sequential execution. In the worst case when a single compact region of the mesh is refined, speedup increased from 8- to 44-fold by repartitioning the mesh using the edge-marking information. We are currently in the process of combining this parallel mesh adaption code with a dynamic partitioner and load balancer [4].

References

1. Biswas, R., Strawn, R.: A new procedure for dynamic adaption of three-dimensional unstructured grids. Appl. Numer. Math. **13** (1994) 437–452
2. Hendrickson, B., Leland, R.: The Chaco user's guide — Version 2.0. Sandia National Laboratories Technical Report SAND94-2692 (1994)
3. Purcell, T.: CFD and transonic helicopter sound. 14th European Rotorcraft Forum (1988) Paper 2
4. Sohn, A., Biswas, R., Simon, H.: A dynamic load balancing framework for unstructured adaptive computations on distributed-memory multiprocessors. 8th ACM Symposium on Parallel Algorithms and Architectures (1996) to appear
5. Strawn, R., Biswas, R., Garceau, M.: Unstructured adaptive mesh computations of rotorcraft high-speed impulsive noise. J. Aircraft **32** (1995) 754–760
6. Van Driessche, R., Roose, D.: Load Balancing Computational Fluid Dynamics Calculations on Unstructured Grids. AGARD Report R-807 (1995)

Solution of Large, Sparse, Irregular Systems on a Massively Parallel Computer

Will Dearholt
Steven Castillo
Gary Hennigan
Klipsch School of Electrical and Computer Engineering
New Mexico State University
Box 30001, Dept. 3-O
Las Cruces, NM 88003

Abstract. A set of tools is introduced which allow engineers and scientists to obtain solutions to large finite-element problems by utilizing multiple-instruction, multiple-data (MIMD) parallel computers. The finite-element mesh is decomposed so that each resulting sub-domain is connected to at most two other subdomains. The node-numbering of the decomposed mesh is such that the resulting set of finite element equations will have a border-block diagonal structure. A parallel algorithm is used to assemble, factor and solve the set of simultaneous algebraic equations that result from the finite-element method (FEM). In this paper, we demonstrate the method on a message passing parallel computer for two- and three-dimensional electrostatic problems, governed by Laplace's equation. Results and performance data for the algorithm as applied to electrostatics problems are given. The current work is an extension of the algorithm described and implemented in Reference [1].

1 Introduction

The finite-element method (FEM) is a general technique used for solving partial differential equations that are commonly encountered in engineering and science problems. Despite the generality of the method, its applicability to many problems is limited by the computational power available. This limitation is particularly evident in three-dimensional problems where both the number of unknowns and the complexity of three-dimensional elements contribute greatly to the computational resources required to solve a given problem. To overcome this limitation, many engineers and scientists have been examining the usefulness of multiple-instruction, multiple-data (MIMD) parallel computers.

While much work has been done in the area of dense-matrix factorization on MIMD architectures (See Refs. [2, 3, 4]), relatively little has been done in the area of sparse-matrix factorization. The fact that there is a lack of results in the area of sparse-matrix factorization on MIMD architectures can be attributed to the complexity of the task of programming such algorithms.

Much of the work that is currently being done in sparse-matrix factorization on MIMD computers focuses on distributing rows or columns of the matrix to different processors in the MIMD architecture. While this allows for a relatively efficient algorithm, it is not well suited to an FEM implementation where it would be advantageous to not only parallelize the factorization of the resulting matrix, but to actually parallelize the process which generates the coefficient matrix. A summary of much of what has been accomplished in the area of sparse-matrix factorization on MIMD architectures can be found in Reference [5].

While the study of such sparse-matrix factorization techniques is important, for many engineers and scientists it is the application of these factorization techniques to the efficient modeling of science and engineering problems that is the ultimate goal. As previously stated, the FEM generates a sparse system of equations which can lead to significant savings in memory requirements, as well as reducing the number of computations, and thus execution time as compared to methods which result in full, dense systems of equations. Both of these are important considerations on MIMD architectures which are generally configured with 8–64MB of memory per processor and are utilized as time-shared resources.

In a previous paper [1], we described a method for solving sparse, positive-definite systems of equations which have a border-block diagonal structure. However, the algorithmic implementation of the factorization suffered because of a lack of scalability. Therefore, the size of the problem that could be solved was limited not by the number of processors available, but by the available memory on each processor. In this paper, we discuss an improved algorithm which overcomes the previously mentioned scaling limitation. The problem size that can be solved on the MIMD computer with the new algorithm is limited only by the number of computational nodes and the total available computational power. The efficiency of the algorithm is determined by the decomposition that is performed. That is, the relative load balance as determined by the number of finite-element nodes and connectivity in each subdomain as well as the ratio of the number of internal nodes to subdomain boundary nodes for the total problem are the factors that will determine the speed of the parallel solution.

2 Automatic Domain Decomposition

One-way dissection is a simple means of obtaining a bordered, block-diagonal system of equations (see Figure 1).

In one-way dissection, a number of distinct dissectors (adjacent FEM nodes), also referred to here as separation boundaries, or s-boundaries, are chosen such that nodes not lying on these dissectors are numbered first, followed by numbering the nodes that make up the dissectors. A simple geometry illustrating this concept is shown in Figure 2.

Consider Figure 2. Internal FEM nodes in each of the four subdomains, 0–3, are consecutively numbered. Since the FEM nodes internal to a given subdomain are not directly connected to FEM nodes internal to other subdomains, their contribution to the system of equations takes the form of a diagonal block. Blocks 0–3 in Figure 3 correspond directly to the FEM nodes internal to each of the subdomains in Figure 3.

Fig. 1. Bordered, block diagonal system of equations generated by a one-way dissection

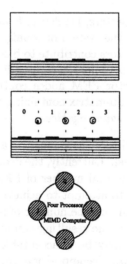

Fig. 2. Mapping from FEM problem to parallel MIMD computer

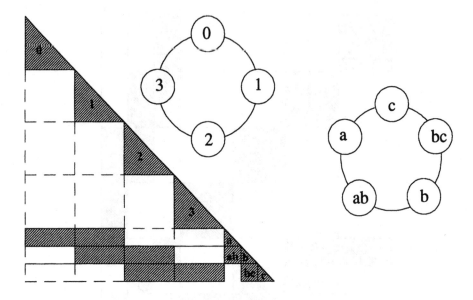

Fig. 3. Factored system of equations as it resides on the processors of a MIMD computer for a 4 subdomain problem.

FEM nodes lying on the dissectors, labeled a, b, and c in Figure 3, are consecutively numbered. Entries in the system of equations corresponding to FEM nodes lying entirely on the dissectors contribute to blocks a, b, and c in Figure 3. Finally, entries in the system of equations corresponding to interactions between internal FEM nodes and dissector FEM nodes contribute to the off-diagonal blocks in Figure 1. The square sub-matrix containing the sub-blocks, a, b, and c will be referred to here as the *s-boundary block*.

To be an effective and useful tool there must be an automatic means of decomposing the finite-element mesh. Currently, the decomposition algorithm uses only the simple criteria that the total number of FEM nodes residing between dissector levels be nearly equal to attempt to achieve an optimal load balance. No consideration is given to minimize the number of nodes that will fall on subdomain boundaries and therefore the resulting communication to computation ratio on the parallel computer may be unacceptable for complex geometrical structures. Details of the one-way decomposition are beyond the scope of this paper but can be found in reference [8].

For most of the meshes, the decomposition code runs on a variety of local serial workstations. The largest meshes are decomposed on a Cray YMP-EL.

3 Parallel FEM Implementation

Once the FEM problem domain has been decomposed, the next step is to actually carry out the finite-element method for the problem on the Massively Parallel Processor (MPP). The algorithm uses two distinct groups of processors on the parallel computer for the purpose of scalability. Here, we refer to the two groups of processors as the lower and upper subcubes. (The term subcube is a misnomer carried over from the earlier days of hypercube parallel computers).

The lower subcube of processors corresponds to the diagonal blocks of the system of equations in Figure 1. The mapping of lower-subcube processors for the simple example given earlier is shown in Figure 3 (Figure 3 shows only the lower half of the system. For indefinite matrices, the upper half of the matrix has to be stored and is assumed to be structurally symmetric to the lower half). Each of the processors in the lower subcube will read in the mesh data for its particular subdomain. After the input files for each subdomain have been read by each of the corresponding processors on the MPP, each processor finds the graph for its mesh and reorders it to reduce local storage and computational requirements. In the current implementation, this is accomplished with the standard reverse Cuthill-McKee (RCM) algorithm. Each processor then performs an elemental assembly to fill its particular diagonal block. The diagonal block is locally stored in envelope form using the connectivity of the reordered subgraph. The steps required to find the subgraph, reorder the subgraph and fill the corresponding diagonal block in envelope form require no inter-processor communication. Communication is necessary only to complete the diagonal terms in the s-boundary block.

The s-boundary block is mapped to the upper subcube of processors. The s-boundary block, consisting of sub-blocks a, b, and c in Figure 1, poses a problem when attempting to find the fill-in pattern of the envelope. In order to determine the fill-in pattern of the s-boundary block, reachable sets must be used [8]. If such sets were used in the parallel algorithm, an inordinate amount of inter-processor communication would be necessary to completely determine the envelope structure of the s-boundary block. To avoid the problem of determining the envelope associated with the s-boundary block, it is assumed to be "block-full".

The advantages of this simplified form for fill-in pattern of the s-boundary block are that it requires little computation and no inter-processor communication. Another advantage is that the factorization can exploit one of several parallel full-block factorization algorithms that are available. The disadvantage of this approach is that the storage requirements can be significantly larger than those of an envelope storage method.

The equation entries for the s-boundary block are first generated on the lower subcube processors and are then communicated to the upper subcube. In the current implementation, the distribution of the s-boundary block is performed by distributing each of the sub-blocks, block a, b, and c in Figure 1, to a separate, independent processor. Blocks a, b, and c receive the equation coefficients for the nodes on the dissectors. Blocks ab and bc will be used for additional storage required because of fill-in that occurs during the algorithm. Figure 3 only shows the lower half of the s-boundary block as is applicable for symmetric matrices. For matrices that are numerically nonsymmetric, two more fill-in blocks are needed above the diagonal. For a problem decomposed into n subdomains the number of processors required to solve the problem is then given by

$$p = 3n - 3. \tag{1}$$

Since the only communication that is necessary in this algorithm is in distributing, factoring, and solving the system of equations for the s-boundary block, the amount of communication is directly proportional to the size of this block. An example of the factored set of equations and it's distribution on a MIMD computer with a torus topology is shown in Figure 3.

4 Parallel Factorization of the System of Equations

The system of equations to be solved is represented by

$$\mathbf{Ax} = \mathbf{b} \tag{2}$$

where $\mathbf{A}$ is the coefficient, or stiffness matrix, $\mathbf{b}$ is a vector representing the discretization of the forcing function, or right-hand side, and $\mathbf{x}$ is the vector of unknowns. First, consider the application of the FEM to an elliptic system (Laplace's equation) which results in $\mathbf{A}$ being symmetric and positive definite. For such a system, the decomposition of $\mathbf{A}$ is written as

$$\mathbf{A} = \mathbf{LU} = \mathbf{LL}^T \tag{3}$$

The system of equations shown in Figure 1 can be partitioned as

$$\mathbf{A} = \begin{bmatrix} \mathbf{B} & \mathbf{V} \\ \mathbf{V}^T & \bar{\mathbf{C}} \end{bmatrix} \tag{4}$$

For the example used here, $\mathbf{B}$ contains the main diagonal blocks, 0, 1, 2, and 3, $\bar{\mathbf{C}}$ contains the group of sub-blocks a, b and c viewed as a single diagonal block, and $\mathbf{V}$ contains the off-diagonal entry adjacent to the corresponding diagonal block.

Next a factorization of the coefficient matrix given in Equation 4 must be found. The form of this partitioned factor is

$$\mathbf{L} = \begin{bmatrix} \mathbf{L}_B & \mathbf{0} \\ \mathbf{Z}^T & \mathbf{L}_C \end{bmatrix} \tag{5}$$

where $\mathbf{L}_B$ and $\mathbf{L}_C$ are the Cholesky factors of the sub-matrices $\mathbf{B}$ and $\mathbf{C}$, respectively, and $\mathbf{C}$ is given by

$$\mathbf{C} = \bar{\mathbf{C}} - \mathbf{V}^T \mathbf{B}^{-1} \mathbf{V} \tag{6}$$

The subtraction in Equation 6 is referred to as the modification of $\overline{\mathbf{C}}$ with the modification matrix given as

$$\mathbf{V}^T \mathbf{B}^{-1} \mathbf{V} = \mathbf{V}^T \mathbf{L}_B^{-T} \mathbf{L}_B^{-1} \mathbf{V} = \mathbf{Z} \mathbf{Z}^T \tag{7}$$

This yields a complete factorization for the stiffness matrix **A**. It is important to note that in the current implementation, the sub-matrix **Z** in Equation 5 is never explicitly stored, but is calculated as needed via an implicit scheme described in References [1] and [8].

The factorization is performed for each of the main diagonal blocks in the block-partitioned system of equations. Using the matrix in Figure 3 as an example, each of the main diagonal blocks, blocks 0–3, are factored simultaneously on processors 0–3 which yields L_B. Note that the factorization of the main diagonal blocks requires no inter-processor communication. While the factorization of the main diagonal blocks proceeds, and if the particular MIMD architecture supports it, the unfactored s-boundary block entries can be simultaneously distributed to the secondary group of processors, overlaying an "expensive" communication with computation.

Once the factorization of the main diagonal blocks is completed, and the s-boundary block is completely distributed to the secondary group of processors, the next step is to modify the s-boundary block given in Equation 7. On the MIMD computer, each processor associated with a main diagonal block can calculate the necessary modification vectors simultaneously. Once a processor calculates a modification vector, it then distributes this information to the appropriate processor in the upper-subcube. At this point fill-in occurs and the additional processors (*ab* and *bc* in Figure 3) are used for the additional storage.

After the modification is complete, the s-boundary block processors must factor the s-boundary block. Currently this is accomplished with a semi-parallel, inner-product scheme. The process of factoring a matrix with this scheme is described as follows (p. 20, Ref. [8]).

For $j = 1, 2, ..., N$

$$\text{Compute } l_{j,j} = \left(a_{j,j} - \sum_{k=1}^{j-1} l_{j,k}^2 \right)^{\frac{1}{2}}.$$

For $i = j+1, j+2, ..., N$

$$\text{Compute } l_{i,j} = \left(a_{i,j} - \sum_{k=1}^{j-1} l_{i,k} l_{j,k} \right) / l_{j,j}.$$

In the case that the coefficient matrix is indefinite and not numerically symmetric, a lower-upper (LU) factorization algorithm is used. The partitioned coefficient matrix is

$$A = \begin{bmatrix} B & V \\ Z^T & \bar{C} \end{bmatrix}. \tag{8}$$

The lower and upper factors are written, respectively as

$$L = \begin{bmatrix} L_B & 0 \\ W^T & L_C \end{bmatrix} \tag{9}$$

and

$$U = \begin{bmatrix} U_B & G \\ 0 & U_C \end{bmatrix}. \tag{10}$$

Proceeding in a way similar to computing the modification to $\overline{C}$ in the Cholesky factorization, write

$$C = \overline{C} - Z^T U_B^{-1} L_B^{-1} V. \tag{11}$$

With a few algebraic manipulations, the modification computation becomes

$$Z^T U_B^{-1} L_B^{-1} V = Z^T U_B^{-1} L_B^{-1} L_B G = Z^T \widetilde{G}. \tag{12}$$

To find the columns of $\widetilde{G}$, solve the system $U_B \widetilde{G} = G$ for each column $\widetilde{g}_i$ of matrix $\widetilde{G}$ and finally write the modification of $\overline{C}$ as

$$C = \overline{C} - Z^T \widetilde{G}. \tag{13}$$

Similar to the Cholesky case, each column of Z^T and $\widetilde{G}$ can be computed as they are needed and no two-dimensional matrices need to be stored thus cutting down on memory requirements.

When the modifications are complete, the s-boundary block has to be factored using a semi-parallel adaptation of the algorithm used for the diagonal blocks on the lower subcube. The lower and upper factors are computed with the formulas

$$l_{i,j} = \frac{a_{i,j} - \sum_{k=1}^{j-1} l_{i,k} u_{k,j}}{u_{j,j}}$$

and

$$u_{i,j} = a_{i,j} - \sum_{k=1}^{i-1} l_{i,k} u_{k,j}.$$

A summary of the algorithm is shown as a flow diagram in Figure 4.

5 Results

The parallel FEM algorithm has been implemented on a Cray T3D with 256 processors. All interprocessor communication on the T3D was accomplished using the native message passing library implemented in an ANSI C code. Mesh generation was done using the MSC Patran FEM package on an HP 730 workstation. The decomposition of each mesh was done on one of several available workstation platforms with the exception of the very largest meshes which were decomposed on a Cray YMP-EL.

For the geometries considered here, the problem considered is that of the electrostatic field distribution for two- and three-dimensional domains governed by Laplace's equation:

$$\nabla \cdot \epsilon(x, y, z) \nabla \phi = 0 \tag{14}$$

where

$$\begin{aligned}
\phi &= V_0 \text{ on } \Gamma_0 \\
\phi &= V_1 \text{ on } \Gamma_1 \\
&\vdots \\
\phi &= V_n \text{ on } \Gamma_n
\end{aligned} \tag{15}$$

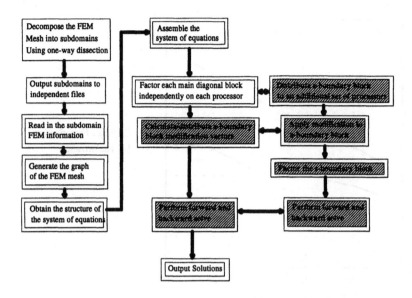

Fig. 4. Summary of parallel FEM algorithm. Double boxes indicate execution on the MIMD computer. Shaded boxes indicate operations which require inter-processor communication.

and ϵ is the electrical permittivity of the physical region, V is the unknown voltage within that region, and the Γ_i are the boundaries of the conductors in the region. A common application of Equation 14 is to obtain capacitance values for specific geometric configurations used in printed circuit boards and transistor layouts in IC's. The algorithm was executed for four geometries:

- a two-dimensional rectangular geometry discretized with first-order quadrilateral elements,

- a three-dimensional rectangular geometry discretized with first-order hexahedral elements,

- a three-dimensional coaxial transmission-line cable discretized with first-order hexahedral elements, and

- a two-dimensional six-strip microstrip transmission line, similar to the geometry illustrated in Figure 2, discretized with first-order quadrilateral elements.

The rectangular geometries were used to verify that the algorithm produced correct results for a problem whose analytic solution is easily obtainable. The values obtained from the solution of Laplace's equation over the rectangular region agreed within 0.05% of those calculated using the analytic solution.

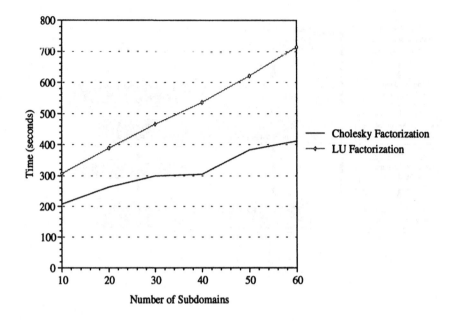

Fig. 5. Scaled speedup for two-dimensional rectangular geometry

Figures 5 and 6 show the scaled speedup timings for the two- and three-dimensional rectangular geometries. For both the two- and three-dimensional geometries, the number of finite element nodes per processor was kept constant at 10,000. Ideally, the total run time should stay constant since the load per processor is constant. However, the communication overhead increases as the number of processors is increased resulting in a longer run time with increasing problem size.

Figures 7 and 8 show the unscaled speedup for a problem of fixed size. The two-dimensional rectangular problem contains 500,000 elements and 503,002 nodes. The three-dimensional rectangular problem contains 320,000 elements and 387,321 nodes.

Figure 9 shows the unscaled speedup for a coaxial transmission-line cable of finite length. The problem was discretized with 382,653 hexahedral finite elements and 320,000 nodes.

Figure 10 shows the unscaled speedup for a two-dimensional six-conductor microstrip transmission-line. The problem was discretized with 132,616 quadrilateral finite elements and 133,679 nodes.

6   Conclusions and Future Research

A scalable FEM parallel algorithm using both direct Cholesky and LU solvers for large, sparse, irregular systems of equations has been introduced in this paper.

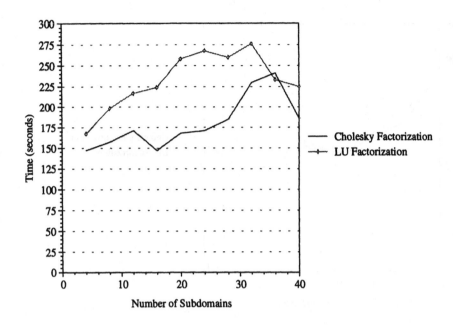

Fig. 6. Scaled speedup for three-dimensional rectangular geometry

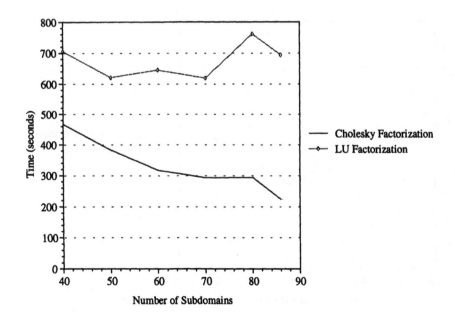

Fig. 7. Unscaled speedup for two-dimensional rectangular geometry

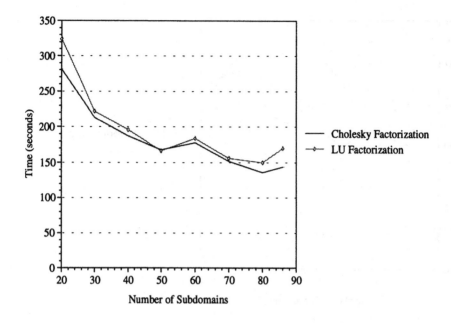

Fig. 8. Unscaled speedup for three-dimensional rectangular geometry

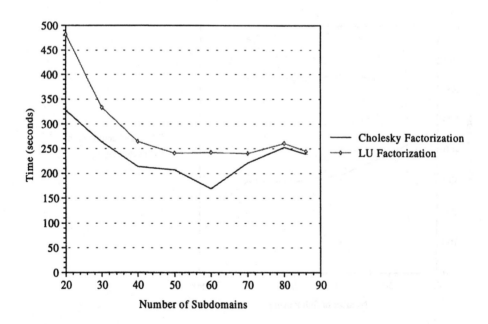

Fig. 9. Unscaled speedup for coaxial cable

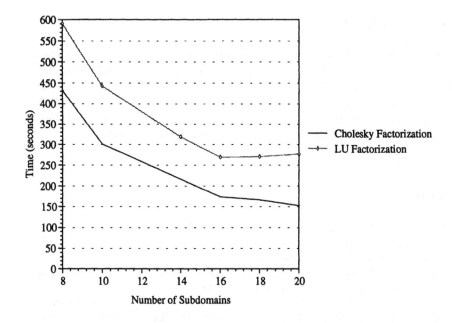

Fig. 10. Unscaled speedup for six conductor microstrip transmission line

The scalability of the code was demonstrated for several simple two- and three-dimensional electrostatic problems. The use of a rooted level structure to achieve a one-way dissection of the FEM mesh worked well for each of these problems.

Use of a MPP for finite-element analysis allows one to solve problems of unprecedented size and complexity which surpass the limitations of a conventional serial computer. These machines offer engineers and scientists a powerful tool for solving difficult problems.

One difficulty that should be mentioned is in obtaining some of the other standard parallel performance measurements such as scaled speedup. This measurement is obtained by holding the per-processor load constant and increasing the number of processors used and thus the problem size. Such measurements are difficult to obtain for algorithms in which different processors perform completely different tasks. For example, in the current implementation of the algorithm discussed here the lower n processors are responsible for, I/O, elemental assembly, diagonal block factorization, etc., while the upper $2n - 3$ processors are responsible only for the factorization of the s-boundary block. The need for standard and simple benchmarking methods for MIMD computers continues to be a problem.

7 Acknowledgments

This research was sponsored by the National Science Foundation under grant #ECS-9158504 and by the National Aeronautics and Space Administration and the Jet Propulsion Laboratory under contract #959913. Additionally, the authors would like to thank the people at Sandia National Laboratories and the Jet Propulsion Laboratories for the use of their valuable time and computational resources, without which this research would not have been possible.

References

1. G. L. Hennigan, S. P. Castillo, and E. C. Hensel, Using domain decomposition to solve symmetric, positive-definite systems on the hypercube computer, *Inter. j. numer. methods eng.*, **33**, No. 9, 1940–1954 (1992).
2. K. Gallivan, R. Plemmons, and A. Sameh, Parallel algorithms for dense linear algebra computations, *SIAM Rev.*, **32**, 54–135 (1990).
3. B. A. Hendrickson and D. E. Womble, The torus-wrap mapping for dense matrix calculations on massively parallel computers, Tech. Rep. SAND92-0792, Sandia National Laboratories, 1992.
4. D. B. Davidson, Large parallel processing revisited: A second tutorial, *IEEE Ant. & Prop. Mag.*, **34**, 9–21 (1992).
5. M. T. Heath, E. Ng, and B. W. Peyton, Parallel algorithms for sparse linear systems, *SIAM Rev.*, **33**, 420–460 (1991).
6. M. L. Barton and J. R. Rattner, Parallel computing and its impact on computational electromagnetics, *IEEE Trans. on Mag.*, **28**, 1690–1695 (1992).
7. G. A. Lyzenga and A. Raefsky, Implementing finite element software on hypercube machines, *Assoc. Comput. Mach.*, 1755–1761 (1988).
8. A. George and J. W. Liu, *Computer Solution of Large Sparse Positive Definite Systems*, Prentice-Hall, Englewood Cliffs, N.J., 1981.

Parallel Implementation of a Sparse Approximate Inverse Preconditioner

Vaibhav Deshpande[1], Marcus J. Grote[2], Peter Messmer[1] and William Sawyer[1]

[1] Swiss Center for Scientific Computing (CSCS/SCSC), CH-6928 Manno, Switzerland
[2] Courant Institute of Mathematical Sciences, New York, NY 10012, USA

Abstract. A parallel implementation of a sparse approximate inverse (SPAI) preconditioner for distributed memory parallel processors (DMPP) is presented. The fundamental SPAI algorithm is known to be a useful tool for improving the convergence of iterative solvers for ill-conditioned linear systems. The parallel implementation (PARSPAI) exploits the inherent parallelism in the SPAI algorithm and the data locality on the DMPPs, to solve structurally symmetric (but non-symmetric) matrices, which typically arise when solving partial differential equations (PDEs). Some initial performance results are presented which suggest the usefulness of PARSPAI for tackling such large size systems on present day DMPPs in a reasonable time.

The PARSPAI preconditioner is implemented using the Message Passing Interface (MPI) and is embedded in the parallel library for unstructured mesh problems (PLUMP).

1 Introduction

We consider the linear system of equations

$$Ax = b, \quad x, b \in \mathbb{R}^n . \tag{1}$$

Here A is a large and sparse matrix and may be non-symmetric. Due to the size of A, direct solvers become prohibitively expensive because of the amount of work and storage required. As an alternative we consider iterative methods such as CGS, GMRES, BCG, and BI-CGSTAB applied to the normal equations [2]. Given the initial guess x_0, these algorithms compute iteratively new approximations x_k to the true solution $x = A^{-1}b$. The iterate x_m is accepted as a solution if the residual $r_m = b - Ax_m$ satisfies $\|r_m\|/\|b\| \leq$ tol. In general, convergence is not guaranteed or may be extremely slow. Hence, the original problem (1) is transformed into a more tractable form, by applying a preconditioning matrix M either to the right or to the left of the linear system

$$AMy = b, \quad x = My, \quad \text{or} \quad MAx = Mb . \tag{2}$$

M should be chosen such that AM (or MA) is a good approximation of the identity I. As the ultimate goal is to reduce the total execution time, both the computation of M and the matrix-vector product My should be done in parallel. Since the matrix-vector product must be performed at each iteration, the number of nonzero entries in M should not greatly exceed that in A.

The most successful preconditioning methods in reducing solver iterations, e.g., incomplete LU factorizations or SSOR, are notoriously difficult to implement on a parallel architecture, especially for unstructured matrices. ILU, for example, can lead to breakdowns. In addition, ILU computes M implicitly, namely in the form $M = U_{approx}^{-1} L_{approx}^{-1}$, and its application therefore involves solving upper and lower triangular sparse linear systems, which are inherently sequential operations. Polynomial preconditioners with $M = p(A)$, on the other hand, are inherently parallel, but do not lead to as much improvement in the convergence as ILU. For a complete discussion see [2].

A relatively new approach is to minimize $\|AM - I\|$ in the Frobenius norm, which exploits the inherent parallelism, because the columns m_k of M can be computed independently of one another. Indeed, since

$$\|AM - I\|_F^2 = \sum_{k=1}^{n} \|(AM - I)e_k\|_2^2 , \qquad (3)$$

the solution of (3) separates into n independent least squares problems

$$\min_{m_k} \|Am_k - e_k\|_2 , \quad k = 1, \ldots, n , \qquad (4)$$

where $e_k = (0, ..., 0, 1, 0, ..., 0)^T$. Thus, we can solve (4) in parallel and obtain an explicit approximate inverse M of A. If M is sparse, (4) reduces to n small least squares problems, which can be solved very quickly [10, 16]. Thus M is computed explicitly and is then applied with a sparse matrix-vector multiplication — an operation which can also be performed in parallel.

The difficulty lies in determining a good sparsity structure of the approximate inverse, otherwise the solution of (4) will not yield an effective preconditioner. Yeremin et al. compute a factorized sparse approximate inverse [15, 14, 16], but only consider fixed sparsity patterns. Simon and Grote [10] solve (4) explicitly, but only allow for a banded sparsity pattern in M. The approach of Cosgrove, Diaz, and Griewank [5], Chow and Saad [4], and Grote and Huckle [12, 11] all suggest methods which capture the sparsity pattern of the main entries of A^{-1} automatically and at a reasonable cost, but stop short of an actual parallel implementation. Gould and Scott [9] present results of a simulated parallel implementation based on a shared-memory paradigm.

In this paper we build on the sequential version of Grote and Huckle [12, 11] and assume that A is (nearly) structurally symmetric (true for partial differential equations solved on meshes). The resulting PARSPAI algorithm offers a high degree of data locality, and its implementation on a distributed memory parallel processor (DMPP) architecture with the Message Passing Interface (MPI) [17] is described in detail. In Sect. 2 we review the SPAI algorithm, which computes a sparse approximate inverse of A. In Sect. 3 we discuss some of the numerous considerations in the parallel implementation. We briefly describe the PARSPAI algorithm in Sect. 4 and present indications about the preconditioner's quality and performance results on a DMPP in Sect. 5. Finally we draw some conclusions about its usefulness in the parallel solution of partial differential equations (PDEs) on very large unstructured meshes.

2 SPAI Algorithm Review

The SPAI algorithm is explained in detail in [12, 11]; we summarize it here briefly for the sake of completeness.

The matrix M is the solution of the minimization problem (4). Since the columns of M are independent of one another, the algorithm for only one of them, m_k, is sufficient. An initial sparsity of M is assumed, i.e., $\mathcal{J}$ is the set of indices j such that $m_k(j) \neq 0$. In reality the initial $\mathcal{J}$ could be very simple, e.g., $\mathcal{J} = \{k\}$. The reduced vector of unknowns $m_k(\mathcal{J})$ is denoted by $\hat{m}_k$. Next, let $\mathcal{I}$ be the set of indices i such that $A(i, \mathcal{J})$ is not identically zero, denote the resulting submatrix $A(\mathcal{I}, \mathcal{J})$ by $\hat{A}$, and define $\hat{e}_k = e_k(\mathcal{I})$. Solving (4) for m_k is equivalent to solving

$$\min_{\hat{m}_k} \|\hat{A}\hat{m}_k - \hat{e}_k\|_2 \tag{5}$$

for $\hat{m}_k$. The $|\mathcal{I}| \times |\mathcal{J}|$ least squares problem (5) is extremely small because A and M are very sparse matrices. Equation (5) is solved, e.g., with the QR decomposition (among other methods — see [8] for details) for each $k = 1, \ldots, n$ and $m_k(\mathcal{J}) = \hat{m}_k$. This yields an approximate inverse M, which minimizes $\|AM - I\|_F$ for the given sparsity structure.

The sparsity pattern $\mathcal{J}$ is then augmented to obtain a more effective preconditioner by reducing the current error $\|AM - I\|_F$, i.e., reducing the norm of the residual

$$r = A(., \mathcal{J})\,\hat{m}_k - e_k \ . \tag{6}$$

If $r = 0$, m_k is exactly the k-th column of A^{-1} and cannot be improved upon. Otherwise, since A and m_k are sparse, most components of r are still zero. $\mathcal{L}$ is the set of remaining indices ℓ for which $r(\ell) \neq 0$ (typically equal to $\mathcal{I}$). To every $\ell \in \mathcal{L}$ corresponds an index set $\mathcal{N}_\ell$, which consists of the indices of the nonzero entries of $A(\ell, .)$ that are not in $\mathcal{J}$ yet. The potential new candidates to augment $\mathcal{J}$ are contained in

$$\tilde{\mathcal{J}} = \bigcup_{\ell \in \mathcal{L}} \mathcal{N}_\ell \ . \tag{7}$$

Grote and Huckle [12, 11] consider for each $j \in \tilde{\mathcal{J}}$ the one-dimensional minimization problem

$$\min_{\mu_j} \|r + \mu_j A e_j\|_2 \ , \tag{8}$$

whose solution is $\mu_j = -\frac{r^T Ae_j}{\|Ae_j\|_2^2}$. They then calculate for each j the 2-norm ρ_j of the new residual $r + \mu_j Ae_j$, namely,

$$\rho_j^2 = \|r\|_2^2 - \frac{(r^T Ae_j)^2}{\|Ae_j\|_2^2} , \qquad (9)$$

and take those j which lead to smallest ρ_j, e.g., those whose ρ_j is less than the mean $\bar{\rho}$.

Using the augmented set of indices $\mathcal{J}$, the sparse least squares problem (4) is solved again. This yields a better approximation m_k of the k-th column of A^{-1}. This process is repeated for each $k = 1, \ldots, n$ until the residual satisfies a prescribed tolerance $\|r\|_2 \leq \epsilon$ or a maximum amount of fill-in $maxfill$ has been reached in m_k . [3]

The SPAI (Sparse Approximate Inverse) Algorithm:

For every column m_k of M:

(a) Choose an initial sparsity $\mathcal{J}$, e.g., $\mathcal{J} = \{k\}$.
(b) Compute the row indices $\mathcal{I}$ of the corresponding nonzero entries and the QR decomposition (5) of $A(\mathcal{I}, \mathcal{J})$. Then compute the solution m_k of the least squares problem (4), and its residual r given by (6).
While $\|r\|_2 > \varepsilon$ and $|\mathcal{J}| \leq maxfill$:

    (c) Set $\mathcal{L}$ equal to the set of indices ℓ for which $r(\ell) \neq 0$.
    (d) Set $\tilde{\mathcal{J}}$ equal to the set of all new column indices of A that appear in all $\mathcal{L}$ rows but not in $\mathcal{J}$.
    (e) For each $j \in \tilde{\mathcal{J}}$ solve the minimization problem (8).
    (f) For each $j \in \tilde{\mathcal{J}}$ compute ρ_j given by (9), and delete from $\tilde{\mathcal{J}}$ all but the most profitable indices.
    (g) Determine the new indices $\tilde{\mathcal{I}}$ and update the QR decomposition using (5). Then solve the new least squares problem, compute the new residual $r = Am_k - e_k$, and set $\mathcal{I} = \mathcal{I} \cup \tilde{\mathcal{I}}$ and $\mathcal{J} = \mathcal{J} \cup \tilde{\mathcal{J}}$.

3 Considerations for Parallel Implementation

While the least squares minimizations in (4) for each k clearly can be performed independently on different processing elements (PEs), each PE must have access to the data required to solve its subproblem. Thus the parallel implementation on a shared-memory machine is more straightforward than that on a DMPP, on which the algorithm is not communication-free or even necessarily minimal in communication.

---

[3] If the process is not stopped, the algorithm will eventually compute the k-th column of A^{-1} .

To consider problems of interest with n very large (e.g., $> 100,000$) on a DMPP, it must be assumed that the matrix A and all the n-vectors used in the calculation are distributed over all PEs. An expedient way is to distribute the vector element-wise over all PEs, and distribute the rows of A in the same manner.

One possible approach is the use of the ITPACK [2] format in distributed form (DIS) as shown in the Fig. 1 and used in the PLUMP library [3]. This distribution assures that the kernel operation for the solver $y \leftarrow Ax$ can be implemented relatively easily, and that communication can be partially overlapped with computation for efficiency.

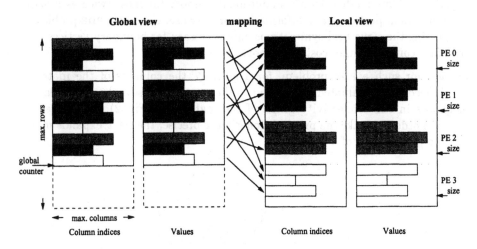

Fig. 1. The distributed ITPACK storage assumes that there is a maximum number of non-zero matrix entries per row, and that the graph is adequately partitioned such that no PE fills its local two-dimensional array. In addition to the matrix value array, there is a corresponding array with column indices for each matrix entry.

Given A in DIS format, step **(d)** in the SPAI algorithm implies that the residuals r or at least the set $\mathcal{J}$ from any given PE's ongoing column m_k calculation has to be broadcasted to all other PEs, since for this PE it is not known a priori whether $r^T A e_j$ in (9) will be non-zero, i.e., whether non-zero positions specified by the set $\mathcal{L}$ will correspond to non-zero entries in the jth column of A. Since all PEs are concurrently working on a different m_k, this would mean a frequent all-to-all communication which would necessarily incur a large amount of unscalable overhead.

For a very large class of problems, namely the solution of a partial differential equations over a (possibly unstructured) mesh, the above-mentioned problem is not as difficult to overcome as it may seem. The problem to be solved is to find the function values $u(x) \in \mathbb{R}$ at any point $x \in \mathbb{R}^n$ in the domain Ω, where u fulfills

$$Lu = f . \tag{10}$$

Here $f(x)$ is defined in Ω, and suitable boundary conditions are applied on $\partial\Omega$. A feature of such problems is that, when Ω is discretized into a finite number of mesh points and the operator L described through a discrete operator, they lead to a nearly or entirely *structurally symmetric* matrix A, i.e., $A(i,j) \neq 0 \rightarrow A(j,i) \neq 0$, even though $A(i,j) \neq A(j,i)$. Such problems provide an opportunity to efficiently determine which columns have to be evaluated, since now the index set $\mathcal{N}_l$ from (7) consists of the indices of the nonzero entries of $A(.,l)$ (as well as $A(l,.)$) which all reside on one PE for given l. If, on the other hand, A is sparse but not inherently structurally symmetric, the matrix can be stored in a structurally symmetric form by storing a zero in $A(i,j)$ for $A(j,i) \neq 0$. This method requires additional memory (at most twice as much), but provides important graph information for later use. Usually in PDE problems, completing the structural symmetry is only necessary for boundary vertices and therefore comes at small cost of memory.

In fact, for such a PDE problem, for a given $\mathcal{J}$ the columns of the matrices which need to be evaluated correspond to the set of the first and second nearest neighbors in the connectivity graph of the matrix (see Fig. 2). As the set $\mathcal{J}$ grows in order to make the preconditioner more precise, the set $\mathcal{I}$ expands much like the propagation of a wavefront.

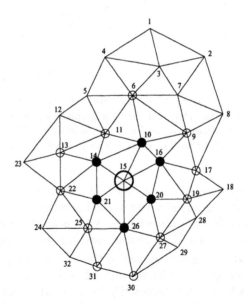

Fig. 2. In structurally symmetric problems the vertices $\tilde{\mathcal{J}}$ to evaluate are the set of first (in black) and second (in white) neighbors of $\mathcal{J}$ (here $\mathcal{J}$ is the vertex marked 15).

To ensure that the "wavefront" crosses a processor boundary as rarely as possible, we assume that the mesh (which is highly correlated with the connectivity graph in Fig. 2) is partitioned over the PEs in an efficient way, i.e., such that the load assigned to each PE is roughly even, and the number of cut edges (or the "surface area") of the individual partitions is minimized. As there is extensive literature on this subject [1, 18, 13] we do not expound on this topic here. If the mesh is partitioned cleverly on many PEs, the PE calculating m_k will, even in the worst case — e.g., if a graph vertex is on a PE boundary — only communicates with one or a few other PEs, depending on how the wavefront progresses. Even if A is an ill-conditioned matrix from a PDE problem, the wavefront should not propagate too far through the graph.

This is supported by the Green's function interpretation of the PDE problem as discussed in detail in [6] and is encouraging for the parallel implementation. The nearest neighbors of the graph vertex k are the best candidates for minimizing $\|Am_k - e_k\|_2$. Also we expect the wavefront to fade out as it propagates, thus limiting the range of partitions (and thus PEs) which have to be addressed.

Tests show that it is sufficient to consider the first nearest neighbors of the set $\mathcal{J}$, i.e., the set $\mathcal{L} - \mathcal{J}$, as possible extensions to the set $\mathcal{J}$. If that set provides a preconditioner of insufficient quality, the second nearest neighbors will most likely be evaluated in subsequent propagations of the wavefront. This is the basis of the simplification in the parallel code which affects the quality and performance of the preconditioner compared to the original SPAI implementation.

4   Realization of PARSPAI

The PARSPAI algorithm has been implemented in FORTRAN 77 using MPI. It is embedded in the PLUMP library which provides a complete environment to describe a matrix A in DIS format, solve the system of equations for a given finite element mesh problem and later to support dynamic refinement of the mesh. At the same time, the implementation of PARSPAI is modular enough to allow its integration with other distributed data formats with little effort. The current implementation of PARSPAI can be outlined as follows:

On every PE for a set of m_k of M:

(**A**) Choose an initial sparsity $\tilde{\mathcal{J}}$, e.g., $\tilde{\mathcal{J}} = \{k\}$.
   While $\|r\|_2 > \epsilon$ and $|\mathcal{J}| \leq maxfill$ and number of iterations $\leq \gamma$:
   (**B**) Given the set $\tilde{\mathcal{J}}$, determine the new set $\tilde{\mathcal{I}}$ to update the matrix $\hat{A}$, using the local entries of A or receiving them from other PEs. Set $\mathcal{I} = \mathcal{I} \cup \tilde{\mathcal{I}}$ and $\mathcal{J} = \mathcal{J} \cup \tilde{\mathcal{J}}$.
   (**C**) Solve the least squares problem (5) and set $\mathcal{L}$ equal to the set of indices ℓ for which $r(\ell) \neq 0$.
   (**D**) Send the residual $r = Am_k - e_k$ and the set $\mathcal{L}$ to other PEs requiring them to compute ρ_j.
   (**E**) Determine the local set $\tilde{\mathcal{J}}$ and for each $j \in \tilde{\mathcal{J}}$ compute ρ_j given by (9). Gather ρ_j from other PEs involved and compute $\bar{\rho}$.

(F) Set $\tilde{\mathcal{J}} = \{j \in \tilde{\mathcal{J}} | \rho_j \leq \beta \cdot \bar{\rho}\}$

In the above description, γ denotes the maximum number of graph extensions for one m_k.

The PEs which receive the residual r and the set $\mathcal{J}$ determine independently the sets $\mathcal{N}_l$ and the solutions of the minimization problem (8). Where SPAI increases $\tilde{\mathcal{J}}$ at most by a fixed number s during one iteration, PARSPAI considers all j with $\rho_j \leq \beta \cdot \bar{\rho}$ for a given parameter β. This allows to determine $\tilde{\mathcal{J}}$ on the involved PEs and avoids additional communication of $\tilde{\mathcal{J}}$.

In the above procedure, steps **(B)** and **(D)** involve exchange of variable amounts of information among the different PEs. This can be realized by using the MPI function **MPI_Alltoallv**. But as mentioned earlier, only nearest neighbors are considered for graph extension. Hence a better approach would be to determine the subset of all PEs which actually require the requisite information and then exchange it using MPI point-to-point communication primitives. The current implementation follows this approach and to improve performance non-blocking send and receive operations are used. Although no comparison has been made, the performance of the two approaches may vary, depending on the underlying MPI library.

Substantial saving in computational effort could be achieved by solving the least squares problem only for the updated part of $\hat{A}$ [12, 11] instead of solving the problem for the entire updated matrix as in the current implementation.

5 Results and Discussion

The implementation of PARSPAI as per its quality and performance was investigated on a wide variety of problems, including test matrices from the Harwell-Boeing Collection [7]. The NEC Cenju-3, a distributed-memory machine with up to 128 nodes, each having a R4400 processor and 64MB memory, was used for this purpose with the NEC-CSCS MPI library.

Numerical experiments were performed on various test cases to determine the controlling parameters in the implementation. We discuss one specific test case from the Harwell-Boeing Collection in this paper. Interested readers may refer to [6] for some additional results.

Table 1 shows the convergence characteristics for the ORSIRR_2 886×886 matrix from an oil reservoir simulation, for SPAI (taken from [12, 11]) and PARSPAI using CGS as a solver. The initial guess was always $x_0 = 0$, $\tilde{r}_0 = r_0 = b$, and the stopping criterion

$$\frac{\|b - A x_m\|_2}{\|b\|_2} \leq 10^{-8}, \quad x_m = M y_m.$$

In line with the sequential SPAI algorithm, the number of iterations decreases as ϵ is reduced, confirming the robustness of the algorithm with respect to this parameter.

Table 1. Number of iterations for ORSIRR_2, using CGS and varying ϵ: unpreconditioned ($M = I$) and preconditioned ($0.1 \leq \epsilon \leq 0.5$, $\gamma = 4$), comparison between SPAI and PARSPAI.

	SPAI	PARSPAI			
		1 PE	2 PE	4 PE	8 PE
$M = I$	653	722	868	691	881
$\epsilon = 0.5$	70	55	55	58	71
$\epsilon = 0.4$	41	41	37	40	54
$\epsilon = 0.3$	32	33	33	32	46
$\epsilon = 0.2$	18	30	29	32	45
$\epsilon = 0.1$	–	27	29	29	44

As per the discussion in Sect. 3, the performance of PARSPAI depends on the maximum number of graph extensions γ. The numerical experiments (Tab. 2) confirm that increasing γ reduces the number of iterations.

Table 2. Number of iterations for ORSIRR_2, using CGS for varying γ ($\epsilon = 0.1$)

	1 PE	2 PE	4 PE	8 PE
$\gamma = 2$	148	151	165	123
$\gamma = 3$	55	63	55	95
$\gamma = 4$	27	29	29	44
$\gamma = 5$	17	18	22	27

The quality of the parallel preconditioner was assessed by evaluating the eigenvalue spectrum of the preconditioned system AM and the condition number. Since the methods to determine $\tilde{\mathcal{J}}$ are not identical, the eigenvalue spectrum of SPAI and PARSPAI differ, as shown in Fig. 3.

The condition numbers obtained using PARSPAI ($\mathrm{cond}_2(AM) = 84.8$) compare favorably with that of SPAI ($\mathrm{cond}_2(AM) = 74.2$) for the same value of $\epsilon = 0.4$. The sparsity pattern and the amount of fill-in however varies considerably, reflecting again the different approaches to augment $\tilde{\mathcal{J}}$.

The speedup for building the preconditioner using PARSPAI for ORSIRR_2 is shown in Fig. 4. In spite of the small size of the test matrix, the results indicate good scaling behavior of PARSPAI. Since the number of iterations remains fairly constant with an increase in the number of PEs (Tab. 1), and because of the known scaling behavior of the matrix-vector product in the CGS solver [3], a good speedup in the preconditioning phase translates into reduced overall execution time.

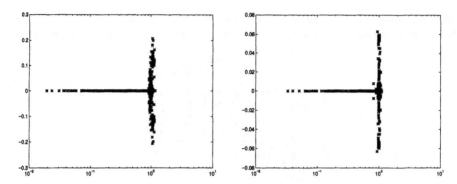

Fig. 3. The eigenvalue spectra of AM_{SPAI} (left) and AM_{PARSPAI} (right) showing the similar quality of both SPAI and PARSPAI ($\epsilon = 0.4$ and $\gamma = 4$).

The true benefit of PARSPAI is apparent from Fig. 5, which shows its performance when applied to a large system of linear equations ($n = 16,384$) as resulting from a PDE on a rectangular mesh. This problem could not be solved on a single processor because of memory limitations; hence the speedup is computed based on the timing on 16 PEs.

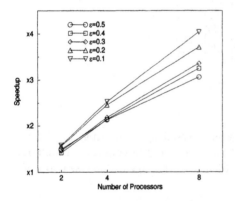

Fig. 4. Speedup for building the preconditioner of the ORSIRR_2 matrix for different number of PEs and $0.1 \le \epsilon \le 0.5$.

Fig. 5. Speedup for building the preconditioner for a matrix of dimension $n = 16,384$.

The scaling behavior of the preconditioner seems to be promising for tackling larger size systems. A good partitioning of the mesh, however, is important to exploit the data locality on each processor and to ensure a good compute-to-communication ratio on the DMPPs. The performance of the preconditioner could be substantially improved by optimizing the communication, tuning the different parameters, and by improving the basic algorithm used in PARSPAI, as suggested in Sect. 4. The results in this paper are indicative of the synergistic coupling of the preconditioner with the underlying data structure for achieving good performance on large size problems.

6 Conclusions

Iterative methods themselves are not difficult to parallelize or necessarily communication-bound on parallel machines, as they only require vector operations and global communication of single values for scalar products and norms. Parallelizing the required matrix-vector product and calculating a preconditioner are the difficult tasks involved. By limiting ourselves to non-symmetric matrices which are structurally symmetric, e.g., those which result from the solution of PDEs on a computational mesh, we have exploited the data locality and the inherent parallelism in the SPAI algorithm.

With the PLUMP library, in which PARSPAI is integrated, the matrix-vector product and the preconditioner are provided in a transparent way. We have presented some initial benchmarks which indicate that parallel iterative solvers along with the PARSPAI preconditioner will be able to tackle very large and ill-conditioned problems beyond the reach of single processor machines and current sparse direct solvers.

Acknowledgments We graciously acknowledge the NEC Corporation for financial support during the realization of this project.

References

1. S. T. Barnard and H. D. Simon. A Fast Multilevel Implementation of Recursive Spectral Bisection for Partitioning Unstructured Problems. Technical Report RNR-092-033, NASA Ames Research Center, Moffett Field, CA 94035, November 1992.
2. R. Barrett, M. Berry, T. Chan, J. Demmel, J. Donato, J. Dongarra, V. Eijkhout, R. Pozo, C. Romine, and H. van der Vorst. *TEMPLATES for the Solution of Linear Systems: Building Blocks for Iterative Methods.* SIAM Publications, 1994.
3. Oliver Bröker, Vaibhav Deshpande, Peter Messmer, and William Sawyer. Parallel Library for Unstructured Mesh Problems. Technical Report CSCS-TR-96-15, Centro Svizzero di Calcolo Scientifico, CH-6928 Manno, Switzerland, May 1996.
4. E. Chow and Y. Saad. Approximate Inverse Preconditioners for General Sparse Matrices. In *Proc. Colorado Conf. on Iterative Meth.*, 1994.
5. J. D. F. Cosgrove, J. C. Diaz, and A. Griewank. Approximate Inverse Preconditionings for Sparse Linear Systems. *Intern. J. Computer Math.*, 14:91–110, 1992.
6. Vaibhav Deshpande, Marcus J. Grote, Peter Messmer, and William Sawyer. Parallel Sparse Approximate Inverse Preconditioner. Technical Report CSCS-TR-96-14, Centro Svizzero di Calcolo Scientifico, CH-6928 Manno, Switzerland, May 1996.
7. I. Duff, R. G. Grimes, and J. Lewis. *User's Guide for the Harwell-Boeing Sparse Matrix Collection (Release I).* Available from http://math.nist.gov:80/MatrixMarket/collections/hb.html.
8. G. H. Golub and C. F. Van Loan. *Matrix Computations.* Johns Hopkins, second edition, 1989.
9. N. I. M. Gould and J. A. Scott. On Approximate-Inverse Preconditioners. Technical Report RAL 95-026, Rutherford Appleton Laboratory, 1995.

10. M. Grote and H. Simon. Parallel Preconditioning and Approximate Inverses on the Connection Machine. In *Proc. of the Scalable High Performance Computing Conference (SHPCC), Williamsburg, VA*, pages 76–83. IEEE Comp. Sci. Press, 1992.

11. Marcus J. Grote and Thomas Huckle. Parallel Preconditioning with Sparse Approximate Inverses. *SIAM Journal on Scientific Computing*. In press.

12. Marcus J. Grote and Thomas Huckle. Effective Parallel Preconditioning with Sparse Approximate Inverses. In *Proc. SIAM Conf. on Parallel Processing for Scientific Comp., San Francisco*, pages 466–471. SIAM, 1995.

13. George Karypis and Vipin Kumar. MeTiS: Unstructured Graph Partitioning and Sparse Matrix Ordering System. Available from http://www.cs.umn.edu/~karypis/metis/references.html.

14. L. Yu. Kolotilina, A. A. Nikishin, and A. Yu. Yeremin. Factorized Sparse Approximate Inverse (FSAI) Preconditionings for Solving 3D FE Systems on Massively Parallel Computers II. In R. Beauwens and P. de Groen, editors, *Iterative Meth. in Lin. Alg., Proc. of the IMACS Internat. Sympos., Brussels*, pages 311–312, 1991.

15. L. Yu. Kolotilina and A. Yu. Yeremin. Factorized Sparse Approximate Inverse Preconditionings. *SIAM Journal on Matrix Analysis and Applications*, 14(1):45–58, 1993.

16. Ju. B. Lifshitz, A. A. Nikishin, and A. Yu. Yeremin. Sparse Approximate Inverse Preconditionings for Solving 3D CFD Problems on Massively Parallel Computers. In R. Beauwens and P. de Groen, editors, *Iterative Meth. in Lin. Alg., Proc. of the IMACS Internat. Sympos., Brussels*, pages 83–84, 1991.

17. Message Passing Interface Forum. MPI: a message-passing interface standard (version 1.1). Revision of article appearing in the *International Journal of Supercomputing Applications*, 8(3/4):157–416, 1994, June 1995.

18. C. Walshaw, M. Cross, M. Everett, and S. Johnson. A Parallelisable Algorithm for Partitioning Unstructured Meshes. In Alfonso Ferreira and Jose D. P. Rolim, editors, *Parallel Algorithms for Irregular Problems: State of the Art*, chapter 2, pages 25–44. Kluwer Academic Publishers, Dordrecht, Netherlands, August 1995. Collection of extended papers from Irregular'94 conference. [ISBN: 0-7923-3623-2].

Decomposing Irregularly Sparse Matrices for Parallel Matrix-Vector Multiplication*

Ümit V. Çatalyürek and Cevdet Aykanat
Computer Engineering Department, Bilkent University
06533 Bilkent, Ankara, Turkey

Abstract. In this work, we show the deficiencies of the graph model for decomposing sparse matrices for parallel matrix-vector multiplication. Then, we propose two hypergraph models which avoid all deficiencies of the graph model. The proposed models reduce the decomposition problem to the well-known hypergraph partitioning problem widely encountered in circuit partitioning in VLSI. We have implemented fast Kernighan-Lin based graph and hypergraph partitioning heuristics and used the successful multilevel graph partitioning tool (Metis) for the experimental evaluation of the validity of the proposed hypergraph models. We have also developed a multilevel hypergraph partitioning heuristic for experimenting the performance of the multilevel approach on hypergraph partitioning. Experimental results on sparse matrices, selected from Harwell-Boeing collection and NETLIB suite, confirm both the validity of our proposed hypergraph models and appropriateness of the multilevel approach to hypergraph partitioning.

1 Introduction

Iterative solvers are widely used for the solution of large, sparse, linear system of equations on multicomputers. Three basic types of operations are repeatedly performed at each iteration. These are linear operations on dense vectors, inner product(s) of dense vectors, and sparse-matrix vector product of the form $\mathbf{y} = \mathbf{A}\mathbf{x}$, where $\mathbf{y}$ and $\mathbf{x}$ are dense vectors, and $\mathbf{A}$ is a matrix with the same sparsity structure as the coefficient matrix [5, 12]. All of these basic operations can be performed concurrently by distributing either the rows or the columns of the matrix $\mathbf{A}$ and the components of the dense vectors in the same way. These two decomposition schemes are referred here as *rowwise* and *columnwise* decomposition schemes, respectively. Note that these two decomposition schemes are one-dimensional decomposition of matrix $\mathbf{A}$ which is a two-dimensional data structure. Both of these two decomposition schemes induce a computational distribution such that each processor is held responsible for updating the values of those vector components assigned to itself. With this data distribution scheme, linear vector operations and inner-product operations can be easily and efficiently parallelized by an even distribution of vector components to processors [5, 12]. Linear vector operations do not necessitate communication, whereas

* This work is partially supported by the Commission of the European Communities, Directorate General for Industry under contract ITDC 204-82166, and Turkish Science and Research Council under grant EEEAG-160.

inner-product operations introduce global communication overhead which does not scale up with increasing problem size.

Sparse-matrix vector product computations constitute the most time consuming operation in iterative solvers. In parallel matrix-vector multiplication, rowwise and columnwise decomposition schemes necessitate communication just before and after the local matrix-vector product computations, respectively. Hence, these two schemes can also be considered as the pre and post communication schemes, respectively. In rowwise decomposition scheme, processors need some nonlocal components of the global **x**-vector, depending on the sparsity pattern of their local rows, just before the local matrix-vector product computations. Each processor send some of its local **x**-vector components to those processor(s) which need them. After receiving the needed nonlocal **x** components, each processor can concurrently compute its local components of the global **y**-vector by performing a local matrix-vector product. In columnwise decomposition scheme, after local matrix-vector product computations, processors send the non-local components of their computed **y**-vectors to those processor(s) which need them, depending on the sparsity pattern of their local columns. After receiving the needed **y** components, each processor can concurrently complete the computation of its local **y**-vector by simply adding these received values to its appropriate local **y**-vector locations. Hence, by weighting each row or column by its nonzero entry count, load balancing problem can be considered as the *number partitioning* problem. However, different row or column partitionings with good load balance may also significantly differ the communication requirement. Unfortunately, the communication requirement scales up with increasing problem size. The minimization of the communication overhead while maintaining the computational load balance reduces to the *domain decomposition problem*, where the sparse matrix **A** constitutes the domain of problem.

Almost all domain decomposition methods proposed in the literature employ *graph model* [9, 13]. In this work, we show the deficiencies of the graph model for decomposing sparse matrices for parallel matrix vector multiplication. The first deficiency is that it can only be used for symmetric square matrices. The second deficiency is the fact that the graph model does not reflect the actual communication requirement which will be described in Section 2.3. In this work, we propose two *hypergraph models* which avoid all deficiencies of the graph model. The proposed models enable the representation and hence the decomposition of unsymmetric square and rectangular matrices as well as symmetric matrices. Furthermore, they introduce a much more accurate representation for the communication requirement. The proposed models reduce the decomposition problem to the well-known *hypergraph partitioning* problem widely encountered in circuit partitioning in VLSI layout design. Hence, the proposed models will be amenable to the advances in the circuit partitioning heuristics and tools to be developed in VLSI community.

Domain decomposition is a preprocessing introduced for the sake of efficient parallelization of the given problem. Hence, heuristics used for decomposition should run in low order polynomial time. Kernighan-Lin (KL) based heuristics are widely used for graph and hypergraph partitioning because of their short run-times and good quality results. Therefore, we selected and implemented fast k-way KL-based graph and hypergraph partitioning heuristics for experimenting the validity of our proposed hypergraph models. Here, k represents the number of processors on the target multicomputer. Recently, multilevel graph partitioning heuristics are proposed leading to successful graph partitioning tools Chaco [8] and Metis [10]. We have also exploited the multilevel partitioning methods for the experimental verification of our proposed hypergraph models in two approaches. In the first approach, Metis graph partitioning tool is used as a black box by transforming hypergraphs to graphs using the traditional clique-net model. In the second approach, lack of existence of multilevel hypergraph partitioning tool led us to develop a multilevel hypergraph partitioning heuristic, for fair comparison of two models.

2 Graph Model and Its Deficiencies

In this section, we discuss the deficiencies of graph model for decomposing sparse matrices for parallel matrix-vector multiplication.

2.1 Graphs and Graph Partitioning Problem

An undirected graph $\mathcal{G} = (\mathcal{V}, \mathcal{E})$ is defined as a set of vertices $\mathcal{V}$ and a set of edges $\mathcal{E}$. Every edge $e_{ij} \in \mathcal{E}$ connects a pair of vertices v_i and v_j. The degree d_i of a vertex v_i is equal to the number of edges incident to v_i. Let w_i and c_{ij} denote the weight of vertex $v_i \in \mathcal{V}$ and the cost of edge $e_{ij} \in \mathcal{E}$, respectively.

$\Pi = (P_1, \ldots, P_k)$ is a k-way partition of $\mathcal{G}$ if the following conditions hold: each part $P_\ell, 1 \leq \ell \leq k$, is a nonempty subset of $\mathcal{V}$, parts are pairwise disjoint ($P_i \cap P_j = \emptyset$ for all $1 \leq i < j \leq k$), and union of k parts is equal to $\mathcal{V}$. In a partition Π of $\mathcal{G}$, an edge is said to be cut if its pair of vertices belong to two different parts, and otherwise uncut. The set of cut (external) edges for a partition Π are denoted as $\mathcal{E}_E$. The cutsize definition for representing the cost $\chi(\Pi)$ of a partition Π is

$$\chi(\Pi) = \sum_{e_{ij} \in \mathcal{E}_E} c_{ij} \tag{1}$$

In (1), each cut edge e_{ij} contributes its cost c_{ij} to the cutsize. In a partition Π of $\mathcal{G}$, the size of a part is defined as the sum of the weights of the vertices in that part. Hence, graph partitioning problem can be defined as the task of dividing a graph into two or more parts such that the cutsize is minimized, while a given balance criterion among the part sizes is maintained.

2.2 Graph Model for Decomposition

Graph representation of only structurally symmetric matrices will be discussed in the decomposition context, since graph model is restricted to symmetric matrices. A symmetric sparse matrix $\mathbf{A}$ can be represented as an undirected graph $\mathcal{G}_A = (\mathcal{V}, \mathcal{E})$. The vertices in the vertex set $\mathcal{V}$ correspond to the rows/columns of the matrix $\mathbf{A}$. In the pre-communication scheme, each vertex $v_i \in \mathcal{V}$ corresponds to the atomic task i of computing the inner product of row i with the column vector $\mathbf{x}$. In the post-communication scheme, each vertex $v_i \in V$ corresponds to the atomic task i of computing the sparse SAXPY/DAXPY operation $\mathbf{y} = \mathbf{y} + x_i \mathbf{a}_{*i}$, where $\mathbf{a}_{*i}$ denotes the i-th column of matrix $\mathbf{A}$. Hence, in both pre and post communication schemes, each nonzero entry in a row and column of $\mathbf{A}$ incurs a multiply-and-add operation during the local matrix-vector product computations in the pre and post communication schemes, respectively. Thus, computational load w_i of mapping row/column i to a processor is the number of nonzero entries in row/column i.

In the edge set $\mathcal{E}$, $e_{ij} \in \mathcal{E}$ if and only if a_{ij} and a_{ji} of matrix $\mathbf{A}$ are nonzeros. Hence, the vertices in the adjacency list of a vertex v_i denote the column (row) indices of the off-diagonal nonzeros in row i (column i) of $\mathbf{A}$. In the pre-communication scheme, each edge $e_{ij} \in \mathcal{E}$ corresponds to the exchange of updated x_i and x_j values between the atomic tasks i and j, just before the local matrix-vector product computations. In the post-communication scheme, each edge $e_{ij} \in \mathcal{E}$ corresponds to the exchange of partial y_i and y_j results between the atomic tasks i and j, just after the local matrix-vector product computations. In both schemes, each edge represents the bidirectional interaction between the respective pair of vertices. Hence, by setting $c_{ij} = 2$ for each edge $e_{ij} \in \mathcal{E}$, both rowwise and columnwise decomposition of matrix $\mathbf{A}$ reduces to the k-way partitioning of its associated graph $\mathcal{G}_A$ according to the cutsize definition given in (1). Thus, minimizing the cutsize according to (1) corresponds to the goal of minimizing the total volume of interprocessor communication. Maintaining the balance among part sizes corresponds to maintaining the computational load balance during local matrix-vector product computations.

2.3 Deficiencies of the Graph Model

As mentioned earlier, graph model is restricted to representing structurally symmetric matrices. Furthermore, the graph model does not reflect the actual communication requirement. Graph model treats all cut edges in an identical manner while computing the cutsize (i.e., 2 words per cut edge). However, r cut edges stemming from a vertex v_i in part P_ℓ to r vertices $v_{i_1}, v_{i_2}, \ldots, v_{i_r}$ in part P_m incur only $r+1$ communications instead of $2r$ in both pre and post communication schemes. Because, in the pre-communication (post-communication) scheme, P_ℓ (P_m) sends x_i ($y_{i_1}, y_{i_2}, \ldots, y_{i_r}$) to processor P_m (P_ℓ) while P_m (P_ℓ) sends $x_{i_1}, x_{i_2}, \ldots, x_{i_r}$ (y_i) to processor P_ℓ (P_m).

3 Hypergraph Models for Decomposition

In this section, we propose two *hypergraph models* for mapping sparse-matrix vector multiplication which avoids the deficiencies of the graph model.

3.1 Hypergraphs and Hypergraph Partitioning Problem

A hypergraph $\mathcal{H} = (\mathcal{V}, \mathcal{N})$ is defined as a set of vertices $\mathcal{V}$ and a set of nets (hyperedges) $\mathcal{N}$ among those vertices. Every net $n_j \in \mathcal{N}$ is a subset of vertices, i.e., $n_j \subseteq \mathcal{V}$. Vertices in a net n_j are called its *pins* and denoted as $pins[n_j]$. The size of a net is equal to the number of its pins, i.e., $s_j = |nets[n_j]|$. The set of nets connected to a vertex v_i is denoted as $nets[v_i]$. The degree of a vertex is equal to the number of nets it is connected to, i.e., $d_i = |nets[v_i]|$. Let w_i and c_j denote the weight of vertex $v_i \in \mathcal{V}$ and the cost of net $n_j \in \mathcal{N}$, respectively.

Definition of k-way partition of hypergraphs is identical to that of graphs. In a partition Π of $\mathcal{H}$, a net that has at least one pin (vertex) in a part is said to connect that part. Let δ_j denotes the number of parts connected by net n_j. A net n_j is said to be cut if it connects more than one part (i.e., $\delta_j > 1$), and uncut (i.e., $\delta_j = 1$) otherwise. The set of cut (external) nets for a partition Π are denoted as $\mathcal{N}_E$. There are various cutsize definitions for representing the cost $\chi(\Pi)$ of a partition Π. Two relevant definitions are:

$$(a) \quad \chi(\Pi) = \sum_{n_j \in \mathcal{N}_E} c_j \quad and \quad (b) \quad \chi(\Pi) = \sum_{n_j \in \mathcal{N}_E} c_j(\delta_j - 1). \quad (2)$$

In (2.a), cutsize is equal to the sum of the costs of the cut nets. In (2.b), each cut net n_j contributes $c_j(\delta_j - 1)$ to the cutsize. Hence, hypergraph partitioning problem can be defined as the task of dividing a hypergraph into two or more parts such that the cutsize is minimized, while a given balance criterion among the part sizes is maintained.

3.2 Two Hypergraph Models for Decomposition

We propose two hypergraph models for the decomposition. These models are referred to here as the column-net and row-net models. In the column-net model, matrix $\mathbf{A}$ is represented as the hypergraph $\mathcal{H}_C(\mathcal{V}_R, \mathcal{N}_C)$. The vertex and net sets $\mathcal{V}_R$ and $\mathcal{N}_C$ correspond to the rows and columns of matrix $\mathbf{A}$, respectively. There exist one vertex v_i and one net n_j for each row i and column j, respectively. Net n_j contains the vertices corresponding to the rows which have a nonzero entry on column j. That is, $v_i \in n_j$ if and only if $a_{ij} \neq 0$. Each vertex $v_i \in \mathcal{V}_R$ corresponds to the atomic task i of computing the inner product of row i with the column vector $\mathbf{x}$. Hence, the weight $w_i = d_i$ is associated with each vertex $v_i \in \mathcal{V}_R$. Nets of $\mathcal{H}_C$ represent the dependency relations of the atomic tasks to the $\mathbf{x}$-vector components in the pre-communication scheme. That is, each net $n_j \subseteq \mathcal{V}_R$ denotes the set of atomic tasks that need x_j.

The row-net model can be considered as the dual of the column-net model. In this model, matrix $\mathbf{A}$ is represented as the hypergraph $\mathcal{H}_R(\mathcal{V}_C, \mathcal{N}_R)$. The vertex and net sets $\mathcal{V}_C$ and $\mathcal{N}_R$ correspond to the columns and rows of the matrix $\mathbf{A}$, respectively. There exist one vertex v_i and one net n_j for each column i and row j, respectively. Net n_j contains the vertices corresponding to the columns which have a nonzero entry on row j. That is, $v_i \in n_j$ if and only if $a_{ji} \neq 0$. Each vertex $v_i \in \mathcal{V}_C$ corresponds to the atomic task i of computing the sparse SAXPY/DAXPY operation $\mathbf{y} = \mathbf{y} + x_i \mathbf{a}_{*i}$. Hence, the weight $w_i = d_i$ is associated with each vertex $v_i \in \mathcal{V}_C$. Nets of $\mathcal{H}_R$ represent the dependency relations of the computation of $\mathbf{y}$-vector components to the atomic tasks represented by vertices of $\mathcal{H}_R$ in the post-communication scheme. That is, each net $n_j \subseteq \mathcal{V}_C$ denotes the set of atomic task results needed to compute y_j.

By assigning unit costs to the nets (i.e., $c_j = 1$ for each net n_j), the proposed column-net and row-net models reduce the decomposition problem into k-way hypergraph partitioning problem according to the cutsize definition given in (2.b) for the pre and post communication schemes, respectively. Part size definition is identical to that of the graph model. Assume that part P_ℓ is assigned to processor ℓ. Let $C[i]$ denotes the *connectivity* set of net n_i which is defined as the set of parts (processors) connected by the net n_i. Note that $\delta_i = |C[i]|$. In the column-net model together with the pre-communication scheme, a cut net n_i indicates that processor $part[x_i] \in C[i]$ should send its local x_i to those processors in the connectivity set of net n_i except itself (i.e., to processors in the set $C[i] - \{part[x_i]\}$. Hence, processor $part[x_i]$ should send its local x_i to $\delta_i - 1$ distinct processors. Here, $part[x_i]$ denotes the part (processor) assignment for x_i. In the row-net model together with the post-communication scheme, a cut net n_i indicates that processor $part[y_i] \in C[i]$ should receive the partial y_i results from those processors in the connectivity set of net n_i except itself (i.e., from processors in the set $C[i] - \{part[y_i]\}$). Hence, processor $part[y_i]$ should receive partial y_i results from $\delta_i - 1$ distinct processors. Thus, in column-net and row-net models, minimizing the cutsize according to (2.b) corresponds to minimizing the actual volume of interprocessor communication during pre and post communication phases, respectively. Maintaining the balance among part sizes corresponds to maintaining the computational load balance during local matrix-vector product computations. Note that row-net and column-net models become identical in symmetric square matrices.

Figure 1 illustrates 4-way graph and hypergraph partitions corresponding to the partial decomposition of a symmetric matrix. Here, assume that part P_ℓ is assigned to processor ℓ for $\ell = 1, 2, 3, 4$. As seen in Fig. 1(a), cutsize in the graph model is $2 \times 5 = 10$ since there are 5 cut edges. However, actual volume of communication is 7 in both pre and post communication schemes. For example, in the pre-communication scheme, processor 1 should send x_1 to both processors 2 and 4 only once, whereas processors 2 and 4 should send 3 and 2 local x_i values to processor 1, respectively. As seen in Fig. 1(b), each cut-net n_i, for $i = 2, 3, \ldots, 6$, contributes 1 to the cutsize since $\delta_2 = \delta_3 = \ldots = \delta_6 = 2$, and cut-net n_1 contributes 2 to the cutsize since $\delta_1 = 3$. Hence, the cutsize in the hypergraph model is 7 thus leading to an accurate modeling of the communication requirement.

4 Decomposition Heuristics

Kernighan-Lin (KL) based heuristics are widely used for graph and hypergraph partitioning because of their short run-times, and good quality results. KL algorithm is an iterative improvement heuristic originally proposed for 2-way graph partitioning (bipartitioning) [11]. This algorithm became the basis for most of the subsequent partitioning algorithms, all of which we call the KL-based algorithms. KL algorithm performs a number of passes until it finds a locally minimum partition. Each pass consists of a sequence of vertex swaps. The same swap strategy was applied to hypergraph partitioning problem by Schweikert-Kernighan [14]. Fiduccia-Mattheyses (FM) [6] introduced a faster implementation of KL algorithm for hypergraph partitioning. They proposed vertex move concept instead of vertex swap. This modification as well as proper data structures, e.g., bucket

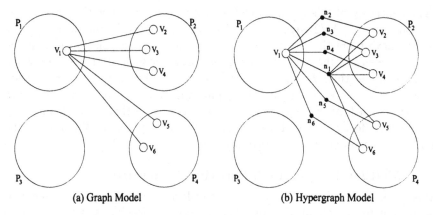

(a) Graph Model   (b) Hypergraph Model

Fig. 1. A partial 4-way decomposition of a symmetric matrix in (a) graph, (b) hypergraph models

lists, reduced the time complexity of a single pass of KL algorithm to linear in the size of the graph and the hypergraph. Here, *size* refers to the number of edges and pins in a graph and hypergraph, respectively. In this work, we have implemented k-way FM-based graph and hypergraph partitioning heuristics for experimenting the validity of our proposed hypergraph models.

The performance of FM deteriorates for large and/or too sparse and/or dense graphs/hypergraphs. Many clustering algorithms have been proposed especially for hypergraphs to alleviate this problem [2]. Clustering corresponds to coalescing highly interacting vertices to supernodes as a preprocessing to FM. Recently, *multilevel* graph partitioning methods have been proposed leading to successful graph partitioning tools Chaco [8] and Metis [10]. These multilevel heuristics consists of 3 phases, namely *coarsening*, *initial partitioning*, and *uncoarsening*. In the first phase, multilevel clustering is successively applied starting from the original graph by adopting various matching heuristics until number of vertices in the coarsened graph reduces below a predetermined threshold value. In the second phase, coarsest graph is partitioned using various heuristics including FM. In the third phase, partition found in the second phase is successively projected back towards the original graph by refining the projected partitions on intermediate level uncoarser graphs using various heuristics including FM.

4.1 Clique-Net Model for Graph Representation of Hypergraphs

The goal in this approach is to exploit the Metis graph partitioning tool as a black box. So, we use the traditional clique-net model to transform hypergraphs to graphs. In this transformation model, the vertex set of the target graph is equal to the vertex set of the given hypergraph. Each net of the given hypergraph is represented by a clique of vertices corresponding to its pins. Vertex weights of the hypergraph become the vertex weights of the graph. Costs of the edges are equal to the sum of the costs of the nets that they represent. If an edge is in the cut set of a graph partitioning then all nets represented by this edge are in the cut set of hypergraph partitioning and vice versa.

The deficiency of this graph model is that it treats a net with size s in the hypergraph as $s(s-1)/2$ edges. This strategy exaggerates the importance of the nets that have more than two terminals and the exaggeration grows with the square of the size of the net [14]. In our current implementation, we remove all nets of size larger than T during the transformation. Furthermore, for each net n_j, we select $F \times s_j$ random pairs of its pins and add an edge with cost one to the graph for each selected pair of pins (vertices). Note that this scheme is an experimental effort to alleviate the above mentioned problem. We use $T = 50$ and $F = 5$ in accordance to the recommendations given in [1].

4.2 A Multilevel Hypergraph Partitioning Heuristic

In this work, we exploit the successful multilevel methodology proposed and implemented for graph partitioning (Metis [10]) to develop a new multilevel hypergraph partitioning tool, called PaToH (PaToH: **P**artitioning **To**ols for **H**ypergraphs). We should note that current implementation is just an initial implementation to experiment both the validity of our hypergraph models and the performance of multilevel approach on hypergraph partitioning.

Coarsening Phase In this phase, the given hypergraph $\mathcal{H} = \mathcal{H}_0$ is coarsened into a sequence of smaller hypergraphs $\mathcal{H}_1 = (\mathcal{V}_1, \mathcal{N}_1)$, $\mathcal{H}_2 = (\mathcal{V}_2, \mathcal{N}_2), \ldots, \mathcal{H}_m = (\mathcal{V}_m, \mathcal{N}_m)$ satisfying $|\mathcal{V}_0| > |\mathcal{V}_1| > |\mathcal{V}_2| > \ldots > |\mathcal{V}_m|$. This coarsening is achieved by combining vertex pairs of hypergraph $\mathcal{H}_i$ into *supernodes* of next level hypergraph $\mathcal{H}_{i+1}$. The weight of each supernode of $\mathcal{H}_{i+1}$ is set equal to the sum of its constituent vertices in $\mathcal{H}_i$. Also, the net set of each supernode is set equal to the union of the net sets of its constituent vertices. Coarsening phase terminates when number of vertices in the coarsened hypergraph reduces below 100 (i.e., $|\mathcal{V}_m| \leq 100$) following the recommendation given in [10].

In the current implementation, we use a randomized vertex matching for coarsening. In this scheme, an un-matched vertex u of hypergraph $\mathcal{H}_i$ is selected randomly. Then, we consider all un-matched vertices which share nets with vertex u for matching. We match u with the vertex v such that the sum of the costs of the shared nets between u and v is maximum among all considered vertices. If there exists no un-matched vertex which shares net(s) with the selected vertex u, then vertex u is left un-matched. In rowwise matrix decomposition context (i.e., column-net model), this matching scheme corresponds to combining rows or row groups with similar row sparsity patterns. This in turn corresponds to combining rows or row groups which need similar sets of **x**-vector components in the pre-communication scheme. A dual discussion holds for columnwise matrix decomposition using the row-net model.

Partitioning Phase The goal in this phase is to find a partition on the coarsest hypergraph $\mathcal{H}_m$. In the current implementation we use k-way FM algorithm with the cutsize definition (2.b) for partitioning $\mathcal{H}_m$. Since the coarsest hypergraph $\mathcal{H}_m$ is small, we run the k-way FM heuristic more than once and take the minimum. We set this number of trials to 5 in PaToH.

Uncoarsening Phase At each level i (for $i = m, m-1, \ldots, 1$), partition Π_i found on $\mathcal{H}_i$ is projected back to the partition Π_{i-1} on $\mathcal{H}_{i-1}$. The constituent

Table 1. Properties of test matrices. d and s denote the vertex degree and net size in graph and hypergraph models, respectively. Z denotes the total number of non-zeros in matrices.

name	$|\mathcal{V}|=|\mathcal{N}|$	$|\mathcal{E}|$	d_{avg}	Z	s_{avg}	s_{min}	s_{max}
bcspwr7	1612	2106	1.31	5824	3.61	2	13
bcspwr10	5300	8271	1.56	21842	4.12	2	14
lshp2614	2614	7683	2.94	17980	6.88	4	7
lshp3466	3466	10215	2.95	23896	6.89	4	7
dwt2680	2680	11173	4.17	25026	9.34	4	19
bcsstk21	3600	11500	3.19	26600	7.39	4	9
ganges	1681	10932	6.50	23545	14.01	3	86
perold	1376	23675	17.21	48726	35.41	3	86
sctab2	1880	28963	15.41	59806	31.81	3	62
sctab3	2480	38263	15.43	79006	31.86	3	79

vertices of each supernode of $\mathcal{H}_i$ is assigned to the part of their supernode. Obviously, this new partition Π_{i-1} has the same cutsize with the previous partition Π_i. Then, we refine this partition by running our k-way FM algorithm on $\mathcal{H}_{i-1}$ starting from the initial partition Π_{i-1}. However, in this phase, we limit the maximum number of passes to 2. We also put an early termination rule into one pass of k-way FM. A pass is terminated whenever last $0.25 \times |\mathcal{V}_i|$ moves do not decrease the cut.

5 Experimental Results

We have implemented k-way FM graph and hypergraph partitioning heuristics and a multilevel k-way hypergraph partitioning algorithm PaToH, and used Metis[10] graph partitioning tool for the experimental evaluation of the validity of the proposed hypergraph models. FM heuristics iteratively improve initial feasible partitions. A partition is said to be feasible if it satisfies the load balance criterion $W_{avg}(1-\varepsilon) \leq W_p \leq W_{avg}(1+\varepsilon)$, for each part $p = 1, 2, \ldots k$. Here, $W_{avg} = (\sum_{i=1}^{n} w_i)/k$ denotes the part sizes of each part under perfect load balance condition, and ε represents the predetermined maximum load imbalance ratio allowed. We have used $\varepsilon = 0.04$ in all heuristics.

Symmetric sparse matrices selected from Harwell-Boeing collection [4] and linear programming problems in NETLIB suite [7] are used for experimentation. Note that test matrices are restricted to symmetric matrices since graphs cannot be used to model unsymmetric square and rectangular matrices. Table 1 displays the characteristics of the selected test matrices. BCSPWR07 and BCSPWR10 matrices come from the sparse matrix representation of power networks. LSHP2614 and LSHP3466 matrices come from the finite element discretizations of L-shaped regions. DWT2680 and BCSSTK21 are structural engineering problems. The sparsity patterns of GANGES, PEROLD, SCTAB2 and SCTAB3 are obtained from the NETLIB suite by multiplying the respective constraint matrices with their transposes. Power matrices, structural engineering matrix DWT2680, and NETLIB matrices GANGES and PEROLD have unstructured sparsity pattern. Finite element matrices, structural engineering matrix BCSSTK21, and NETLIB matrices SCTAB2 3 have rather structured sparsity pattern.

The graph and hypergraph representations of these matrices are partitioned to 4, 8, 16, and 32 parts by running the heuristics on a Sun UltraSparc 1/140. Each heuristic were run 50 times for each decomposition instance using random initial seeds. Minimum communication volume values of these 50 runs are displayed in Table 2 together with the average run-times. Communication volume values displayed in this table correspond to the communication cost computed according to (2.b).

We will refer to the FM heuristics using the graph and hypergraph models as FM-G and FM-H, respectively. As seen in Table 2, FM-H usually finds better decompositions than FM-G (8% better on the overall average). As also seen in this table, FM-H always finds drastically better decompositions than FM-G on unstructured test matrices with small net sizes (e.g., power matrices). However, the relative performance of FM-H with respect to FM-G deteriorates on structured matrices with large net sizes (e.g., finite element matrices and NETLIB matrices SCTAB2–3). This experimental finding can be attributed to the following reason. FM-H algorithm encounters large number of zero move gains during the decomposition of such matrices. FM-H algorithm randomly resolves these ties. However, on such cases, FM-G algorithm tends to gather the adjacent vertices although they do not decrease the actual communication requirement at that point in time. However, as seen in the table, PaToH overcomes the large net size problem because of the multilevel clustering (matchings) performed during the coarsening phase (e.g., PEROLD, SCTAB2–3).

In multilevel heuristics, clique-net approach does not perform very well compared to the graph model Metis (only 3% better on the overall average) as expected. As seen in Table 2, our multilevel hypergraph partitioning heuristic (PaToH) almost always performs better than the graph model Metis (13% better on the overall average). However, our current implementation of PaToH is 1.14 to 22.09 times slower than graph model Metis (6.55 times slower on the overall average). As described in Section 4.2, current implementation of the PaToH is just an initial implementation to experiment the performance of multilevel approaches on hypergraph partitioning.

6 Conclusion and Future Research

Two hypergraph models were proposed for decomposing sparse matrices for parallel matrix-vector multiplication. The proposed models avoid all deficiencies of the graph model. The proposed models enable the representation and hence the decomposition of unsymmetric square and rectangular matrices as well as symmetric matrices. Furthermore, they introduce a much more accurate representation for the communication requirement. The proposed models reduce the decomposition problem to the well-known *hypergraph partitioning* problem thus enabling the use of existing circuit partitioning heuristics and tools widely used in VLSI design. Fast Kernighan-Lin based graph and hypergraph partitioning

Table 2. Minimum communication costs for 50 runs and average run-times (in seconds). Numbers in parentheses represent values normalized with respect to the graph model results found by the same class of heuristics. Bold values indicate the best communication volume values with respective heuristics.

| | | k-way FM Heuristics | | Multilevel Heuristics | | | | | |
| | | Graph Model | Hypergraph Model | Graph Model Metis | | Clique-Net Metis | | PaToH | |
name	k	cost	cost	cost	time	cost	time	cost	time
bcspwr7	4	312	**55** (0.18)	33	0.25	32 (0.97)	(1.12)	**27** (0.82)	(1.14)
	8	466	**193** (0.41)	87	0.39	86 (0.99)	(1.00)	**83** (0.95)	(1.74)
	16	630	**359** (0.57)	176	0.61	177 (1.01)	(0.93)	**174** (0.99)	(3.73)
	32	677	**506** (0.75)	**304**	1.02	307 (1.01)	(0.87)	315 (1.04)	(8.37)
bcspwr10	4	1260	**384** (0.30)	124	0.71	126 (1.02)	(1.11)	**117** (0.94)	(1.73)
	8	1935	**727** (0.38)	231	0.87	**229** (0.99)	(1.08)	238 (1.03)	(3.31)
	16	2328	**1417** (0.61)	422	1.11	**413** (0.98)	(1.07)	414 (0.98)	(7.37)
	32	2570	**1739** (0.68)	707	1.56	**690** (0.98)	(1.07)	720 (1.02)	(19.25)
lshp2614	4	206	**204** (0.99)	234	0.47	243 (1.04)	(1.31)	**207** (0.88)	(1.37)
	8	392	**386** (0.98)	420	0.64	420 (1.00)	(1.25)	**396** (0.94)	(2.24)
	16	641	**638** (1.00)	687	0.91	691 (1.01)	(1.14)	**662** (0.96)	(4.64)
	32	1024	**998** (0.97)	1064	1.36	1069 (1.00)	(1.03)	**1048** (0.98)	(14.27)
lshp3466	4	235	**234** (1.00)	275	0.54	268 (0.97)	(1.30)	**237** (0.86)	(1.57)
	8	449	**447** (1.00)	492	0.68	483 (0.98)	(1.25)	**451** (0.92)	(2.75)
	16	**728**	**728** (1.00)	803	0.92	773 (0.96)	(1.21)	**759** (0.95)	(5.88)
	32	1171	**1135** (0.97)	1219	1.36	1190 (0.98)	(1.12)	**1169** (0.96)	(16.27)
dwt2680	4	222	**189** (0.85)	205	0.50	199 (0.97)	(1.57)	**186** (0.91)	(1.90)
	8	623	**506** (0.81)	497	0.65	469 (0.94)	(1.44)	**440** (0.89)	(3.01)
	16	1119	**970** (0.87)	879	0.91	844 (0.96)	(1.31)	**836** (0.95)	(6.06)
	32	1606	1624 (1.01)	1438	1.37	1370 (0.95)	(1.09)	**1369** (0.95)	(17.18)
bcsstk21	4	244	**240** (0.98)	281	0.91	**240** (0.85)	(1.05)	**240** (0.85)	(1.24)
	8	1064	**1026** (0.96)	707	1.09	587 (0.83)	(1.07)	**554** (0.78)	(2.27)
	16	2021	**1859** (0.92)	1244	1.37	1061 (0.85)	(1.06)	**993** (0.80)	(5.05)
	32	2692	**2405** (0.89)	2088	1.88	1763 (0.84)	(1.02)	**1674** (0.80)	(15.33)
ganges	4	733	**379** (0.52)	395	0.54	357 (0.90)	(1.19)	**297** (0.75)	(2.04)
	8	1236	**787** (0.64)	713	0.73	724 (1.02)	(1.13)	**589** (0.83)	(4.06)
	16	1771	**1730** (0.98)	1204	1.02	1348 (1.12)	(1.02)	**1139** (0.95)	(8.82)
	32	**2550**	2792 (1.09)	2167	1.49	2331 (1.08)	(0.94)	**2122** (0.98)	(22.09)
perold	4	1320	**1286** (0.97)	1041	0.96	1017 (0.98)	(3.65)	**868** (0.83)	(2.29)
	8	2283	**2216** (0.97)	2233	1.23	2198 (0.98)	(3.04)	**1652** (0.74)	(4.29)
	16	4044	**3537** (0.87)	3750	1.62	3737 (1.00)	(2.44)	**2656** (0.71)	(7.38)
	32	5780	**4778** (0.83)	5471	2.29	5170 (0.94)	(1.89)	**4111** (0.75)	(14.58)
sctab2	4	**1095**	1840 (1.68)	1106	1.31	1060 (0.96)	(4.17)	**901** (0.81)	(1.78)
	8	**1930**	2882 (1.49)	1976	1.78	1859 (0.94)	(3.28)	**1522** (0.77)	(2.80)
	16	**3672**	4213 (1.15)	3245	2.33	3058 (0.94)	(2.66)	**2563** (0.79)	(4.94)
	32	6653	**6019** (0.90)	5624	3.08	5414 (0.96)	(2.18)	**4151** (0.74)	(11.69)
sctab3	4	**1397**	2511 (1.80)	1396	1.61	1281 (0.92)	(3.49)	**1119** (0.80)	(1.99)
	8	**2642**	3788 (1.43)	2534	2.02	2315 (0.91)	(2.97)	**1943** (0.77)	(3.13)
	16	**4484**	5439 (1.21)	4007	2.54	3907 (0.98)	(2.52)	**3163** (0.79)	(5.87)
	32	**7531**	7619 (1.01)	6802	3.27	6417 (0.94)	(2.12)	**4944** (0.73)	(16.46)

heuristics were implemented and the successful multilevel graph partitioning tool (Metis) was used for the experimental evaluation of the validity of the proposed hypergraph models. An initial version for a multilevel hypergraph partitioning heuristic was also implemented for experimenting both the validity of the proposed models and the performance of the multilevel approach on hypergraph partitioning. Experimental results on sparse matrices, selected from Harwell-Boeing collection and NETLIB suite, confirmed the validity of our proposed hypergraph models. Initial experimental results were also found to be promising for the performance of multilevel approaches on hypergraph partitioning. We are currently working on improving both the speed and quality performance of our multilevel hypergraph partitioning heuristic.

References

1. C. J. Alpert, L. W. Hagen, and A. B. Kahng. A hybrid multilevel/genetic approach for circuit partitioning. Technical report, UCLA CS Dept., 1996.
2. C. J. Alpert and A. B. Kahng. Recent directions in netlist partitioning: A survey. *VLSI Journal*, 19(1-2):1–81, 1995.
3. Ü. V. Çatalyürek and C. Aykanat. A hypergraph model for mapping repeated sparse matrix-vector product computations onto multicomputers. In *Proceedings of International Conference on Hyperformance Computing*, December 1995.
4. I. S. Duff, R. Grimes, and J. Lewis. Sparse matrix test problems. *ACM Transactions on Mathematical Software*, 15(1):1–14, march 1989.
5. F. Erçal, C. Aykanat, F. Özgüner and P. Sadayappan. Iterative algorithms for solution of large sparse systems of linear equations on hypercubes. *IEEE Transactions on Computers*, 37:1554–1567, 1988.
6. C. M. Fiduccia and R. M. Mattheyses. A linear-time heuristic for improving network partitions. In *Proceedings of the 19th ACM/IEEE Design Automation Conference*, pages 175–181, 1982.
7. D. M. Gay. Electronic mail distribution of linear programming test problems. *Mathematical Programming Society COAL Newsletter*, 1985.
8. B. Hendrickson and R. Leland. A multilevel algorithm for partitioning graphs. Technical report, Sandia National Laboratories, 1993.
9. B. A. Hendrickson, W. Camp, S. J. Plimpton and R. W. Leland. Massively parallel methods for engineering and science problems. *Communication of ACM*, 37(4):31–41, April 1994.
10. G. Karypis and V. Kumar. A fast and high quality multilevel scheme for partitioning irregular graphs. Tech. report, CS Dept., University of Minnesota, 1995.
11. B. W. Kernighan and S. Lin. An efficient heuristic procedure for partitioning graphs. *The Bell System Technical Journal*, 49(2):291–307, February 1970.
12. C. Pommerell, M. Annaratone, and W. Fichtner. A set of new mapping and coloring heuristics for distributed-memory parallel processors. *SIAM Journal of Scientific and Statistical Computing*, 13(1):194–226, January 1992.
13. J. Ramanujam, F. Erçal and P. Sadayappan. Task allocation onto a hypercube by recursive mincut bipartitioning. *J. Parallel and Dist. Comput.*, 10:35–44, 1990.
14. D. G. Schweikert and B. W. Kernighan. A proper model for the partitioning of electrical circuits. In *Proceedings of the 9th ACM/IEEE Design Automation Conference*, pages 57–62, 1972.

Dynamic Spectral Partitioning

Horst D. Simon[1], Andrew Sohn[2]

[1] Lawrence Berkeley National Laboratory, University of California, Berkeley, Ca
94720
[2] Computer and Information Science Department, New Jersey Institute of
Technology, Newark, NJ 07102-1982

Abstract. Recursive Spectral Bisection (RSB) has been proposed as
an efficient heuristic algorithm for partitioning problem for unstructured
problems about six years ago, and has since become a widely used tool
when implementing finite element applications on parallel processors.
However, many applications have a dynamically changing communication pattern, e.g. unstructured grid problems with adaptive refinement.
In this talk we will outline a method which combines the advantages of
RSB with the capability of quickly updating a partitioning, if the under-
lyng grid is dynamically changing. We call this method dynamic spectral
partitioning (DSP). We will discuss the derivation of DSP, and motivate
it with applications from structural analysis and computational chemistry. Then, using an adaptive grid refinement 3d Navier-Stokes code
on the IBM SP-2, we will demonstrate how DSP can be applied to the
solution of practical problems.

Dynamic Spectral Partitioning

Abstract: Dynamic Spectral Partitioning...

Fast Distributed Genetic Algorithms for Partitioning Uniform Grids*

Ioannis T. Christou[1] and Robert R. Meyer[1]

Computer Sciences Department, University of Wisconsin, Madison, Wisconsin 53706.

Abstract. In this paper we present a new method for partitioning general large uniform 5-point grids into sub-domains of given areas having minimum total perimeter. For applications in scientific computing in parallel environments, this problem corresponds to minimizing the communication overhead between processors while observing load balancing constraints dictated by the speed of each individual processor. For a large class of grid shapes we show that the partition produced by our method is asymptotically optimal as the problem parameters grow to infinity. A new distributed Genetic Algorithm based on this decomposition theory significantly outperforms other well-known methods such as the spectral bisection (or quadrisection) methods and the geometric mesh partitioner.

1 Introduction

Minimum Perimeter (MP) problems are a class of NP-complete problems that arise in the solution of finite-difference schemes in parallel environments or the simulation of molecule behavior in Chemical Engineering. They also find applications in low level computer vision (edge detection in image processing). In such applications, one must perform some computational task over a grid of unit cells and the computations performed in each cell require the value of its four immediate neighbors. Such schemes are called 5-point grids because the update of the value of each cell involves its previous value and the value of its northern, southern, eastern and western neighbors. In a parallel computing environment, distributing the grid cells among the available processors will inevitably lead to communication between the processors at the common boundaries of the regions that each processor will occupy. It is therefore necessary to partition the grid in such a way so as to minimize communication penalties (especially as the trend in parallel computing shifts towards networks of workstations where these penalties can be very high).

In its most general form, the Minimum Perimeter problem $MP(\mathcal{G}, P)$ can be stated as follows: *Given a Grid $\mathcal{G}$ of unit cells, a number of processors P, and an associated load a_i for each processor, find an assignment of the grid cells to the processors so that the perimeter of the partition is minimized while*

---

* This research was partially supported by the Air Force Office of Scientific Research under grant F49620-94-1-0036, and by the NSF under grants CDA-9024618 and CCR-9306807.

observing the load balancing constraint that processor i is assigned a_i cells. The perimeter of a partition is the sum of the lengths of the boundaries of the regions that each processor occupies, while the load of each processor is the area of the region it occupies. The problem is therefore a Graph Partitioning problem, and as such, it can be formulated as a Quadratic Assignment problem ([PRW93]), with $|\mathcal{G}|P$ binary variables and $|\mathcal{G}| + P$ constraints. Letting $\mathcal{I}$ denote the set of pairs of adjacent cells, and $\mathcal{A}_p$ the area for processor p, the QAP formulation is as follows:

$$\min. \sum_{i,j \in \mathcal{G}} \sum_{\substack{p,p'=1 \\ p \neq p'}}^{P} c_{ij} x_i^p x_j^{p'}$$

$$s.t. \begin{cases} \sum_{i \in \mathcal{G}} x_i^p = \mathcal{A}_p & p = 1 \ldots P \\ \sum_{p=1}^{P} x_i^p = 1 & i \in \mathcal{G} \\ x_i^p \in \mathbf{B} = \{0,1\} \end{cases}$$

$$\text{where } c_{ij} = \begin{cases} 1 & \text{if } (i,j) \in \mathcal{I} \\ 0 & \text{else} \end{cases}$$

MP is an NP-complete problem (see [Yac93]) and as such there is little hope of solving it exactly with a polynomial time algorithm. Instead, motivated by the results obtained in [CM96a], we develop a fast solution technique, snake decomposition, that for a large class of grids can be shown to produce partitions whose relative distance from a computable lower bound converges to zero as the problem size tends to infinity. For this purpose, we have developed a new Distributed Genetic Algorithm (DGA) that runs on a Cluster of Workstations (COW) and we have compared the performance of our algorithm in terms of solution quality as well as running time against the performance of well known algorithms for graph partitioning such as the spectral methods ([HL95a]) and the geometric mesh partitioner ([GMT95]). The results show clearly the superiority of the performance of our method against those of established methods for a large class of test problems.

Because of its practical significance, many algorithms have been proposed for solving the MP. Kernighan and Lin's heuristic ([KL70]) for partitioning a graph into two components is a very well known technique that is still used in many modern codes as a subroutine but has the disadvantage of requiring a relatively good initial partition upon which it attempts to improve. It is a standard local refinement routine incorporated in the Chaco package ([HL95a]). Pothen et. al. ([PSL90]) developed the spectral method in the context of general graph partitioning; discussion of improved spectral partitioning algorithms including spectral quadrisection or octasection can be found in [HL95b]. Laguna et. al. ([LFE94]) also developed a GRASP heuristic for partitioning a general graph into two pieces; and in [CQ95] Crandall and Quinn presented a heuristic for decomposing non-uniform rectangular grids among a number of heterogeneous processors. On the other hand, Miller et. al. ([MTTV93]) have designed a domain decomposer for meshes based on geometric ideas. Finally, Genetic Algorithm approaches to the graph partitioning problem have been proposed ([vL91]) where the length of each individual in the population is at least as big as the size of the graph. Our GA is a high-level approach that uses relatively few variables.

2   Asymptotically Optimal Equi-partitions

In this section we prove that under some rather mild assumptions, one can partition a 5-point uniform grid into any number of equal-sized components in such a way that the total perimeter of the partition approaches a computable lower bound as the problem parameters tend to infinity. The decomposition concepts that form the basis of this theory are then employed (as described in the following sections) in algorithms that outperform current approaches for graph partitioning. The theory makes use of the fact [Yac93] that a lower bound on the perimeter of the equi-partition of any 5-point grid into P regions, each with area $\mathcal{A}_p = \frac{A}{P}$ is given by

$$(1) \qquad\qquad L(A, P) = 2P \left\lceil 2\sqrt{\frac{A}{P}} \right\rceil .$$

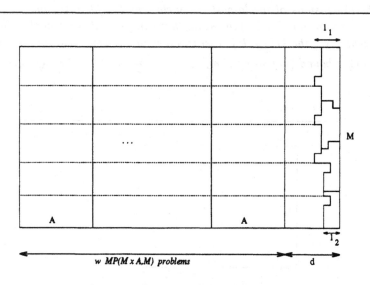

Fig. 1. MP($M \times N, P$), $P \geq max(M, N)$

The theorems below also extend a result reported in [CM96a, CM96b] which shows how to obtain a good partition of a rectangular grid of dimensions $M \times N$ among P processors with $P \geq \max(M, N)$ and $\mathcal{A}_p = \frac{MN}{P}$. This is accomplished by decomposing the problem into $w = N \div A_p$ sub-grids of area $M \times A_p$ which can be partitioned among M processors each, and a leftover area in the rightmost part of the grid (which will be assigned the remaining processors). Except for the last area, each of the sub-grids can be efficiently partitioned into a series of stripes, by using the concept of optimal heights ([YM92]) defined as the solution h^* of the following problem

$$\min_{h,w} \ h + w$$

$$s.t. \begin{cases} hw \geq A_p \\ h, w \in \mathbb{N}. \end{cases}$$

These stripes are filled with processor indices in a continuous fashion (filling the columns of the stripe left to right). The last area is filled using a "reverse" stripe filling process. It can then be shown that the relative distance of this solution from the lower bound is

(2)
$$\delta_r < \frac{1}{A_p} + \frac{1}{\sqrt{A_p}}$$

Figure 1 shows the stripe decomposition process.

Theorem 1. *Let $\mathcal{G}$ denote a 5-point uniform grid with total area $A(\mathcal{G})$, to be equi-partitioned among P processors, each having an area $A_p = \frac{A(\mathcal{G})}{P}$. Let (M_0, N_0) denote the dimensions of the largest rectangle that can fit in $\mathcal{G}$, and let P_0 denote the maximum number of processors that can fit in this rectangle. Then, if $P_0 \geq \max(M_0, N_0)$ the MP($\mathcal{G}, P$) possesses a solution whose relative distance δ_G from the lower bound (1) satisfies $\delta_G < \frac{1}{A_p} + \frac{1}{\sqrt{A_p}} + \left[1 - \frac{P_0 A_p}{A(\mathcal{G})}\right] \sqrt{A_p}$.*

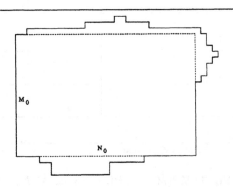

Fig. 2. The Embedded Rectangle

Proof. As mentioned above, any rectangular grid of dimensions $M_0 \times N_0$ can be partitioned among $P \geq \max(M_0, N_0)$ processors (using stripe decomposition) in such a way so that the relative distance of the perimeter of the solution from the lower bound is less than the RHS of (2), where A_p is simply the area of each processor. Now, consider a general grid $\mathcal{G}$ (see for example figure 2); the number of processors that can be assigned to the largest rectangle $M_0 \times N_0$ that can fit in this grid is $P_0 = \left\lfloor \frac{M_0 N_0}{A_p} \right\rfloor$ and this number is by hypothesis greater than or equal to $\max(M_0, N_0)$. Using stripe decomposition, it is possible therefore to assign P_0 processors in this rectangular area with a total relative error δ_0 in perimeter that is less than the expression in the RHS of (2). The rest of the grid (as well as possibly the right bottom part of the rectangle that might have been left unassigned using the P_0 processors) will be assigned using the remaining $P - P_0$ processors. In the worst possible case, each of the unassigned cells will have a perimeter of 4 and there are

$$A_0^c(\mathcal{G}) = A(\mathcal{G}) - P_0 A_p$$

cells left unassigned. So the total relative error of the solution from the lower bound is bounded from above by

$$\delta_G < \delta_0 + \frac{4 A_0^c(\mathcal{G}) - 2(P - P_0) \left\lceil 2\sqrt{A_p} \right\rceil}{2P \left\lceil 2\sqrt{A_p} \right\rceil}$$

$$< \delta_0 + \frac{(P - P_0) A_p}{P \sqrt{A_p}}$$

$$< \frac{1}{A_p} + \frac{1}{\sqrt{A_p}} +$$

$$+ \left[1 - \frac{P_0 A_p}{A(\mathcal{G})} \right] \sqrt{A_p}$$

which ends the proof.

As an easy corollary we obtain the following:

Corollary 2. *Let $\mathcal{G}^k$ be a sequence of 5-point uniform grids. Assume that $\mathcal{G}^k$ has total area $A(\mathcal{G}^k)$, (which contains a rectangle of dimensions (M_0^k, N_0^k)) to be equi-partitioned among P^k processors each having an area A_p^k. If $P_0^k :=$ $\left\lfloor \frac{M_0^k N_0^k}{A_p^k} \right\rfloor \geq \max(M_0^k, N_0^k)$, then if $\left[1 - \frac{P_0^k A_p^k}{A(\mathcal{G}^k)} \right] \sqrt{A_p^k} \to 0$ as $A_p^k \to \infty$ the sequence $MP(\mathcal{G}^k, P^k)$ has solutions with relative distances from the lower bound $\delta_G^k \to 0$.*

Essentially, the theorem guarantees the existence of partitions that are asymptotically optimal as long as the grid is near-rectangular. Such grids might be elongated trapezoids to be partitioned among a large number of processors (such grids arise from simulations in chemical engineering). For example consider a sequence of trapezoids with embedded rectangles of size $N^2 \times N$ to be equipartitioned among N^2 or more processors. This sequence of trapezoids satisfies the conditions of the corollary for any given angle of the remaining triangles in its top and bottom ends.

The theorem however does more than that; it provides a very efficient method for constructing such solutions, namely the stripe decomposition method equipped with a termination phase where after the P_0 processors have been assigned to the $M_0 \times N_0$ rectangle, the remaining cells of the grid are assigned to the $P - P_0$ processors left in a scanning fashion (scan the grid and for each cell unassigned assign it to the first processor that hasn't yet occupied $\mathcal{A}_p$ cells).

It is easy to extend the ideas behind the previous theorem, to include 5-point uniform grids that contain a finite number of relatively large disjoint rectangular areas by essentially applying stripe decomposition to each one of the embedded rectangles.

Theorem 3. *Let $\mathcal{G}$ denote a 5-point uniform grid with total area $\mathcal{A}(\mathcal{G})$, to be equi-partitioned among P processors, each having an area $\mathcal{A}_p = \frac{\mathcal{A}(\mathcal{G})}{P}$. For a finite n and $i = 1 \ldots n$ let (M_i, N_i) denote the dimensions of the n largest disjoint rectangles whose union fits in $\mathcal{G}$, and let P_i denote the maximum number of processors that can fit in each of these rectangles. Then, if $P_i \geq \max(M_i, N_i)$ the $MP(\mathcal{G}, P)$ possesses a solution whose relative distance δ_G from the lower bound (1) satisfies*

$$\delta_G < n \left[\frac{1}{\mathcal{A}_p} + \frac{1}{\sqrt{\mathcal{A}_p}} \right] + \left[1 - \frac{\sum_{i=1}^{n} P_i \mathcal{A}_p}{\mathcal{A}(\mathcal{G})} \right] \sqrt{\mathcal{A}_p}.$$

3   Snake Decomposition

Motivated by the result of the previous section, we can now present a new method for equi-partitioning the grid among any number of processors (a feature lacking from many other codes which require the number of processors to be a power of two). Note that stripe decomposition applied to rectangular grids partitions the rows of the grid into stripes of optimal height (for the given area $\mathcal{A}_p$) and then fills these stripes with processor indices. The snake decomposition method extends this idea by allowing non-optimal heights to be considered, and by allowing processor indices to "overflow" to the next stripe if necessary. This overflow procedure generally produces solutions that are better those considered in the previous section, although a precise comparison is difficult. It also extends the original stripe decomposition by being applicable to *any* uniform 5-point grid, and we have experimented with various grid shapes such as toroidal domains, elliptical or diamond domains of quite different sizes. A key advantage is that this high-level approach reduces the dimensionality of the problem to that of determining values for the stripe heights. Furthermore, it can be easily expanded to include non-uniform grids by recursively applying it within the non-unit grid cells, as we briefly discuss in the last section of this paper.

To describe the snake decomposition method, observe that any 5-point uniform grid can be represented by an $M \times N$ rectangle with some of its cells having

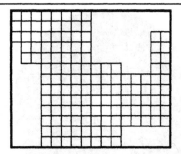

Fig. 3. Rectangular Hull Representation of a Grid

a certain value to indicate that they are not part of the grid, or "unavailable". This super-grid is the smallest rectangular grid that can accommodate our given grid; in the combinatorics literature [Mel94], this rectangle is sometimes called the convex hull of the grid. Snake decomposition accepts as input a partition of the rows of this super-grid (see the thick rectangle in figure 3) into a set of near optimal heights, and then fills the grid with the required number of processors by filling the columns of each stripe consecutively in a way that resembles the movement of a snake. The first stripe's columns are filled left to right, then the second stripe's columns are filled going right to left, and then the process repeats. If the end of a stripe has been reached, but the processor that was used to fill the last part of it still hasn't been assigned A_p cells, then part of the stripe(s) immediately below the area that the current processor occupies are assigned to this processor in a row-by-row fashion. This is done in order to keep the perimeter small.

Figure 4 shows a partition of a torus into 64 equi-area sub-domains obtained by our algorithm. The torus is a disk of radius 50 with a hole of radius 7 in its center. The horizontal lines that are formed at the boundaries of the partitions correspond to the various stripe heights. The partition of the torus has an associated relative gap of 11% from the lower bound, the best found by any method we have tried. (Because of the irregular boundary of the torus, the lower bound (1) is not expected to be close to the optimal value, so the distance of this solution from optimality should be much less than 11%.)

The running time of the procedure **snake(...)** is $O(|\mathcal{G}|)$ making it a very fast routine for partitioning arbitrary uniform 5-point grids. The key to obtaining high-quality solutions is the determination of a partition of the rows of the grid that will produce stripes that can be filled with minimal deviation from optimal perimeter. For this end, we have developed two methods and we have tested their performance. (See also [Mar96], which describes a very fast knapsack approach to stripe height determination for rectangular grids meeting certain conditions.) The first, called R-SNAKE, simply picks at random optimal heights (and with a small probability it picks near-optimal ones) to create a valid partition of stripes. The process is repeated a certain number of times, and the best of these trials is kept as the final solution. The second is a new distributed Genetic Algorithm that

Fig. 4. Snake partition of torus among 64 procs

breeds such row-partitions with the hope of finding better and better partitions. The fitness function for this GA is a scaled variant of the total perimeter of the feasible solution produced by the snake decomposition procedure.

4 DGA: a new Distributed GA

Genetic Algorithms traditionally operate on a fixed population of individuals, each one representing a solution to a given problem [Hol92, Mic94]. At each iteration, the population is replaced by new individuals created using two genetic operators, the recombination operator (crossover) and the mutation operator that act upon the chromosomes of two parent individuals that have been selected for mating.

DGA is a new, fully asynchronous, distributed Genetic Algorithm following the "island" model of computation. When started, DGA spawns a certain number of processes (each of which is called an *island*) on the platform on which it is running, and each island is initialized with a certain number of individuals created randomly. It uses the steady state approach as the mechanism for creating the next generation of individuals, but it also includes a new feature, namely age, in order to control the population and to maintain diversity of the population and prevent premature convergence. Furthermore, each DGA island has a variable population size, and each individual in the population may have different chromosome (DNA) length.

A main iteration in each island performs the following steps:

- For a certain number of times select two individuals, apply crossover and mutation to create a new offspring, evaluate it and place it in the island (replacing another individual if there is no empty space in the island).
- Increase the age of each individual and remove "olds" according to a probability distribution.

- Broadcast the island's population.
- If migrating criteria are satisfied, select qualified individuals for migration to other islands and send them.
- Probe for incoming individuals and receive all that have arrived.

The algorithm is fully asynchronous in that all send and receives are done asynchronously, i.e. when a process sends a message to another process, it does not wait until the receiving process receives the message. Instead, it resumes computation as soon as the outgoing message is safely on its way on the network. The criteria for sending individuals to other islands are based on workload values: if an island's population has dropped too much then a decision is made to send the best individuals from another island to the depopulated island.

All processes during the probing step simply probe their buffer pool to check for pending messages, and if there are any, they are received, else computation is resumed from the point it was left. Thus, an individual sent to a process during an early generation might actually get there several generations later. However, the approach offers the advantage of not wasting network and CPU resources waiting for ACK/NACK signals. In the probing step, any incoming individuals are ranked according to their fitness value and inserted in the population.

Indirectly, the criterion for sending individuals to other islands helps increase the average fitness of the depopulated islands, because islands become deserted when individuals are deleted because of old age. But the age at which an individual is deleted is proportional to its fitness value and, thus, one would expect that islands with high fitness individuals never become deserted while islands where the average fitness is low tend to shrink in population size, and thus become fertile ground for highly fit individuals to migrate.

The age mechanism also helps maintain diversity of the population within each island by eventually removing any individual no matter how well fit. This prevents an elitist strategy from finding an individual representing a good but not even near optimal solution and then driving the whole population towards this solution (a phenomenon well-known in GA literature as *premature convergence*).

Finally, we have introduced variable chromosome length individuals because our solution space consists of integer arrays (collections of stripe heights) of various lengths with the property that the sum of each array's components is fixed (and equal to the number of rows of the grid to be partitioned). One can imagine many other applications where varying chromosome lengths are best for representing the search space. DGA's fitness function is the snake filling procedure since we are interested in the performance of snake decomposition given good quality inputs. However, there is nothing preventing DGA from being applied to other problem domains given suitable fitness functions.

5 Computational Results

In order to evaluate the performance of our method we make comparisons with other well known methods on two classes of problem sets. The first class comprises of a set of rectangular grids to be partitioned among a certain number of processors. The second class is a set of irregular-boundary uniform 5-point grids.

We compare the performance of DGA against that of recursive spectral bisection (RSB) and quadrisection (RSQ) as implemented in the Chaco package [HL95a], a well-known package for graph partitioning developed at Sandia National Laboratories; for all experiments with Chaco, the Kernighan-Lin procedure was used as a post-processing phase. On the class of rectangular grids we also make comparisons with the geometric mesh partitioner [MTTV93, GMT95], another well known mesh partitioner. Finally, we test DGA against R-SNAKE to check whether a Genetic Algorithm outperforms random selection in finding good inputs to the snake procedure, and we also make comparisons with PERIX-GA [CM96a, CM96b], a GA based on a different tiling approach. (Branch-and-bound (CPLEX) and GRASP approaches were also tested, but the results and run times for these methods were unsatisfactory for problem sizes much smaller than even the smallest of the problems considered below. See [CM96b] for GRASP results, which were better than those obtained with branch-and-bound.)

R-SNAKE was written in ANSI C, compiled with the -O2 optimization option and run on a Sun SPARC Server 20 workstation. The same holds true for the Chaco package. The implementation of the geometric mesh partitioner that was available to us was written in MATLAB, which partly explains the very long times of the method for many of the test problems. DGA was also written in ANSI C, and utilizes the PVM 3.3.10 message passing interface for inter process communication [GBD+94]. DGA runs on a cluster of Sun SPARC Server 20 workstations (COW) available at the Computer Sciences Dept. at the University of Wisconsin - Madison.

R-SNAKE was allowed to try 100 random valid stripe arrays and it reports the best partition found. DGA requires more parameters. Each DGA island (process) maintains a maximum of 16 individuals per generation. There are 4 and 8 islands spawned (using the hostless programming paradigm). Whenever an individual arrives at an island, it replaces the worst individual in the population if there is no empty space in the island by the time it arrives. One-point crossover was used, with the rate set at 0.85. The mutation rate was set at 0.15. Since the product of the crossover and mutation operators may result in something that is not a legal individual, a *repair strategy* was used. Each new individual is given as input to a repair routine that modifies as few alleles as possible (sometimes even changing the length of the individual) so that the resulting individual is legal, i.e., represents an exact partition of the rows of the grid. Finally, as the algorithm follows the steady-state approach, approximately 70% of the populations new individuals are born in each generation (not necessarily replacing an equal number of old individuals, because whenever empty space exists, a new individual is inserted without replacing any existing individual). Each individual's lifespan is determined as a random variable that follows the Gaussian distribution $N(5 * fitness(individual), 0.09)$. DGA was allowed to run for 20 generations. Experimentation showed that the above parameters resulted in good overall GA behavior.

PROBLEM			SPECTRAL		GEOMETRIC		PERIX-GA	
M	N	P	Time	Gap%	Time	Gap%	Time	Gap%
32	31	8	1.8	6.52	43.6	5.43	84.0	2.71
32	31	256	4.3	6.73	152.3	-2.73*	80.4	0.00
32	30	64	3.0	6.25	90.4	6.25	50.9	0.00
100	100	8	9.0	9.33	111.0	7.39	81.9	2.64
128	128	128	85.5	14.13	539.9	7.13	67.6	1.65
256	256	256	227.8	13.25	3304.2	4.15	105.1	0.00
512	512	512	-	-	-	-	279.0	1.63

Table 1. Spectral Bisection, Geometric and PERIX-GA on 9 procs

In table 1 we compare recursive spectral bisection and geometric mesh partitioner against PERIX-GA [CM96a], a synchronous GA following the host-node programming paradigm running on a 9-node partition of the COW. PERIX-GA assigns 2 individuals per processing node and a host processor co-ordinates the evolutionary process. The times on all tables are in seconds. The columns labeled "Gap" show the relative distance of the solution from the lower bound. An asterisk in table 1 indicates the fact that the partition found was not balanced (i.e. there were components that had at least two more nodes than other components). Also, note that for the last problem, both the geometric and the spectral method ran out of memory when trying to construct the adjacency matrix of the graph. PERIX-GA outperforms both methods in solution quality, but takes longer to finish on the smaller grids. On the other hand, R-SNAKE and DGA, significantly outperform PERIX-GA in response time, and find the same quality or better partitions (and consequently outperform the spectral and the geometric method as well) as is evident from table 2.

PROBLEM			PERIX-GA		R-SNAKE		DGA (4 islands)		DGA (8 islands)	
M	N	P	Time	Gap%	Time	Gap%	Time	Gap%	Time	Gap%
32	31	8	84.0	2.71	1.3	1.08	6.9	1.08	9.2	1.08
32	31	256	80.4	0.00	0.8	0.00	7.1	0.00	10.1	0.00
32	30	64	50.9	0.00	0.5	0.00	7.8	0.00	9.4	0.00
100	100	8	81.9	2.64	2.4	2.28	17.7	2.28	20.4	2.28
128	128	128	67.6	1.65	3.5	1.90	15.5	1.63	16.5	1.63
256	256	256	105.1	0.00	16.9	0.00	36.9	0.00	38.5	0.00
512	512	512	279.0	1.63	58.7	0.68	123.8	0.56	103.7	0.63

Table 2. PERIX-GA on 9-procs vs. R-SNAKE and DGA on 4 or 8 procs

As can be easily seen from tables 1 and 2, R-SNAKE significantly outperforms recursive spectral bisection and quadrisection as well as the geometric mesh partitioner in solution quality, and in most cases in response time as well on all the rectangular domains we tested. On the more difficult irregular boundary problems, R-SNAKE and DGA have times that are comparable to the ones given by RSB and RSQ, but the solution quality difference here is more dramatic, rising up to 22 percentage units for the diamond domain partitioned among 16 processors. The sole exception to this is the (small) elliptical domain partitioned among 64 processors, where RSB found a marginally better solution than R-SNAKE or DGA. Comparing R-SNAKE with DGA, we observe that DGA finds better (but by no more than 1%) solutions but requires more time. Also, since the times for DGA with 8 islands running on 8 COW nodes (see table 4) are almost the same as those for DGA running with 4 islands on 4 nodes, the communication penalties incurred by our method are minimal compared to other random network factors.

PROBLEM		RSB		RSQ		R-SNAKE		DGA (4 islands)	
Shape	P	Time	Gap%	Time	Gap%	Time	Gap%	Time	Gap%
circle	16	23.3	24.44	9.1	21.80	9.7	8.33	19.8	8.33
circle	64	34.7	16.87	14.5	28.34	11.7	6.35	19.4	6.21
ellipse	16	2.3	10.83	1.4	13.33	5.4	8.33	8.37	8.33
ellipse	64	3.5	5.16	2.2	15.10	4.9	5.56	9.4	5.36
torus	16	27.3	28.97	12.5	32.67	16.8	11.50	18.8	11.50
torus	64	36.5	22.86	18.5	34.3	9.9	11.08	17.2	11.08
diamond	16	14.0	38.67	6.5	35.74	14.6	17.70	10.7	16.40
diamond	64	18.7	29.78	9.0	28.80	13.2	14.60	16.2	13.37

Table 3. Spectral Methods vs. R-SNAKE and DGA on non-rectangular grids

The size of the irregular boundary grids in our test suite varies; the circle has 7800 cells, the torus 7696 cells. The diamond domain is smaller, with 4019 cells, and the elliptical domain is the smallest in our test suite with only 823 cells. A partition of the torus among 64 processors as found by DGA is shown in figure 4. Finally, we run DGA with one island only but leaving all the other parameters intact, disabling all communication (we don't even start PVM) so as to further check the effect of communication on response times of the algorithm. The results (shown under the columns labeled "DGA pop16" of table 5) suggest that indeed the communication overhead of the algorithm is almost negligible. The quality of the resulting partitions is comparable to that of R-SNAKE or the DGA with four (eight) islands, but not as good, and quite logically so, as more processes imply that more individuals are created and tested.

To isolate the effect of the island model on the evolution process, we also run DGA with 1 island but this time allowing a maximum of 64 or 128 individuals on the island (as opposed to the previous experiments where each island could maintain only up to 16 individuals). As expected, the solution times increase,

PROBLEM		DGA (8 islands)	
Shape	P	Time	Gap%
circle	16	20.29	8.47
circle	64	17.5	5.87
ellipsis	16	6.4	8.33
ellipsis	64	7.5	5.56
torus	16	16.7	11.50
torus	64	13.8	11.00
diamond	16	10.4	16.40
diamond	64	14.7	13.37

Table 4. DGA on 8 COW nodes on non-rectangular grids

PROBLEM		DGA pop16		DGA pop64		DGA pop128	
Shape	P	Time	Gap%	Time	Gap%	Time	Gap%
circle	16	12.2	9.02	31.8	8.47	60.1	10.27
circle	64	11.3	8.74	31.9	7.03	56.8	6.83
ellipsis	16	1.2	8.33	4.2	9.58	6.6	9.58
ellipsis	64	2.5	5.36	4.7	6.16	7.8	6.75
torus	16	11.4	11.79	30.2	12.78	67.2	12.78
torus	64	11.5	11.08	30.9	11.60	67.2	12.71
diamond	16	5.4	17.18	19.9	16.70	41.5	18.75
diamond	64	7.4	14.06	20.7	13.55	39.9	14.25

Table 5. DGA with 1 island

but what is interesting is the fact that DGA running with a single population that is roughly 4 or 8 times bigger than the population on each of the islands of the previous experiments fails to find the same quality solutions. Occasionally, it beats DGA with one island and a maximum population size of 16, but it never finds the same quality solutions as DGA with 4 or 8 islands. This effect may be partly due to a premature convergence phenomenon: an initial good solution tends to have many offspring during its lifetime thus drives the rest of the population into a homogeneous state that is only locally optimal. The island model helps avoid this phenomenon by keeping separate populations which preserve the overall diversity, which in turn later enables the algorithm to find better solutions.

6 Concluding Remarks and Future Directions

We have presented snake decomposition, an extension of the stripe decomposition method for partitioning arbitrary uniform 5-point grids among any number of processors so as to minimize the total perimeter of the partition. To find good input heights for the snake decomposition routine, we have designed and implemented DGA, a new distributed GA that breeds multiple populations that inhabit islands of finite capacity. Its main feature that distinguishes it from traditional GAs is the fact that individuals "live" for a certain number of "years" (GA iterations) and throughout their lifetime, they mate with other individuals or migrate to other islands with a probability that is proportional to their fitness value. The overall GA (equipped with a snake decomposition routine as its fitness function) produces solutions that are better (and often significantly better) than the ones found by recursive spectral bisection or quadrisection or the geometric mesh partitioner, and the times are comparable or better than those of the other methods, which are themselves established as excellent methods for graph partitioning.

It is easy to extend snake decomposition to handle *any arbitrary 5-point grid* since any non-uniform 5-point grid can be thought of as a uniform grid of cells that are either unit cells or are themselves grids of finer granularity, in which case snake decomposition can be applied (recursively) to any such grid-cell when it tries to assign a processor index to such a grid-cell. Indeed, one of our immediate goals is to allow snake decomposition to handle any non-uniform, irregular-boundary 5-point grid to be partitioned among any number of processors. Another goal is to extend the theorems that we have developed for the uniform case, to the non-uniform one. So far, we have restricted our attention to equi-partitioning of the domain; however, in a heterogeneous environment workstations might have different processing speeds and therefore partitions with unequal loads between the processors might be desired. Modifying snake decomposition to work efficiently with radically different area sub-domains is another goal, as is the possibility of including a knapsack routine for specifying promising strings when initializing the population of each island. Experiments with a knapsack approach for rectangular domains have been recently performed and the results in [Mar96] are quite impressive. Finally, modeling this new distributed GA with the "aging" mechanism and studying the dynamics of the populations thus generated is our last (but certainly not least) current goal.

7 Acknowledgments

Again, we would like to thank B. Hendrickson and R. Leland for providing us with version 2.0 of the Chaco package. We obtained the MATLAB code for the geometric mesh partitioner from the anonymous ftp site referenced in Gilbert et al. ([GMT95]).

References

[CM96a]   I. T. Christou and R. R. Meyer. Optimal and asymptotically optimal equipartition of rectangular domains via stripe decomposition. In H. Fischer, B. Riedmuller, and S. Schaffler, editors, *Applied Mathematics and Parallel Computing - Festschrift for Klaus Ritter*, pages 77–96. Physica-Verlag, 1996.

[CM96b]   I. T. Christou and R. R. Meyer. Optimal equi-partition of rectangular domains for parallel computation. *Journal of Global Optimization*, 8:15–34, January 1996.

[CQ95]   P. Crandall and M. Quinn. Non-uniform 2-d grid partitioning for het-
            erogeneous parallel architectures. In *Proceedings of the 9th International
            Symposium on Parallel Processing*, pages 428–435, 1995.

[GBD+94]   A. Geist, A. Beguelin, J. Dongarra, W. Jiang, R. Manchek, and V. Sun-
            deram. *PVM 3 User's Guide and Reference Manual.* Oak Ridge National
            Laboratory, 1994.

[GMT95]   J. R. Gilbert, G. L. Miller, and S. H. Teng. Geometric mesh partitioning:
            Implementation and experiments. In *Proceedings of the 9th International
            Symposium on Parallel Processing*, pages 418–427, 1995.

[HL95a]   B. Hendrickson and R. Leland. *The Chaco User's Guide Version 2.0.* San-
            dia National Laboratories, July 1995.

[HL95b]   B. Hendrickson and R. Leland. An improved spectral graph partitioning
            algorithm for mapping parallel computations. *SIAM J. on Sci. Comput.*,
            16:452–469, 1995.

[Hol92]   John Holland. *Adaptation in Natural and Artificial Systems.* MIT Press,
            1992.

[KL70]   B. W. Kernighan and S. Lin. An effective heuristic procedure for partition-
            ing graphs. *Bell Systems Tech. Journal*, pages 291–308, February 1970.

[LFE94]   M. Laguna, T. A. Feo, and H. C. Elrod. A greedy randomized adaptive
            search procedure for the two - partition problem. *Operations Research*,
            July - August 1994.

[Mar96]   W. Martin. Fast equi-partitioning of rectangular domains using stripe de-
            composition. Technical Report MP-TR-96-2, University of Wisconsin -
            Madison, February 1996.

[Mel94]   M. Bousquet Melou. Codage des polyominos convexes et equation pour
            l'enumeration suivant l'aire. *Discrete Applied Mathematics*, 48:21–43, 1994.

[Mic94]   Zbigniew Michalewicz. *Genetic Algorithms + Data Structures = Evolution
            Programs.* Springer-Verlag, 1994.

[MTTV93]   G. L. Miller, S. H. Teng, W. Thurston, and S. A. Vavasis. Automatic mesh
            partitioning. In A. George, J. R. Gilbert, and J. W. H. Liu, editors, *Graph
            Theory and Sparse Matrix Computation.* Springer-Verlag, 1993.

[PRW93]   P. M. Pardalos, F. Rendl, and H. Wolkowicz. The quadratic assignment
            problem: A survey and recent developments. In P. M. Pardalos and
            H. Wolkowicz, editors, *Quadratic Assignment and Related Problems.* Amer-
            ican Mathematical Society, 1993.

[PSL90]   A. Pothen, H. D. Simon, and K. P. Liu. Partitioning sparse matrices with
            eigenvectors of graphs. *SIAM Journal on Matrix Analysis and Applications*,
            11:430–452, 1990.

[vL91]   G. von Laszewski. Intelligent structural operators for the k-way graph
            partitioning problem. In R. Belew and L. Booker, editors, *Proceedings of
            the Fourth Intl. Conference on Genetic Algorithms*, pages 45–52. Morgan
            Kaufmann Publishers, Los Altos, CA, 1991.

[Yac93]   J. Yackel. *Minimum Perimeter Tiling in Parallel Computation.* PhD thesis,
            University of Wisconsin - Madison, August 1993.

[YM92]   J. Yackel and R. R. Meyer. Optimal tilings for parallel database design. In
            P. M. Pardalos, editor, *Advances in Optimization and Parallel Computing*,
            pages 293–309. North - Holland, 1992.

Toward Efficient Unstructured Multigrid Preprocessing (Extended Abstract)

Susan E. Dorward[1,2], Lesley R. Matheson[1], Robert E. Tarjan[1,2]

[1] NEC Research Institute
4 Independence Way
Princeton, NJ, 08540
[2] Department of Computer Science
Princeton University
Princeton, NJ 08544 **

Abstract

The *multigrid method* is a general and powerful means of accelerating the convergence of discrete iterative methods for solving partial differential equations (PDEs) and similar problems. The adaptation of the multigrid method to unstructured meshes is important in the solution of problems with complex geometries. Unfortunately, multigrid schemes on unstructured meshes require significantly more preprocessing than on structured meshes. In fact, preprocessing can be a major part of the solution task, and for many applications, must be done repeatedly. In addition, the large computational requirements of realistic PDEs, accurately discretized on unstructured meshes, make such computations candidates for parallel or distributed processing, adding problem partitioning as a preprocessing task.

We report on a project to apply ideas from graph theory and geometry to the solution of the preprocessing tasks required for the parallel implementation of unstructured multigrid methods. Our objective is to provide conceptually simple, efficient, and unified methods. In a previous conference paper, we proposed two bottom-up, graph-based methods and one top-down method. In this paper, we report on several sets of experiments designed to explore the practical aspects of one of the methods, based on independent dominating sets. The experiments studied the empirical properties of the mesh hierarchies generated by the method and the numerical performance of the multigrid method solving Laplace's equation using these mesh hierachies. The experiments also studied the domain partitions generated by the method. Our conclusion based on these preliminary experiments is that our simple, automatic methods provide excellent multigrid performance at low preprocessing cost.

1 Introduction

Standard iterative methods for solving partial differential equations can suffer from slow convergence, caused by the need to propagate information all the way across a finely discretized mesh. The *Multigrid Method* [5, 27] provides a way to overcome this difficulty. (Alternative techniques include *Spectral* and

---

** Research at Princeton University partially supported by the National Science Foundation, Grant No. CCR-8920505, and the Office of Naval Research, Contract No. N0014-91-J-1463.

Conjugate Gradient methods [2, 7].) The PDE is discretized not once, but several times, with different amounts of coarseness, and a *mesh hierarchy*, consisting of the original fine mesh and successively coarser meshes, is constructed. In addition to standard iterative steps on each individual level of the hierarachy, information about partial solutions is periodically transferred from a finer level to the next coarser level (*restriction*) and from a coarser level to the next finer level (*prolongation*). The exact arrangement of such steps is a parameter of the method, leading to such versions of multigrid as the V-cycle, the F-cycle, and the W-cycle [1]. There has been an enormous amount of work on multigrid methods in recent years; see the excellent tutorial of Briggs [1] and the proceedings of the biennial Copper Mountain Multigrid Conference, e.g.[19, 11, 12, 20].

Whereas the implementation and behavior of multigrid methods on structured (gridlike) meshes is reasonably well understood, the same is not true for unstructured meshes, such as triangulations of arbitrary planar regions. Such meshes are important in solving large practical problems with complicated geometries, such as accurately computing the airflows around an aircraft. For such problems the preprocessing required to construct the mesh hierarchy can be a major part of the computational task. In such applications the preprocessing tasks must be re-executed frequently. Furthermore, solving such problems is computationally expensive, making them good candidates for parallel or distributed implementation. Such implementation imposes another preprocessing task, that of partitioning the problem to achieve balanced computation and low communication costs.

Our goal in this work is to explore the use of simple graph-theoretic and computational-geometric ideas in performing the preprocessing tasks of unstructured multigrid methods. We assume that one is given the finest mesh, and the task is to construct the mesh hierarchy, the inter-mesh transfer operators, and, if necessary for parallel implementation, the problem partition. These tasks are discussed in somewhat more detail in section 2. We sought efficient, flexible, and unified methods for carrying out these tasks. In a previous conference paper [3] (see also [13]) we proposed two bottom-up, graph-based methods, the *dominating set method* and the *independent set method*, and one top-down, geometry-based method, the *bifurcation method*. These methods are described in section 3. This paper reports on experimental work to determine the properties of the mesh hierarchies produced by the first of these methods, to test whether the resulting meshes lead to fast multigrid convergence, and the quality of the domain partitions. These experiments are described in section 4. Section 5 contains our conclusions.

As noted above, there has been relatively little work on unstructured multigrid preprocessing. We comment on two approaches different from ours that have been considered. The first is to generate completely unrelated and independent meshes for each level of the hierarchy [15, 16]. This method is flexible but expensive: each mesh must be generated by hand and other preprocessing tasks require the relationships between the meshes to be computed and stored. The second method is the *agglomeration method* [9, 25, 26], which considers the dual of the graph of the fine mesh and obtains coarser meshes by combining regions. This method has many similarities with our graph-based methods. Notes by Mavriplis [18] give a nice survey of these methods, and of unstructured multigrid in general.

We describe our ideas for the two-dimensional case, and all our experiments deal with this case. But our ideas generalize to three dimensions.

2 Multigrid Preprocessing Steps

We assume that we are given a fine mesh consisting of a triangulation of a planar region. For simplicity and because it is usually the method of choice we shall assume the triangulation is a constrained Delaunay triangulation, though more general triangulations are possible. The multigrid preprocessing tasks are the following.

1. **Point Set Generation**
   Generate a hierarchy of coarser and coarser point sets covering the same region (or approximately the same region) as the original point set. Each successive level of points should have a constant factor smaller size than the previous (finer) level. Our goal is a coarsening ratio in the vicinity of four (two per dimension), since this coarsening ratio is regarded as best in the structured case. Special care must be taken to preserve region boundaries.

2. **Triangulation**
   Each level of the point set hierarchy must be triangulated, giving a hierarchy of triangulations of the original region (subject to boundary approximations). This can be done using a constrained Delaunay triangulation algorithm for each level, which is what we used in our experiments. The triangulation process can possibly be sped up using coherence among the point sets, a topic we ignore here.

3. **Construction of Intra-grid and Inter-grid Transfer Operators**
   An iterative equation-solving scheme must be set up that defines how information about an approximate solution is propagated between points (a point-based scheme) or triangles (a cell-based scheme) in the same level of the hierarchy and between adjacent levels of the hierarchy. In this paper, we only consider point-based schemes. Within a grid, each point has a *stencil* that includes all adjacent points and possibly other nearby points, depending upon details of the numerical method. Finding such a stencil for each point is routine. But large stencils imply expensive computation; thus there is some benefit in keeping the degree of all vertices small. (Of course in a planar triangulation, the average vertex degree is less than six). Computing the inter-grid transfer operators requires knowing, for each point, where it lies in the next finer and next coarser meshes. See [18] for details concerning the construction of the numeric operators. Computing point locations for all points in both adjacent meshes can be done in linear time using a systematic search of each mesh; simpler methods may suffice depending on the point set generation method.

4. Partitioning

For parallel or distributed implementation, the computation must be subdivided into pieces to fit on each processor. We consider direct iterative schemes,in which the next value at a point depends only on the previous values at its neighbors. Our task is to subdivide the meshes into point sets of roughly equal size (to achieve load balancing) and with small boundaries (to minimize communication costs). Since there is some evidence that intra-grid communication costs dominate inter-grid communication costs [18, 13], we concentrate on partitioning individual levels of the hierarchy; but our partitioning schemes give coherent partitions that tend to reduce inter-grid as well as intra-grid communication. This issue deserves more study.

Since tasks 2 and 3 are relatively routine we focus here on tasks 1 and 4. All three of our schemes generate coarser point sets by discarding points from the original point set while trying to maintain uniform coverage. The fact that each point set is a strict subset of the next finer one can simplify preprocessing tasks 2 and 3, but we do not explore this issue further here.

3   Point Selection and Partitioning Schemes

3.1   Bottom-Up Schemes

Our first schemes are bottom-up methods that use local information based on graph-theoretic concepts, specifically those of dominating sets and independent sets. A *Dominating Set D* in a graph is a set of vertices such that every vertex is either in D or adjacent to a vertex in D. Such a set is *minimal* if no proper subset is a dominating set. An *Independent Set* is a set of vertices no two of which are adjacent. It is *maximal* if no proper subset is independent.

The Dominating Set Scheme Our first scheme for coarsening is simple: choose an independent dominating set as the next point set. Such a set is automatically minimal. Our discussion and our experiments focus on dominating sets chosen by the sequential greedy algorithm, defined as follows. Choose one point at a time to be in the dominating set. Upon picking a point, delete it and all of its neighbors. Stop when all points are deleted. Related parallel schemes also exist [10]. The sequential greedy algorithm provides a simple framework into which rules for point selection can be inserted in order to meet multigrid-related criteria. We mention three such rules:

Randomized Greedy: *Select the next dominating set point at random among the available points. The probability distribution can be uniform or can be weighted to favor certain regions such as the region boundary.*

Maximum Degree: *Always select the next available point of highest degree. In applying this method, we can use either the original degree or the current degree (decreased by deletions).*

The third rule is related to our basic partitioning method and requires some additional introduction. Once a dominating set is chosen, we triangulate it, by finding a constrained Delaunay triangulation; this generates the next coarser mesh. We iterate this process of choosing a dominating set and retriangulating until we have the desired number of levels of the hierarchy. As we construct this hierarchy, we grow a forest, *the partition forest*, whose leaves are the initial points and whose nodes at height i are the points in the ith dominating set. The children of a node corresponding to dominating point p are the corresponding node in the next finer level, and all nodes corresponding to points adjacent to p that were deleted when p was chosen. Each level of this forest gives a partition of all the finer levels defined by the descendant relation.

Subtree Balance: *Choose a dominating point based on its number of descendant leaves in the partition forest, attempting to balance all the subtrees. We leave this rule deliberatively vague, since there are many ways to try to obtain balance.*

We comment here on some theoretical properties of dominating sets. The results of experiments with various versions of these rules are discussed in section 4. Any triangulated disc (a planar graph all of whose faces but one are triangles) has a dominating set of at most 1/3 of the vertices; this bound is tight [14]. We conjecture that any large enough triangulated planar graph has a dominating set of at most 1/4 of the vertices; no upper bound less than 1/3 is known. The triangulated disc result yields a linear-time algorithm for finding a suitable dominating set. But in practice this algorithm seems overly complicated. Furthermore, our experiments yield good results for the (simpler) greedy algorithm.

We can also prove that if the original triangulation has some appropriate geometric uniformity condition, then so does the triangulation of an independent dominating set. The numerical quality of the uniformity degrades, however, as one might expect. See [13].

The Independent Set Scheme In contrast to the dominating set scheme, which explicitly chooses points to save, the independent set scheme explicitly chooses points to discard. Specifically, we find a maximal independent set, discard it, and retriangulate the remaining points. Since any planar graph is four-colorable, such a planar graph contains a maximal independent set of at least 1/4 of the points, leaving at most 3/4 of the points. To achieve the desired coarsening we must apply the independent set coarsening step several times, approximately 4 or 5. We considered various heuristics for generating independent sets; see [3, 13] for further details.

3.2 A Top-Down Method

A completely different approach to generating the point set hierarchy is a top-down approach we call the *bifurcation strategy*. We divide the points in half by slicing along a vertical or horizontal line, and repeat in each half, continuing until each point is in its own region. This defines a tree analogous to a $k - d$ tree. At each level, each cell contains approximately the same number of points. We choose within each cell one *representative point*; the representative points at each level define the point set hierarchy. See [3, 13] for further details.

In the next section we present a selection of experimental results. While experiments have been performed on all three methods, in this paper we focus exclusively on the dominating set strategy. This choice is motivated by a lack of space, by the more mature state of the dominating set experimental data, and by our belief that this method will perform quite well in practice. But all three strategies merit further investigation.

4 Experiments

Experimental evidence confirms that dominating sets can potentially provide a basis for automatically generating coarse meshes from a given fine mesh. Once chosen, the dominating set (DS) can also facilitate the construction of inter-mesh transfer operators and the partition of the mesh hierarchy for parallel implementation. Generally we found that a purely topological method such as the DS method can generate a very good hierarchy of meshes simply, quickly and automatically. Boundary conditions introduce complication but not more so than for alternative methods. Experiments suggest that the method can also provide a partition of every mesh that is within a small constant factor of optimum. The main drawback is some lack of fine control over the size and shape of the regions of the domain partition.

4.1 Dominating Set Size

As mentioned above, a complicated dominating set algorithm can guarantee a set size of 1/3 [14] for any planar triangulated disc. But our experiments suggest that simple greedy approaches guided by the appropriate heuristic can yield coarse mesh point sets that are close to optimal. The simplest algorithm, for example, the randomized greedy algorithm produces set sizes of approximately 1/4 on simple random meshes. The coarsening ratio (the ratio of fine mesh points to coarse mesh points) is consistently greater than 4 throughout the mesh hierarchy. Table 1 shows the coarsening ratios for the hierarchy generated from a 10,000-point random mesh using the randomized rule.

Meshes for practical applications, however, can differ substantially from those generated from random point sets. We tested the dominating set heuristics on meshes generated by a software tool used for finite element problems [17]. Our objective was to replicate some practical mesh qualities while considering only simple boundary problems. Complex boundaries are an important issue that deserves further study. In the results presented here the fine mesh input is accompanied by a small set of permanant boundary points. We consider meshes

Table 1. Coarsening Ratios

Coarsening Ratios						
Heuristic & Graph	**1st**	**2nd**	**3rd**	**4th**	**5th**	**6th**
Randomized & 10,000 random	4.1	4.2	4.2	4.1	4.0	4.3
Maximum Degree & 10,000 Random	5.2	5.2	5.2	5.2	4.9	5.0
Subtree Balance & 10,000 Random	3.7	3.6	3.8	3.8	3.8	3.5
39857 Square	3.7	3.7	3.7	3.6	3.1	
42735 Rectangle	3.7	3.7	3.8	3.6	3.2	
6587 Hydrofoil	3.6	3.7	3.7	3.3		

Table 2. Convergence Rates

Graph	Size	Convergence Rate
Square	9984	.1630
Square	39857	.1618
Rectangle	1757	.1720
Rectangle	42735	.1631

Comparison to hand–optimized meshes:

Square 1589

Hand Optimized	Dominating Set
.1660	.1633

Straight iteration: .9932

with 1 to 4 continuous boundaries generated for finite element computation. Figure 1 shows a small example.

Table 1 shows ratios of dominating set size to original set size produced by the subtree balance heuristic on four sample meshes. This heuristic produces dominating sets that are slightly larger than 1/4 the size of the original set. Because the goal of this heuristic is to produce a load-balanced partition, the set size increases as compared to alternative heuristics. Preliminary experiments suggest that this slight increase does not have any substantial impact on performance. (See section 4.3).

4.2 Properties of the Coarse Meshes

The coarse mesh point sets must not only be the right size but they must be well-distributed and yield *good* meshes when triangulated. The relationship between mesh quality and convergence rates of iterative methods, in general, is complicated and involves properties specific to the particular numerical method. This relationship is not well understood. Experimentation most often provides guidance for practical applications.

Our experiments suggest that the greedy dominating set heuristics all produce reasonably well-shaped coarse meshes. Inspection of the meshes suggests that the coarse meshes faithfully reflect the distribution of the fine mesh and the resulting Delaunay triangulations are well-behaved. Figure 1 is an example mesh hierarchy from an approximately 1757 point rectangle within a square domain. Histograms showing coarse mesh angle sizes reveal that only a small proportion of angles are unusually large or small, with the proportion growing as the mesh becomes coarser. Figure 2 shows a histogram of five coarse meshes produced from a 49,924-point fine mesh. In the figure, each angle unit is ten degrees. Our performance experiments suggest that this degradation does not affect performance.

Fig. 1. Fine Mesh and Coarse Meshes Produced by a Dominating Set Scheme

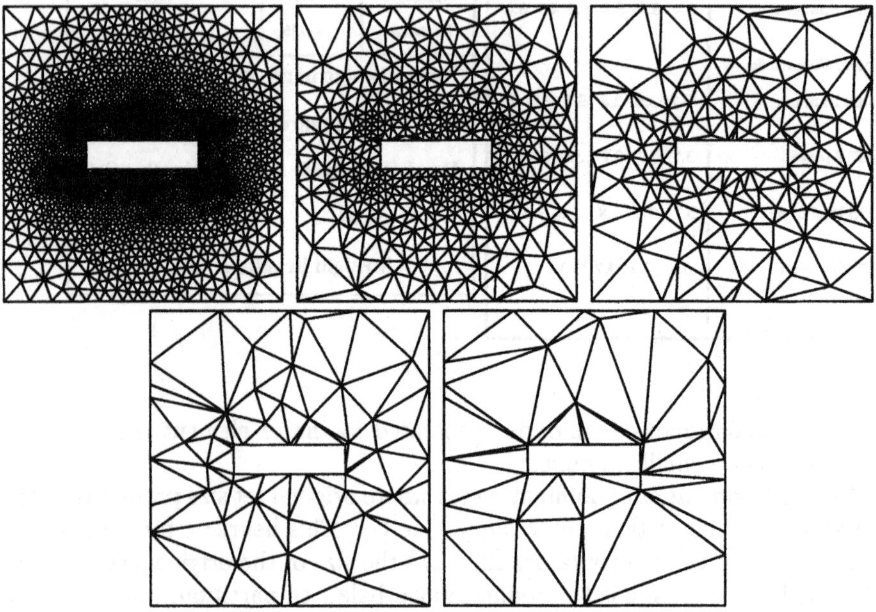

4.3 Performance

The overriding objective of multigrid preprocessing is to produce efficient numerical behavior. Thus evaluation of the discrete preprocessing algorithms requires feedback from numerical schemes.

Experimentation involves a host of complicated issues, however. One is the tremendous range of potential testbeds (elliptic, hyperbolic and parabolic PDEs, explicit, implicit, hybrid iterative schemes, hundreds of applications, and many different multigrid methods). To combat the profusion we first chose a model equation (Laplace's) which is elliptic (not time dependent). We solved the equation on simple domains with a few practical characteristics. Dimitri Mavriplis [17] provided the solution code, a close relative of the suite of so-called FLO codes, developed by Luigi Martinelli, Antony Jameson and others at Princeton University. These codes are well established for high accuracy fluid dynamics applications. The choice to use these codes in part reflects the importance we

Fig. 2. Histogram of Angles Sizes

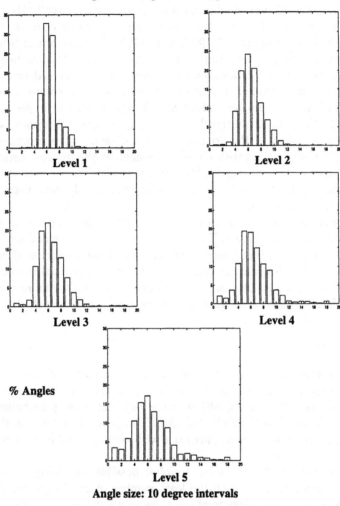

Level 1

Level 2

Level 3

Level 4

% Angles

Level 5

Angle size: 10 degree intervals

attribute to better understanding the complications of employing computational ideas in practical well-entrenched software environments.

The code solves the Laplace equations using a weighted-Jacobi iterative scheme, linear interpolation and restriction operators, and V-cycle and W-cycle multigrid algorithms. It uses residual averaging, a coarse grid correction scheme and performs a constant number of sweeps at each level. It does not solve the coarsest level directly. In the experiments termination accuracy was set at 10^{-10}.

On our fine meshes with 1500 to 50,000 points, mesh hierarchies generated automatically by a dominating set scheme produce convergence rates (the percentage of error returned after a complete cycle) as low as those produced on hand generated meshes with no loss of accuracy. For example, solution on a square within a square, with 1589 points on the fine mesh, and 4 coarse meshes produced work-normalized convergence rates [3] of approximately .1633. Hand-generated meshes yield very similar rates of approximately .1660. The solution required approximately 14 cycles. (It is interesting to note that convergence rates with one mesh were approximately .9932 after 1000 iterations, and still not close to termination accuracy). This result is indicative of the results obtained in similar comparisons that varied the geometry, point distribution and problem size of the initial fine grid. Table 2 provides a sample of W-cycle convergence rates.

A multigrid method can be evaluated by how consistently it decreases the error per cycle. Structured multigrid methods require $O(logN)$ cycles, where N is the number of points in the domain of the problem, to reach discretization accuracy. This implies a logarithmic improvement in the approximation, or a constant number of bits, per cycle. We can use this metric to evaluate an unstructured multigrid scheme. Our experiments consistently demonstrated this steady logarithmic error reduction.

Our experiments suggest that to achieve rapid convergence, the coarsest mesh must have sufficiently few points. This is a consequence of the standard iterative solution method used on the coarsest grid, and may hinder solution of problems with complex geometries, which require many points to represent the boundary. For such problems, it may be wise to use a more accurate (but more expensive) solution method on the coarsest grid. This issue deserves further study.

4.4   Partitions

Our experiments suggest that a partition forest constructed with the dominating set scheme produces *both* good meshes and good domain partitions. While many strategies (including [21, 22, 23, 24]) generate very high quality partitions, most require a significant amount of computation. The partition forest, on the other hand, generates reasonably good partitions with very little additional computation.

We obtained the partitions in the simplest possible way using the partition forest, by choosing the level with the least number of points greater than the number of processors and then combining the smallest regions. Many smarter, tree-based hueristics are possible. We chose the simplest method to better understand what level of quality could be obtained without any additional work. The good quality of these partitions strongly motivates further study of such heuristics.

Consistently, the partitions obtained by the dominating set strategy were load-balanced to within 20% − 30%. Table 3 presents a sample of ratios of the maximum to the ideal region sizes, measured in terms of the numbers of points. The ratios are representative of those obtained over the entire testspace of fine meshes. The ratios in the table are averaged over partition sizes in the range of 64 − 256, for a particular mesh.

The subdomains tend to be moderately well-shaped, minimizing communication by keeping the border sizes small relative to the size of the the the subdomain.

---

[3] convergence rates normalized for comparison to one-level iterative schemes

Table 3. Ideal Partition Ratios

Dominating Set : Ideal		
Graph & Size	Max Load / Ideal	Max Cut/ Ideal
Square		
9984	1.32	2.53
39857	1.29	2.81
Rectangle		
42267	1.28	2.73
49924	1.21	2.71
Airfoil		
16267	1.29	2.66
33108	1.30	2.86
Off optimal:	20%–30%	factor of 2–3

Table 4. Metis Partition Ratios

Dominating Set : Metis			
Graph & Size (# regions)	Max Cut	Total Cuts	Load
Square 39857			
(16)	2.6	1.9	1.4
(64)	1.6	1.6	1.2
Square 9984			
(16)	2.1	1.4	1.6
(64)	2.0	1.4	1.4
Rectangle 42735			
(16)	1.5	1.5	1.7
(64)	.9	1.6	1.2
Rectangle 49924			
(16)	.5	.5	1.3
(64)	.6	.95	1.6
Airfoil 16267			
(64)	1.6	2.3	1.5
	.5–2.6		1.2–1.7

Analysis suggests that the communication requirements of the partitions are within a factor of 2 to 3 of conservative estimates of optimal (for a more detailed description of the optimal lower bound see [4]). Table 3 presents a sample of representative ratios.

One drawback to the method is that it offers little control over the shape of the subdomains. Figure 3 shows a partition that is indicative of most of the experimental results. The fine mesh, pictured in figure 4, is denser around the boundaries of the internal rectangle.

We compared the partitions generated by our simple scheme with those generated by a state-of-the-art multi-level partitioning code [8]. On most examples,

Fig. 3. A Sample Mesh

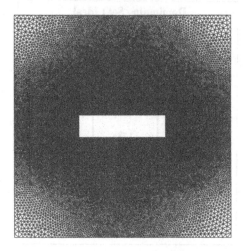

Fig. 4. A Dominating Set Partition

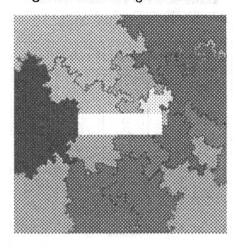

our partitions compare well with those produced by the code. Table 4 gives a representative sample of the ratios of the dominating set-based method to the best multi-level algorithm for load balance, total edge cuts and maximum edge cuts. Generally, the dominating set method was within a factor 20% − 70% of the load balance produced by the multi-level algorithm. (This is slightly higher than the ratios to the ideal because the multi-level algorithm experiments were restricted to partition sizes that were a power of two.) While the multi-level partitions were highly load-balanced (usually to within 1%), moderate variability in the quality of the edge cuts was observed. The ratios of the edge cuts (total and maximum) of the dominating-set-based partitions to those of the multi-level partitions ranged from .5 − 2.6. The multi-level algorithm requires a significant amount of computation, employing optimization steps such as Kernighan-Lin local improvement techniques. The addition of similar refinement techniques could be expected to noticably reduce communications costs (boundary size) of the dominating-set-based partitions.

5 Conclusions

We have reported on an ongoing project to apply ideas from graph theory and geometry to a practical parallel application. We looked specifically at the pre-processing tasks required for unstructured multigrid methods. The size and complexity of the applications demand fast, simple algorithms and efficient parallel implementations. Such algorithms and the intended applications motivate experimental and theoretical evaluation.

We summarized experimental results for a bottom-up strategy. The *Dominating Set Strategy* creates a hierarchy of dominating sets from a fine mesh and uses this data structure to help solve the preprocessing tasks automatically and efficiently. The strategy generates suitable mesh hierarchies and good domain partitions. The relationship between the meshes can also be used to expedite the construction of intergrid transfer operators.

Perhaps the most important conclusion to be drawn from our theoretical and experimental results is that discrete algorithm ideas can have an impact on important numerical applications. All of the strategies mentioned here merit further investigation. Our experiments also suggest the importance of balancing computational effort against results achieved. Specifically, simple, fast partitioning schemes may well generate results good enough to avoid the need for more accurate but more expensive methods.

References

1. Briggs, W., " *A Multigrid Tutorial,*" SIAM, 1987.
2. Boyd, J., *"Chebyshev and Fourier Methods,"* Springer-Verlag, New York, 1989.
3. Dorward, S., Matheson, L., and Tarjan, R., "Unstructured Multigrid Strategies on Massively Parallel Computers: A Case for Integrated Design," *Proceedings of the 27th Annual Hawaii International Conference on Systems Sciences,* pp. 169-178, 1994.
4. Dorward, S., Matheson, L., and Tarjan, R., "Toward Efficient Unstructured Multigrid Preprocessing," Technical Report, NEC Research Institute, 1996.
5. Fedorenko, R., " Relaksacionnyi Metod Resenija Raznostynch Ellipticeskich Uravenija," *CISL Matem i Matem Fiz,* vol. 1, pp. 922-27, 1961.
6. Fletcher, C., " *Computational Galerkin Methods,*" Springer-Verlag, 1984.
7. Golub, G., and Van Loan, C., *"Matrix Computations,"* Johns Hopkins University Press, 1989.
8. Karypis, G., and Kumar, V., "A Fast and High Quality Multilevel Scheme for Partitioning Irregular Graphs," Technical Report no. 95-035, Department of Computer Science, University of Minnesota, 1995.

9. Lallemand, M., Steve, H., and Dervieux, A., "Unstructured Multigridding by Volume Agglomeration: Current Status," *Computers and Fluids*, vol. 21, no. 1, pp.1-21, 1992.

10. Luby, M., "A Simple Parallel Algorithm for the Maximal Independent Set Problem," *SIAM Journal on Computing*, vol. 15, pp. 1036-1053, 1986.

11. Mandel, J., McCormick, S., Dendy, J., Farhat, C., Lonsdale, G., Parter, S., Ruge, J., Stuben, K., eds., *"Proceedings of the Fourth Copper Mountain Conference on Multigrid Methods*, SIAM, Philadelphia, 1989.

12. Manteuffel, T., McCormick, S., Program Chairmen, *"Proceedings of the Fifth Copper Mountain Conference on Multigrid Methods"*, SIAM, 1991.

13. Matheson, L., "Multigrid Algorithms on Massively Parallel Computers, " *PhD. Dissertation, Department of Computer Science, Princeton University*, 1994.

14. Matheson, L. and Tarjan, R., "Dominating Sets in Planar Graphs, " *European Journal of Combinatorics*, to appear.

15. Mavriplis, D., and Jameson, A., "Multigrid Solution of the Two-Dimensional Euler Equations on Unstructured Triangular Meshes", *AIAA Journal*, vol. 26, no.7, pp. 824-831, 1988.

16. Maviriplis, D., " Three Dimensional Multigrid for the Euler Equations", *Proc. of the AIAA 10th Comp. Fluid Dynamics Conference*, Honolulu, Hawaii, pp. 239-248, 1991.

17. Mavriplis, Dimitri, NASA ICASE, *Private Communication*, 1995.

18. Mavriplis, D., "Lecture Notes ", *26th Computational Fluid Dynamics Lecture Series Program of the von Karman Institute (VKI) for Fluid Dynamics*, Rhodes-Saint-Genese, Belgium, 1995.

19. McCormick, S., ed., " *Multigrid Methods,"* (Proceedings of the Third Copper Mountain Conference on Multigrid Methods), Marcel Dekker, 1988.

20. Melson, N., Manteuffal, T., McCormick, S., eds., *"Proceedings of the Sixth Copper Mountain Conference on Multigrid Methods"*, NASA (CP-3224), 1993.

21. Miller, G., Teng, S., Thurston, W., and Vavasis, S., "Automatic Mesh Partitioning", *Sparse Matrix Computations: Graph Theory Issues and Algorithms*, The Insitute of Mathematics and Its Applications, 1992.

22. Miller, G., and Vavasis, S., "Density Graphs and Separators", *Proceedings of the Second ACM- SIAM Symposium on Discrete Algorithms*, pp.331-336, 1991.

23. Pothen, A., Simon, H., and Liou, K., "Partitioning Sparse Matrices with Eigenvectors of Graphs", *SIAM Journal of Matrix Analysis and Applications*, vol. 11, no. 3, pp. 430-452, 1990.

24. Simon, H., "Partitioning Unstructured Problems for Parallel Processing," *Computing Systems in Engineering*, vol. 2, pp. 135-148, 1991.

25. Smith, W., "Multigrid Solution of Transonic Flow on Unstructured Grids," *Recent Advances and Applications in Computational Fluid Dynamics*, 1990.

26. Venkatakrishnan, V., and Mavirpilis, D., "Agglomeration Multigrid for the Three Dimensional Euler Equations," *AIAA Journal*, to appear.

27. Wesseling, P., *An Introduction to Multigrid Methods*, John Wiley and Sons, 1991.

Domain Decomposition for Particle Methods on the Sphere

Ömer Eğecioğlu and Ashok Srinivasan

Department of Computer Science, University of California,
Santa Barbara, CA 93106

Abstract. We present an algorithm for efficient parallelization of particle methods when the domain is the surface of a sphere. Such applications typically arise when dealing with directional data. We propose a domain decomposition scheme based on geometric partitioning that provides domains suitable for practical implementation. This algorithm has the advantage of being fast enough to be applied dynamically, and at the same time provides good partitions, comparable in quality to those produced by spectral graph partitioning schemes.

1 Introduction

Particle methods are widely used in several applications [1, 5, 4, 3]. These typically involve a set of particles represented as points in some space, and a function that describes the interaction between pairs of particles. For each particle, one independently sums the interaction between it and all other particles, and a new state for each particle is then computed. This new state typically is a new position and velocity, and the calculations are repeated several times to observe the evolution of the system. This leads to an irregular computational problem in which the set of particles which interacts with any given particle changes with time in an unpredictable manner. Furthermore, in applications involving directional data such as certain complex fluid flow problems, the natural domain of representation is the unit sphere [17, 14].

In a parallel implementation, particles are assigned to processors by first breaking the domain into subdomains, and then mapping these subdomains to different processors. Each processor proceeds to compute the interactions of all the particles in the system with the particles in its subdomain. The interactions with particles that lie outside its subdomain require a processor to obtain the states of those particles from other processors. We call the particles in the subdomain of a processor the points *owned* by the processor. The points owned by a given processor that are needed by other processors are *shared* points. In many applications such as molecular dynamics and Smoothed Particle Hydrodynamics based methods, the interacting forces between the particles are short range and the effect of particles that are farther away than a certain cut-off distance can be ignored [4, 3]. In order to further mitigate high communication costs, one usually tries to overlap computation with communication. Hence, processors first send their shared data to the processors that need them, and following this perform their local computations. Subsequently, they receive the shared data they themselves need and perform their remaining computations, and update the states of the points in their subdomain. Some updating of the domains can also be done at this stage. Usually a full domain decomposition is not performed at the end of each iteration since the cost of the decomposition can be prohibitive. The basic scheme of such calculations is outlined in Figure 1.

---

1. Domain Decomposition.
2. Map domains to processors.
3. Start loop
   (a) Determine shared points.
   (b) Send shared points to processors that need them.
   (c) Compute using interior data.
   (d) Receive shared data needed from other processors.
   (e) Compute using received data and update state.
   (f) Update domain data.
   End loop

Fig. 1. Outline of a general parallel particle method calculation.

Efficient parallelization requires the selection of subdomains for each processor in such a way that only few particles outside interact with particles within the subdomain. It is also necessary to efficiently determine the set of shared particles at each processor. An important aspect of the computations is to be able to perform effective dynamic range searching so that interactions with only those particles that are within the cut-off distance of the short range interactions are computed.

The outline of this paper is as follows. Sect. 2 describes graph-theoretical and geometric domain decomposition strategies as they apply to particle methods on the sphere. The algorithm we present in Sect. 3 is essentially a geometric partitioning based on Orthogonal Recursive Bisection [2]. However, we take advantage of the geometry of the sphere to produce partitions with quality comparable to sophisticated methods such as spectral partitioning. Experimental results and comparisons with other popular schemes available in Chaco, version 2.0 [9] and Metis, version 2.0.3 [11] are presented in Sect. 4. These experiments show that our algorithm is an order of magnitude faster than even the relatively fast inertial method for large problem sizes, and demonstrate the high quality of the partitions obtained. Conclusions are given in Sect. 5.

2 Domain Decomposition

Domain decomposition has been widely studied [9, 10, 11, 12, 13] and several types of methods for its solution have been proposed: graph-theoretical and geometric, for example. Graph-theoretical schemes ignore coordinate information and treat domain decomposition as a general graph partitioning problem. Geometric algorithms, in contrast, use coordinate information of the points to divide the domain into contiguous regions.

The quality of the partitions produced can be judged by the load imbalance introduced and the communication cost incurred. We try to keep the load balanced, i.e., ensure that the amount of computation performed by each processor is about equal. Subject to this restriction, we further wish to keep the communication cost low. There are several measures for estimating the communication cost. Before describing the criterion used in our algorithm, we shall briefly describe the communication pattern implied by Figure 1. In order to overlap computation and communication, each processor determines the shared data it needs to send to other processors. It is appropriate to send the required data to each processor as a single message. This reduces the startup time and is especially advantageous in systems that support long messages. If n_i is the number of processors that need the data of point i, excluding the processor to which i has been assigned, then we define the communication cost as $\sum n_i$. This measure ignores the startup time and can be justified if the messages are sufficiently long. It differs from the *hop* metric in that the number of links traversed are ignored, providing an architecture independent measure. With cut-through routing being widely prevalent, this criteria seems justified. However, it should be noted that too many messages in the system could cause network congestion and the number of links traversed could affect the true communication cost [9]. Our communication measure also differs from the commonly used edge-cut metric in graph partitioning which tries to minimize the number of edges cut. If more than one point in a particular processor needs data related to one point from another processor, the remote processor need send the data only once. The processor that receives the data can store this and reuse it when needed. In contrast to the edge-cut metric, our communication cost takes this factor into account as well.

Graph-theoretical algorithms such as spectral methods produce high quality partitions especially when combined with a local refinement strategy [13], but require too much time. When combined with multilevel methods, these give good partitions much faster [10], however, they are still not fast enough to be used frequently. Since the distribution of the points could change significantly in the types of applications we are considering, the quality of the partitions may degrade quickly.

Geometric algorithms make use of the coordinates of the points to find partitions fast. In this case the quality of the partitions obtained is usually not very good. Orthogonal Recursive Bisection (ORB) for example, bisects the domain along a coordinate. This is recursively applied using different coordinates. This scheme is fast, though the quality, as judged by the communication cost incurred, could be poor. Another method that uses coordinate information is the Inertial Method. This method produces partitions which are usually of a higher quality than those produced by ORB, at the expense of a slight increase in the computational effort required to produce the partitions. Alternate approaches to parallelization of particle methods can be found in [15]. Our scheme resembles ORB, but takes advantage of certain metric properties of the surface of the sphere to give good partitions.

Before describing our algorithm, we note that one can consider stereographically projecting the points on the sphere onto the plane and then using an existing partitioning algorithm for the plane. However, points close to the projecting pole are widely separated in the projection. This distortion on locality makes geometric algorithms unsuitable.

3 The Algorithm

We propose an essentially geometric scheme for decomposing the surface of the sphere into regions bounded by a pair of latitudes and and a pair of longitudes. The input to the domain decomposition algorithm consists of: (i) the number P of processors available, (ii) the cut-off distance h for the short-range interactions, and (iii) a set of N points defined by their coordinates (latitude and longitude) on the unit sphere. We assume that each point is dynamically assigned a positive weight which is proportional to the computational effort required for computing the new state of the point. Each point represents a particle in the system.

The computational effort for a given point is roughly proportional to the number of points within a distance h of the given point. There are different options available to obtain a reasonable estimate of what the weight should be. A large class of problems involves compressible fluid flow calculations in which the density of the fluid has to be determined [4]. For sufficiently small h, the number of points within a distance h of any point is approximately proportional to the density at the point. Thus, one may take the weight to be proportional to the density. If such data is not available, one may use non-parametric density estimation techniques to estimate the density [6]. In our implementation of the domain decomposition algorithm on the sphere we have used positive integral weights, though using floating point weights does not present any additional difficulty.

As its output, the domain decomposition algorithm associates an integer in the interval $[0, P - 1]$ with each point, which indicates which partition (subdomain) a point belongs to. In addition, the algorithm can also produce a mapping of partitions to processors, thus determining the processor to which each point is assigned. Our algorithm produces a mapping for a tree topology, with the processors located at the leaves of the tree. This is not unduly restrictive since efficient schemes for embedding trees into other topologies exist [8].

We use a recursive bisection procedure. At each stage,

1. we first consider a cut on the subregion along the latitude that gives a balanced load, and also a longitudinal cut that gives a balanced load;
2. we then calculate and compare the communication cost of each cut, and choose the one that with the lower cost.

Thus initially, one of the first two types of cuts shown in Figure 2 is made. Being

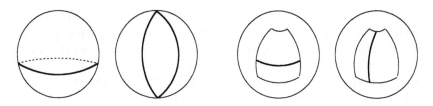

Fig. 2. Initial latitudinal and longitudinal cuts; generic latitudinal and longitudinal cuts.

on the surface of the sphere adds an additional complication if the region we are currently considering has not been cut by a longitude before. Such regions look either like rings or polar caps, as shown in Figure 3 (a). In this case there is no unique pair of longitudes that balances the load. In fact if there are n points in such a region, then there are $O(n^2)$ possible pairs of longitudes, and $O(n)$ possible pairs among these along which we can perform a cut while keeping the load balanced. A naive strategy would determine for each fixed choice of the starting longitude of the region, the corresponding longitude to end the region which gives a balanced load. This can be done by using a sorted array of longitudes in $O(\log n)$ time per initial choice. Since there are $O(n)$ possible initial choices, the overall time appears to be $O(n \log n)$ for the determination of the cut. However, we show that this type of a longitudinal cut can actually be determined using only $O(n)$ operations. Our algorithm requires a preprocessing overhead of $O(N \log N)$. However $O(N \log N)$ preprocessing is required for sorting the N points in the system according to a number of parameters anyway, so this does not add to the overall complexity. In this way, the rest of the computation takes only linear time at each level of the recursion.

The algorithm is outlined in greater detail below. Being on the surface of the sphere leads to some complicated boundary conditions to maintain. In order to ensure the clarity of the presentation, these are not elaborated on here.

3.1 Latitudinal cut

We first describe latitudinal cuts since they are the simpler of the two. For a latitudinal cut, we wish to divide the sphere into two parts along a certain latitude. If we sweep a latitude from the South to the North Pole, then the load balance of the two parts it divides changes discontinuously, and does so exactly at those latitudes at which the data points are located. Hence, we need to consider only these latitudes. In the preprocessing step, we keep a list of the points sorted in ascending order of latitude. We traverse this array, and perform a prefix computation to calculate the cumulative weights of all those points that have been encountered so far, including the current location. In order to find the latitude at which to cut, we perform a binary search on the array of cumulative weights to find the location that gives the best load balance, i.e., has cumulative weight closest to half the total weight of the partition. It is possible for two adjacent locations to have equally good load balance. In this case we choose one of the cuts arbitrarily. We observe that if several points have the same latitude, they may fall in different partitions. In order to compute the cost of the chosen partition, we need to know the number of points that lie within a distance h of the closest latitudes of either region. We use the property that the shortest distance between a point and a latitude is the absolute value of their differences in latitude. We locate the farthest points within the cut-off distance of the latitudes defining the boundaries of the two regions. This is performed by binary search on the sorted array of latitudes. The number of points that will be communicated is one more than the difference in the positions of these points in the sorted list.

3.2 Longitudinal cut

There are two cases to consider for a longitudinal cut. If any ancestor (in the recursion tree) of the region being cut has been subjected to a longitudinal cut before, then this case leads to a simpler algorithm since cutting along a single longitude will necessarily divide the region into two parts. We choose this longitude in a manner analogous to that of the latitude, using a pre-sorted array of longitudes. Computing the cost requires a little more attention since the shortest distance between a point and a longitude is in general not the difference of their longitudes. If we sweep a longitude around the sphere and consider the neighborhood within distance h of this longitude, then points may enter and leave this neighborhood at different values of the longitude. We can calculate the longitudes at which any point enters and leaves this neighborhood. If a point is within distance h of all longitudes (near the poles), then we consider it as entering at $-\infty$ and leaving at ∞. We have a preprocessing step in which we create two sorted arrays based on the longitudes at which a point enters and leaves the neighborhood respectively. In order to compute the number of points within distance h of a given longitude, we find the last point that has just joined the neighborhood and the next point that leaves the neighborhood. These points are found by binary search on the two sorted arrays constructed above. The difference between the number of points that have joined the neighborhood and the number that have already left gives the number of points still in the neighborhood.

In the second type of longitudinal cut, no ancestor of the region has been subjected to a longitudinal cut before. Now we need to decide on two longitudes at which to perform the cut, since one longitude alone will not divide the region into two pieces (see Figure 3 (a)). We start with the first longitude, say A_1, in the sorted list of longitudes, and find the corresponding longitude A_2 that balances the load if we start the region defined by the cut at A_1. We compute the cost as in the case of a cut which requires a single longitude; however, we now need to add the number of points on both boundaries. We next look at the longitude B_1 that comes second in the sorted list of longitudes. We find the other end B_2 of the possible cut not by performing a binary search on the list, but by incrementing the location of A_2 until we achieve load balance. This construction is as shown in Figure 3 (b). A similar procedure is carried out in computing the

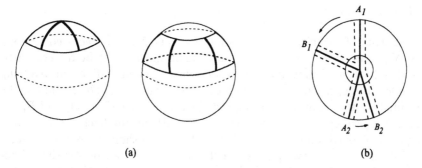

Fig. 3. (a) Longitudinal cuts that require a pair of longitudes; (b) Pairs of longitudes that balance the load. The center is the North Pole.

communication cost as well. We proceed in this manner around the sphere and choose the cut that has the lowest communication cost.

An example of a sequence of various latitudinal and longitudinal cuts made using this decomposition scheme is given in Figure 4.

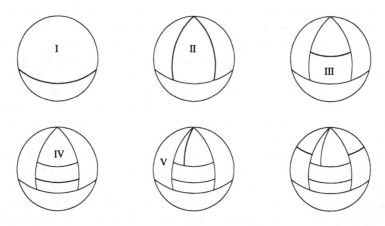

Fig. 4. An example: The first cut is latitudinal, producing domain I and its complement. Sample subsequent cuts on some of the subdomains are: longitudinal cut on I, latitudinal cuts on II and III, longitudinal cut on IV, and latitudinal cut on V.

3.3 Partitioning

After we decide on a particular cut, we need to partition the set of points. An important step here is to obtain the sorted arrays for each partition without needing to perform an extra $O(n \log n)$ sorting step. We can get the sorted arrays in linear time by scanning each already sorted array in order and placing a point at the end of the array of whichever partition it belongs too. In addition, if we performed the longitudinal cut involving two longitudes, we need to change the values of the longitudes of certain points in one of the partitions by subtracting 2π from their coordinates, so that if we sweep a longitude from one end of the partition to the other, we will remain within the partition. Getting the sorted arrays in this case also requires two passes over the sorted arrays, rather than

3.4 Complexity

The complexity of the initial preprocessing step is $O(N \log N)$ required for sorting the N points. If there are n points in a partition that is to be further partitioned, then locating the latitude, or the longitude in a longitudinal cut involving only one longitude, can be done in $O(\log n)$ time. This takes $O(n)$ time for the longitudinal cut that requires two longitudes, since the "arms" A_1, A_2 and B_1, B_2 of Figure 3 (b) sweep through the points once, without any backtracking. Generating the new partition requires $O(n)$ time for any of these types of cuts, since we need to make one or two passes to extract the sorted arrays for the subdomains themselves. Thus each level of the recursion requires $O(N)$ time, leading to $N \log P$ complexity for the recursion if P parts are needed (assuming P is a power of 2). In addition, we have $O(N \log N)$ preprocessing time, which gives a total complexity of $O(N \log N + N \log P) = O(N \log N)$.

4 Experimental Results

We performed experiments to test the performance of our algorithm, and also to compare it with existing algorithms. As a measure of the load imbalance, we considered the quantity: tP/T where P is the number of processors desired, T is the sum of the weights of all the points, and t is the sum of the weights of all the points in the processor with the largest such sum. If the load were perfectly balanced, then this quantity would be 1. In all of the experiments, we found that all the methods tested gave well balanced partitions, especially with a large number of particles. Thus we do not report further on this aspect of the experiments, and judge the quality of the partitioning based only on the communication cost incurred. In the rest of this section, the term *quality* refers to the communication cost incurred. The ratio of the communication costs that appear in our plots to $P \cdot N$ is the average communication cost incurred between pairs of processors, as a fraction of the total number of points. We obtained our data points on the sphere by generating samples from two probability density distributions. We used the rejection-acceptance technique to generate the points. We assigned weights to each point proportional to the density of the distribution at the point. The weights were rounded to integers with a minimum value of 1. We chose a value of h such that it gave a reasonably good estimate when using kernels for non-parametric estimation of the probability density. This was done on the basis of practical applications in which our scheme is particularly useful [14].

We compared our algorithm with general graph partitioning algorithms, since these have been found to give good quality partitions [10]. We also compared our scheme with the inertial method, since this is a geometric method which is much faster than the general graph partitioning methods. For problems of large size, even the multilevel graph partitioning algorithms were at least two orders of magnitude slower than our algorithm. Therefore we have presented timing results comparing our algorithm only with the inertial method. The inertial method used was that implemented by Chaco, version 2.0. The spectral bisection method used the multilevel spectral eigensolver implemented in Chaco, version 2.0. The multilevel spectral bisection scheme implemented in Metis, version 2.0.3 gave partitions of similar quality, and requiring a similar run time, as that of Chaco. However, the latter was marginally faster and gave partitions of slightly better quality in a few tests, and so was used in our experiments. It should be noted that though the number of vertices in our graphs is not very high compared with many of the graphs used for tests in current literature, the relative denseness of our graphs results in a large number of edges. Many of our larger graphs have millions of edges.

Experiment 1: We first performed experiments to observe how the speed of our method scales with the number of points. The experiments were performed on Sun SPARCstation 5, and the timing results are reported in seconds. We present results showing the total time required, and also the time required by just the partitioning phase, ignoring the initial preprocessing time. We compare it in Figure 5 with the inertial method implemented in Chaco, version 2.0, without the Kernighan-Lin refinement. The time reported is that taken just for the partitioning. We did not use the Kernighan-Lin refinement for the inertial method because this increased the time taken significantly. Since speed is the major advantage of a geometric algorithm, we decided not to use this refinement. It can be seen that as the number of points increases, the inertial method is about an order of magnitude slower than our scheme. We also note that our scheme scales well as the number of points increases. It should also be noted that with a large number of points, the majority of the time is spent in the initial sorting, which can be easily parallelized.

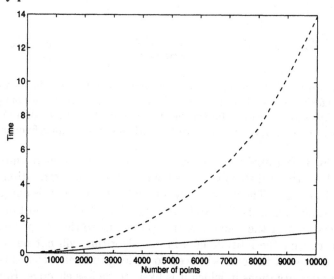

Fig. 5. Comparison of the speed of our algorithm and inertial partitioning into $P = 32$ parts, without Kernighan-Lin refinement. The solid line shows the time taken by our algorithm. The dotted line shows the time taken in just the partitioning phase. The dashed line shows the results for the inertial method. Time is in seconds.

Experiment 2: We next investigated the quality of the partitions obtained. In all the experiments reported below, the data was partitioned into $P = 32$ parts. We consider points generated on the unit sphere with the distribution: $\psi(\phi, \theta) = \exp\left(U \sin^2 \phi\right)/A$, where U is a parameter, A normalizes ψ to a probability density, and ϕ and θ are the latitude and the longitude respectively. This particular function arises in the solution of a certain problem in complex fluids [14], and the distribution depends only on the latitude. Here, $-\pi/2 \le \phi \le \pi/2$, and $0 \le \theta < 2\pi$. In our experiments, we have used the special case of $U = 4.6$, $A = 25.6$. The value of h was taken to be 0.2.

We can see from Figure 6 that our method, inertial partitioning, and the multilevel spectral method give partitions of comparable quality for this distribution, though the spectral method gives slightly better partitions.

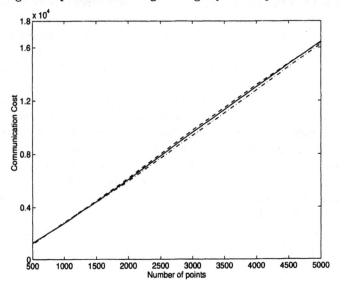

Fig. 6. Comparison of the quality of the partitions, as judged by the communication cost incurred for the ψ distribution. The solid line presents the results for our algorithm. The dashed line shows the same for the inertial method. The dashed-dotted line shows the results for the multilevel spectral method with Kernighan-Lin refinement.

Experiment 3: Our final comparison is with the distribution given by: $\cos(\phi) \cdot \beta(\theta, 6, 2)$ where the β distribution is similar to the *beta* distribution, with the range scaled to $[0, 2\pi]$. The value of h was taken to be 0.3. This is non-uniform in both the latitude and in the longitude. It should be noted that most of the points are concentrated near the equator of the sphere due to the $\cos(\phi)$ term. Hence, we can expect that the latitude cuts in our algorithm will not be particularly effective and most of the cuts will need to be longitudinal. Thus, this tests our algorithm under situations in which it is likely to be less effective. However, the results presented in Figure 7 show that our algorithm performs almost as well as the other algorithms in this case, though it is slightly worse than the multilevel spectral method.

The experiments conducted show that all the methods considered here give partitions with good load balance. It also appears that the communication cost incurred are comparable. However, the scheme we have presented is much faster. This is probably due to the fact that our method has been specifically designed for points on the surface of the sphere, whereas the other methods are much more general.

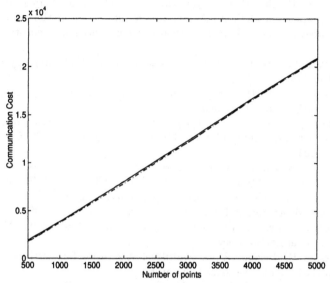

Fig. 7. Comparison of the quality of the partitions, as judged by the communication cost incurred, for the distribution proportional to $\cos(\phi) \cdot \beta(\theta, 6, 2)$. The solid line presents the results for our algorithm. The dashed line shows the same for the inertial method. The dashed-dotted line shows the results for the multilevel spectral method with Kernighan-Lin refinement.

5 Conclusions

We have presented a geometric domain decomposition algorithm that partitions data on the surface of the sphere and gives partitions suitable for particle method applications. Experiments have shown that the quality of the partitions obtained are comparable to more sophisticated schemes. The method has the advantage of being extremely fast, even compared with the inertial method. This good performance is to be expected since the graph edges in our problem are a function of geometric locality, and therefore suitable for geometric algorithms. Furthermore, high storage costs associated with graph algorithms for dense graphs (which is typical for our applications) are avoided.

The method produces partitions such that other operations on the data can be implemented by fast algorithms [7]. The domains produced by the algorithm can be parameterized well using four coordinates. This property is useful for other operations, which are described in [7]. The source code of the implementation can be obtained from the authors.

References

1. Barnes, J., Hut, P.: A hierarchical $O(N \log N)$ force-calculation algorithm. Nature **3** (1986) 446-449
2. Berger, M.J., Bokhari, S.H.: A partitioning strategy for nonuniform problems on multiprocessors. IEEE Transactions on Computers **C-36** (1987) 570-80
3. Young, W.S., Brooks III, C.L.: Implementation of a Data Parallel, Logical Domain Decomposition Method for Interparticle Interaction in Molecular Dynamics of Structured Molecular Fluids. Journal of Computational Chemistry **15** (1994) 44-53
4. Monaghan, J.J.: Particle Methods for Hydrodynamics. Computer Physics Reports **3** (1985) 71-124
5. Harlow, F.H.: The Particle-in-Cell Computing Method for Fluid Dynamics. Meth. Comput. Phys. **3** (1964) 319-343
6. Eğecioğlu Ö., Srinivasan, A.: Efficient Nonparametric Estimation of Probability Density Functions. Technical Report TRCS95-21, University of California at Santa Barbara, 1995
7. Eğecioğlu Ö., Srinivasan, A.: Parallelization of Particle Methods on the Sphere, Technical Report TRCS96-10, University of California at Santa Barbara, 1996
8. Leighton, F.T.: Introduction to parallel algorithms and architectures : arrays, trees, hypercubes. M. Kaufmann Publishers, San Mateo, California, 1992
9. Hendrickson, B., Leland, R.: The Chaco User's Guide, Version 2.0. SAND95-2344, Sandia National Laboratories
10. Hendrickson, B., Leland, R.: A Multilevel Algorithm for Partitioning Graphs. SAND93-1301, Sandia National Laboratories
11. Karypis, G., Kumar, V.: METIS, Unstructured Graph Partitioning and Sparse Matrix Ordering System, Version 2.0. Dept. of Computer Science, University of Minnesota, 1995
12. Williams, R.D.: Performance of Dynamic Load Balancing Algorithms for Unstructured Mesh Calculations. Concurrency **3** (1991) 457-481
13. Kernighan, B.W., Lin S.: An Efficient Heuristic Procedure for Partitioning Graphs. Bell System Technical Journal, 1970
14. Chaubal, C., Leal, L.G.: The Effect of Flow Type on the Rheology of Liquid Crystalline Polymers. Society of Rheology, 67th Annual Meeting, Sacramento, CA Oct 8-12, 1995
15. Plimpton, S.: Fast Parallel Algorithms for Short-Range Molecular Dynamics. J. Comp. Phys. **117** (1995) 1-19
16. Barnard, S.T., Simon, H.: A parallel implementation of multilevel recursive spectral bisection for application to adaptive unstructured meshes. In: Proceedings of the Seventh SIAM Conference on Parallel Processing for Scientific Computing, San Francisco, CA, USA, 15-17 Feb. 1995. Edited by: Bailey, D.H.; Bjorstad, P.E.; Gilbert, J.R.; Mascagni, M.V.; and others. Philadelphia, PA: SIAM, 1995, 627-32
17. Szeri, A., Leal, L.G.: A new computational method for the solution of flow problems of microstructured fluids. Part 2. Inhomogeneous shear flow of a suspension. Journal of Fluid Mechanics **262** (1994) 171-204

Coordination of Distributed/Parallel Multiple-grid Domain Decomposition

C.T.H. Everaars and F. Arbab

CWI, P.O. Box 94079, 1090 GB Amsterdam, The Netherlands

Abstract. A workable approach for the solution of many (numerical and non-numerical) problems is domain decomposition. If a problem can be divided into a number of sub-problems that can be solved in a distributed/parallel fashion, the overall performance can significantly improve. In this paper, we discuss one of our experiments using the new coordination language **MANIFOLD** to solve an instance of the classical optimization problem by domain decomposition. We demonstrate the applicability of **MANIFOLD** in expressing the solutions to domain decomposition problems in a generic way and its utility in producing executable code that can carry out such solutions in both distributed and parallel environments.

The multiple-grid domain decomposition method used in this paper is based on adaptive partitioning of the domain and results in highly irregular grids as shown in the examples. The implementation of the distributed/parallel approach presented in this paper looks very promising and its coordinator modules are generally applicable.

1 Introduction

In sciences, engineering, and economics, decision problems are frequently modeled as optimizing the value of a function under some constraints. The problem in its generic form is formulated as follows:

$$\min f(x) \quad \text{subject to } x \in D \subset \mathbb{R}^n. \tag{1}$$

There is an enormous amount and variety of literature about the theory and implementation of this problem. This variety is essentially due to different assumptions about the underlying problem structure. It is not our aim to offer the reader a tour through this literature, nor do we intend to present a very sophisticated algorithm for a certain class of global optimization problems. We consider solving an instance of (1) in a *distributed/parallel* fashion only as an example of the application of the domain decomposition method in the field of numerical computing. As a concrete example, we use a multi-extremal function in two variables, which is to be minimized in a certain domain. We use this function to illustrate the applicability of our generic domain decomposition coordinator module to implement irregular, adaptive multiple-grid methods. The same coordinators can be used without change for higher-dimensional functions as well as other non-numeric domain decomposition problems.

If a problem can be divided into a number of sub-problems that can be solved on a cluster of parallel computers and workstations, we may be able to significantly improve the performance of our solution. The new brand of coordination languages[5] presents a viable approach to this kind of problem decomposition. In this paper, we discuss one of our experiments using the new coordination language MANIFOLD to decompose an instance of the classical optimization problem and solve it using irregular grids in a distributed/parallel fashion.

MANIFOLD is a coordination language developed at CWI (Centrum voor Wiskunde en Informatica) in the Netherlands. It is very well suited for managing complex, dynamically changing interconnections among sets of independent concurrent cooperating processes. Although parallel computing and distributed computing are quite distinct in nature, they can both serve to improve performance. Distributed computing is related to the emergence of computer networks: computer applications move from single stand-alone mainframes to multiple communicating local workstations. Parallel computing arose from the quest to fundamentally improve the speed of sequential computation by using multiple processing units. From the language point of view, MANIFOLD does not make a distinction between a multiprocessor mainframe and a simple one-processor workstation. This feature makes MANIFOLD a very powerful tool for problem solving in heterogeneous computing environments.

MANIFOLD is based on the IWIM model of communication[2]. The basic concepts in MANIFOLD are *processes*, *events*, *ports*, and *streams*. A MANIFOLD application consists of a (potentially very large) number of (light- and/or heavyweight) processes (which may be written in different programming languages) running on a network of heterogeneous hosts, some of which may be parallel systems. The MANIFOLD system which has been ported to several different platforms, consists of a compiler, a run-time system library, a number of utility programs, libraries of builtin and predefined processes, a link file generator called MLINK and a run-time configurator called CONFIG.

Due to space limitation, we refer to[1] for a short introduction to MANIFOLD and for a comparison with other coordination languages. [1]

In next section we present our optimization problem and describe the parallel/distributed domain decomposition. We close this paper with a short conclusion in section 3.

2   Domain Decomposition

As an instance of (1) we take the Goldstein and Price function:

$$\min z = (1 + (x + y + 1)^2(19 - 14x + 3x^2 - 14y + 6xy + 3y^2)) \qquad (2)$$
$$(30 + (2x - 3y)^2(18 - 32x + 12x^2 + 48y - 36xy + 27y^2))$$
$$\text{with } (x, y) \in [-2.0, 2.0]$$

---

[1] See also our html pages located at http://www.cwi.nl/cwi/projects/manifold.html.

Figure 1 shows the landscape formed by this function in its domain. Although at this scale the detailed "bumpiness" of this function cannot be seen, this figure still shows the potential difficulty of the general problem (1).

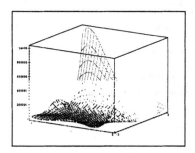

Fig. 1. The Goldstein and Price function

Analytical solutions to such problems are, in general, non-existent and domain decomposition is a common search technique used to solve them through numerical methods. Domain decomposition imposes a grid on the domain of the function, splitting it into a number of sub-domains, as determined by the size of the grid. Next, we obtain a (number of) good rough estimate(s) for the lowest value of z in each sub-domain. Then, we either use the best obtained estimate for the optimum z value, or select the sub-domains with the most promising z values and decompose them into smaller sub-domains. In iterative refinement methods, new estimates for the lowest value of z in each of these sub-domains, recursively, narrow this search process further and further into smaller and smaller regions that (hopefully) tend towards the area with the real minimum z, while the estimates for the obtained minimum z values become more and more accurate. In iterative single-grid domain decomposition, the same grid is imposed on all successive sub-domains. Multiple-grid adaptive domain decomposition techniques allow a different grid for each sub-domain, whose granularity and other properties may depend on the attributes of the sub-domain and those of the function within that region.

A simple domain decomposition program is presented in section 2.1. In section 2.2 we modify this program to handle iterative refinement and multiple, adaptive grids. In section 2.3 we visualize the numerical results of this program, and in section 2.4 we evolve our program into a simple computational steering application.

2.1 Single-grid Domain Decomposition

The following **MANIFOLD** program shows a non-iterative single-grid domain decomposition application.

```
1 manifold PrintObjects atomic {internal.}.
2 manifold Split atomic {internal.}.
```

```
 3  manifold AtomicEval(event, port in) atomic {internal.}.
 4  manifold Eval forward.
 5  manifold Merger port in a, b. atomic {internal.}.
 6
 7  /*************************************************************/
 8  manifold Main
 9  {
10    auto process split is Split.
11    auto process eval is Eval.
12    auto process print is PrintObjects.
13
14    begin: <<1, -2.0, -2.0, 2.0, 2.0, 5, 5>> -> split -> eval -> print.
15  }
16
17  /*************************************************************/
18  manifold Eval()
19  {
20    event filled, flushed, finished.
21
22    process atomeval is AtomicEval(filled, 1000).
23
24    stream reconnect KB input -> *.
25
26    priority filled < finished.
27
28    begin:
29      {
30        activate(atomeval), input -> atomeval,
31        guard (input, a_everdisconnected ! empty, finished) // no more input
32      }.
33
34    finished:
35      {
36        ignore filled. //possible event form atomeval
37
38        begin: atomeval -> output.  //your output is only that of atomeval
39      }.
40
41    filled:
42      {
43        process merge<a, b | output> is Merger.
44
45        stream KK * -> (merge.a, merge.b).
46        stream KK merge -> output.
47
48        begin:
49          {
50            activate(merge), input -> Eval -> merge.a,
51            atomeval -> merge.b, merge -> output
52          }.
53
54        finished:. //do nothing and leave this block
55      }.
56
57    end:
58      {
59        begin:
60          {
61            guard(output, a_disconnected, flushed), // ensure flushing
62            terminated(void) //wait for units to flush through output
63          }.
64
65        flushed: halt.
66      }.
67  }
```

The main manifold in this application creates split, eval, and print as instances of manifold definitions Split, Eval, and PrintObjects, respectively (line 10-12). It then connects the output of a process instance which produces a unit that describes a domain and its decomposition (in our case, 5 × 5), to the input port of split; the output port of split to the input port of eval; and the output port of eval to the input port of print. The process main terminates when all three connections are broken.

The code for Split is a C function. An instance of Split reads from its input port a unit that describes a (sub-)domain and the specification of a grid, produces units on its output port that describe the sub-domains obtained by imposing the grid on this input domain, and terminates.

An instance of Eval is expected to read all the sub-domains (in this case, there are 25) from its **input** port. It then finds the best estimate for the optimum z value in each of its sub-domains, produces through its **output** port an ordered sequence of units describing the best solutions it has found, and terminates.

The process **PrintObjects** is implemented as a C function. An instance of **PrintObjects** simply prints the units it reads from its **input**, each of which describes a (sub-)domain and the x, y, and z values for the estimated minimum z value found at the point (x, y) in that domain.

An instance of **Eval** coordinates the cooperation of instances of two other manifolds, namely **AtomicEval** and **Merger**.

AtomicEval is implemented as a C function. An instance of **AtomicEval** reads a bucket of $s > 0$ sub-domains (for simplicity, let $s = 1$) from its **input** port and raises a specific event, which it receives as a parameter, to inform other processes that it has filled up its input bucket with s sub-domain descriptions. It then finds the best estimate for the optimum z value in each of its sub-domains, producing an ordered sequence of units describing the best solutions it has found through its **output** port, and terminates. The algorithm used by **AtomicEval** to find the estimates for the optimum z value in a sub-domain is completely internal to this computation module and is irrelevant for our purposes in this paper. In our example, we use sampling: we simply evaluate z for a number of (say 1000) sample points in each sub-domain and consider the sample point with the minimum z as the best estimate for that sub-domain.

Merger is also implemented as a C function. An instance of **Merger** reads from its ports **a** and **b** two ordered sequences of units describing sub-domains and their best estimates, and produces a sequence of one or more of its best sub-domains on its **output** port.

As noted above, an instance of Eval receives through its **input** port an unknown number of units that describe (sub-)domains. It is supposed to feed as many of its own input units to an atomic evaluator as the latter can take; feed the rest of its own input as the input to another copy of itself; merge the two output sequences (of the atomic evaluator and its new copy); and produce the resulting sequence through its own **output** port. Let us follow the source code of the manifold Eval in more detail.

In its **begin** state, an instance of Eval connects its own **input** to an instance of the **AtomicEval**, it calls **atomeval**. It also installs a *guard* on of its own **input** port. This guard posts the event **finished** if it has an empty stream connected to its departure side, after the arrival side of this port has no more stream connections, following a first connection. This means that the event **finished** is posted in an instance of Eval after a first connection to the arrival side of its **input** is made, then all connections to the arrival side of its **input** are severed, and all units passed through this port are consumed. The connections in this state are shown in Figure 2.a.

Two events can preempt the **begin** state of an instance of Eval: (1) if the incoming stream connected to **input** is disconnected (no more incoming units) and **atomeval** reads all units available in its incoming stream, the guard on **input** posts the event **finished**; and (2) the process **atomeval** can read its fill

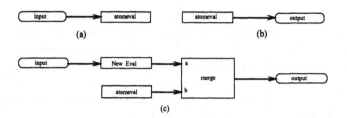

Fig. 2. The connections made in the different states of **Eval**

and raise the event **filled**. Normally, only one of these events occurs; however, when the number of input units is exactly equal to the bucket size, s, of **atomeval**, both **finished** and **filled** can occur simultaneously. In this case, the priority statement makes sure that the handling of **finished** takes precedence over **filled**.

Assume that the number of units in the input supplied to an instance of **Eval** is indeed less than or equal to the bucket size s of an atomic evaluator. In this case, the event **finished** will preempt the **begin** state and cause a transition to its corresponding state in **Eval**. In this state, we ignore the occurrence of **filled** that may have been raised by **atomeval** (if the number of input units is equal to the bucket size s); and deliver the output of **atomeval** as the output of the **Eval**. The connections in this state are shown in Figure 2.b.

Now suppose the number of units in the input supplied to an instance of **Eval** is greater than the bucket size s of an atomic evaluator. In this case, the event **filled** will preempt the **begin** state and cause a transition to its corresponding state in **Eval**. In this state we create an instance of the merger process, called **merge**. A new instance of the **Eval** is created in the **begin** state of the nested block. The rest of the input is passed on as the input to this new **Eval**, its output is merged with the output of the atomic evaluator, and the result is passed as the output of the **Eval** instance itself. The connections in this state are shown in Figure 2.c. An occurrence of **finished** in this state preempts the connected streams and causes a transition to the local **finished** state in this block. This preemption is necessary to inform the new instance of **Eval** (by breaking the stream that connects **input** to it) that it has no more input to receive, so that it can terminate. The empty body of the **finished** state means that it causes an exit from its containing block.

In the **end** state, an **Eval** instance installs a guard on its **output** port to post the event **flushed** after there is no stream connected to the arrival side of this port following its first connection. This means that the event **flushed** is posted in an instance of **Eval** after a connection is made to its arrival side, and all units arriving at this port have passed through. The **Eval** instance then waits for the termination of the special predefined process **void**, which will never happen (the special process **void** never terminates). This effectively causes the **Eval** instance to hang indefinitely. The only event that can terminate this indefinite wait is an occurrence of **flushed** which indicates there are no more units pending to go through the output port of the Eval instance.

The output of our program consist of 25 lines showing the results produced by 25 instances of AtomicEval, each taking in the description of a single subdomain. Due to space limitation, we show here only the top line representing the best estimate for the global minimum to be 3.126 at point (0.006, -1.015) and the last line, which represents the worst result.

```
domain = (-0.400, -1.200) ( 0.400, -0.400) point = ( 0.006, -1.015), z =    3.126
domain = (-1.200,  1.200) (-0.400,  2.000) point = (-0.440,  1.219), z = 102644.133
```

The recursive way in which the coordinator process Eval creates and coordinates its atomic workers is interesting. These atomic workers (the numerical evaluators and the mergers, together with the atomic workers created in the coordinator process main) and their connections are shown in figure 3. Here e_i (m_i) denotes the ith evaluator (merger), dashed lines represent the (re)connections of the same stream, and n is the recursion depth of Eval. Note that all these processes run concurrently with each other. This means that, depending on the installation configuration of the MANIFOLD system, they can run truly in parallel with each other on a distributed and/or parallel platform.

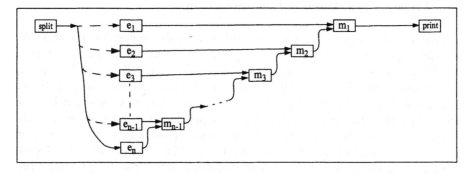

Fig. 3. The atomic processes at work.

Each MANIFOLD process runs as a separate thread (a light-weight process). In our installation of the MANIFOLD system on Sun and SGI machines, thirty or so of these threads are bundled together and comprise a MANIFOLD task. Each task instance is an operating-system-level (heavy-weight) process that runs somewhere on a distributed platform. The actual host(s) where these tasks run are specified in a configuration file which is read at runtime. If, e.g., we impose a 100×100 grid on the domain (so when the bucket size s of AtomicEval is 10, the recursion depth of Eval is $n = 1000$) and the configuration file contains a number of SGIs, a number of SUNs, an IBM SP/2, and some Linux machines, etc., more than 67 MANIFOLD task instances are created and spread over this heterogeneous environment and run in a distributed/parallel fashion. For instance, on a multi-processor machine such as SGI, thirty or so threads in the same task can run concurrently. At most k of these threads can actually be running (truly) in parallel with each other, where k is the number of processors on the machine.

An interesting aspect of our application is the dynamic way in which Eval switches connections among the process instances it creates (see figure 2). Perhaps more interesting, is the fact that, in spite of its name, Eval knows nothing about evaluating functions! What Eval embodies is, not any computation, but only a protocol that describes how instances of two process definitions (e.g., AtomicEval and Merger in our case) should communicate with each other (see [3] for a detailed treatment of this phenomenon). A logical consequence of this clear separation of coordination and computation concerns into distinct modules is that we can use this same protocol for a completely different pair of process definitions than AtomicEval and Merger. In fact, this same module is used to implement a parallel/distributed bucket sort program as well [3]. An interesting use of this protocol would be to optimize a multi-extremal function f in n variables for large n's in a distributed/parallel fashion. To accomplish this, we only need to change the atomic workers; no change to the coordinators (Eval and Main) is necessary, which means they do not even have to be recompiled for this new application.

2.2 Multiple-grid Domain Decomposition

In this section we discuss a multiple-grid domain decomposition method. We initially impose a 2×2 grid on the domain of the function and start on each sub-domain an evaluator (AtomicEval). The evaluator finds a rough estimate for the lowest value of z in its sub-domain and determines a suitable grid (in our example, either 4×2 or 2×4) for its further decomposition, should that become necessary later. Our version of the evaluator proposes a 4×2 grid for the sub-domain under its consideration if the function is more hilly in the x-direction than in the y-direction in this sub-domain; otherwise, it proposes a 2×4 grid. With these grids we always have eight evaluators which can (in principle) run concurrently. Of course the relationship between the domain, the function, and the splitting scheme may be considered more carefully to yield better grids, perhaps with more variety and more adaptively. Our particular choice of grids and the simple criterion we use to select between them are good enough for our demonstration purposes. Note, however, that the choice of grids, their sizes, their number, their degree of adaptivity, as well as the criteria used for selecting among them, are all details that are internal to AtomicEval and, thus, irrelevant to our coordination modules (Eval and Main).

Eval simply continues with selecting the sub-domain with the most promising z value and the splitter imposes the recommended grid on it for its decomposition. New estimates for the lowest value of z in each of these sub-domains, recursively, narrow this search process further and further into smaller and smaller regions that (hopefully) tend towards the area with the real minimum z, while the estimates for the obtained minimum z values become more and more accurate. We stop this iterative decomposition algorithm when the relative improvement of the best solution found in two successive iteration steps falls below a certain threshold. The result is a highly irregular grid which shows the search path through the domain. The following MANIFOLD program shows the multiple-grid domain decomposition:

```
 1 manifold pass1 import.
 2 manifold variable import.
 3 manifold Eval import.
 4
 5 manifold PrintObjects atomic {internal.}.
 6 manifold Split atomic {internal.}.
 7 manifold AtomicEval(event, port in) atomic {internal.}.
 8 manifold Merger port in a, b. atomic {internal.}.
 9 manifold Checker(port in, port in, port in, event, event) atomic {internal.}.
10
11 #define TOL 1.0e-5
12 #define IDLE terminated(void)
13
14 /*****************************************************************/
15 manifold Main
16 {
17   event checkit, goon, stop.
18
19   auto process best1 is variable.
20   auto process best2 is variable.
21   auto process pr is PrintObjects.
22   stream reconnect BK * -> pr.
23
24   begin:
25     {
26       auto process p1 is pass1.
27
28       begin:
29         {
30           <<1, -2.0, -2.0, 2.0, 2.0, 2, 2>> -> Split -> Eval -> (-> pr, -> p1),
31           best2 = p1
32         );
33         post(goon).
34     }.
35
36   goon:
37     best1 = best2;
38     {
39       auto process p1 is pass1.
40
41       begin:
42         {
43           getunit(best1) -> Split -> Eval -> (-> pr, -> p1),
44           best2 = p1
45         );
46         post(checkit).
47     }.
48
49   checkit:
50     (
51       Checker(best1, best2, TOL, goon, stop),
52       IDLE
53     ).
54
55   stop:.
56 }
```

Lines 1-3 declare the manifolds pass1 and variable and Eval from the previous section. The keyword import states that the real definition (i.e. the body) of these manifolds are given elsewhere (in a library or in another source file). An instance of the predefined manifold pass1 remains idle until its input is connected to a stream. Once this connection is made, it passes the unit it receives on its input through its output port and terminates. An instance of the predefined manifold variable repeatedly reads a unit from its input port. It remembers the unit it reads, and if the departure side of its output is connected, it passes the unit on through its output port. Lines 11-12 define some preprocessor macros, in the same syntax as that of the C preprocessor. These macros define our symbolic constants. The main manifold contains four states (line 24, 36, 49 and 55). In the begin state the stream configuration on line 30 is constructed. The output of Eval is fanned out to the processes pr and p1, which are respectively instances of PrintObjects (line 21) and pass1 (line 26). Because we initially impose a 2×2 grid (line 30) on the domain, the first output of Eval consist of an ordered sequence of four units describing the best solutions found in the four sub-domains. The first unit of this sequence, containing the most promising sub-domain to find the minimum, is fed to p1, which delivers it to best2 (line 31) and terminates. When all the connections set up in lines 30-11 are broken (this happens when the tuple producer <<1, -2.0, -2.0, 2.0, 2.0, 2, 2>>, Split and Eval are done with their jobs and die, and p1 delivers its value to best1) the goon event is posted (line 33) and we switch to the goon state. There, best2 delivers its value to best1 (line 37). On line 43, a unit is read from the output port of best1 (getunit(best1)) and fed back to a stream configuration similar to the one on the lines 30-31. When the connections set up on lines 43-44 are broken, the checkit event is posted (line 46) and we switch to the checkit state. In this state, an instance of the Checker manifold, which compares best1 and best2, is automatically created and activated and we wait (due to the word IDLE on line 52) until this process raises a goon or a stop event. The Checker instance raises the stop event when the relative improvement to the best solutions found in two successive iteration steps is below a certain threshold (TOL, line 11). This causes a state switch to the stop state (its body is empty) and stops the iterative domain decomposition. In the other case, a transition to the goon state sets up another iteration step (line 37-47). The output of this program is shown below.

```
domain = (-2.000, -2.000) ( 2.000,  2.000) s = (2, 2)

domain = (-2.000, -2.000) ( 0.000,  0.000) point = (-0.035, -1.003), z =   3.303 s = (2, 4)
domain = ( 0.000, -2.000) ( 2.000,  0.000) point = ( 0.054, -0.973), z =   3.708 s = (4, 2)
domain = ( 0.000,  0.000) ( 2.000,  2.000) point = ( 1.778,  0.182), z =  84.152 s = (2, 4)
domain = (-2.000,  0.000) ( 0.000,  2.000) point = (-0.902,  0.011), z = 313.979 s = (4, 4)

domain = (-1.000, -1.000) ( 0.000, -0.500) point = (-0.010, -0.997), z =   3.039 s = (2, 4)
domain = (-1.000, -1.500) ( 0.000, -1.000) point = (-0.044, -1.016), z =   3.462 s = (4, 2)
domain = (-1.000, -0.500) ( 0.000,  0.000) point = (-0.609, -0.395), z =  30.039 s = (2, 4)
domain = (-2.000, -0.500) (-1.000,  0.000) point = (-1.002, -0.085), z = 256.380 s = (2, 4)
domain = (-1.000, -2.000) ( 0.000, -1.500) point = (-0.750, -1.501), z = 311.659 s = (4, 2)
domain = (-2.000, -1.000) (-1.000, -0.500) point = (-1.001, -0.534), z = 496.128 s = (2, 4)
domain = (-2.000, -2.000) (-1.000, -1.500) point = (-1.000, -1.663), z = 647.851 s = (2, 4)
domain = (-2.000, -1.500) (-1.000, -1.000) point = (-1.006, -1.478), z = 1844.802 s = (2, 4)

domain = (-0.500, -1.000) ( 0.000, -0.875) point = (-0.005, -0.995), z =   3.021 s = (2, 4)
domain = (-0.500, -0.875) ( 0.000, -0.750) point = (-0.051, -0.874), z =  10.979 s = (2, 4)
domain = (-0.500, -0.750) ( 0.000, -0.625) point = (-0.223, -0.749), z =  27.162 s = (2, 4)
domain = (-1.000, -0.625) (-0.500, -0.500) point = (-0.501, -0.502), z =  32.732 s = (2, 4)
domain = (-0.500, -0.625) ( 0.000, -0.500) point = (-0.497, -0.509), z =  32.974 s = (2, 4)
domain = (-1.000, -0.750) (-0.500, -0.625) point = (-0.504, -0.632), z =  59.715 s = (4, 2)
domain = (-1.000, -0.875) (-0.500, -0.750) point = (-0.504, -0.750), z = 125.833 s = (4, 2)
domain = (-1.000, -1.000) (-0.500, -0.875) point = (-0.500, -0.881), z = 218.267 s = (2, 4)

domain = (-0.250, -1.000) ( 0.000, -0.969) point = (-0.005, -0.999), z =   3.008 s = (4, 2)
domain = (-0.250, -0.969) ( 0.000, -0.938) point = ( 0.000, -0.968), z =   3.440 s = (4, 2)
domain = (-0.250, -0.938) ( 0.000, -0.906) point = (-0.007, -0.937), z =   4.772 s = (4, 2)
domain = (-0.250, -0.906) ( 0.000, -0.875) point = (-0.003, -0.906), z =   7.113 s = (4, 2)
domain = (-0.500, -0.906) (-0.250, -0.875) point = (-0.251, -0.880), z =  31.002 s = (4, 2)
domain = (-0.500, -0.938) (-0.250, -0.906) point = (-0.252, -0.908), z =  33.062 s = (4, 2)
domain = (-0.500, -0.969) (-0.250, -0.938) point = (-0.250, -0.940), z =  34.270 s = (4, 2)
domain = (-0.500, -1.000) (-0.250, -0.969) point = (-0.250, -0.999), z =  34.737 s = (4, 2)

domain = (-0.062, -1.000) ( 0.000, -0.984) point = ( 0.000, -1.000), z =   3.000 s = (2, 4)
domain = (-0.062, -0.984) ( 0.000, -0.969) point = ( 0.000, -0.984), z =   3.109 s = (2, 4)
domain = (-0.125, -1.000) (-0.062, -0.984) point = (-0.063, -0.998), z =   4.066 s = (2, 4)
domain = (-0.125, -0.984) (-0.062, -0.969) point = (-0.063, -0.984), z =   4.301 s = (2, 4)
domain = (-0.188, -1.000) (-0.125, -0.984) point = (-0.126, -0.999), z =   8.004 s = (2, 4)
domain = (-0.188, -0.984) (-0.125, -0.969) point = (-0.125, -0.982), z =   8.319 s = (2, 4)
domain = (-0.250, -1.000) (-0.188, -0.984) point = (-0.188, -0.995), z =  17.092 s = (2, 4)
domain = (-0.250, -0.984) (-0.188, -0.969) point = (-0.188, -0.981), z =  17.473 s = (2, 4)

domain = (-0.031, -1.000) ( 0.000, -0.996) point = ( 0.000, -1.000), z =   3.000 s = (4, 2)
```

```
domain = (-0.031, -0.996) ( 0.000, -0.992) point = (-0.001, -0.996), z =   3.008 s = (4, 2)
domain = (-0.031, -0.992) ( 0.000, -0.988) point = ( 0.000, -0.992), z =   3.027 s = (4, 2)
domain = (-0.031, -0.988) ( 0.000, -0.984) point = ( 0.000, -0.988), z =   3.059 s = (4, 2)
domain = (-0.062, -1.000) (-0.031, -0.996) point = (-0.031, -1.000), z =   3.250 s = (4, 2)
domain = (-0.062, -0.996) (-0.031, -0.992) point = (-0.032, -0.996), z =   3.286 s = (4, 2)
domain = (-0.062, -0.992) (-0.031, -0.988) point = (-0.032, -0.992), z =   3.333 s = (4, 2)
domain = (-0.062, -0.988) (-0.031, -0.984) point = (-0.031, -0.988), z =   3.382 s = (4, 2)
```

As shown in the output above, the description of a single sub-domain is extended with the recommended grid to be imposed on it if it is selected for further decomposition. The first line in this output is our initial input unit representing the whole domain and its desired splitting which is initially set to 2×2 (s = (2, 2)). Each succeeding group of eight lines then represents one iteration. The best sub-domain found in each iteration is fed as input to the next iteration. The first line of the last group (representing the 6th iteration) shows the best solution found ($z = 3.000$) to be at $(0.000, -1.000)$, which is much better than the best solution we found using our single 5×5 grid ($z = 3.1261$) in section 2.1.

It is quite common in global optimization to first apply a purely random search – a very simple and popular "folklore" approach to global optimization – as a preliminary search phase for reducing the initially chosen search domain. The current estimate of the global optimum found in this search can then form a starting point for a local search algorithm (e.g., the method of steepest descent, Newton, the conjugate gradient method, etc.). If we consider the work done in Eval as the preliminary search phase and define another manifold, LocalMinimizer, to implement our choice of a local search method, we can easily modify our coordinator module to accommodate such a hybrid scheme. All we need to do is change line 55 into stop: getunit(best2) -> LocalMinimizer -> pr.

2.3 Adding a Visualizer

Visualizing the results of our parallel/distributed application of the previous section can be very informative. With **MANIFOLD**, this can be done in a straightforward way. We simply make another atomic manifold (called Show) and make some drain cocks in the **MANIFOLD** code of section 2.2 with the stream constructor -> and the = operator (which in a hidden way uses the stream constructor). This results in the **MANIFOLD** program below, which is almost the same as the code in section 2.2.

```
 1 manifold pass1 import.
 2 manifold variable import.
 3 manifold Eval import.
 4
 5 manifold PrintObjects atomic {internal.}.
 6 manifold Split atomic {internal.}.
 7 manifold AtomicEval(event, port in) atomic {internal.}.
 8 manifold Merger port in a, b. atomic {internal.}.
 9 manifold Checker(port in, port in, port in, event, event) atomic {internal.}.
10 manifold Show atomic {internal.}.
11
12 #define TOL 1.0e-5
13 #define IDLE terminated(void)
14
15 /***************************************************************/
16 manifold Main
17 {
18   event checkit, goon, stop.
```

```
19
20    auto process best1 is variable.
21    auto process best2 is variable.
22    auto process pr is PrintObjects.
23    process show is Show.
24
25    stream reconnect BK * -> (show, pr).
26
27    begin:
28      {
29        auto process p1 is pass1.
30
31        begin:
32          {
33            activate(show),
34            <<1, -2.0, -2.0, 2.0, 2.0, 2, 2>> ->
35            (-> show, -> Split -> Eval -> (-> pr, -> p1) ),
36            best2 = p1
37          );
38          post(goon).
39      }.
40
41    goon:
42      best1 = best2; show = best2;
43        {
44          auto process p1 is pass1.
45
46          begin:
47            {
48              getunit(best1) -> Split -> Eval -> (-> pr, -> p1),
49              best2 = p1
50            );
51            post(checkit).
52        }.
53
54    checkit:
55      (
56        Checker(best1, best2, TOL, goon, stop),
57        IDLE
58      ).
59
60    stop: show = best2.
61  }
```

The irregular grid in figure 4 shows the iterative search process in the domain towards the best solution ($z = 3.000$) at point (0.000, -1.000). In this figure we can (partly) follow the splitting sequence which, as we know from the previous section, uses the grids 2×2, 2×4, 2×4, 4×2, 2×4, and 4×2. Due to the scale of this figure, only a part (the first three grids) of this irregular splitting can be seen clearly.

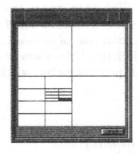

Fig. 4. The visualizer

The Show manifold is simple to implement in C using a portable graphic library (e.g. Phigs, GKS, OpenGL) and a portable widget library.

The adding of the visualizer clearly shows the "plumbing" aspect of MANIFOLD

programming: no explicit action is necessary to "move" information around in
MANIFOLD – provide the pipes (with -> or/and =) and the units will flow.

2.4 Computational Steering Through a GUI

In this section we extend the Show manifold of section 2.3 with a simple graphical
user interface (GUI) with some steering facilities. With this GUI we can select a
domain by mouse (by drawing a rectangle) and start (by pressing mouse buttons)
the iterative recursive domain decomposition of section 2.2 on that domain. We
call the work which has to be done on such a selected domain a "cluster." The
processes contained in clusters are spread out over the computers specified in a
configuration file (see section 2.2). This is completely transparent to the user. A
user only needs to supply a list of his favorite machines in a configuration file.
Once a cluster is started by a mouse click, it sends its identification back to the
GUI, which is shown in the area above the "show" button. In figure 5, we see
three clusters (c0, c1 and c3). Selecting, e.g., c0 and c1 (whose identifications
are highlighted) and pressing the show button results in the GUI as shown in
figure 5. In this figure, in addition to the global minimum of 3.000 at (0.000,
-1.000) which we know from the previous section, a local minimum of 84.000 at
(1.800, 0.200) is also shown.

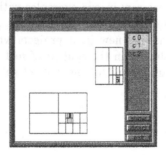

Fig. 5. The simple GUI

Another facility of the GUI is its ability to deactivate a cluster (by selecting
the cluster and clicking on the deactivate button). Consequently, the selected
area of a deactivated cluster gets a black border to indicate its termination.
Also, the clusters which terminate normally get the same black border.

With this simple GUI we can interactively explore the domain of the optimization problem in a distributed/parallel fashion. The manifold source code
for this distributed/parallel computational steering example is available via our
html pages and shows, once again, the flexibility of the MANIFOLD language.

3 Conclusions

MANIFOLD is a new coordination language for orchestration of the cooperation among large sets of concurrent processes that comprise parallel and/or distributed applications. One of the advantages of **MANIFOLD** is that it makes no distinction (that is visible to a programmer) between distributed and parallel environments: the same **MANIFOLD** code can run in both. A unique characteristic of **MANIFOLD** is its separation of computation concerns from communication concerns into distinct program modules. This leads to reusable pure-computation and reusable pure-coordination modules with little dependency on their application environments. All these features make **MANIFOLD** a suitable framework for the construction of modular software to solve irregular problems on parallel and/or distributed platforms.

Our experiment using **MANIFOLD** for this type of applications deals with an instance of the classical optimization problem. The emphasis of our work is on the construction and validation of the protocol modules necessary for this and other (numeric and non-numeric) applications. **MANIFOLD** allows such coordination modules to be compiled separately (and in isolation from any computation code), and stored in protocol libraries, whereby they can be subsequently linked with various separately compiled pure-computation modules to build running applications. Thus, the same coordinator modules described in this paper can be (and, indeed, are) used in various other domain decomposition applications as well as other non-numeric applications that use a similar splitting scheme.

Another important feature of **MANIFOLD** is its underlying plumbing paradigm which makes it easy – as we saw in our examples with the addition of Show – to compose and recompose **MANIFOLD** applications and adapt them to new requirements. We are beginning new joint projects where the practical utility of **MANIFOLD** will be evaluated in the context of real commercial applications, many of which involve parallel and/or distributed solutions to irregular problems.

References

1. F. Arbab. Coordination of massively concurrent activities. Technical Report CS-R9565, Centrum voor Wiskunde en Informatica, Kruislaan 413, 1098 SJ Amsterdam, The Netherlands, november 1995. Available on-line: http://www.cwi.nl/ftp/CWIreports/IS/CS-R9565.ps.Z.
2. F. Arbab. The IWIM model for coordination of concurrent activities. In P. Ciancarini and C. Hankin (eds.), *Coordination '96*, Lecture Notes in Computer Science #1061, Springer-Verlag, April 1996.
3. F. Arbab, C.L. Blom, F.J. Burger, and C.T.H. Everaars. Reusable coordinator modules for massively concurrent applications. In *Euro-Par '96*, Lecture Notes in Computer Science, Springer-Verlag, August 1996.
4. P. Bouvry and F. Arbab. Visifold: A visual environment for a coordination language. In *Coordination '96*, Lecture Notes in Computer Science, Springer-Verlag, April 1996.
5. D. Gelernter and N. Carriero. Coordination languages and their significance. *Communication of the ACM*, 35(2):97–107, February 1992.

Systems Support for Irregular Parallel Applications

Kathy Yelick

Computer Science Division, University of California at Berkeley
yelick@cs.berkeley.edu

Abstract. Software developers for distributed memory multiprocessors often complain about the lack of libraries and tools for developing and performancing tuning their applications. While some tools exist for regular array-based computations, support for applications with pointer-based data structures, asynchronous communication patterns, or unpredictable computational costs is seriously lacking. The Multipol distributed data structure library addresses this need.

The purpose of this talk is to describe our experience building Multipol and associated software. First, I will describe several irregular applications that helped motivate the Multipol design and are now part of a challenging new irregular application benchmark suite. The Multipol application benchmarks are medium sized applications from CAD, Cell Biology, Symbolic Algebra, and Genetics. Second, I will present an overview of the Multipol design, which is built on a lightweight runtime layer with support for multi-threading, remote invocation, application-specific caching, global snapshots, dynamic message aggregation, and scheduling. The Multipol data structures include sets, queues, lists, hash tables, and graphs, with each data structure used in at least one application. The library is designed for flexibility and performance portability: rather than setting system-wide policies for load balancing, caching, or communication, it provides several alternatives that the application programmer may select and mechanism for extending the library. Finally, I will describe some of the scheduling and load balancing algorithms used in our applications.

Systems Support for Irregular Parallel Applications

Computer Science Division, University of California, Berkeley,
yelick@cs.berkeley.edu

Distributed Object Oriented Data Structures and Algorithms for VLSI CAD

John A. Chandy[1], Steven Parkes[2], and Prithviraj Banerjee[1]

[1] Coordinated Science Laboratory, University of Illinois, Urbana, IL 61801, USA
[2] Sierra Vista Research, 236 N Santa Cruz Avenue, Los Gatos, CA 95030, USA

Abstract. ProperCAD II is a C++ object oriented library supporting actor based parallel program design. The library easily allows the design of data structures with parallel semantics for use in irregular applications. Inheritance mechanisms allow creation of the distributed data structures from standard C++ objects. This paper discusses the use of such distributed data structures in the context of a particular VLSI CAD application, standard cell placement. The library and associated runtime system currently run on a wide range of platforms.

1 Introduction

The use of parallel platforms, despite increasing availability, remains largely restricted to well-structured numeric codes. Irregular applications in terms of data access patterns as well as control flow are difficult to effectively and efficiently parallelize. The use of object-oriented design techniques and the actor model of computation can address the use of parallel platforms for unstructured problems. ProperCAD II is an object oriented library supporting the design of actor based parallel programs [1, 2]. The library easily allows the design of data structures with parallel semantics for use in irregular applications. Because the foundation is based on C++, inheritance mechanisms allow creation of the distributed data structures from standard C++ objects.

The domain of VLSI CAD provides a rich class of irregular problems. The computational intensity of VLSI CAD tools makes parallel processing an attractive solution [3]. However, most applications in this area are characterized by complex inter-related data structures as well as irregular access patterns across these objects. These properties make VLSI CAD applications particularly difficult to efficiently parallelize. The use of the ProperCAD II library as well as C++ design techniques help alleviate this problem. The approach has been used on several VLSI CAD problems including test generation [4], fault simulation [5], and VHDL simulation [6]. In this paper, we demonstrate the use of these techniques in a specific VLSI CAD problem, standard cell placement.

2 ProperCAD II

The major goal of the ProperCAD project [7] is to develop portable parallel algorithms for VLSI CAD applications on a range of parallel machines including shared memory multiprocessors such as the Sun SparcServer 1000E and the SGI Challenge, distributed memory multicomputers such as the Intel Paragon, IBM SP-2, and Thinking Machines CM-5, and networks of workstations. ProperCAD II provides C++ library-based machine independent runtime support in an object–oriented manner [1, 2] (Figure 1).

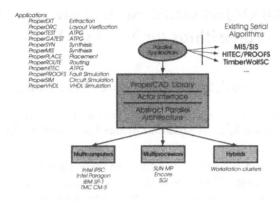

Fig. 1. An overview of the ProperCAD project.

2.1 Actor basics

The ProperCAD II library expresses parallelism through a statically-typed high level C++ interface based on actors. The interface is class library-based and allows multiple levels of abstraction as well as incremental parallelization. Through the use of a fundamental object called an actor [8], the library provides mechanisms necessary for achieving concurrency. An actor object consists of a thread of control that communicates with other actors by sending messages, and all actor actions are in response to these messages. Specific actor methods are invoked to process each type of message.

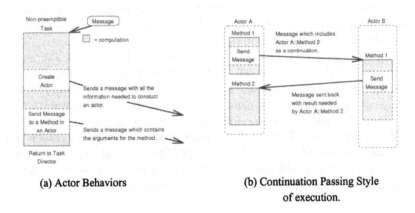

(a) Actor Behaviors

(b) Continuation Passing Style of execution.

Fig. 2. Actor model with continuation passing.

Figure 2(a) shows the three basic actions that an actor method actor can take: create new actors, send messages to actors, and perform computations that change its state. When a method creates an actor, a message is sent to the run time system with all the information needed to construct an actor. When a method sends a message, a message containing the arguments and the identity of the method to be invoked is sent to the runtime system for later execution. Both actor creation and message sends are non-blocking calls. The model only specifies that the actor be created or the task be run sometime in the future. Once a task starts, it runs to completion and cannot be preempted.

The actor model lacks explicit sequencing primitives. Synchronization is implicit and derives from the single-threaded nature of individual actors. The return executed at the completion of an actor method is an implicit wait; the actor automatically becoming available for any pending method invocations. Since an actor cannot suspend execution implicitly in the middle of a computation, *continuation-passing style* (CPS) [9] is used to express control and data dependencies. Figure 2(b) shows an example of continuation passing style. The actor model is a message-driven model in which the method name is in the message and the method is the code invoked upon message reception.

2.2 ProperCAD II interface

Applications created with ProperCAD II use five basic classes provided by the library: `Actor`, `ActorName`, `ActorMethod`, `Continuation`, and `Aggregate`.

All actor types are derived from the library-supplied class, `Actor`. Adding the `Actor` base to a class in a sequential object-oriented program enables the creation of actor methods and continuations as described below. These features allow the expression of parallelism. For example, a user class may be created as follows.

```
class Foo : public Actor { ... };
```

`ActorNames` serve the role of pointers and references for instances of actor classes. Because normal pointers are not valid across processor boundaries, actor names provide the mechanism for access of actors in a global namespace.

```
Foo* actorPtr = ...;
ActorName<Foo> fooName = actorPtr;
```

`ActorMethods` are member functions which may be invoked asynchronously and remotely. They are executed via `Continuations`, the concurrent equivalent of member function pointers. The definition and use of these constructs is shown below.

```
class Foo : public Actor {
  void bar( barArgs& );
  class bar : public ActorMethod<barArgs> {};
}

barArgs &args;
Foo::bar::Continuation cont ( fooName );
cont( args );
```

The Foo actor has a method bar which takes barArgs as an argument. This is easily designated as an actor method by creating a new nested class bar derived from a templated `ActorMethod`. In order to invoke the bar method asynchronously, we simply create a `Continuation` cont bound to a particular `ActorName`. We can now treat cont as member function pointer and execute it directly thereby causing an implicit message send. Since Continuations are first-class, cont may also be passed to another method.

Individual actors express neither internal parallelism nor data distribution. Collection types, based on aggregates, allow both concurrency within the object as well as data distribution. An aggregate is simply a collection of actors which share a common name [10]. An example of an aggregate would be a distributed array where different elements are stored on different actors. The use of aggregate representations removes the serialization step that would be required because of a gateway actor. The Aggregate interface is similar to that of the Actor class, and the creation and use of names and actor methods is accomplished similarly.

```
class FooAggr : public Aggregate { ... };
```

Aggregates provide the necessary mechanisms for distributed data structures. Because of the standard C++ interface, access to these distributed data structures is efficient. The benefit of aggregates is apparent in the following section in the presentation of an example application built using the ProperCAD II library.

3 Example: Standard Cell Placement

The VLSI cell placement problem involves placing a set of cells on a VLSI layout, given a netlist which provides the connectivity between each cell and a library containing layout information for each type of cell. This layout information includes the width and height of the cell and the relative position of each pin. The primary goal of cell placement is to determine the best locations of each cell so as to minimize the total area of the layout and the length of the nets connecting the cells together. Standard cell layouts are organized into equal height rows, and the desired placement should have equal length rows, as shown in Figure 3.

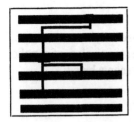

Fig. 4. Wirelength cost function.

Fig. 3. Standard cell placement.

3.1 Serial Algorithm

We have developed the parallel algorithm based on the serial TimberWolfSC program. TimberWolfSC's core algorithm, simulated annealing, is a suitable approach to problems like VLSI cell placement since they lack good heuristic algorithms. Briefly, simulated annealing is an iterative improvement strategy that starts with a system in a disordered state, and through perturbations of the state, brings the system gradually to a low energy, and thus optimal, state. One of the unique features of simulated annealing is that, unlike greedy algorithms, perturbations that increase the energy of the system are sometimes accepted with a probability related to the temperature of the system [11]. In the context of cell placement, and TimberWolfSC in particular, perturbations are simply moves of the cells to different locations on the layout, and the energy is an approximated layout cost function. The major component of the cost function in TimberWolfSC is the sum of all nets bounding box perimeters as an estimate of net wirelength (Figure 4).

In order to understand the use of aggregates in parallelization, some further explanation of the data structures used is necessary. The circuit information is described primarily with the use of three arrays: the list of cells, the list of nets, and finally an array describing row information. Each cell data structure contains positional information as well as a linked list of pins that belong to the cell. Likewise, each net data structure has bounding box information as well as a linked list of pins that belong to the net. The pin data structures are shared by both the cell and net linked lists.

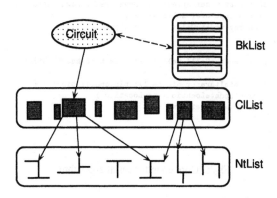

Fig. 5. Relationships between objects.

In an object-oriented framework, these data structures are C++ objects. The cell and net structures are thus placed in Cell and Net C++ classes respectively. Of particular interest are the cell and net arrays, which now become the ClList and NtList C++ objects. A BkList object is used to keep track of row information as well as the bins used for overlap penalty calculation. All the objects are integrated together in an object called Circuit which manages the core annealing algorithm. In addition, the Circuit object also contains many of the global parameters and flags that are relevant during annealing. The relationships between these objects is shown graphically in Figure 5.

The core algorithm is shown in the Circuit::anneal() code fragment in Figure 6. The Circuit object makes requests to the ClList object through the pickACell() method to pick a Cell to move. A new position for the cell is chosen by making a request to the BkList data structure. The Circuit object then asks the ClList to evaluate the delta cost of the move of the chosen `Cell`. If the move is accepted, then the data structures are updated through `updateCell()` which updates each net attached to `Cell`, through the `updatePin()` method.

```
class Circuit {
  ClList &carray;
  NtList &netarray;
  BkList &barray;
  // ...
};

Circuit::anneal()
{
  while ( terminationNotReached() )
    tryCellMove();
  finishUp();
}

Circuit::tryCellMove()
{
  Cell &cell = carray.pickACell();
  newLocation = barray.newLocation();
  deltaCost = carray.evaluateMove( cell, newLocation );
  if ( acceptMove( deltaCost ) )
    carray.updateCell( cell, newLocation );
}

ClList::updateCell( Cell &cell, Position &newLocation )
{
  for ( pinIterator pin(cell); pin.end(); pin++ ) {
    pin->updateLocation( newLocation );
    netarray.updatePin( *pin );
  }
}
```

Fig. 6. Core code for serial algorithm

3.2 Parallel algorithm

Parallelism through inheritance. In order to remain compatible with the arrays in the sequential code, we need arrays with distributed semantics. This is accomplished easily with the use of aggregates. For example, we can simply create a new distributed class, `CellAggr`, that is derived from the `ClList` class as well as the aggregate class, as below.

```
class CellAggr : public ClList, public Aggregate {
  Cell &pickACell();
  // ...
};
```

By doing so, the `CellAggr` class has representative actors on each processor that are responsible for the cells allocated to that particular processor. Thus, a request made to access a particular cell can be made to the local representative actor which will then forward it on to the actor on the thread where the cell is actually present. A similar transformation is done for the net array. In total, there are aggregates for the cells (CellAggr), nets (NetAggr), and rows (BlockAggr), as well as the CktAggr that is derived from Circuit. The dashed line in Figure 7 indicates the separation between two threads. Notice that the individual cells and nets are not replicated.

How does this data distribution affect the code? The main operations performed by the Circuit::anneal() method are the selection of a cell, evaluating the move, deciding whether to accept, and updating the cell. The evaluation and decision phases are independent of location of the cell. Picking a cell should be made only from the local pool of cells. To accomplish this, we make ClList::pickACell() a virtual base function, and rewrite the implementation as shown in Figure 8.

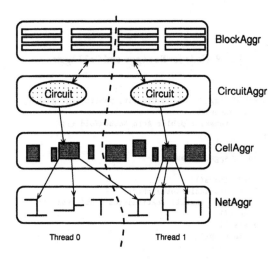

Fig. 7. Relationships between distributed objects.

Likewise, although updating cells is a local operation, the updating of nets can not be performed locally since the adjacent nets are distributed. Therefore, updatePin() is made virtual and rewritten as in Figure 8. We use the continuation invocation mechanism to invoke a remote NetAggr::updatePin(). The invocation of the remote method is asynchronous, so the update is in effect a "lazy" update.

The presence of the updates causes an interesting problem. Since actor methods are run to completion without preemption, if Circuit::anneal() is left as it is, the while loop will run to completion before any update messages can be serviced by the run time system. In order to allow these messages to be received, the while loop must be transformed into message driven code. As seen in Figure 9, through the use of virtual functions again, the anneal() method is modified to try only only one move, and then reenable itself by executing an asynchronous continuation to itself. Similar transformations have been discussed in [12].

```
Cell &CellAggr::pickACell()
{
  Cell cell = ClList::pickACell();
  while ( !isLocalCell( cell ) )
    cell = ClList::pickACell();
}

class NetAggr : public NtList, public Aggregate {
  void updatePin( Pin& );
  class updatePin : public ActorMethod<Pin> {};
};

void NetAggr::updatePin( Pin &p, Position &location )
{
  if ( isLocalNet( p ) {
    NtList::updatePin( p, location );
  } else {
    updatePin::Continuation cont ( ownerOf( p ) );
    cont( p, location );
  }
}
```

Fig. 8. Code for `NetAggr` and `CellAggr`

```
class CktAggr : public Circuit, public Aggregate {
  void anneal();
  class anneal : public ActorMethodVoid {};
};

void CktAggr::anneal()
{
  tryCellMove();
  if ( terminationNotReached() ) {
    CktAggr::anneal::Continuation cont( *this );
    cont();
  } else {
    finishUp();
  }
}
```

Fig. 9. Code for `CktAggr`

Data distribution. The circuit is read in on a single thread, and as each cell and net is read in, the associated data structures are distributed to the other threads. The process of determining which cells are assigned to which processor is done using a prepartitioning phase. There are two primary concerns in our partitioning. First, the load balance must be maintained, i.e. each partition should have roughly the same number of cells. Secondly, the number of nets cut should be minimized to decrease the interaction between partitions. Ratio cut partitioning methods have long been used in the CAD community because of their effectiveness at reducing the cut size. However, these methods are inappropriate for our use because they do not provide well balanced partitions. We have instead used a partitioning algorithm based on the Sanchis modification of the Fiduccia-Mattheyses algorithm [13].

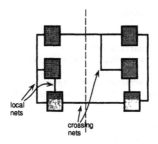

Fig. 10. Crossing nets.

When a request is made to evaluate the cost of a cell move, the connected Net objects may be located on another thread. One option would be for the NetAggr to send a message to the appropriate representative to request a calculation of the cost. The overhead involved in the communication makes this prohibitive. Therefore, copies of these nets that span multiple threads are replicated locally. An example of these "crossing" nets is shown in Figure 10. Consistency is maintained through the updatePin() method.

Dynamic redistribution. The final element of our parallel algorithm is the dynamic redistribution. As the annealing schedule proceeds, the initial partition becomes more and more irrelevant since it corresponds very little to the geographic partitioning of the rows. While the initial partitioning does reduce the amount of communication in terms of pin updates, the fact that the partition is spread across many rows affects the row penalty calculations as well as cell mobility. Therefore, it is reasonable to repartition the cells so that the partition reflects the geographical row-based partition. The repartitioning is started only after the cells have settled within some proximity of their final locations.

In the sample code in Figure 11, CktAggr::anneal() has been modified to execute a continuation to start up the repartition process. The details of the repartitioning are not shown, but is achieved through two phases of message sends which synchronize all the representatives of the aggregates. Notice that the anneal() re-enabling continuation is not executed. After the repartitioning has been completed, the anneal() method can then be re-enabled, and the asynchronous behavior starts again.

Experimental Results. We ran the parallel implementation on a shared memory multiprocessor Sun SparcServer 1000E as well as the Intel Paragon, a distributed memory machine. The speedups and wirelengths for a set of benchmark circuits are shown in Figures 12 and 13. The speedup graphs show an average speedup of 5 on 8 processors on the SparcServer and an average speedup of over 11 on 32 processors on the Paragon. The tables indicate the wirelength cost of the resultant placement relative to the cost from sequential TimberWolfSC. There is moderate (7-10%) degradation of the quality of the placement. The dashed lines on the Paragon results indicate that the circuit could not be run because of excessive memory requirements. These larger circuits (biomed, industry2, avq.large) show the advantage of using a distributed circuit approach to exploit the memory resources on multiple processors. For these larger circuits, the speedups are de-

```
void CktAggr::anneal()
{
  tryCellMove();
  if ( timeToRepartition() ) {
    CellAggr::repartition::Continuation cont( *this );
    cont();
  } else if ( terminationNotReached() ) {
    CktAggr::anneal::Continuation cont( *this );
    cont();
  } else {
    finishUp();
  }
}

void CellAggr::repartition()
{
  // perform repartitioning steps
  // ...
  CktAggr::anneal::Continuation cont( cktName );
  cont();
}
```

Fig. 11. Code for repartitioning

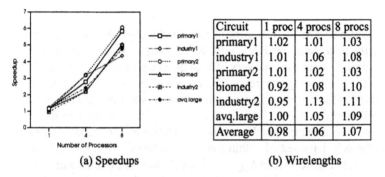

Circuit	1 proc	4 procs	8 procs
primary1	1.02	1.01	1.03
industry1	1.01	1.06	1.08
primary2	1.01	1.02	1.03
biomed	0.92	1.08	1.10
industry2	0.95	1.13	1.11
avq.large	1.00	1.05	1.09
Average	0.98	1.06	1.07

(a) Speedups   (b) Wirelengths

Fig. 12. Results on a Sun SparcServer 1000E (Shared Memory Multiprocessor)

rived from uniprocessor times extrapolated from a SUN4/690MP, a machine with comparable uniprocessor performance.

4 Related work

Several other researchers have produced work in environments to support irregular applications in object oriented environments, such as Charm++ [14], pC++ [15], CC++ [16]. Charm++ provides similar run time support for message driven applications to Proper-CAD II. The primary differences are Charm++'s lack of support for static message typing, as represented by first-class continuations, and composability. pC++ is a language extension of C++ with support for data parallel semantics in much the same manner as HPF [17]. Since it presents a data parallel view of the world, it is difficult to express irregular problems such as VLSI CAD in this framework. CC++ achieves concurrency

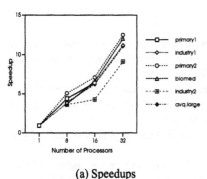

Circuit	1 proc	8 procs	16 procs	32 procs
primary1	1.01	1.00	1.08	[a]
industry1	0.95	1.03	1.13	1.12
primary2	1.00	1.04	1.13	1.09
biomed	-	1.03	1.06	1.07
industry2	-	1.06	1.08	1.13
avq.large	-	1.05	1.05	1.08
Average	0.99	1.04	1.09	1.10

[a] Circuit was not large enough to be effectively partitioned over 32 processors

(a) Speedups   (b) Wirelengths

Fig. 13. Results on an Intel Paragon (Distributed Memory Multicomputer)

through parallel constructs which direct particular code fragments to be performed on different processing threads. This task parallelism approach can mimic many of the features in actor model. However, the ProperCAD II library does provide extra meta programmability features that allow the program designer to change the behavior of the run time system such as queuing policies, memory usage, load balancing, etc.

Other work to support irregular applications but not targeted toward object-oriented environments include Multipol [18] and PARTI/CHAOS [19]. Multipol provides a library of distributed data structures for use with a message driven run time system, based on atomic threads, the functional equivalent of actor methods. PARTI/CHAOS offers irregular run-time support for iterative irregular computation where the communication pattern is unchanged and predictable, but not resolvable at compile time. Neither Multipol or PARTI/CHAOS allow parallelism via derivation as available in ProperCAD II.

5 Conclusions

In this paper, we have presented a methodology for creating parallel programs and distributed data structures through simple inheritance mechanisms present in C++ and the use of the ProperCAD II library. The approach has been used on a wide variety of applications. The distributed data structures presented in this paper for standard cell placement are effectively being reused through object-oriented methodologies for global routing and timing driven placement.

Acknowledgements

Our sincere thanks to Dr. Carl Sechen for providing us with the `TimberWolfSC` 6.0 placement code. We are also grateful to the San Diego Supercomputing Center for providing us access to their Intel Paragon, and also to Intel Corporation for the donation of an Intel Paragon. This research was supported in part by the Semiconductor Research Corporation under contract 95-DP-109 and the Advanced Research Projects Agency under contract DAA-H04-94-G-0273 administered by the Army Research Office.

References

1. S. Parkes, J. A. Chandy, and P. Banerjee, "A library-based approach to portable, parallel, object-oriented programming: Interface, implementation, and application," in *Proceedings of Supercomputing '94*, (Washington, DC), pp. 69–78, Nov. 1994.

2. S. M. Parkes, "A class library approach to concurrent object-oriented programming with applications to VLSI CAD." Ph.D. Dissertation, University of Illinois at Urbana-Champaign, Sept. 1994. Tech. Rep. CRHC-94-20/UILU-ENG-94-2235.

3. P. Banerjee, *Parallel Algorithms for VLSI Computer Aided Design Applications*. Englewoods Cliffs, NJ: Prentice Hall, 1994.

4. S. Parkes, P. Banerjee, and J. H. Patel, "ProperHITEC: A portable, parallel, object–oriented approach to sequential test generation," in *Proceedings of the Design Automation Conference*, (San Diego, CA), pp. 717–721, June 1994.

5. S. Parkes, P. Banerjee, and J. Patel, "A parallel algorithm for fault simulation based on PROOFS," in *Proceedings of the International Conference on Computer Design*, (Austin, TX), Oct. 1995.

6. V. Krishnaswamy and P. Banerjee, "Actor based parallel VHDL simulation using Time Warp," in *Proceedings of the 1996 Workshop on Parallel and Distributed Simulation*, (Philadelphia, PA), May 1996.

7. B. Ramkumar and P. Banerjee, "ProperCAD: A portable object-oriented parallel environment for VLSI CAD," *IEEE Trans. Computer-Aided Design*, vol. 13, pp. 829–842, July 1994.

8. G. A. Agha, *Actors: A Model of Concurrent Computation in Distributed Systems*. Cambridge, MA: The MIT Press, 1986.

9. A. W. Appel, *Compiling with Continuations*. Cambridge, England: Cambridge University Press, 1992.

10. A. A. Chien, *Concurrent Aggregates: Supporting Modularity in Massively Parallel Programs*. Cambridge, MA: The MIT Press, 1993.

11. S. Kirkpatrick, C. D. Gelatt, and M. P. Vecchi, "Optimization by simulated annealing," *Science*, vol. 220, pp. 671–680, May 1983.

12. J. G. Holm, A. Lain, and P. Banerjee, "Compilation of scientific programs into multithreaded and message driven computation," in *Proceedings of the Scalable High Performance Computing Conference*, (Knoxville, TN), pp. 518–525, May 1994.

13. L. A. Sanchis, "Multiple-way network partitioning," *IEEE Trans. Computers*, vol. 38, pp. 62–81, 1989.

14. L. V. Kalé and S. Krishnan, "CHARM++: A portable concurrent object oriented system based on C++," in *Proceedings of OOPSLA '93*, Sept. 1993.

15. D. Gannon and J. K. Lee, "Object-oriented parallelism: pC++ ideas and experiments," *Proc. Japan Society for Parallel Processing*, pp. 315–339, 1993.

16. K. M. Chandy and C. Kesselman, "Compositional C++: Compositional parallel programming," in *Proceedings of Workshop on Compilers and Languages for Parallel Computing*, pp. 79–93, 1992.

17. High Performance Fortran Forum, *High Performance Fortran Language Specification, version 1.1*. Houston, TX, 1994.

18. C.-P. Wen, S. Chakrabarti, E. Deprit, A. Krishnamurthy, and K. Yelick, "Runtime support for portable distributed data structures," in *Workshop on Languages, Compilers and Runtime Systems for Scalable Computers*, May 1995.

19. R. Ponnusamy, J. Saltz, and A. Choudhary, "Runtime-compilation techniques for data partitioning and communication schedule reuse," in *Proceedings of Supercomputing '93*, (Portland, OR), pp. 361–370, Nov. 1993.

Parallel Progressive Radiosity with Adaptive Meshing

Yizhou Yu, Oscar H. Ibarra, Tao Yang

Department of Computer Science, University of California
Santa Barbara, CA 93106, USA

Abstract. Radiosity plays an important role in computer graphics. This paper presents an efficient parallel algorithm for progressive radiosity with adaptive meshing, which adopts a novel static processor assignment strategy and takes advantages of hierarchical computation structure in this problem to minimize communication and balance dynamic load. Our experiments on a Meiko CS-2 distributed memory machine show that this algorithm has achieved good performance for the tested cases.

1 Introduction

The main application of realistic image synthesis in computer graphics is to create simulated scenes of photo realistic quality. Recently radiosity method becomes increasingly popular for determining global illumination in architectural modeling and virtual reality [5, 12] because it accurately portrays illumination effects such as shadows and interreflections in diffuse environments.

An important application requirement is to provide real-time interaction when a user modifies a high-quality synthesized image in a computer aided design process. At the present time, radiosity can be used for such cases but they are too time-consuming to accomplish real-time interaction. A compromise solution to reduce the radiosity time is to use progressive illumination calculation [3, 13]. The basic idea is to conduct a sequence of refinement iterations to improve the image quality. The intermediate result after a few iterations can be used for displaying and a user can revise the design based on this intermediate solution without waiting for the entire computation to end. A further improvement to increase the image quality of radiosity is to incorporate adaptive subdivision [6, 10].

It is important to further reduce the radiosity time since it still takes minutes to see the obvious improvement from one view to another. There have been several parallel algorithms proposed in [1, 2, 9, 11] but speedups for progressive radiosity with adaptive meshing are still low because the computation associated with patches in a 3D space is unstructured and the cost varies during iterations. Furthermore, adaptive refinement of patches may increase the number of patches on some processors dynamically, consequently it worsens the load balance. Thus, load balancing is the main challenge in achieving high speedups [9]. Recent research [2, 9] improves parallel performance by concurrentizing several iterations on different processors. This is called to exploit control parallelism. In this scheme, synchronization is needed when several iterations modify the same patch object and communication overhead is high on distributed memory machines.

In this paper we propose a parallel progressive radiosity algorithm which exploits data parallelism instead of control parallelism. It identifies the hierarchical computational structure in this problem and uses a novel object ordering with static cyclic mapping to achieve load balance and low communication overhead.

2 Progressive Radiosity with Adaptive Meshing

We begin with an overview of the sequential algorithm. The radiosity method assumes that a 3D space contains a set of surfaces, which are perfectly diffuse, i.e. they reflect light with equal radiance in all directions. To get discrete numerical solutions, each surface is further subdivided into a set of patches and this process is called *meshing*. Radiosity is assumed to be constant on each patch and we need to derive this value in order to generate a realistic image. The patch radiosities satisfy the well-known radiosity equation, valid for each sample wavelength:

$$B_i = E_i + \rho_i \sum_{j=1}^{N} F_{ji} B_j \ . \tag{1}$$

The constants and unknown variables are:

- N is the number of patches after meshing.
- B_i is the radiosity(emittance per unit area) of patch i (radiosity) to be solved in the radiosity process.
- E_i is the given self-emitted radiosity of patch i. If $E_i > 0$, patch i is usually called a light source.
- ρ_i is the given reflectivity of patch i.
- F_{ji} is the constant form-factor which is fraction of light flux leaving patch i that arrives at patch j.

This system of simultaneous equations represents the equilibrium energy interchange via multiple interreflections and emissions in the environment.

2.1 Progressive Radiosity

Directly solving (1) is too costly for large N. Progressive radiosity [3] is a kind of iterative method to solve 1. The algorithm is given in Fig. 1. At each iteration, the patch with maximum unshot light flux is chosen to shoot its energy. All patches will receive some part of this flux and update their radiosity values. After each iteration the accuracy of the radiosity for each patch increases, and the partial result can be displayed after several iterations. The complexity of the form-factor calculation is distributed among these iterations and the partial result can be displayed sooner than the Gauss-Seidel based method. Also the computation associated with dark patches with low shooting energy is delayed because they do not contribute light energy significantly in the 3D space.

2.2 Adaptive Meshing

In the first paragraph of Sect. 2, we have assumed that each patch has a constant radiosity. That is actually not true for each patch with a large area. To achieve a good accuracy, adaptive meshing was integrated with radiosity in [4, 6, 10, 15]. In this approach, each patch derived from the initial subdivision (meshing) might be further refined during the course of the computation if the accuracy

```
real Fᵢ[N];        /*Columns of form-factors */
typedef real spectrum[# of wavelengths]; /*RGB tristimuli are usually used.*/
spectrum ΔRad, ΔB[N];
spectrum B[N];        /*Array of radiosities*/
for all patches do        /*Initialization loop*/
   ΔB[i] ≝ Eᵢ;   /*Delta radiosity= self-emittance*/
   B[i] ≝ Eᵢ;
/*The following is the iterative resolution process.*/
while no convergence() do    ·/*Emission loop*/
   i=patch-of-max-flux();
   compute form-factors Fᵢ[j];    /*Form-factor loop*/
   for all patches j do{        /*Update loop*/
      ΔRad ≝ ρⱼΔB[i] × Fᵢ[j]Aⱼ/Aᵢ;
      ΔB[j] ≝ ΔB[j] + ΔRad;
      B[j] ≝ B[j] + ΔRad;
   }        /*End of update loop*/
   ΔB[i] ≝ 0.0;
}        /*End of emission loop*/
```

Fig. 1. The progressive radiosity method where symbols, $\stackrel{v}{=}$, $\stackrel{v}{\times}$ and $\stackrel{v}{+}$, indicate that the operations are applied on vectors.

of each patch radiosity does not meet the standard. There are various criteria for such adaptive meshing. We use the following method which performs well on parametric domain of curved or planar surfaces:

- 1) We first subdivide each surface into a triangular mesh. Only patches produced in this initial meshing are called *superpatches*. Each superpatch may be further adaptively subdivided into smaller patches during iterations using the method described in 2). But the *shooting* patch in progressive radiosity with adaptive meshing is always a *superpatch*.
- 2) In each iteration, for each triangular patch in the current mesh as shown in Fig. 2, we compute the radiosity received from the current shooting patch at four points A, B, C and D which are centers of four smaller triangles obtained by connecting the midpoints of the edges of the larger one.
  Then we obtain the linearly interpolated radiosity at D from the radiosities at A, B and C, and compare it with the previously computed radiosity at D. If the difference is larger than a threshold, subdivide this triangle into smaller ones. Otherwise, test linearity at some sample points on AB, BC and CA. If it is nonlinear for any of them, subdivide this triangular patch. We apply the above process recursively on each newly generated patches.

2.3 Form-factor Calculation

We discuss how each form-factor is computed for the above sequential algorithm. Recall the analytic expression for form-factors:

$$F_{ij} = \frac{1}{\pi A_i} \int_{A_i} \int_{A_j} \frac{cos\theta_i cos\theta_j}{r^2} VIS(P_i, P_j) dA_i dA_j \qquad (2)$$

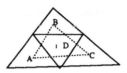

Fig.2. Subdivision within a triangular patch. **Fig.3.** Form-factor from an area to a differential area.

where the cosine functions and visibility testing, $VIS(P_i, P_j)$, are very expensive to evaluate. That is why form-factor calculation is the main concern in radiosity algorithms.

Given area A_1 in the receiving patch and A_2 in the shooting patch, as shown in Fig. 3, [13] proposed a disk formula for approximating the analytic expression for form-factor from area A_2 to a differential area dA_1 on area A_1. The resulting numerical formula for radiosity at dA_1 due to illumination by A_2 is

$$B_1 = \rho_1 B_2 A_2 \frac{1}{l} \sum_{i=1}^{l} \delta_i \frac{cos\theta_{1i} cos\theta_{2i}}{\pi r_i^2 + A_2/l} \tag{3}$$

where l is the number of sample points on A_2 and δ_i expresses the visibility of each sample point from dA_1.

We adopt this formula because it is desirable to obtain the radiosity at some sample point with a known normal on a curved patch rather than the radiosity received by the whole patch. In our algorithm, the radiosity of each triangular patch is approximated by the radiosity at its center. Thus, in the progressive radiosity algorithm, the first statement inside the innermost *for* loop should be modified to: ΔRad= the radiosity received by the center of patch j from patch i obtained by using (3).

3   A Parallel Solution

Our approach is to follow the sequential algorithm semantics, exploit irregular data parallelism instead of control parallelism and provide a carefully designed processor assignment strategy. It parallelizes the *for* loop in the algorithm of Fig. 1. The calculation for each patch needs all surface information but does not need knowledge about patches on other processors.

3.1   Initialization and Data Distribution

At the beginning, the albedo and geometrical information of all surfaces making up the objects in a scene are replicated to all processors. After each processor computes the bounding box for each surface, it sets up an octree-based space partition which will be used in the data distribution and form-factor calculation. Then each processor subdivides each surface into a number of large triangular superpatches of approximately the same size and orders all superpatches used for the processor assignment. Notice that the result of this partitioning process is used for the rest of the iterations, and it only takes a couple of seconds. There is no need to parallelize this process.

In the superpatch distribution stage, our algorithm distributes superpatches cyclically on the given p processors based on their ordering numbers. We will discuss the superpatch ordering and distribution strategy in Sect. 4. Now we have two *hierarchies* of data. The upper level contains the octree partition and geometrical information about all surfaces. The lower level contains radiosity and geometrical information on all patches. After data distribution, each processor only owns a subset of superpatches and it keeps a copy of all upper level information to reduce *communication* arising from data dependency in form-factor calculation. Duplicating the data in upper level has little impact on memory requirement. This is because usually we have several hundred of surfaces in a scene but the number of patches after the initial and adaptive meshing is very large.

3.2 Iterative Radiosity Computation

At the beginning of each iteration, each processor picks up the superpatch with the maximum unshot light flux in its own dataset. Then a global MAX reduction operation which costs about $O(\log p)$ is conducted to select the superpatch with the global maximum unshot light flux. Then each processor only works on its own patches to receive radiosity from the shooting patch. It may subdivide a patch into smaller ones by using the adaptive meshing technique discussed in Sect. 2.2. At the end of each iteration, a barrier is called to synchronize the processors and start the next iteration. To increase granularity, we can shoot more than one superpatch at each iteration.

We discuss a *hierarchical* strategy in reducing the computation cost associated with radiosity calculation in a patch subdivision using adaptive meshing. By observation, we find that the lightness of objects in a scene is contributed mainly by a small number of light sources. After they finish shooting, the changes of lightness in this environment are not substantial. On the other hand, the existence of these light sources causes the adaptive subdivision of other patches. But the resulting fine mesh is only useful when these sources possess a large amount of unshot flux. After shooting from bright light sources completes, coarser patch subdivision may be enough because the dark light sources do not lead to significant changes of radiosity values in destination patches. Thus we maintain the hierarchical structure of subdivision. When a shooting patch is selected, we start to compute the impact of this shooting patch on radiosities of a set of patches represented hierarchically in a top-down fashion. We first start from the superpatch and apply the procedure to its child nodes recursively. When the computation at an internal node x shows that the radiosity distribution for subtree nodes rooted at x is smooth enough, the computation can stop at this point.

This hierarchical computing strategy can eliminate the amount of computation substantially because many iterations involve shooting patches with small unshot energies. It also improves the *load balance* because given a set of superpatches after initial meshing, uneven run-time subdivision of each superpatch is the major reason causing load imbalance. The hierarchical computing method eliminates unnecessary computation in a superpatch with a large subdivision tree, and thus smoothes cost difference between different patch subdivision trees. We will show the effectiveness of this hierarchical strategy in our experiments.

3.3 Form-factor Calculation

It is indicated in [2] that the form-factor calculation and the radiosity update require an access to the information regarding *all* patches. That is actually not necessary. One good method for the form-factor calculation is discussed in [13] and reviewed in Sect. 2.3.

We only need the radiosity and geometrical information of the shooting patch, the albedo and geometrical information of the receiving patches and occluding information implied in the octree space partition. Thus each processor only accesses local patch information and the replicated surface data. No interprocessor communication is needed during the form-factor calculation. For the method discussed in Sect. 2.3, visibility test only uses surface geometry. It is done by casting rays from the current receiving patch to some sample points on the shooting patch. This process can be significantly accelerated by using the octree space partition [8]. To accelerate form-factor calculation, we can also fit a coarser mesh for the shooting patch by combining some of the tiny patches. And a larger patch takes the average radiosity of the smaller ones.

4 Processor Assignment for Patches

Our goal is to distribute the amount of dynamic computation evenly among all processors. Since the amount of computation differs for different patches, it is not sufficient to only make each processor have an equal number of patches. The problem of partitioning irregular data space has been studied in other scientific application areas, for example n-body simulations [7]. Usually the quadtree(octree) partitioning method is used and neighboring leafs are directly mapped to the same processor. This mapping may not be effective for our problem, which will be justified in our performance analysis.

Dynamic load balancing that migrates patches between processors looks reasonable. But in practice it suffers high communication overhead on a distributed memory machine. We will use a static assignment for all superpatches to avoid patch migration overhead: each superpatch and its possible child patches generated during adaptive meshing are assigned to the same processor. The *key idea* is to identify superpatches with similar cost involved in adaptive meshing and distribute these superpatches evenly among different processors.

We study the computation requirement associated with each super or non-super patch. At each iteration, most of the computation is spent on the numerical integration for form-factor calculation (Equation (3)), whose complexity depends on many factors, such as the distance between the shooting and receiving patches, the relative orientation of the patches. The following are some facts that we need to exploit in the design of processor assignment to achieve load balance.

- **F1:** Adjacent patches on the same surface have similar orientation because a surface is usually represented by a continuous mathematical function which has continuous normals;
- **F2:** Patches close to each other have approximately the same distance to the shooting patch;
- **F3:** Most subdivision happens at shadow boundaries. If a patch contains a shadow boundary, another patch nearby is also likely to contain a shadow boundary since shadow boundaries are continuous curves. So both these patches are likely to be subdivided into many smaller patches.

Based on these facts, in addition to make processors have the approximately equal number of superpatches, we propose the following strategies for processor mapping.

- **S1:** Adjacent superpatches on the same surface should be distributed to different processors. This will not incur additional communication because adjacent patches have no extra dependence on each other.
- **S2:** Superpatches in different surfaces close to each other should be distributed to different processors based on F2. This heuristic will be applied after S1 because S2 has less constraints.

Since all surfaces are distributed irregularly in a 3D space, there is no obvious ordering between them. To achieve the goal of S1 and S2, we derive a linear order for all superpatches, and then cyclically distribute superpatches to processors based on this order.

4.1 Ordering of Superpatches within the Same Surface

Each surface is assumed to be bivariate and its parametric domain is a square. A triangular superpatch is always subdivided into two smaller ones at its longest edge during the initial meshing. The ordering of superpatches within a surface is defined recursively during initial meshing using the following three rules:

1. Initially a surface is subdivided into four superpatches. Their ordering is clockwise as depicted in Fig. 4(a).
2. If a superpatch is subdivided, the two newly generated superpatches should be inserted into the ordering at the position occupied by the original superpatch. So if superpatch 2 in Fig. 4(a) is subdivided, the ordering is shown in Fig. 4(b).
3. Given the ordering for the current mesh, there exists a route traversing all superpatches following the ordering. As the directed cycle shown in Fig. 4(a), each superpatch has an entry and an exit edge. An entry edge is the one where the route enters the superpatch. An exit edge is the one where the route leaves the superpatch. If a superpatch in the current mesh is subdivided, the relative order of the two new superpatches is defined as follows.
   (a) If the subdivision happens at the entry edge, the new ordering is shown in Fig. 5(a); **(b)** If the subdivision happens at the exit edge, the new ordering is shown in Fig. 5(b); **(c)** If the subdivision happens at the third edge, the new ordering is shown in Fig. 5(c).

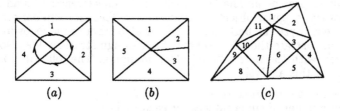

Fig. 4. Ordering after subdivision.

Example:. The ordering for a surface using the above rule is shown in Fig. 4(c). The superpatches on a surface generally have irregular pattern and there is no way to distribute them row-wise or column-wise.

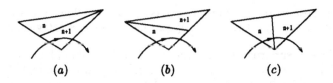

(a) (b) (c)

Fig. 5. Ordering during subdivision.

It can be shown that a continuous route traversing all superpatches following the above ordering always exists after each subdivision. We can see that two consecutive superpatches in the ordering must be adjacent to each other because they share a common edge. This is important because it is most likely that two adjacent superpatches share the same properties, such as there is one shadow boundary on both of them. However, since we are trying to fit a linear ordering onto a 2D or 3D space, we can not guarantee any two adjacent superpatches will be close to each other in the ordering. But this ordering scheme surely can increase this kind of possibility. Another property is that the superpatches within the same larger superpatch are close to each other in the ordering. This means that these superpatches in the same local region, which share the same local properties, are likely to be distributed to different processors.

4.2 Ordering of Superpatches on Different Surfaces

Now we can define the ordering for superpatches on all surfaces using the same octree partition mentioned in Sect. 3.3.

1. Traverse the octree recursively. If a leaf node L_1 is met before L_2, all superpatches on surfaces intersecting L_1 are ordered before those on surfaces intersecting L_2. If a surface intersects more than one leaf, it is only considered the first time it is encountered.
2. If more than one surfaces intersect the same leaf node, they are ordered randomly. But if one surface S_1 is put before S_2, all superpatches on S_1 are also before those on S_2 in the ordering.

4.3 Performance Analysis

It is difficult to provide an analytic result on the effectiveness of load balancing for an arbitrary irregular object distribution in a 3D space and our strategy is a heuristic. We analyze the performance of our algorithm in the following two scenarios to demonstrate the effectiveness of our design strategy. We also compare our approach with the octree-based block mapping. The following parameters will be used in this analysis.

- p is the number of processors.
- T is the number of superpatches for each surface.
- n is the total number of sample points used for all numerical integrations using (3) for a receiving superpatch in one iteration.
- E is the average cost for each sample point when (3) is evaluated.
- γ is the ratio of the number of radiosity updates and patch subdivisions over the total number of sample points for numerical integrations. So $\gamma \ll 1$.
- C is the maximum amount of time needed for each radiosity update or patch subdivision. It is less expensive than each form-factor calculation.

Scenario 1: Loosely distributed light source-pairs. Suppose there are m pairs of flat object surfaces $\{S_1, S_1', S_2, S_2', \cdots, S_m, S_m'\}$ as shown in Fig. 6. These surfaces are exactly the same except for their spatial positions and orientations. The two surfaces in the same pair are placed face-to-face very close to each other.

Each surface is subdivided into the same number (T) of superpatches. We assume that $p << m$ and if the shooting superpatch and the receiving superpatch are on the same pair but different surfaces, we need at least n_2 sample points for the numerical integrations to achieve the desired accuracy. We also assume that the surface pairs are placed far away from each other so that if the shooting patch and the receiving patch are on different pairs, we need at most n_1 sample points for numerical integrations. Notice that $n_1 << n_2$.

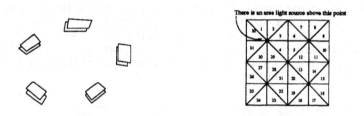

Fig.6. Surface configuration in Scenario 1 **Fig.7.** An example of surface configuration
when $m = 5$.   for Scenario 2.

For one iteration, let the shooting patch be on S_j. By (3), the sequential time for form-factor calculation in one iteration is $Seq_{form} = En_2T + En_1(2m - 2)T$. where the first term is for those superpatches on S_j' and the second term is for those receiving superpatches on other surface pairs.

The sequential time for radiosity updates and patch subdivisions at each iteration is about $\quad Seq_{other} = 2C\gamma n_2 T + 2C\gamma n_1 T(2m - 2)$.

When our method is used, we let α be the cost of communication for each iteration. Then the parallel time for each iteration is approximately equal to

$$Par = (E + 2C\gamma)n_2\frac{T}{p} + (E + 2C\gamma)n_1\frac{(2m - 2)T}{p} + \alpha.$$

So the speedup of K iterations is

$$\frac{Seq_{form} + Seq_{other}}{Par} = \frac{K((E + 2C\gamma)n_2T + (E + 2C\gamma)n_1(2m - 2)T)}{K((E + 2C\gamma)n_2\frac{T}{p} + (E + 2C\gamma)n_1\frac{(2m-2)T}{p} + \alpha)} \approx p$$

if the cost of communication (α) is relatively low. Our experiments show that the communication overhead is small.

If we use octree-based block mapping, then superpatches on the same light source pair are assigned to the same processor. Each processor has $\frac{m}{p}$ pairs of surfaces. At each iteration, the processor in which the shooting patch is selected will have the heaviest CPU load which is $(E+2C\gamma)n_2T+(E+2C\gamma)n_1(\frac{2m}{p} - 2)T$.

Since $n_1 << n_2$ and $p << m$, the speedup is at most

$$\frac{K((E + 2C\gamma)n_2T + (E + 2C\gamma)n_1(2m - 2)T)}{K((E + 2C\gamma)n_2T + (E + 2C\gamma)n_1(\frac{2m}{p} - 2)T + \alpha)} \leq \frac{n_2T + n_1(2m - 2)T}{n_2T + n_1(\frac{2m}{p} - 2)T} \leq \frac{2}{3} + \frac{2}{3}p.$$

Scenario 2: Single light source above a planar surface. The second case has one planar surface. There is a small area light source hanging above the center of the upper left quarter of the planar surface and the position of this light source is very close to that surface. One example is shown is Fig. 7. Based on an analysis [14] similar to that for Scenario 1, we can show our method can reach near optimal speedup(p) while the speedup of octree-based block mapping is much less than p. So our method can balance the load and outperform the octree-based block mapping.

5 Experimental Results

We implemented the parallel radiosity algorithm presented in the previous two sections on a Meiko CS-2 distributed memory machine. Each Meiko node is SUN Sparc Viking with a peak performance 40MFLOP per second and nodes are connected by a fat-tree like fast network with a peak bandwidth 40MB per second. An octree is set up on each processor for data distribution and the acceleration of ray-object intersection.

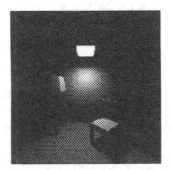 

Fig. 8. The left is a room with a lamp, chair and window. The right is a room with tables, stools and some other objects.

We tested our algorithm on three indoor scenes. Two scenes are shown in Fig. 8. The number of surfaces in each scene is between 200 and 300. The number of superpatches after the initial meshing for each scene is around 10,000. 400 iterations were executed for each scene, which is reasonable for interactive design. The sequential time for each scene is about 3 hours.

Scalability. The parallel time speedup for each test scene is shown in Fig. 9. This result is comparable to the recent results for progressive radiosity[2] *without* adaptive meshing, and is much better than previous results for both adaptive and non-adaptive progressive radiosity[9]. Due to the difficulties arising from adaptive meshing, the above experimental result shows that our algorithm deals with irregular and adaptive load variation very well.

Distribution of computation time, idle time and communication overhead. We will show that the load among processors is approximately the same during the radiosity computation. We measure the CPU time used for arithmetic computation for each processor and we call it workload. The workload distribution on 16 processors for 400 iterations in processing the first scene is shown in Table 1. It can be seen that our algorithm has achieved a good load balance. The workload distribution for other scenes is similar.

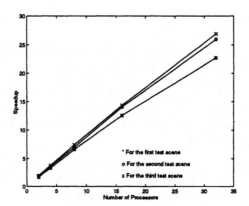

Fig. 9. Speedup for three test scenes.

Table 1. Workload distribution on 16 processors for the first scene.

Proc. ID	1	2	3	4	5	6	7	8
Workload	1314	1308	1303	1332	1313	1509	1286	1334
Proc. ID	9	10	11	12	13	14	15	16
Workload	1577	1291	1303	1259	1572	1301	1659	1314

We have not reached the perfect speedup when $p = 32$ because we lose some performance due to communication overhead and some processor idles caused by small load imbalance. Table 2 lists the average time among all processors spent on communication and the standard deviation of total amount of workload on 32 processors. The communication cost is extremely low, used for selecting the shooting patch and broadcasting the data for the shooting patch. The load imbalance factor is within 10%. That is probably the best we can achieve for a static assignment in responding to the dynamically-changing workload. The previous work [9] using dynamic balancing does not have a good speedup because of high communication overhead.

Table 2. Cost of communication and standard deviation of workload.

	Scene 1	Scene 2	Scene 3
Communication	0.87%	1.21%	1.65%
SDev. of workload	9.94%	7.40%	9.78%

Effectiveness of the hierarchical calculation strategy. We have examined the impact of our hierarchical calculation method which is discussed in Sect. 3.2. In the following, we list the improvement ratio $\left(\frac{Speedup_{with}}{Speedup_{without}} - 1\right)$ when p=32. Here $Speedup_{without}$ is the speedup without using this strategy and $Speedup_{with}$ is the speedup using our method. The improvement is around 22% for scene 1, 16% for scene 2, and 24% for scene 3. That is another reason we can obtain a much better performance compared to [9].

6 Conclusions

We presented an efficient parallel progressive radiosity algorithm with adaptive patch refinement using a hierarchical computing and octree-based cyclic mapping scheme. This algorithm can significantly reduce the time in generating high-quality realistic images for real-time interaction. Our parallel algorithm efficiently exploits irregular and adaptive data parallelism using a carefully designed object assignment method. Our experiments show that it has low communication cost and promising scalability.

Acknowledgments This work was supported in part by a grant from the UCSB committee on research, NSF grants CCR89-18409 and CCR-9409695. We thank the anonymous referees for their valuable comments.

References

1. Baum, D., Winget, J.: Real Time Radiosity Through Parallel Processing and Hardware Acceleration. Computer Graphics **24**(1990), No.2, 67–75.
2. Bouatouch, K., Priol, T.: Data Management Scheme for Parallel Radiosity. Computer-Aided Design **26** (1994) 876–882.
3. Cohen, M., Chen, S., et al.: A Progressive Refinement Approach to Fast Radiosity Image Generation. Computer Graphics **22**(1988), No.4, 75–84.
4. Hanrahan, P., Salzman, D., Aupperle, L.: A Rapid Hierarchical Radiosity Algorithm. Computer Graphics **25**(1991), No.4, 197–206.
5. Kawai, J., Painter, J., Cohen, M.: Radioptimization–Goal Based Rendering. Proceedings of SIGGRAPH'93, 147–154.
6. Lischinski, D., Tampieri, F., Greenberg, D.: Discontinuity Meshing for Accurate Radiosity. IEEE CG&A **12**(1992), No.6, 25–39.
7. Liu, P., Bhatt, S.: Experiences with parallel N-body simulation. Proceedings of 6th Annual ACM Symposium on Parallel Algorithms and Architectures(1994) 122-131.
8. MacDonald, J., Booth, K.: Heuristics for ray tracing using space subdivision. the Visual Computer **6** (1990) 153–166.
9. Paddon, D., Chalmers, A.: Parallel processing of the radiosity method. Computer-Aided Design **26** (1994) 917-927.
10. Paulin, M., Jessel, J.: Adaptive mesh generation for progressive radiosity: A ray-tracing based algorithm. Proceedings of Eurographics'94, C421-C432.
11. Recker, R., George, D., Greenberg, D.: Acceleration Techniques for Progressive Refinement Radiosity. Computer Graphics **24**(1990), No.2, 59-66.
12. Schoeneman, C., Dorsey, J., Smits, B., Arvo, J., Greenberg, D.: Painting with Light. Proceedings of SIGGRAPH'93, 143-146.
13. Wallace, J., Elmquist, K., Haines, E.: A Ray Tracing Algorithm for Progressive Radiosity. Computer Graphics **23**(1989), No.3, 315-324.
14. Yu, Y., Ibarra, O., Yang, T.: Parallel Progressive Radiosity with Adaptive Meshing. UCSB Computer Science Technical Report(1996).
15. Yu, Y., Peng, Q.: Multiresolution B-spline Radiosity. Proceedings of Eurographics'95, C285-C298.

Lineal Feature Extraction by Parallel Stick Growing

Galen C. Hunt * and Randal C. Nelson **

Department of Computer Science
University of Rochester, Rochester, NY 14627, USA

{gchunt,nelson}@@cs.rochester.edu

Abstract. Finding lineal features in an image is an important step in many object recognition and scene analysis procedures. Previous feature extraction algorithms exhibit poor parallel performance because features often extend across large areas of the data set. This paper describes a parallel method for extracting lineal features based on an earlier sequential algorithm, stick growing. The new method produces results qualitatively similar to the sequential method.

Experimental results show a significant parallel processing speed-up attributable to three key features of the method: a large numbers of lock preemptible search jobs, a random priority assignment to source search regions, and an aggressive deadlock detection and resolution algorithm. This paper also describes a portable generalized thread model. The model supports a light-weight job abstraction that greatly simplifies parallel vision programming.

1 Introduction

Finding lineal features in an image is an important step in many object recognition and scene analysis procedures. It is also a time-consuming one. Even with modern workstations, finding all of the lines in a single image can take on the order of tens of seconds. Given the need for speed, lineal feature extraction is an obvious candidate for parallel processing. However, unlike many image processing operations, such as convolution, and more general local area operations such as relaxation and morphological transforms, higher level feature extraction computations do not have a regular structure that can be easily exploited by automatic parallelization techniques. Extended feature detection operations in general, and lineal feature extraction algorithms in particular tend to make disproportionate access to image data elements in the features (e.g., along the lines). It is difficult to predict the computational pattern in advance because feature locations are known only after the computation has finished. Extended feature extraction processes in vision represent an important class of irregularly structured problems for which efficient parallel algorithms are needed.

We present here a parallel method for lineal feature extraction suitable for coarse-grain implementation. The method is a parallel adaptation of the line-segment finding procedure described in [10]. Although we implement an algorithm for the extraction of a specific kind of extended feature (line segments), we think that the general parallel

---

* Galen Hunt was supported by a research fellowship from Microsoft Corporation.
** Randal Nelson was supported in part by ONR grant number N00014-93-I-0221.

approach can be applied to a wide variety of extended feature extraction processes. In particular, the original serial algorithm has been since modified to extract curvilinear boundaries. Carrying over the parallel implementation in this case is trivial.

The layout of the paper is as follows. The remainder of this section gives a brief introduction to lineal-feature extraction methods and previous parallel work. Section 2 briefly describes Nelson's stick-growing method for segment extraction. Section 3 describes our programming model and the parallel stick growing method. In Section 4 we present experimental results demonstrating the strong scalability of the new method. Concluding remarks and future work can be found in Section 5.

1.1 Lineal Feature Extraction

There have been several approaches to extracting lineal primitives. The most widely used involves edgel linking and segmentation. The basic idea is to find local edge pixels using some low-level process, link them into contours on the basis of proximity and orientation, and then segment the contours into relatively straight pieces, again using any of several processes. The classic example of this approach is the Nevatia Babu line detector [11]. Other examples include work by Zhou et al. [15] and Nalwa and Pauchon [9]. Difficulties with the linking approach are basically due to its locality, and include unreliability of the low-level edge finder, instability of segmentation in the presence of bumps or many low-level edges, and difficulty hooking up long features if the data are sparse. Some of these problems can be ameliorated using multi-resolution representations e.g., [4], and grouping techniques [7].

A second method of line detection is based on the Hough transform [2]. Here local edges vote for all possible lines they are consistent with, and the votes are tallied up later to determine what lines are actually present. The main problems with this approach are complexity, coarse resolution, and lack of locality. The method is also expensive to implement, particularly if high resolution is desired, because every edgel must vote for all the lines it is consistent with. This problem is sometimes addressed in a post-processing, verification phase. The method also has trouble finding short segments in busy images. Princen et al. [13] address some of these problems using a hierarchical grouping process in conjunction with a local Hough transform.

A third method of lineal feature detection due to Burns et al. [1] utilizes the gradient direction to partition the image into a set of support regions, each of which will presumably be associated with a single feature. A least-squares fitting procedure is then used to fit a line segment to each region. This method can detect low-contrast features, but the segmentation can be unstable. Also features can rather easily be broken up by local perturbations.

Finally, there are statistical approaches. For example, Mansouri et al. [8] propose a hypothesize and test algorithm to find line segments of a given length by hypothesizing their existence based on local information, and attempting to verify that hypothesis statistically on the basis of a digital model of an ideal segment edge.

The method we implement here, is closest to the linking approaches, but uses a growth rule based upon a non-linear energy minimization scheme over a broad region of support in order to avoid the locality problems of traditional linking methods.

1.2 Previous Parallel Work

Our parallel method is significant because we parallelize an irregular algorithm with robust extraction capabilities. Prior works have parallelized regular algorithms with limited extraction capabilities.

Little [6] describes a feature extraction implementation on the massively parallel Connection Machine with 64K processors. Each pixel in the image is assigned to a separate virtual processor. Edgel detection is performed by convolving the image with a Gaussian operator. Each pixel is linked with any existing neighboring pixel. The pixels in a contour are labeled by an iterative distance-doubling algorithm. Each processor is assigned a fixed unique integer identifier. At every step of the algorithm each processor exchanges with its linked neighbors the maximum identifier known to belong to the contour. Little's algorithm provides edgel detection and linking, but does not segment contours into extended features.

Lin et al. [5] describe a parallel algorithm in which each processor performs a variant of the Nevatia-Babu [11] algorithm on a small region of the image. If the pixels of a contour cross a region boundary, the lines from each region are joined using a linear approximation algorithm credited to Williams [14]. They report a weighted speedup of 78 using 4096 processors on a MasPar MP-2 and a speedup of 307 on a 512 processor CM-5 [12].

Gerogiannus and Orphanoudakis [3] describe a parallel implementation of the Hough transform [2]. The image is broken into discrete regions with each region assigned to a processor. Each processor calculates the votes by the edges within its region for lines in the Hough space. The votes are then summed across processors. Using an iPCS/2, they report speedups of 4 for 64 processors. An implementation of the Hough transform using lock-free increment instructions for voting could achieve significantly higher speedup.

2 Stick Growing

Our parallel algorithm is based on a sequential line finding procedure described in [10]. The essence of the method is to define a metric that assigns a score to any possible line segment, based on the underlying image data, and repeatedly extract the best segment from the image. The practical problems are first, to design an appropriate matching measure, and second, to make the method efficient since it is clearly impractical to look through all possible segments multiple times. The efficiency problem can potentially be dealt with using any of several approximate maximization techniques. In this case, the problem is well enough behaved that a hill climbing method is effective.

The issue of designing a matching criterion for mapping lineal features to line segments is a bit subtle. The main difficulty is that, while a line segment is well defined mathematically, the notion of a lineal feature is a subjective one and must be dealt with as such. Intuitively, a lineal feature consists of a straight part, and two ends. Hence we define a matching criterion that includes explicit representations for the straight section of the feature, and the end stops. These end stops turn out to be extremely important in achieving good performance. We call the combined representation a *stick*.

The matching criterion is applied to the image as follows. The gradient magnitude and direction are determined by local convolution operators. To compute the match-score for a particular stick, the magnitude image is correlated with three templates at the appropriate positions and orientations. One of these represents a straight segment, the other two end stop patterns. The straight segment is a Gaussian whose central profile has been linearly extended, and the end stop patterns are differences of Gaussians with centers separated by two standard deviations. The correlation is computed using only points whose gradient direction is consistent with the direction of the segment. The match score is computed by adding the straight correlation value to any positive response from the end stop measures. Negative values from the end-stop templates are set to zero. This non-linearity prevents a sudden brightening in the line from inhibiting the growth of a stick.

Sticks are fitted to lineal features by first finding a high-gradient starting point. These starting points are edgels, determined by applying non-maximum suppression in the direction of the gradient. Starting with a short initial stick aligned perpendicular to the local gradient and centered at the starting point, a hill climbing procedure is performed, varying the centerpoint, length, and orientation of the stick incrementally to maximize the match score.

A few additional practical details are involved. Since it is inefficient to compute the entire straight correlation at each step for longer sticks, the full match value is computed only for sticks up to a certain length (about 14 pixels in the current implementation). This constitutes a seed segment. Beyond that point, the effect of extension at both ends is explored by probing out from a base point (initially the center point of the seed) with extension templates with a restriction that the orientation can change only slightly from that of the seed. Should extension be indicated, then a new basepoint is selected from among the three adjacent pixels that would increase the length of the stick by finding the best match among the nine permitted basepoint/angle combinations. When a local maximum is finally reached, if the final stick has a length exceeding a selected threshold, the points contributing to the final score are marked, and eliminated from contributing to other segment scores.

In order to find multiple segments, the image is broken up into neighborhoods, and sticks are grown starting at the top N locations in each neighborhood. A new starting location is not selected until completion of the growth phase of the previous stick, since some previously attractive start locations may be subsumed by the new feature. A stick can grow out of its original neighborhood, which can have the effect of eliminating some start-point candidates in others it passes through.

In summary, the stick growing algorithm operates as follows:

1. Preprocess image and extract gradients and local edge points.
2. Break image into small 32x32 pixel regions.
3. For each region:
    (a) Find edgel point with highest gradient.
    (b) Grow segment up to 14 pixels long perpendicular to gradient using template matching.
    (c) If segment is longer than 14 pixels, try to grow the tips as follows:
        i. Start each tip as one half of the segment.

      ii. Perform template match (nonlinear) for possible tip extensions.

     iii. As long as extensions correlate at least as well as original line segment extend the tip.

(d) Record the line segment (stick), erase gradient and edge pixels used in stick construction and look for another segment in the same region.

3 Parallel Stick Growing

Creating a good parallel algorithm requires a sound programming model and a clear insight into where potential parallelizations exist within a program. In this section we describe first, the programming model used for creating our parallel stick growing method. We then describe the parallelization possible within stick growing and our methods for exploiting it.

3.1 Programming Model

Our parallel stick growing method uses a generalized thread model (GTM). GTM abstracts a shared-memory system providing the creation and destruction of parallel threads and re-entrant mutexes. GTM is implemented as a small set of abstract C++ classes defining a system, threads and mutexes. Concrete classes for each operating system inherit and expand these abstract classes. GTM implementations exist for Sun Solaris, SGI IRIX, Digital Unix (OSF/1) and the Win32 API (Windows 95 and Windows NT). Porting GTM to a new system requires modifying only a single file which is normally on the order of 200 lines of well-documented C++ code.

    Although threads are normally considered light-weight, they can be quite expensive when compared to process granularities in most vision algorithms which can be as small as a few hundred CPU cycles. For instance, during preprocessing stick growing uses a 3x3 pixel averaging filter. Theoretically, the optimal granularity would be a set of 9 input pixels and single output pixel. In reality, false sharing effects within cache lines enlarges the smallest practical granularity to something on the order of one hundred input pixels, which corresponds to several thousand CPU cycles. Cache-line effects are small compared to the cost of creating and destroying processor threads. On our SGI Challenge, thread start-up times are usually on the order of 250ms. Given a 100MHz clock cycle, thread creation takes approximately 25 million CPU cycles. Thread creation times dwarf most vision algorithm granularities.

    In order to reduce the smallest possible CPU scheduling granularity, we introduce into our programming model the concept of *jobs*. Abstractly, a *job* is the smallest indivisible unit of work available in an algorithm. In practice, the size of a job is limited by cache-line effects. Jobs normally have a minimal size of a few tens-of-thousands of CPU cycles. We implement jobs as concrete classes derived from an abstract C++ class. All state for a job must be contained within its class instance. In addition to state specific to its work, a job also has a fixed priority assigned at the time of its creation. Runnable jobs are placed in a priority heap. Worker threads, one per processor, remove a single job at a time from the queue. Optimal load balance is guaranteed for any specific job granularity. The worker thread executes the job by calling its run member function.

The job runs non-preemptively until it either finishes or returns itself to the queue. Because all of a job's state is maintained within its class instance, worker threads use a single stack. Another positive benefit is that job don't need any kind of locking of their private state because they can never be preempted. Context switching between jobs consists of nothing more than selecting a job pointer from the heap and calling its run member function. Job creation requires only a single, typically small, dynamic memory allocation for the class instance member functions and a function call to add the job to the queue.

The combination of a highly portable generalized thread model (GTM) and an extremely light-weight job abstraction, provides a powerful programming model for vision algorithms. With GTM, our code is readily runnable on a large number of machines. Jobs strengthen the model by creating a unit of processing with granularity close to that exhibited by most vision problems.

3.2 Parallelization

Parallelism in stick growing exists in two forms, the first is data parallelism in the initialization step. Stick growing correlates line segments using a large set of templates. We reduce algorithm start-up time by creating templates in parallel. Another costly, but parallelizable, task is image preprocessing. The largest fraction of image preprocessing in stick growing consists of a number of 3x3 averaging and gradient calculation operations. We parallelize preprocessing by creating distinct jobs which operate on horizontal strips just 8 pixels wide.

The vast majority of processing time in stick growing is spent finding and growing line segments. The obvious units for parallelization are the 32x32 search regions. We create one job for each search region. The job's task is to extract the lines starting within its region. Each search job is assigned a unique fixed priority. As will be shown in section 4, assigning priorities randomly increases the chance that temporally concurrent jobs are spatially distant. Spatially distant reduces the chance that two jobs will contend for the same region.

Because lines almost always extend beyond a single region, there exists a need to synchronize job access to image regions. The stick search and grow algorithm is implemented using a roll-back enable transaction mechanism. A job searches for a line segment then grows it using a sequence of states. All state information about a line is maintained in such a way that line growing can be suspended or rolled back to the start configuration at any time when a search job attempts to enter a new region.

When a job has found a line, it commits by erasing the gradient and edge information subsumed by that line. Jobs must not erase data being used by another job. Synchronization becomes even more important in light of the fact that lines always have two ends and often cross each other. A job must hold a lock on a region before it can touch any data within the region. A job holds locks to all regions it has touched while growing a line segment until it either commits or is forced to roll back.

Before entering a new region, a job attempts to grab the lock for the region. If the lock is not held by another job, the job continues growing its current stick. If the lock is held by another job, the former job suspends itself. The suspension releases the worker thread to the next job available on the work queue.

Because a job suspends itself whenever it cannot acquire a lock to a region, deadlock conditions are frequent. A deadlock results when one job is waiting on a lock held by another job which is waiting to acquire yet another lock. In most systems job completion is a high priority. Often job completion necessitates conditions that make deadlock detection and prevention extremely complex. In stick growing, however, deadlock often means that two jobs are working on the same line. The optimal choice is to stop one of the jobs as soon as possible so that the other can complete the line.

We detect and recover from deadlock as early as possible by adding a scavenger job to the system. The scavenger job is assigned minimal priority. It runs only when there is a processor available with no outstanding search jobs. The scavenger examines the list of region locks. Whenever it finds a job suspended on a lock waiting for a job that is waiting for another region lock, it compares the priorities of the jobs. If the job holding the region has the highest priority, the scavenger does nothing. If a suspended job has a higher priority, the scavenger forces the job holding the region to roll back its search and release all locks. The scavenger job guarantees that no job is ever suspended waiting for a job with lower priority that isn't making progress.

The combination of aggressive job creation and early deadlock detection by the scavenger creates a system which make continual progress. As will be shown in the next section, our method has good performance in spite of the complex interactions of lines in most images.

4 Experimental Results

Our experimental test suite consists of 4 images ranging from very simple to very complex. Each of image measures 512x512 pixels with 256 gray scales. The test images are: `square`, `group`, `tinytown`, and `tree`. See Figure 1.

First, we conducted qualitative experiments to verify that the results produced using the parallel method where sufficiently similar to those produced by the original method. Figure 2 contains the original image, the lines extracted using the original stick growing method and lines extracted using our parallel stick growing method with 5 processors. There are some discrepancies produced by the nondeterminism of the parallel method. Parallel nondeterminism is a result of the race condition between jobs competing for the same pixels. These differences are most visible in the hexagon and triangle shapes in Figure 2. The discrepancies produced by the parallelism are no greater than those produced by the nondeterminism of the original method (e.g. when run on a shifted version of the image). The results indicate that our parallel method is qualitatively equivalent to the original method.

Our second set of experiments are quantitative in nature. We measure runtime performance of the parallel stick growing method. Runtimes were measured on our 12 processor SGI Challenge using the 20ns memory-mapped hardware clock.

Figure 3 plots the normalized execution times on 11 processors while varying the assigning priorities to search regions. Recall that throughout its lifetime a search job retains the priority assigned to the region from which it originates.

The *column major* algorithm assigns region priorities in column major order from bottom to top moving from left to right. The *row reversal* algorithm assigns regions

Fig. 1. Test images: square (TL), group (TR), tinytown (BL) and tree (BR).

column major priorities, but even rows move from left to right and odd rows move from right to left. The *column interleave* algorithm assigns column major priorities moving from left to right, but even columns all have higher priorities than all odd columns. The *interleave and reversal* algorithm combines the even/odd row reversal with the even/odd column interleaving. For the fifth algorithm, *random* assigns each region a unique random priority. Random priority assignment reduces the probability that that two spatially proximal searches will be active at the same time.

Figure 4 plots the speedup for each of the four sample images. Region priorities were assigned using the random algorithm. Each experiment was repeated 40 times. The average execution time pre image was calculated after discarding the first experiment to remove startup virtual memory paging latencies. Runtimes ranged from 2 seconds for 11 processors on square to 96 seconds for a single processor on tree. Appendix A contains summaries of the experimental data.

The square and group images exhibit poor scalability because their features are restricted both in number and in size. In the extreme case, the method extracts 9 lines from square. Since each line is be extracted by a single processor, almost all of the speed-up for simple images can be attributed to the parallelization of the preprocessing

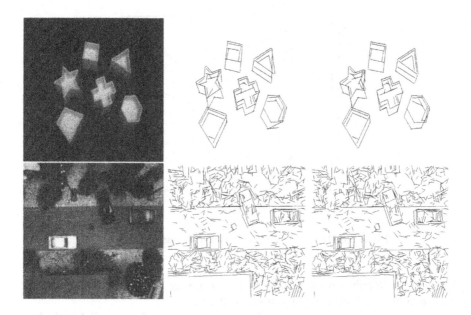

Fig. 2. Group (T) and tinytown (B): Image, Sequential Method, 5 Processor Method.

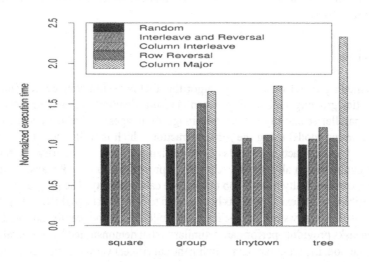

Fig. 3. Normalized execution times on 11 processors for stick growing varying the assignment algorithm.

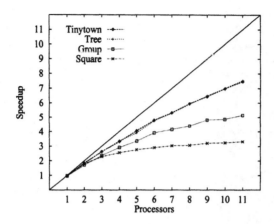

Fig. 4. Speedup of the parallel method on the sample images.

operations. As described in Section 2, the preprocessing is comprised of operations which are readily parallelized by traditional methods.

Tinytown and tree demonstrate the strong scalability of our parallel method on complex images. Since most of the processing time is spent growing line segments, two of factors limit scalability: 1) resource contention, when one or more processors attempt to acquire a lock on the same region, and 2) wasted computation, when two or more jobs attempt to grow the same line from separate regions. These effects are reduced by aggressive deadlock avoidance and priority assignment which temporally isolates spatially proximal tasks.

5 Conclusion

We have presented a parallel stick growing algorithm that is qualitatively equivalent to the sequential stick growing method. Experimental results demonstrate that our method exhibits good parallel scalability for a wide range of images. We also presented a parallel programming model using the *jobs* abstraction which is well suited to vision algorithms. The jobs abstraction provides flexible sizing in task granularity for both regular and irregular vision algorithms. A future improvement to the jobs abstraction would add a processor affinity to each job to improve cache locality. The programming model we describe is very flexible and has been ported to Sun Solaris, SGI IRIX, Digital Unix and Microsoft Windows NT. We believe our model should be readily exploitable by other vision tasks providing performance similar to that demonstrated by our parallel stick growing method. In particular, parallelizing the curvilinear variant of the sequential stick growing method should be a trivial extension of our current work.

Source Code Availability

The C++ sources for the parallelized stick-growing algorithm and the GTM package can be found at http://www.cs.rochester.edu/u/gchunt/ipp.

References

[1] J. B. Burns, A. R. Hanson, and E. M. Riseman. Extracting Straight Lines. In *Proc. DARPA IU Workshop*, pages 165–168, New Orleans, LA, 1984.

[2] R. O. Duda and P. E. Hart. Use of the Hough Transform to Detect Lines and Curves in Pictures. *Communications of the ACM*, 15:11–15, 1972.

[3] D. Gerogiannus and S. C. Orphanoudakis. Load balancing requirement in parallel implementations of image feature extraction tasks. *IEEE Transactions on Parallel and Distributed Systems*, 4(9):994–1013, 1993.

[4] T. H. Hong, M. O. Shneier, R. L. Hartley, and A. Rosenfeld. Using pyramids to detect good continuation. *IEEE Transactions on Systems, Man and Cybernetics*, 13:631–635, 1983.

[5] C.-C. Lin, V. K. Prasanna, and A. Khokhar. Scalable Parallel Extraction of Linear Features on MP-2. In M. A. Bayoumi, L. S. Davis, and K. P. Valavanis, editors, *Proceedings of the IEEE Workshop on Computer Architectures for Machine Perception*, pages 352–361, New Orleans, LA, 1993.

[6] J. J. Little. Parallel Algorithms for Computer Vision on the Connection Machine. AIM-928, Massachusetts Institute of Technology, Artificial Intelligence Laboratory, 1986.

[7] D. G. Lowe. *Perceptual Organization and Visual Recognition*. Kluwer Academic Publishers, Hingham, MA, 1985.

[8] A. Mansouri, A. S. Malowany, and M. D. Levine. Line Detection in Digital Pictures: A Hypothesis Prediction / Verification Paradigm. *Computer Vision, Graphics, and Image Processing*, 40:95–114, 1987.

[9] V. S. Nalwa and E. Pauchon. Edgel Aggregation and Edge Description. *Computer Vision, Graphics, and Image Processing*, 40:79–94, 1987.

[10] R. C. Nelson. Finding Line Segments by Stick Growing. *IEEE Transactions on Pattern Analysis and Machine Intelligence*, 16(5):519–523, 1994.

[11] R. Nevatia and K. R. Babu. Linear Feature Extraction and Description. *Computer Vision Graphics and Image Processing*, 13:257–269, 1980.

[12] V. K. Prasanna, C.-L. Wang, and A. Khokhar. Low Level Vision Processing on Connection Machine CM-5. In M. A. Bayoumi, L. S. Davis, and K. P. Valavanis, editors, *Proceedings of the IEEE Workshop on Computer Architectures for Machine Perception*, pages 117–126, New Orleans, LA, 1993.

[13] J. Princen, J. Illingworth, and J. Kittler. A hierarchical approach to line extraction based on the Hough transform. *Computer Vision Graphics and Image Processing*, 52:57–77, 1990.

[14] C. M. Williams. An Efficient Algorithm for the Piecewise Linear Approximation of Planar Curves. *Computer Graphics and Image Processing*, 8:286–293, 1978.

[15] Y. T. Zhou, V. Venkateswar, and R. Chellappa. Edge Detection and Linear Feature Extraction Using a 2-D Random Field Model. *IEEE Trans. Pattern Analysis and Machine Intelligence*, 11:84–95, 1989.

A   Execution Times

The following table contains maximum, average and minimum execution times for each of the test images. Also shown are the average number of line segments found in each image and the average number of aborts initiated by the scavenger thread to avoid deadlock.

	square						group				
	Execution Time (secs.)						Execution Time (secs.)				
P	Max.	Avg.	Min.	Seg.	Aborts	P	Max.	Avg.	Min.	Seg.	Aborts
1	7.1267	7.0184	6.9748	9	0	1	23.5426	22.3784	21.5262	107	0
2	4.3798	3.8457	3.6324	9	7	2	14.5387	12.5891	11.2854	108	57
3	3.2556	3.0442	2.9078	9	21	3	10.6219	9.1392	7.7385	108	154
4	2.8744	2.7182	2.6418	9	26	4	8.1085	7.4060	6.2877	108	201
5	2.8162	2.5118	2.4569	9	25	5	7.5025	6.4209	5.4747	108	230
6	2.7215	2.3908	2.3309	9	26	6	6.6728	5.5070	5.2807	109	295
7	2.5799	2.2835	2.2239	9	29	7	6.2184	5.1825	4.5674	109	313
8	2.8202	2.2562	2.1422	9	29	8	5.8441	4.8979	4.4045	109	333
9	2.2166	2.1591	2.1142	9	28	9	5.4492	4.4756	3.8098	109	336
10	2.5150	2.1361	2.1035	9	28	10	5.5447	4.4283	3.7731	109	349
11	2.1337	2.0871	2.0632	9	28	11	5.2645	4.1880	3.5121	109	337

	tinytown						tree				
	Execution Time (secs.)						Execution Time (secs.)				
P	Max.	Avg.	Min.	Seg.	Aborts	P	Max.	Avg.	Min.	Seg.	Aborts
1	71.2920	69.8364	67.6445	886	0	1	96.0055	94.6899	92.9571	1075	0
2	38.6185	36.8806	35.4569	886	207	2	51.9263	49.6628	48.2414	1077	387
3	26.5888	25.6757	24.7986	884	403	3	37.3478	35.5521	33.1753	1078	1 859
4	21.3605	20.4401	19.5630	885	655	4	28.8391	27.6471	26.0316	1078	11176
5	17.8572	16.6815	15.6954	887	11014	5	28.4120	23.7589	21.4923	1078	11502
6	15.3411	14.1217	12.8148	887	11158	6	20.9000	19.5797	18.3607	1079	21781
7	14.0021	12.7300	11.7680	888	11418	7	18.3213	17.5979	16.4599	1078	22024
8	12.6716	11.3598	10.2568	889	11590	8	16.4218	15.7018	14.7241	1078	22199
9	11.9200	10.5001	9.1272	889	11700	9	15.0749	14.3241	13.4812	1079	22286
10	11.0740	9.6792	8.8570	889	11767	10	13.7033	13.2774	12.6115	1080	22343
11	10.5673	9.0596	8.2577	890	11792	11	13.1274	12.3223	11.5535	1079	22390

A Simple Parallel Algorithm for the Single-Source Shortest Path Problem on Planar Digraphs*

Jesper L. Träff, and Christos D. Zaroliagis

Max-Planck-Institut für Informatik
Im Stadtwald, D-66123 Saarbrücken, Germany
E-mail: {traff,zaro}@mpi-sb.mpg.de

Abstract. We present a simple parallel algorithm for the *single-source shortest path problem* in *planar digraphs* with nonnegative real edge weights. The algorithm runs on the EREW PRAM model of parallel computation in $O((n^{2\epsilon} + n^{1-\epsilon}) \log n)$ time, performing $O(n^{1+\epsilon} \log n)$ work for any $0 < \epsilon < 1/2$. The strength of the algorithm is its simplicity, making it easy to implement, and presumably quite efficient in practice. The algorithm improves upon the work of all previous algorithms. The work can be further reduced to $O(n^{1+\epsilon})$, by plugging in a less practical, sequential planar shortest path algorithm. Our algorithm is based on a region decomposition of the input graph, and uses a well-known parallel implementation of Dijkstra's algorithm.

1   Introduction

The shortest path problem is a fundamental and well-studied combinatorial optimization problem with a wealth of practical and theoretical applications [1]. Given an n-vertex, m-edge directed graph $G = (V, E)$ with real edge weights, the *shortest path problem* is to find a path of minimum weight between two vertices u and v, for each pair u, v of a given set of vertex pairs; the weight of a u-v path is the sum of the weights of its edges. The weight of a shortest u-v path is called the *distance* from u to v. The shortest path problem comes in different variants depending on the given set of u, v vertex pairs, and the type of edge weights [1].

Although efficient sequential algorithms exist for many variants, there is a certain lack of efficient parallel algorithms; that is, of algorithms that perform *work* (total number of operations performed by the available processors) which is close to the number of operations performed by the best known sequential algorithm. Designing efficient parallel algorithms for shortest path problems constitutes a major open problem in parallel computing. One possible reason for the lack of such algorithms could be that most of the emphasis so far has been put on obtaining very fast (i.e. NC) algorithms. However, in most practical situations, where the number of available processors p is fixed and much smaller than the

---

* This work was partially supported by the EU ESPRIT LTR Project No. 20244 (ALCOM-IT), and by the DFG project SFB 124-D6 (VLSI Entwurfsmethoden und Parallelität).

sizes of the problems at hand, it is more important to have work-efficient (rather than very fast) parallel algorithms, since the running time will be dominated by the work divided by p. Moreover, this seems to be of particular importance if such algorithms can be shown to have other practical merits (simplicity, ease of implementation).

An important variant of the shortest path problem is the *single-source* problem: given G as above and a distinguished vertex $s \in V$, called the *source*, the problem is to find shortest paths from s to every other vertex in G. The single-source shortest path problem has efficient sequential solutions, especially when G has nonnegative edge weights. In this case, the problem can be solved by Dijkstra's algorithm in $O(m + n \log n)$ time using the Fibonacci heap or another priority queue data structure with the same resource bounds [3, 5]. If in addition G is planar, then the problem can be solved optimally in $O(n)$ time [9].

In the following we consider the single-source shortest path problem in planar digraphs with nonnegative real edge weights. Despite much effort, no sublinear time, work-optimal parallel algorithm has been devised even for this case. The best previous algorithm is due to Cohen [2] and runs in $O(\log^4 n)$ time using $O(n^{3/2})$ work on an EREW PRAM. There are two cases where the work is better. Both cases, however, require edge weights to be nonnegative integers and in one case the algorithm is not deterministic. More specifically, in [11] an $O(\text{polylog}(n) \log L)$-time, $O(n)$-processor *randomized* EREW PRAM algorithm was given, where L is the largest (integral) edge weight of G. In [9], a deterministic parallel algorithm was given that runs in $O(n^{2/3} \log^{7/3} n(\log n + \log D))$ time using $O(n^{4/3} \log n(\log n + \log D))$ work, where D is the sum of the integral edge weights. All of the above algorithms use sophisticated data structures which make them difficult to implement.

In this paper we present a simple, easily implementable, parallel algorithm for the single-source shortest path problem on planar digraphs G. By compromising on parallel running time, we obtain a (deterministic) algorithm which in terms of work-efficiency improves upon the previous algorithms. More precisely, our algorithm runs in $O((n^{2\epsilon} + n^{1-\epsilon}) \log n)$ time and performs $O(n^{1+\epsilon} \log n)$ work on an EREW PRAM, for any $0 < \epsilon < 1/2$. A choice of $\epsilon = 1/3$ improves the bounds in [9] by a logarithmic factor at least, while a choice of $\epsilon = 1/4$ improves the work in [2] by a factor of $n^{1/4}$. The work of our algorithm can be further improved to $O(n^{1+\epsilon})$, if the sequential algorithm of [9] is used as a subroutine. However, we cannot claim that this version of the algorithm is easily implementable.

Like previous planar single-source shortest path algorithms, our algorithm is based on a so-called region decomposition of G [4], coupled with a reduction of the problem to a collection of shortest path problems on the regions of G. Given a region decomposition, our algorithm mainly consists in the concurrent application of Dijkstra's sequential single-source shortest path algorithm to the regions of the graph, followed by a final application of a simple parallel version of Dijkstra's algorithm to an auxiliary (non-planar) graph constructed using the shortest path information computed in the regions. By suitable copying of the edges of the graph, concurrent reading and writing can be avoided. For computing the region decomposition presupposed by our shortest path algorithm, we also sketch an EREW PRAM implementation of the algorithm in [4]. This implementation (somewhat more complicated than that of the shortest path algorithm) computes a specific representation of the region decomposition as required for the shortest path algorithm.

The main advantage of our algorithm is its simplicity which makes it easy to implement and presumably also efficient in practice (i.e. capable of giving good speedups in parallel machines with a modest number of processors). We intend to incorporate the algorithm into a library of basic PRAM algorithms and data structures, called PAD [8], currently under development.

2 Preliminaries

Let for the remainder of this paper $G = (V, E)$ be a directed planar graph with nonnegative, real edge weights, $n = |V|$ vertices and $m \leq 3n - 6 = O(n)$ edges. In the following, when we speak about separator properties of G, we are referring to the *undirected version* of G (i.e. ignoring the direction of the edges). When we speak of shortest paths, however, we take the direction of edges into account.

A *separator* of a graph $H = (V_H, E_H)$ is a subset C of V_H whose removal partitions V_H into two disjoint subsets A and B such that any path from a vertex in A to a vertex in B contains at least one vertex from C. Lipton and Tarjan [12] showed that planar graphs have small separators.

Theorem 1 (Planar separator theorem). *Let $G = (V, E)$ be an n-vertex planar graph with nonnegative costs on its vertices summing up to one. Then, there exists a separator S of G which partitions V into two sets V_1, V_2, such that $|S| = O(\sqrt{n})$ and each of V_1, V_2 has total cost at most 2/3.*

We call such a separator S, a $\frac{1}{3}$-$\frac{2}{3}$ separator of G. The cost of a subset V' of V, denoted by $wt(V')$, is defined as the sum of the costs of the vertices of V'.

A *region decomposition* of a graph G is a division of the vertices of G into *regions*, such that each vertex is either *interior*, belonging to exactly one region, or *boundary*, and shared among at least two regions. For any integer $1 \leq r \leq n$, an *r-division* is a region decomposition of G into $\Theta(n/r)$ regions such that each region has at most $c_1 r$ vertices and at most $c_2\sqrt{r}$ boundary vertices, for some constants c_1 and c_2.

By recursively applying the planar separator theorem, Frederickson [4] gave a sequential $O(n \log n)$ time algorithm for computing an r-division. Our single-source shortest path algorithm – like many others, see e.g. [9] – is based on Frederickson's r-division of a planar graph. A parallel implementation of Frederickson's approach for computing an r-division is briefly described in Section 4. This implementation is based on recursive applications of the optimal parallel algorithm of Gazit and Miller [6] for finding a $\frac{1}{3}$-$\frac{2}{3}$ separator in a planar graph, whose implementation is also sketched.

The other two main subroutines used by our algorithm are: (a) Dijkstra's sequential algorithm [1]. We shall denote a call of the algorithm on a digraph H with source vertex s as Seq-Dijkstra(s, H). (b) A parallel version of Dijkstra's algorithm [3], applied to a digraph $G' = (V', E')$, and running in time $O(m'/p + n' \log n')$ using $p \le m'/n'$ EREW PRAM processors, where $n' = |V'|$ and $m' = |E'|$. The parallelization of Dijkstra's algorithm is straightforward and obtained by doing distance label updates in parallel, with each processor maintaining a local heap. We shall denote a call of the parallel Dijkstra algorithm on a digraph G' with source vertex s as Par-Dijkstra(s, G'). Note that any elementary heap data structure with $O(\log n)$ worst-case time operations suffices for our purposes. This is so because the work performed, $O(m' \log n')$, by such an implementation of parallel Dijkstra is asymptotically smaller than the work performed by the other steps of our algorithm (since $m' = O(n)$).

3 The planar shortest path algorithm

We now present our parallel algorithm for the single-source shortest path problem on planar digraphs G with nonnegative edge weights. We assume that G is provided with an r-division. In Section 4 we sketch how such an r-division can be found.

Let $s \in V$ be the source vertex. Our algorithm works as follows. Inside every region compute, for every boundary vertex v, a shortest path tree rooted at v. These single-source computations are done concurrently using Dijkstra's sequential algorithm. For the region containing s an additional single-source computation starting at s is performed, if s is not a boundary vertex. Then, G is contracted to a graph G' having as vertices the source vertex s and all boundary vertices of the decomposition of G, and having edges between any two boundary vertices belonging to the same region (of G) with weight equal to their distance inside the region (if a path does not exist, the corresponding edge weight is set to ∞). Furthermore, there are edges from s to the boundary vertices of the region containing s, say R_1, with weight equal to their distance from s in R_1. In G' a single-source shortest path computation is performed, using the parallel Dijkstra algorithm, producing shortest paths from s to all other vertices of G', that is, to all boundary vertices of G. Finally, the shortest paths and distances from s to the rest of the vertices in G (i.e. to all the interior vertices) are computed in parallel, using for each (interior) vertex the shortest path information obtained for the boundary vertices of the region it belongs to.

Algorithm Planar single-source shortest path.

Input: A weighted planar digraph $G = (V, E)$, a distinguished source vertex $s \in V$, and an r-division of G into regions R_i, $1 \le i \le t$, $t = O(n/r)$. Let $V(R_i)$ (resp. $B(R_i)$) be the vertex set (resp. boundary vertex set) of R_i. Let $B = \bigcup_{1 \le i \le t} B(R_i)$ be the set of all boundary vertices and let $B(v)$, for $v \in B$, denote the set of regions to which the boundary vertex v belongs. W.l.o.g. assume that $s \in V(R_1)$. (If s is a boundary vertex, then pick R_1 arbitrarily from the regions to which s belongs.) The r-division is computed by the algorithm given in Section 4, and is provided with the following information. Each set $B(R_i)$ is represented as an array, and every interior vertex (i.e. a vertex in $V(R_i) - B(R_i)$) has a label denoting the region it belongs to. There is also an array containing all boundary vertices $v \in B$, and for each such v there is an array of length $|B(v)|$ containing the regions for which v is a boundary vertex. Each boundary vertex $u \in B(R_i)$ has a pointer to its position in the array $B(u)$. All adjacent vertices of a boundary vertex $v \in B$ that belong to the same region are assumed to form a consecutive segment of vertices in the adjacency list of v. Finally, every vertex $u \in B(R_i)$ has two pointers to u's adjacency list, pointing to the first and the last vertex in the (consecutive) segment of vertices that belong to R_i.

Remark: The segmentation of the adjacency lists of the boundary vertices allows to associate a processor with each boundary vertex of R_i, and thus to avoid concurrent reads or writes for boundary vertices belonging to many regions.

Output: A shortest path tree in G rooted at s. The shortest path tree is returned in arrays $D[1:n]$ and $P[1:n]$. The distance from s to v is stored in $D[v]$ and the parent of v in the shortest path tree is stored in $P[v]$.

Method:

1. INITIALIZATION

Comment: We make $|B(R_i)|$ copies of every region R_i. This is needed to avoid concurrent memory accesses in Step 2. Let R_i^k denote the k-th copy of region R_i which will be associated with the k-th boundary vertex $v_i^k \in B(R_i)$. With every $v \in V(R_i)$, a distance (resp. parent) array $D_v[1:|B(R_i)|]$ (resp. $P_v[1:|B(R_i)|]$) is associated. For boundary vertex $v_i^k \in B(R_i)$ the k-th entry $D_v[k]$ (resp. $P_v[k]$) will be used when a shortest path from v_i^k to v is computed.

1.01 **for all** $1 \le i \le t$ **do in parallel**
1.02   **for all** $1 \le k \le |B(R_i)|$ **do in parallel**
1.03   **for all** $v \in V(R_i) - B(R_i)$ **do in parallel**
1.04   Make a copy of the adjacency list of v and add it to R_i^k;
1.05 $D_v[k] = \infty$; $P_v[k] = null$;
1.06   **od**
1.07   **for all** $v \in B(R_i)$ **do in parallel**
1.08   Make a copy of the segment of the adjacent vertices of v belonging to R_i and add it to R_i^k;
1.09 $D_v[k] = \infty$; $P_v[k] = null$;
1.10   **od**
1.11   **od**
1.12 **od**

2. SHORTEST PATHS INSIDE REGIONS

Comment: For each boundary vertex v_i^k of R_i, a single-source shortest path problem is solved in R_i using Dijkstra's sequential algorithm. Each time, during the execution of the algorithm, if a boundary vertex v_i^j of R_i is selected, then only the segment of its adjacent vertices belonging to R_i is scanned.

2.01 **for all** $1 \le i \le t$ **do in parallel**

2.02   **for all** $v_i^k \in B(R_i)$ **do in parallel**
2.03   Run Seq-Dijkstra(v_i^k, R_i^k);
2.04   **od**
2.05 **od**

Comment: After this step, in every region R_i, the distance from each boundary vertex $v_i^k \in B(R_i)$ to each $u \in V(R_i)$ is stored in $D_u[k]$, and a pointer to the parent of u in the shortest path tree rooted at v_i^k is stored in $P_u[k]$.

3. SHORTEST PATH TREE INSIDE R_1
Comment: If s is not a boundary vertex, solve the single-source shortest path problem inside R_1 with source vertex s, resulting in a distance (resp. parent) array $D^1[v]$ (resp. $P^1[v]$), for all $v \in V(R_1)$.

3.01 **if** $s \notin B(R_1)$ **then** run Seq-Dijkstra(s, R_1), resulting in arrays $D^1[\cdot]$ and $P^1[\cdot]$;

4. CONTRACT G
Comment: Contract G to a graph G' having the source vertex s and all boundary vertices of G as vertices. For any two boundary vertices v_i^k and v_i^j belonging to the same region R_i there is an edge in G' from v_i^k to v_i^j with weight equal to their distance in R_i. If s is not a boundary vertex, there are edges from s to all boundary vertices of R_1 with weights equal to the distances found in Step 3. The single-source shortest path problem is then solved on G' with source s, using the parallel Dijkstra algorithm, resulting in distance and parent arrays $D'[1 : |V'|]$ and $P'[1 : |V'|]$. $D'[v]$ stores the distance from s to v in G', and $P'[v]$ stores a pointer to the parent of v in the shortest path tree in G' rooted at s. After step 4 the distance from s to each boundary vertex of G has been computed.

4.01 $V' = (\bigcup_{1 \le i \le t} B(R_i)) \bigcup \{s\}$; $E' = \emptyset$;
4.02 **for all** $1 \le i \le t$ **do in parallel**
4.03   **for all** pairs $v_i^k, v_i^j \in B(R_i)$ **do in parallel**
4.04   Add edge (v_i^k, v_i^j) to E' with weight equal to $D_{v_i^j}[k]$;
4.05   **od**
4.06 **od**
4.07 **if** $s \notin B(R_1)$ **then**
4.08   **for all** $v_1^k \in B(R_1)$ **do in parallel**
4.09   Add edge (s, v_1^k) to E' with weight equal to $D^1[k]$;
4.10   **od**
4.11 $G' = (V', E')$;
4.12 Run Par-Dijkstra(s, G'), resulting in arrays $D'[\cdot]$ and $P'[\cdot]$;

Comment: The adjacency list representation of E' (Steps 4.04 and 4.09) is constructed as follows. An array of size $|B(R_i)|$ is associated with each boundary vertex $v_i^k \in B(R_i)$; the edge (v_i^k, v_i^j) is stored in the j-th position of this array. Now recall that vertex $v = v_i^k$ belongs to different regions. Using the array $B(v)$ of the regions to which v belongs, an array containing the edges of E', in which all edges adjacent to v form a consecutive segment, can be constructed by a prefix computation. Note that this representation of E' may contain multiple edges, namely in the case where boundary vertices v_i^k and v_i^j both belong to the same regions, but this does not affect neither the correctness nor the complexity of running the parallel Dijkstra algorithm in Step 4.12. (The latter is true, because every edge in G' belongs only to one region.) Moreover, each time a pointer $P'[v]$ is updated, $v \in V'$, we store together with the parent vertex of v the region to which the edge $(P'[v], v)$ belongs. This allows us in Step 5 to recover the parent pointers for the required shortest path tree in G.

5. FINAL STEP

Comment: A shortest path tree T_s in G rooted at s is now computed as follows.

For each interior vertex $u \in V(R_i) - B(R_i)$ of a region R_i, scan through its distance array and find the boundary vertex v_i^k which minimizes the sum of the distance from s to v_i^k (as computed in Step 4) and the distance from v_i^k to u (as computed in Step 2). The parent of u, $P[u]$, in T_s is the parent of u in the shortest path tree in R_i rooted at v_i^k. These computations, concerning the interior vertices of the regions, are done in Steps 5.10-5.13.

For each boundary vertex $v_i^k \in B(R_i)$ we look up its parent $v_j^l = P'[v_i^k]$ in the shortest path tree T_s' in G' rooted at s. If the edge (v_j^l, v_i^k) belongs to R_i (this information was saved by the parallel Dijkstra algorithm in Step 4), and v_j^l is not the source vertex, then the s-v_i^k distance is simply the s-v_i^k distance in G', and the parent of v_i^k in T_s is the parent of v_i^k in the shortest path tree in R_i rooted at v_j^l which is stored in $P_{v_i^k}[l]$. Note that if the parent of v_i^k in T_s' happens to be the source vertex s, and s is not a boundary vertex, then the required distance and parent of v_i^k in T_s are those stored in $D^1[v_i^k]$ and $P^1[v_i^k]$, respectively, as computed in Step 3. These computations, concerning the boundary vertices, are done in Steps 5.14-5.22.

Finally, in the case where s is not a boundary vertex, the distance and parent information computed so far for the interior vertices in R_1 may not be correct, because $D[u]$, for $u \in V(R_1) - B(R_1)$, stores the weight of a (shortest) s-u path passing through at least one boundary vertex and the actual shortest s-u path may stay entirely in R_1. This is rectified by updating $D[u]$ (resp. $P[u]$) to $D^1[u]$ (resp. $P^1[u]$) in the case where $D^1[u] < D[u]$. These computations, regarding the interior vertices of R_1, are done in Steps 5.23-5.27.

A preprocessing step is necessary in order to avoid concurrent memory accesses. To avoid concurrent reading of the array D' in Step 5.11, $|V(R_i) - B(R_i)|$ copies of each value $D'[v_i^k]$ has to be made for each boundary vertex v_i^k (Steps 5.01-5.05). To avoid concurrent reading of the parent pointers in array P' in Step 5.15, a copy of $P'[v]$ is made for each of the $|B(v)|$ regions to which the boundary vertex $v \in B$ belongs (Steps 5.06-5.08).

When Step 5 is completed, distances and parent pointers for all vertices $v \in V$ are stored in arrays $D[1:n]$ and $P[1:n]$ as required.

5.01 **for all** $1 \le i \le t$ **do in parallel**
5.02   **for all** $v_i^k \in B(R_i)$ **do in parallel**
5.03   Make $|V(R_i) - B(R_i)|$ copies of $D'[v_i^k]$;
        let $D_u'[v_i^k]$ denote the u-th copy of $D'[v_i^k]$ for $u \in V(R_i) - B(R_i)$;

5.04   **od**
5.05 **od**
5.06 **for all** $v \in B$ **do in parallel**
5.07   Make $|B(v)|$ copies of $P'[v]$; let $P'_i[v]$ denote the copy of $P'[v]$ for region R_i;
5.08 **od**
5.09 **for all** $1 \leq i \leq t$ **do in parallel**
5.10   **for all** $u \in V(R_i) - B(R_i)$ **do in parallel**
5.11 $D[u] = \min_{v_i^k \in B(R_i)} \{D'_u[v_i^k] + D_u[k]\}$;
5.12 $P[u] = P_u[k]$;
5.13   **od**
5.14   **for all** $v_i^k \in B(R_i)$ **do in parallel**
5.15   Let $v_j^l = P'_i[v_i^k]$;
5.16   **if** edge (v_j^l, v_i^k) belongs to R_i **then**
5.17   **if** $v_j^l = s$ and $s \notin B(R_1)$ **then**
5.18 $D[v_i^k] = D^1[v_i^k]; P[v_i^k] = P^1[v_i^k]$;
5.19   **else**
5.20 $D[v_i^k] = D'[v_i^k]; P[v_i^k] = P_{v_i^k}[l]$;
5.21   **od**
5.22 **od**
5.23 **if** $s \notin B(R_1)$ **then**
5.24   **for all** $u \in V(R_1) - B(R_1)$ **do in parallel**
5.25   **if** $D^1[u] < D[u]$ **then**
5.26 $D[u] = D^1[u]; P[u] = P^1[u]$;
5.27   **od**

End of algorithm.

The correctness of the above algorithm is not hard to establish and is omitted due to space limitations (the interested reader is referred to [15]). For the resource bounds, it is clear from the description of the algorithm that all steps can be done without concurrent read or write. In Step 1, $O(\sqrt{r})$ copies of $O(r)$ edges are made within each region, using a prefix computation. Hence, Step 1 takes $O(\log n)$ time and $O(n\sqrt{r})$ work. The shortest path computations in Step 2 take $O(r \log r)$ time and require $O(n\sqrt{r} \log r)$ work. One additional single-source shortest path computation may be needed in Step 3 taking $O(r \log r)$ time. The contraction of the graph in Step 4 results in a graph of $O((n/r)\sqrt{r}) = O(n/\sqrt{r})$ vertices and $O((\sqrt{r})^2(n/r)) = O(n)$ edges, on which the single-source shortest path problem is solved in parallel in $O((n/\sqrt{r}) \log n)$ time and $O(n \log n)$ work, using the parallel Dijkstra algorithm. Finally, in Step 5, copying the D' values takes $O(n\sqrt{r})$ work, and copying the P' values takes $O(n/\sqrt{r})$ work, since the total size of the lists $B(v)$ is $O(n/\sqrt{r})$; both copying operations take $O(\log n)$ time. The remainder of Step 5 can be done in constant time and $O(n)$ work. Hence, the total time of the algorithm is $O(r \log r + (n/\sqrt{r}) \log n)$, and the total work is $O(n\sqrt{r} \log n)$. By letting $r = n^{2\epsilon}$, for any $0 < \epsilon < 1/2$, we have:

Theorem 2. *On an n-vertex planar graph the single-source shortest path problem can be solved in* $O(n^{2\epsilon} \log n + n^{1-\epsilon} \log n)$ *time and* $O(n^{1+\epsilon} \log n)$ *work.*

The work bound of the above result can be improved by a logarithmic factor, if we substitute the calls of the sequential Dijkstra algorithm in Step 2 with the linear-time algorithm for planar digraphs [9].

4 Obtaining a region decomposition

In this section we briefly discuss the EREW PRAM implementation of the algorithm in [4] for finding an r-division of a planar graph G. The main procedure is an algorithm for finding a separator in G. A simple and optimal parallel algorithm for the latter problem was given by Gazit and Miller [6]. Their algorithm is a clever parallelization of the sequential approach by Lipton and Tarjan [12], and runs in $O(\sqrt{n}\log n)$ time using $O(n)$ work on a CRCW PRAM.

We start by sketching the implementation on an EREW PRAM of the algorithm in [6], running in $O(\sqrt{n}\log n)$ time and performing $O(n\log n)$ work. Then, in Section 4.2, we give the implementation of the algorithm for finding the r-division. (For simplicity, we relax in the following the constant in the size of the separator.) Detailed descriptions of these implementations (along with simplifications and proofs of correctness) can be found in [15].

4.1 The Gazit-Miller separator algorithm

To better understand how the Gazit-Miller algorithm works, we have to recall the Lipton-Tarjan approach. Let $G = (V, E)$ be an embedded planar graph. The Lipton-Tarjan algorithm starts by choosing an arbitrary vertex $s \in V$ and then performs from s a BFS (breadth first search) in G. The vertices of V are assigned a *level* numbering (with s having level 0) w.r.t. the level they belong to in the BFS tree constructed. Let $V(\ell)$ be the set of vertices at level ℓ. The crucial property of BFS is that every $V(\ell)$ is a separator of G. Let ℓ_1 be the *middle level*, i.e. $wt(\bigcup_{\ell<\ell_1} V(\ell)) < 1/2$, but $wt(\bigcup_{\ell\leq\ell_1} V(\ell)) \geq 1/2$. Consequently, $wt(\bigcup_{\ell>\ell_1} V(\ell)) < 1/2$. If $|V(\ell_1)| = O(\sqrt{n})$, then the algorithm stops since $V(\ell_1)$ is clearly the required separator. Otherwise, there are levels $\ell_0 \leq \ell_1$ (*first cut*) and $\ell_2 > \ell_1$ (*last cut*) such that $|V(\ell_0)| \leq \sqrt{n}$, $|V(\ell_2)| \leq \sqrt{n}$, $\ell_2 - \ell_0 \leq \sqrt{n}$, and ℓ_0 (resp. ℓ_2) is the largest (resp. smallest) such level. Removal of the first and last cuts partitions V into three sets: $A = \bigcup_{\ell<\ell_0} V(\ell)$, $B = \bigcup_{\ell_0<\ell<\ell_2} V(\ell)$, and $C = \bigcup_{\ell>\ell_2} V(\ell)$. If $wt(B) \leq 2/3$, then the required separator is $S = V(\ell_0) \cup V(\ell_2)$, V_1 is the largest of A, B, C, and V_2 is the union of the remaining two (smaller) sets. However, if $wt(B) > 2/3$, then B has to be further split. Since $wt(A) + wt(C) < 1/3$, it suffices to find a separator S' of B with $O(\sqrt{n})$ vertices such that each part into which B is separated has cost at most 2/3. For if we have it, then the required separator S is $V(\ell_0) \cup V(\ell_2) \cup S'$ and $|S| = O(\sqrt{n})$, V_1 is the larger part of B, and V_2 is the union of A, C and the smaller part of B. Clearly, both V_1 and V_2 will have cost at most 2/3.

To construct S', remove from G all vertices in A and C (along with their incident edges) and add to the resulting graph the vertex s with edges from s to all vertices in $V(\ell_0 + 1)$. Call the new graph G_B. The crucial property that gives the required size for S' is that G_B has a spanning tree T of diameter $\leq 2\sqrt{n}$. Let

E_T be the edges of T and let E_T^* be their corresponding dual edges in the dual graph $G_B^* = (V_B^*, E_B^*)$ of G_B. Then, the set of edges $E_B^* - E_T^*$ (i.e. the duals of the non-tree edges of T) form a spanning tree of G_B^*. By observing that every non-tree edge $e = (u, v)$ of T forms a cycle, say $C(e)$, with the unique u-v path in T and by working on T^*, we can compute for each $C(e)$ its size as well as the total cost of the vertices which are strictly inside $C(e)$. This information can be computed in $O(n)$ time by performing a bottom-up traversal of T^*. It is not hard to see that there exists a cycle $C(e)$ which is the required separator S'.

The difficulty in parallelizing the above approach is the computation of the BFS tree rooted at (an arbitrary vertex) s: either one has to pay in time $(O(n))$ resulting in a parallel algorithm with actually no speedup, or one has to pay in work (close to $O(n^3)$) which makes the parallel algorithm highly work-inefficient. In order to avoid the expensive BFS computation, Gazit and Miller proposed a different partitioning of V into levels. Their approach is summarized as follows: perform a normal BFS, but if at some level there are only a few vertices then "augment" its size by adding more vertices into it. This so-called *augmented BFS* must be done in a way such that successive augmented levels are connected, otherwise G_B may not have a small diameter; connectedness is achieved by taking augmentation vertices in preorder from a spanning tree of G.

By the description of Lipton-Tarjan algorithm, it suffices to find the levels ℓ_0 (first cut), ℓ_1 (middle level) and ℓ_2 (last cut). The problem of finding a separator S' in G_B can be solved by choosing one of the following approaches: (a) a straightforward parallelization of the Lipton-Tarjan approach which takes $O(\sqrt{n})$ time and $O(n)$ work, since T and T^* have depth $O(\sqrt{n})$; (b) a fast parallelization of approach (a) in $O(\log n)$ time and $O(n)$ work using parallel tree contraction [7]; (c) the approach described in [13] and which also takes $O(\log n)$ time and $O(n)$ work. For our purposes, the approach (a) is the most appropriate.

Hence, the bulk of the work in the Gazit-Miller algorithm is the computation of the three levels ℓ_0, ℓ_1 and ℓ_2. (Note that these levels may not be the same as those computed by the Lipton-Tarjan algorithm; however, they will have the same crucial properties.) The algorithm consists of three phases: An INITIALIZATION PHASE (which initializes an array $A[1 : n]$, finds a spanning tree T of G rooted at an arbitrary vertex s, computes the preorder numbering of the vertices in T, and finally stores the vertices of G in A w.r.t. their preorder number); PHASE A (which finds levels ℓ_0 and ℓ_1); and PHASE B (which computes level ℓ_2). We now briefly sketch the implementations of PHASE A and PHASE B.

PHASE A:
01. $\ell = 0$; $V(0) = \{s\}$;
02. **while** $wt(\bigcup_{\ell' < \ell} V(\ell')) < 1/2$ **do** (* main loop *)
03.   NEXT-LEVEL$(\ell, V(\ell))$;
04. $\ell = \ell + 1$; $j = 2\ell + 1$; (* Now ℓ represents the next level *)
05.   **while** $|V(\ell)| < j$ **do** (* augment level ℓ *)
06.   Pop the top $\sqrt{n}$ elements from A and store them temporarily into an array A';
07.   Mark in A' those vertices that belong to any level $i < \ell$;
08.   Using a parallel prefix computation, remove the marked vertices

09.   from A' and count the number, R, of the remaining vertices;
               $\rho = \min\{j - |V(\ell)|, R\}$;
10.   Add the first ρ elements of A' to $V(\ell)$ and push the
               remaining $R - \rho$ to the top of A;
11.   **od** (* augment level ℓ *)
12.   **if** $|V(\ell)| = j$ **then** $\ell_0 = \ell$;
13. **od** (* main loop *)
14. $\ell_1 = \ell$;
END OF PHASE A.

The procedure NEXT-LEVEL is a straightforward parallelization of one BFS step: Every vertex in $V(\ell)$ is substituted by its list of adjacent vertices. All vertices belonging to levels smaller than $\ell + 1$ are removed (using a prefix computation) and finally all duplicate vertices are removed using sorting.

PHASE B starts at level ℓ_1 and by performing a normal BFS computes the level ℓ_2, which is the first level (during the BFS process) satisfying $|V(\ell)| \leq \sqrt{n - k}$ where $k = |\bigcup_{0 \leq \ell \leq \ell_1} V(\ell)|$. We can prove the following (the proof is given in [15]).

Theorem 3. *Let $G = (V, E)$ be an n-vertex planar graph with nonnegative costs on its vertices summing up to one. Then, a partition of V into three sets V_1, V_2, S, such that S is a separator of G, $|S| = O(\sqrt{n})$, and each of V_1, V_2 has total cost at most $2/3$, can be computed in $O(\sqrt{n} \log n)$ time using $O(n \log n)$ work on an EREW PRAM.*

4.2   The parallel algorithm for finding an r-division

The algorithm for finding an r-division of a planar graph $G = (V, E)$ is based on recursive applications of Theorem 3. First every region R is partitioned recursively by calling the Gazit-Miller algorithm with vertex cost $\frac{1}{|V(R)|}$ until it has the required size. If some region R has the appropriate size, but the number of its boundary vertices, $|B(R)|$, is large, then we call recursively the Gazit-Miller algorithm in R with vertex cost 0 for the interior vertices and cost $\frac{1}{|B(R)|}$ for every boundary vertex. Since each invocation of the Gazit-Miller algorithm gives rise to only two new regions and all concurrent calls work on disjoint parts of V, it is easy to construct the representation of the region decomposition required by the shortest path algorithm (Section 3). Let an invocation of the Gazit-Miller algorithm on region R yield partition R_1, R_2 and S. By a prefix computation the adjacency lists of each new boundary vertex $v \in S$ can be split into vertices belonging to R_1 and vertices belonging to R_2. The pointers to these segments are computed at the same time. The algorithm is then called recursively on regions R_1 and R_2. Finally, the array $B(v)$ of regions to which vertex v belongs is computed by a scan of v's segmented adjacency list.

Theorem 4. *An r-division of an n-vertex planar graph G can be computed in $O(\sqrt{n} \log^2 n)$ time using $O(n \log^2 n)$ work on an EREW PRAM.*

Note that both time and work required to find the region decomposition is within that of the shortest path algorithm (Theorem 2).

5 Final remarks

It has tacitly been assumed that the input to the separator algorithm is a planar graph with an embedding. This of course begs the question of the existence of a parallel planarity testing and embedding algorithm, or of a parallel separator algorithm without requiring an embedding as part of the input. We are not aware of any parallel algorithm for the latter case. Work-efficient, NC algorithms for planarity testing have been given in [10, 14], but neither of these algorithms seems to be easily implementable. Designing a simple, easily implementable, parallel algorithm for planarity testing and embedding is an interesting open problem.

Acknowledgement. We are grateful to Hillel Gazit for providing us with [6].

References

1. R. Ahuja, T. Magnanti, and J. Orlin, *Network Flows*, Prentice-Hall, 1993.
2. E. Cohen, Efficient parallel shortest-paths in digraphs with a separator decomposition, *Proc. 5th Symp. on Par. Alg. and Archit. (SPAA)*, pp.57-67, 1993.
3. J. Driscoll, H. Gabow, R. Shrairman, and R.E. Tarjan, Relaxed heaps: An alternative to Fibonacci heaps with applications to parallel computation, *Comm. of the ACM*, 31(11):1343-1354, 1988.
4. G. Frederickson, Fast algorithms for shortest paths in planar graphs with applications, *SIAM Journal of Computing*, 16(6):1004-1022, 1987.
5. M. Fredman and R.E. Tarjan, Fibonacci heaps and their uses in improved network optimization algorithms, *Journal of the ACM*, 34(3):596-615, 1987.
6. H. Gazit and G. Miller, An $O(\sqrt{n}\log(n))$ optimal parallel algorithm for a separator for planar graphs, Unpublished manuscript, 1987.
7. J. JáJá, *An Introduction to Parallel Algorithms*, Addison-Wesley, 1992.
8. C. Keßler and J. Träff, A library of basic PRAM algorithms and its implementation in FORK, *Proc. 8th Symp. on Par. Alg. and Archit. (SPAA)*, to appear, 1996.
9. P. Klein, S. Rao, M. Rauch, and S. Subramanian, Faster shortest-path algorithms for planar graphs, *Proc. 26th Symp. on Theory of Comp. (STOC)*, pp.27-37, 1994.
10. P. Klein and J. Reif, An efficient parallel algorithm for planarity, *Journal of Computer and System Sciences*, 37:190-246, 1988.
11. P. Klein and S. Subramanian, A linear-processor, polylog-time algorithm for shortest paths in planar graphs, *Proc. 34th Symp. on Foundations of Computer Sc. (FOCS)*, pp.259-270, 1993.
12. R. Lipton and R.E. Tarjan, A separator theorem for planar graphs, *SIAM Journal on Applied Mathematics*, 36(2):177-189, 1979.
13. G. Miller, Finding small simple cycle separators for 2-connected planar graphs, *Journal of Computer and System Sciences*, 32:265-279, 1986.
14. V. Ramachandran and J. Reif, Planarity testing in parallel, *Journal of Computer and System Sciences*, 49(3):517-561, 1994.
15. J.L. Träff and C.D. Zaroliagis, A simple parallel algorithm for the single-source shortest path problem on planar digraphs, Tech. Rep. MPI-I-96-1-012, Max-Planck-Institut für Informatik, Saarbrcken, June 1996.

A Regular VLSI Array
for an Irregular Algorithm

Florent de Dinechin[1], Doran K. Wilde[2], Sanjay Rajopadhye[1],
Rumen Andonov[3]

[1] IRISA, Campus de Beaulieu, 35042 Rennes France
[2] Brigham Young University, Provo Utah
[3] ISTV, University of Valenciennes, France

Abstract. We present an application specific, asynchronous VLSI processor array for the dynamic programming algorithm for the 0/1 knapsack problem. The array is derived systematically, using correctness-
preserving transformations, in two steps: the standard (dense) algorithm
is first transformed into an irregular (sparse) functional program which
has better efficiency. This program is then implemented as a modular
VLSI architecture with nearest neighbor connections. Proving bounds
on buffer sizes yields a linear array of identical asynchronous processors,
each with simple computational logic and a pair of *fixed size* FIFOs. A
modular solution can be obtained by additional load-time control, enabling the processors to pool their buffers.

1 Introduction

The *0/1 knapsack problem* is a classic, NP-complete, combinatorial optimization
problem with many applications [7, 12]. In this paper we concentrate on the *dynamic programming* approach to this problem [4, 7], since it has more regularity
than the dual *branch-and-bound*. It is well known that naive dynamic programming performs a lot of redundant computation, which can be avoided by using
a *sparse representation* of the data, yielding a significant improvement in the
average case performance [6]. Many authors have investigated parallel solutions
in the dense or sparse case. Software parallel implementations of the dense approach may be found in [11]. Lee et al. implement the sparse algorithm on a
hypercube using a divide and conquer strategy [10], which takes $O(mc/q + c^2)$
time on q processors, and uses $O(mc)$ storage in the worst case[4]. Chen et al.
present a pipelined linear array which uses $\Theta(mc)$ storage, $\Theta(c)$ on each of m
processors [5]. These authors, however, all assume that the target is a general
purpose multiprocessor, in particular, each processor has unbounded memory.

In this paper, we present a dedicated VLSI array architecture for the forward
phase of the sparse algorithm. This architecture is a *wavefront array processor*

---

[4] Lee, Shragowitz and Sahni point out that this could be worse than the sequential
algorithm [10]. The average behavior, however, is expected to be better because of
sparsity.

(WAP) which is similar to a systolic array, except that the processors are asynchronous, and communicate through FIFO queues [9].

Our contributions are twofold. First, we *systematically derive* the sparse algorithm from the (dense) recurrence of the dynamic programming algorithm. Our derivation is similar to that used in [3] for the *unbounded* knapsack problem. Second, our implementation on dedicated VLSI is fully modular with respect to problem parameters. For this purpose we first show that buffer sizes are bounded by the maximum object weight. This is itself a problem parameter, but we then show how an appropriate number of PE's, each with the same amount of memory, may be configured so that they "pool" this memory (a similar idea was previously used for the dense algorithm [2]). Thus it is possible to solve a larger problem instance by simply adding more PEs to the array, without having to redesign the PE itself. Furthermore, we also discuss the problem of choosing the buffer sizes optimally.

The paper is organized as follows. In Sect.2 we introduce the problem and the sparse representation. In Sect.3 we present the transformation of the recurrence equation of the dense algorithm into a stream functional program. Sect.4 deals with the implementation of this program as a WAP, and the choice of the buffer sizes. Finally, we present our conclusions. Because of space constraints we give neither proofs nor implementation details, which may be found in [1].

2 Problem Definition

The *forward phase* of the dynamic programming algorithm for the 0/1 knapsack problem is defined by the profit function given by the recurrence equation below:

$$\begin{cases} f_k(j) = \max\left(f_{k-1}(j),\ p_k + f_{k-1}(j - w_k)\right) & \forall (k, j) \in \{1 \ldots m\} \times \{1 \ldots c\} \\ f_0(j) = f_k(0) = 0 \\ f_k(j) = -\infty \quad \forall j < 0 \end{cases}$$

$$(1)$$

Table 1 shows an example of the $f_k(j)$, calculated as per (1). The entry at $j = 10$ and $k = 4$ indicates that the maximum profit acheivable for this problem is 19. The backtracking phase (which we do not consider in this paper) would indicate that the maximum profit is achieved by placing objects 1, 2 and 4 in the knapsack.

Table 1. Values of $f_k(j)$ for $m = 4$; $c = 10$; $w_i = 5, 4, 6, 1$; $p_i = 7, 8, 9, 4$.

j / k	1	2	3	4	5	6	7	8	9	10
1	0	0	0	0	7	7	7	7	7	7
2	0	0	0	8	8	8	8	8	15	15
3	0	0	0	8	8	9	9	9	15	17
4	4	4	4	8	12	12	13	13	15	19

There is considerable redundancy in this table. It is easy to prove [1] that each f_k (each row) is a monotonically increasing function, which can be efficiently represented as a set of *critical points* $[j, f_k(j)]$ (the boxed values in Table 1). This *sparse representation* of f_k is also illustrated by Fig.1.a.

The sparse algorithm [13] uses (1) to build this sparse representation iteratively: given the set (or sequence) S_{k-1} of critical points representing f_{k-1}, first compute an auxillary set S'_{k-1} by adding $[w_k, f_k]$ to each element of S_{k-1}. Then take the union of S_{k-1} and S'_{k-1}, which contains all the critical points of f_k, plus some that are *dominated* (not critical): a point $[j_1, f_1]$ dominates another point $[j_2, f_2]$ iff $j_1 \leq j_2$ and $f_1 \geq f_2$, (i.e., if it has less weight and more profit).

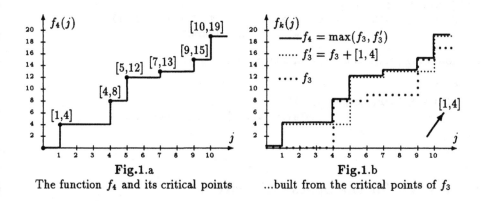

Fig.1.a
The function f_4 and its critical points

Fig.1.b
...built from the critical points of f_3

The set S_k of the critical points of f_k is obtained by removing all the dominated points from the union set, as illustrated in Fig.1.b.

3 Derivation of the Stream Functional Program

We derive a stream functional program to implement the recurrence equation (1), computing the stream (sequence) of critical points S_k from the stream S_{k-1}.

We use the following notations: braces { ... } are used to group sequences. The operator ˆ denotes the concatenation of an element to a sequence. Parentheses are used for function application and square brackets are used to form tuples.

The initial function $f_0 = 0$ can be trivially represented by the sequence $S_0 = \{[0, 0]\}$. Then the term $p_k + f_{k-1}(j - w_k)$ is represented by the sequence S'_{k-1} obtained by adding the pair $[w_k, p_k]$ to each pair element in $[0, 0]ˆS_{k-1}$. The resulting sequence is clipped so that no accumulated weight exceeds the knapsack capacity c. This yields $S'_k = \text{AddTest}([w_k, p_k], [0, 0]ˆS_{k-1}, c)$, where AddTest is defined as follows:

```
AddTest([w,p], {}, c)       = {}
AddTest([w,p], [j,f]^S, c) = if j+w>c : {}
                             else  : [j+w, f+p] ^ AddTest([w,p], S, c)
```

The max function used in (1) is implemented as a stream operator computing the sparse sequence for the maximum of two functions given as sparse sequences. This is done by a merge sort based on the j elements (the Merge function below), followed by a removal of the pairs that are dominated by an earlier pair in the sequence (the Filter function below).

```
Merge({}, S) = S
Merge(S, {}) = S
Merge([j1,f1] ^ S1 , [j2,f2] ^ S2) =
    if        j1 < j2  :  [j1,f1] ^ Merge(S1 , [j2,f2] ^ S2)
    else if   j1 > j2  :  [j2,f2] ^ Merge([j1,f1] ^ S1 , S2)
    else if   j1 = j2  :  [j1, max(f1,f2)] ^ Merge(S1 , S2)

Filter({}, t) = {}
Filter([j,f]^S, t) =  if  f > t  :  [j,f] ^ Filter(S, f)
                          else   :  Filter(S ,t)
```

The following program then computes S_k from S_{k-1}:

```
S(0)={}
S(k) = Filter( Merge( S(k-1),
                AddTest( [wk,pk], [0,0]^S(k-1), c ) ),
           0 )
```

4   A WAP for the Sparse Algorithm

It is well known [8] that a stream functional program corresponds to a network of processes communicating over asynchronous FIFO channels. Hence the above program for calculating the recurrence (1) can be implemented on an *asynchronous array processor* with m cells. The cell k receives the sequence S_{k-1} and computes the sequence S_k. The structure of such a cell is shown in Fig.2. The FIFO buffer between two consecutive cells is optional: its purpose is to improve the overall throughput, therefore its size depends on statistical considerations. Simulations showed, however, that small internal buffers lead to near-optimal efficiency: for random values of (w_i, p_i) in the range $(10 \cdots 100, 10 \cdots 100)$ and $c = 3000$, for instance, the optimal throughput was reached with only 10 registers.

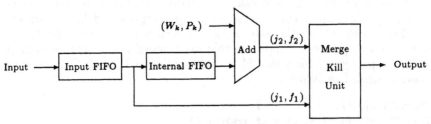

Fig.2. Basic Processor

The internal FIFO, on the other hand, may lead to problems: as the merge-kill unit consumes $[j_1, f_1]$ from the input FIFO, a copy must be saved in the internal queue for later use in the second input of the merge-kill unit. If this queue is too small, the circuit will fail due to FIFO overflow. The crucial fact allowing a VLSI implementation using fixed size buffers is based on the fact that *the maximal size of the internal queue on any cell is* w_{max} (see proof in [1]). As this result still limits such a processor to operate on objects of weight smaller than its internal FIFO size, we extend the design, by the means of a configuration bit, to allow the FIFOs of consecutive processors to be connected to form one single logical processor[5]. Thus the array is extensible with respect to w_{max}. It is also extensible with respect to m by simply adding new processors to the array, or by using multiple passes: it is easy to implement a LPGS partitioning scheme for this WAP, with an external buffer (e.g. in a host) bounded by c, the knapsack capacity. The choice of the size α of the internal FIFO then leads to a classical trade-off: a large FIFO increases the average efficiency of the processors but also their area, leading to fewer processors on a given silicon area. The optimal value of α is very data-dependent and should thus be determined by an extensive simulation using sample data. A worst-case analysis is also possible and leads to the following equation which gives, for each value of $\beta = \log_2 \alpha$, the maximal size m of the knapsack problem which may be handled by the architecture.

$$ m \leq \beta + \left\lfloor \log_2 \left(1 - \beta + \left\lfloor \frac{S}{2^\beta s_r + s_0} \right\rfloor \right) \right\rfloor \tag{2} $$

Here s_r is the area of one FIFO register, and s_0 the area of one processor, excluding the internal FIFO. An extensive search over the values of β (from 0 to 16 is obviously sufficient) gives the optimal value of α in the worst case.

5 Conclusion

We have presented a systematic derivation of a wavefront array processor from a recurrence equation specifying the (forward phase of the) dynamic programming algorithm for the 0/1 knapsack problem. The final array is interesting in its own right (although it remains an open problem whether it is possible to perform the backtracking phase with similar space/time complexity).

The main advantage of this approach is to combine the strong points of an irregular algorithm (time efficiency due to asynchrony, and space efficiency due to sparsity) with the strong points of a parallel regular array (simplicity of the design and efficiency due to potential massive parallelism). Thus the methodology consists of two systematic, independent transformations: the first transforms regular to irregular (and thus increases algorithmic efficiency), and the second transforms irregular to regular (and thus increases implementation efficiency). Problems, however, arise when we try to generalize both steps:

The first transformation uses some property of the data (here sparsity and monotonicity) to lead to an irregular algorithm, expressed as a stream functional

---

[5] The price to pay for this is roughly doubling the number of pins per chip.

program, which is more efficient in average than the regular one. This is based on manually proving properties of the computations, and is related to program synthesis. It is not likely that it can be automated.

The second transformation is more classical and leads from a irregular stream functional program to a regular (but asynchronous) WAP, whose parameters are derived from properties of the algorithm or data. The crucial problem here is to prove bounds on buffers in order to obtain a VLSI implementation. We conjecture that this can be done systematically, however slight variations in the algorithm can lead to crucial problems (for example, a direct adaptation of the program used in [3] yields an array where buffer sizes cannot be bounded).

We believe that our methodology may be applied to other irregular problems, such as sparse matrix computations.

References

1. R. Andonov, F. de Dinechin, S. Rajopadhye, and D. Wilde. – Systematic design of wavefront array processors : A case study. – Internal Report 743, IRISA, March 1994.
2. R. Andonov and S. Rajopadhye. – An optimal algo-tech-cuit for the knapsack problem. – Technical Report PI-791, IRISA, January 1994. – (to appear in IEEE Transactions on Parallel and Distributed Systems).
3. R. Andonov and S. V. Rajopadhye. – A sparse knapsack algo-tech-cuit and its synthesis. – In *International Conference on Application-Specific Array Processors (ASAP-94)*, pages 302–313, San Francisco, August 1994. IEEE.
4. R. Bellman. – *Dynamic Programming.* – Princeton University Press, Princeton, NJ, 1957.
5. G.H. Chen and J.H. Jang. – An improved parallel algorithm for 0/1 knapsack problem. – *Parallel Computing*, 18:811–821, 1992.
6. E. Horowitz and S. Sahni. – Computing partitions with aplications to the knapsack problem. – *Journal of the ACM*, 21(2):277–292, April 1974.
7. T. C. Hu. – *Integer Programming and Network Flows.* – Addison-Wesley, 1969.
8. G. Kahn. – The semantics of a simple language for parallel processing. – In *Proceedings of IFIP*, pages 471–475. IFIP, August 1974.
9. S. Y. Kung, K. S. Arun, R. J. Gal-Ezer, and D. V. B. Rao. – Wavefront array processor: Language, architecture and applications. – *IEEE Transactions on Computers*, C-31:1054–1066, 1982.
10. J. Lee, E. Shragowitz, and S. Sahni. – A hypercube algorithm for the 0/1 knapsack problems. – *J. of Parallel and Distributed Computing*, 5:438–456, 1988.
11. J. Lin and J. A. Storer. – Processor-efficient hypercube algorithm for the knapsack problem. – *J. of Parallel and Distributed Computing*, 13:332–337, 1991.
12. S. Martello and P. Toth. – *Knapsack Problems: Algorithms and Computer Implementation.* – John Wiley and Sons, 1990.
13. G. Nemhauser and J. Ullman. – Discrete dynamic programming and capital allocation. – *Management Science*, 15(9):494–505, 1969.

Digital Librarires and Spatial Information Processing

Terence R. Smith

University of California at Santa Barbara
smith@cs.ucsb.edu

Abstract. The process of constructing and supporting general digital libraries offers a rich area for research into, and application of, parallel and distributed computing. The ability of large, distributed digital libraries to perform adequately over the Internet may well depend on the contributions that parallel computing can make to their performance. This is particularly the case for digital libraries that support access to multimedia materials by geographical reference, as compared with more traditional forms of access relating to author, title, and subject matter. We provide a survey of significant classes of problems in the construction and maintenance of such libraries that can benefit from parallel and distributed processing. Particular emphasis is placed on the processing of information that is implicitly or explicitly organized in terms of spatial reference. Such information includes items whose contents are explicitly organized in terms of spatial reference, such as maps, images, and video (and hence in terms of the "vector" and "raster" data models), and items whose contents are only implicitly organized in such terms, such as texts. Key aspects of such information that encourage the application of parallel computation are the large sizes of individual items (often in the gigabyte range); the fact that much of the information contained in the items is in "implicit" form and requires significant computation to make explicit; and possibilities for decomposing a computation into relatively independent components corresponding to some partition of the geographic space.

The survey is organized in terms of the main functional components of a general digital library: the interface, catalog, storage, and ingest components. Examples of the problems discussed in the survey include the use of library servers that take the form of multicomputers and whose scheduling is optimized to support many simultaneous library users; the user of high-performance parallel computing for the extraction of catalog meta-information and the translation of meta-information representation languages; the application of high-performance parallel computing for the preprocessing of large datasets in preparation for storage in appropriate forms; the application of high-performance parallel computing for the processing of spatially-indexed items at query time, in support of user-centered workspaces; and the use of multicomputing in processing user queries over large networks of workstations.

Flexible Communication Mechanisms for Dynamic Structured Applications*

Stephen J. Fink[1], Scott B. Baden[1], and Scott R.Kohn[2]

[1] Department of Computer Science and Engineering, University of California, San Diego, La Jolla, CA 92093-0114
[2] Department of Chemistry and Biochemistry, University of California, San Diego, La Jolla, CA 92093-0340

Abstract. Irregular scientific applications are often difficult to parallelize due to elaborate dynamic data structures with complicated communication patterns. We describe flexible *data orchestration* abstractions that enable the programmer to express customized communication patterns arising in an important class of irregular computations—adaptive finite difference methods for partial differential equations. These abstractions are supported by KeLP, a C++ run-time library. KeLP enables the programmer to manage spatial data dependence patterns and express data motion handlers as first-class mutable objects. Using two finite difference applications, we show that KeLP's flexible communication model effectively manages elaborate data motion arising in semi-structured adaptive methods.

1 Introduction

Many scientific numerical methods employ structured irregular representations to improve accuracy. Irregular representations can resolve fine physical structures in complicated geometries but are difficult to implement due to elaborate, dynamic data structures. Since these structures give rise to unpredictable communication patterns, parallelization is difficult. To ease the programmer's burden, programming languages and libraries can hide many low-level details of a parallel implementation [1, 2, 3, 4, 5, 6]. We present Kernel Lattice Parallelism (KeLP), a C++ class library that provides high-level abstractions to manage data layout and data motion for dynamic irregular block-structured applications [3].

KeLP supports *data orchestration*, a model which enables the programmer to express dependence patterns among dynamic grid collections and to customize the interpretation of those dependences for an application. KeLP's data

---

* This research is supported in part by ONR contract N00014-93-1-0152 and by the DOE Computational Science Graduate Fellowship Program. Computer time on the Intel Paragon at the San Diego Supercomputer Center was provided by a UCSD School of Engineering block grant. Access to the IBM SP2 was provided by the Cornell Theory Center.

[3] The KeLP software and documentation is available at
http://www.cse.ucsd.edu/groups/hpcl/scg/kelp.html.

orchestration model uses two techniques—structural abstraction and the inspector/executor model. *Structural abstraction*, introduced in the LPARX programming system, separates the description of an elaborate computational structure from the data itself [2, 7]. KeLP utilizes structural abstraction to provide intuitive geometric operations for manipulating a high-level description of data dependence patterns.

KeLP relies on a generalization of the inspector/executor model employed in Multiblock PARTI [4]. KeLP encodes data dependence patterns into an object called a *MotionPlan*, and interprets the corresponding data motion using a handler called a *Mover*. The programmer may customize the data motion pattern and interpretation according to the needs of the application.

KeLP's abstractions offer increased flexibility in expressing communication compared to previous block-structured inspector/executor libraries such as Multiblock PARTI. Such flexibility is vital in implementing irregular applications. To understand why, consider an adaptive multigrid method employed in *ab-initio* materials design[8]. In this application dynamic collections of 3D blocks of data are organized into levels. The number of blocks per level will vary at run time, along with their shape, size, and physical location with respect to one another. (See Fig. 1.)

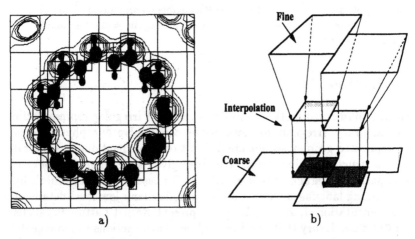

a)   b)

Fig. 1. a) An adaptive discretization of a $C_{20}H_{20}$ molecule. b) Example of inter-level transfer operations required for structured adaptive mesh refinement.

In this application, collections of data communicate in five distinct patterns, both within and between levels. However, data access patterns differ in each adaptive mesh application. For example, a hyperbolic partial differential equation arising in shock hydrodynamics demands a different set of data motion patterns that are compatible with the conservative differencing schemes used in the application. Moreover, specialized boundary conditions may be required in each application. KeLP's data orchestration mechanisms simplify the expression these complex block communication patterns. Additionally, KeLP allows the programmer to customize communication pattern interpretation, allowing affiliated computation to occur along with data motion.

KeLP runs using message-passing (e.g.. MPI[9]) and has been tested on the IBM SP2, Cray T3D, Intel Paragon, clusters of workstations and single processor workstations. We have used KeLP to implement a dynamic irregular multilevel adaptive mesh refinement algorithm and a simple uniform static finite difference calculation. In one application (uniform finite difference), we applied application specific optimizations that reduce absolute communication time by a factor of 2 over the unoptimized case; performance came to within 15% of a carefully hand-coded application.

Performance alone, however, reveals only part of the picture. Because five different communication patterns arose in our adaptive solver, it was necessary to write five different pieces of code to handle them. KeLP abstractions hide much of the detail; the complexity of the programming task would be daunting using message-passing primitives alone.

The remainder of this paper proceeds as follows. Section 2 describes KeLP's data orchestration model. Section 3 validates KeLP on two applications, and makes some comparisons with LPARX, which does not employ orchestration. Section 4 discusses related work and Section 5 summarizes the KeLP results.

2 Data Orchestration

KeLP relies on the LPARX structural abstraction model to provide geometric constructs that facilitate the design. We will give a brief overview of structural abstraction, and then discuss KeLP's data orchestration model.

2.1 Structural Abstraction

Structural abstraction was introduced in the LPARX programming system. Under structural abstraction, the geometry of a block structured data set is stored separately from the data itself. The decomposition of the blocks exists as a first-class object [2, 7]. KeLP extends the notion to communication. That is, communication patterns are first class, mutable objects, along with the handlers that carry out the communication.

KeLP inherits three core data decomposition abstractions from LPARX: *Region*, *Grid*, and *XArray*. KeLP extends the model with a fourth core abstraction, the *FloorPlan*.

A Region is a first-class object that represents a rectangular subset of Z^n. A Region is identified by $[P_1, P_2]$ where P_1 and P_2 are the two Points at the lower and upper corners of the Region. [4] For a Region R, $lwb(R)$ and $upb(R)$ return P_1 and P_2, respectively.

---

[4] A Point is an integer n-tuple representing a point in Z^n. Element-wise addition and scalar multiplication are defined over Points in the obvious way. For a Point P, $P(i)$ returns the ith component of P.

The *Region calculus* is a set of high-level geometric operations provided to help the programmer manipulate index sets. Three useful Region calculus operations are *shift*, *intersect*, and *grow*. For a Region R and a Point P, $shift(R, P)$ denotes R translated by the vector P: $[lwb(R) + P, upb(R) + P]$. *Intersection* between two Regions is defined in the usual geometric way. Given a Point g, $grow(R, g)$ returns the Region that is equivalent to R padded with $g(i)$ cells in the ith direction. If $g(i) < 0$, the Region is shrunk in the obvious way. Note that all Region operations can be implemented efficiently with a small number of integer operations, and Regions are closed under *shift*, *intersection*, and *grow*.

A Grid is dynamic array of objects, all of the same type, whose index space is a Region. A Grid G may not be distributed across multiple processor memories; rather, it exists only in the address space of one processor. A Grid G is identified by its Region and by the common type of its elements. For example, the Fortran-90 array defined as `real A[3:7]` corresponds to a one-dimensional Grid A of `real` with $region(A) = [3, 7]$. A Grid differs from a simple array in that it has a processor assignment and that the run time system provides powerful block copy operations over Grids, described below. For convenience, most KeLP Region calculus operations are defined over Grids. For example, if G_1 and G_2 are Grids, then $G_1 \cap G_2$ returns the Region $region(G_1) \cap region(G_2)$.

An XArray serves as a container class for multiple Grids, which collectively represent a distributed data object. Each Grid element in an XArray may have a different Region, though all must have the same rank and element type (see Fig. 2). We may enumerate an XArray by indexing its elements, i.e. $X(1)$ and $X(2)$ are the first and second (Grid) elements of XArray X.

The KeLP FloorPlan is a one-dimensional array of Regions with processor assignments. The FloorPlan provides a useful first-class abstraction to encapsulate the notion of a data decomposition. The programmer may use Region calculus operations to modify a FloorPlan, and then use the FloorPlan to instantiate an XArray with a given data decomposition. Just as a Region abstracts the index domain of a Grid, a FloorPlan represents the index domain and processor assignments for an XArray.

2.2 Data Orchestration Abstractions

In an irregular application such as adaptive multigrid, a collection of grids (i.e., a KeLP XArray) communicate as a single logical unit. For example, in Fig. 1b, the irregularly-shaped fine level communicates with the irregularly-shaped coarse level over the points falling in the shadow cast by the fine level. KeLP represents a data motion pattern between XArrays using the *MotionPlan* abstraction. The MotionPlan is a first-class communication schedule [3, 4] object representing an atomic block copy between XArrays. The programmer builds and modifies a MotionPlan using Region calculus operations. This functionality gives the user powerful mechanisms to describe highly irregular data motion patterns.

To understand how to build a MotionPlan we must first describe the primitive of communication in KeLP, a block copy operation. Let G_1, G_2 be two Grids, and R_1, R_2 be two Regions. Then G_1 on $R_1 \Rightarrow G_2$ on R_2 denotes a block copy

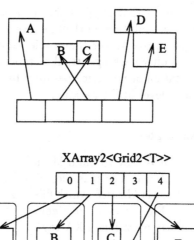

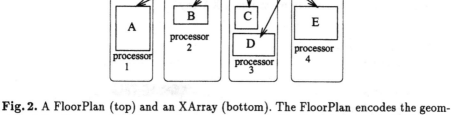

XArray2<Grid2<T>>

Fig. 2. A FloorPlan (top) and an XArray (bottom). The FloorPlan encodes the geometry of the XArray. The XArray is a coarse-grained distributed array of 2D blocks of data. The blocks have different sizes and each is assigned a single processor,

operation, meaning copy the values from G_1 at indices in R_1 into G_2 at indices in R_2. For this operation, we call G_1 the *sender* and G_2 the *receiver*.

With this in mind, we can now describe the incremental construction of a MotionPlan. The programmer adds block copy operations to a MotionPlan, one at a time. For a MotionPlan M, two XArrays X and Y, and Regions R_1 and R_2, $M.copy(X, i, R_1, Y, j, R_2)$ adds the block copy operation $X(i)$ on $R_1 \Rightarrow Y(j)$ on R_2 to M. The programmer may also modify an extant MotionPlan using Region calculus operations. MotionPlan concatenation and record deletion are also possible, along with other modifications enabled by the Region calculus.

Once the MotionPlan has been generated, it is passed to a *Mover*, a first class object that interprets the MotionPlan and performs the data transfer operations described therein. The Mover object translates the MotionPlan and issues matching non-blocking send/receive pairs to effect the data motion pattern. If data for a particular message happens to reside contiguously in memory, the message is sent or received without intermediate buffer-packing.

Since the Mover is a self-contained object, independent of the rest of KeLP, it is possible to extend and replace Mover objects to realize different communication operations. For example, the KeLP distribution includes a Mover that provides message aggregation, concatenating multiple Region copies between a pair of physical processors into one message. (For example, the inter-level transfer in Fig. 1b.) The programmer may also derive objects from Mover to perform numeric operations along with communication. For example, we have implemented a linear multigrid elliptic solver that requires the error on the coarse level to be interpolated and added to the solution on the fine level. The multigrid program derives a specialized object from Mover that copies and adds simultaneously, by overriding the Mover's buffer packing virtual member functions. This facility allows efficient implementation of numeric operators by eliminating temporary storage and additional user-level buffer packing.

2.3 Data Motion Examples

Using the Region calculus, it is easy to build MotionPlans to describe common collective communication patterns. For example, one common pattern that arises in finite difference calculations is *fillpatch*, which fills in ghost cells with data from logically overlapping grids. Fig. 3 shows the algorithm to generate the *fillpatch* MotionPlan for an irregularly partitioned XArray.

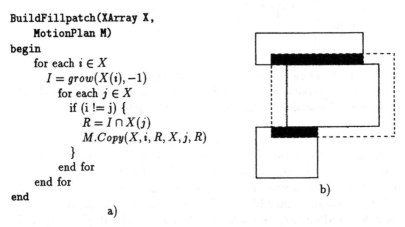

```
BuildFillpatch(XArray X,
    MotionPlan M)
begin
    for each i ∈ X
        I = grow(X(i), −1)
        for each j ∈ X
            if (i != j) {
                R = I ∩ X(j)
                M.Copy(X, i, R, X, j, R)
            }
        end for
    end for
end
```

a)

b)

Fig. 3. a) Pseudocode to generate a `fillpatch` MotionPlan `M` to fill in ghost cells for XArray `X`. b) The dark shaded regions represent ghost regions that are copied into the central Grid.

Since MotionPlans may be constructed incrementally, the programmer may compose complicated collective communication patterns from simpler patterns. For example, suppose an application demands that ghost regions be filled in both between overlapping Grids and across periodic boundary conditions. Independent subroutines could build the fillpatch and periodic communication Motion-Plans, and the first-class MotionPlans can be composed into a single MotionPlan representing the total communication pattern. One advantage of this mechanism is that it is possible to provide a library of pre-defined MotionPlan generators which the programmer can use to build more complicated patterns. Another advantage is that the combined MotionPlan may expose possible communication optimizations (e.g.. message vectorization) that could not be performed if the simpler communication patterns were executed separately.

2.4 Coarse Grain Data Parallelism

KeLP's programming model is based on a coarse-grain data parallel control flow which was also employed in LPARX. Programs begin with a single logical thread of control, whose execution is implemented by distributing and replicating operations across multiple SPMD processes as needed. Periodically, the KeLP program enters a **forall** loop, where each iteration of the **forall** loop executes independently on exactly one SPMD process.

Whereas KeLP and LPARX employ the same coarse grain data parallel computation model, the two systems differ on where data motion operations may occur. In LPARX, each process may initiate block copy operations from within a **forall** loop. Since each SPMD process does not execute all iterations of the loop, block copy operations must be implemented with one-sided communication mechanisms. Coarse grain data-parallel semantics require that all block copy operations complete before executing statements after the **forall** loop. Thus, at the end of the **forall** loop, all processors participate in a global synchronization point to ensure that all block copies complete before the program may proceed.

This asynchronous one-sided communication implementation introduces several overheads on message-passing multicomputers which do not provide native one-sided communication mechanisms. First there is the direct cost of synchronization; a barrier synchronization on current message-passing multicomputers typically takes several hundred microseconds. Additionally, unnecessary global synchronization may exacerbate load imbalance and increase network congestion by forcing all processes to run in close synchrony even when then program's data dependencies do not require it. Furthermore, data transfers conditionally initiated by one partner without the other's knowledge preclude run-time preprocessing of the communication pattern. This prevents some optimizations such as posting for contiguous messages directly into user data structures.

KeLP eliminates the need for one-sided communication by disallowing block copy operations from inside a **forall** loop. Instead, all block copy operations are treated as collective communication. Following the inspector/executor paradigm [4], all processors store a locally relevant piece of the distributed communication pattern (MotionPlan). No costly global synchronization is required to detect termination of data movement. Additionally, the KeLP run-time library may exploit information in the MotionPlan to perform communication optimizations, such as message aggregation and optimized buffer management to avoid unnecessary user-level buffer-packing.

3 Validation

We present results for a dynamic multilevel structured adaptive mesh refinement algorithm and a simple static finite difference application in KeLP. The first application illustrates the expressive power of data orchestration; five separate MotionPlans were required along with one customization of the mover. The second example, which is far less complicated, enables us to compare performance of the KeLP implementation with a carefully hand-coded version. [5]

3.1 Adaptive Multigrid

Lda3d is a 3D adaptive multigrid eigenvalue solver used in *ab initio* materials science simulations [2, 8]. This application was originally coded in LPARX and then ported to KeLP. The lda3d algorithm demands complex irregular communication to transfer data within and between levels of the mesh hierarchy (see Fig. 1b). MotionPlans and the Region calculus provide a natural paradigm to describe these data motion patterns.

Fig. 4 shows performance results for lda3d on the Intel Paragon and IBM SP2. The results show that KeLP's orchestration mechanisms reduce communication time by 40 to 70% compared to LPARX. On the SP2, lda3d is communication bound and KeLP version reduces overall running time by up to 40%. On the Paragon, communication is not the bottleneck and although communication overheads are substantially reduced, Amdahl's law [10] limits overall application improvement to approximately 10%. Clearly the benefits of KeLP would be substantial on workstation clusters that experience high message start times.

In Fig. 4, load imbalance is measured as the time a processor must wait for other processors when entering a communication phase. KeLP's relaxed synchronization requirements expose load imbalance due to unequal *communication* loads as a significant problem in lda3d. In LPARX, since all processors synchronize at the end of a communication phase, the processes exit the communication phase in very close synchrony. Any variance in running time due to unequal communication loads is attributed to communication time in Fig. 4. Since KeLP does not introduce any unnecessary synchronization, the communication load discrepancy propagates out of the communication phase and gets attributed to load imbalance in Fig. 4. Practically, this means that KeLP's relaxed synchronization requirements allow the programmer to try to hide discrepancies in communication load by considering both computation and communication load when assigning work to processors.

3.2 Jacobi

To assess the efficiency of the KeLP communication mechanisms, we now analyze the performance of KeLP on a simple, static regular application. The application is jacobi3d, a seven-point stencil relaxation which solves Laplace's equation over a uniform 3D grid. The 3D grid is distributed blockwise on each axis. In the coarse-grain data parallel programming model, each processor acquires

---

[5] For the Intel Paragon results presented here, the C++ compiler was g++ v2.7.0, with the -O2 -mnoieee flags. The Fortran compiler was if77 R5.0, with -O4 -Knoiee. The Paragon results were under OSF/1 v1.0.4 with the NX mesage-passing library. The IBM SP2 results used xlC v2.1, with -O -Q, and xlf v3.1 with -O3. The operating system was AIX v3.2 with the MPL message-passing library.

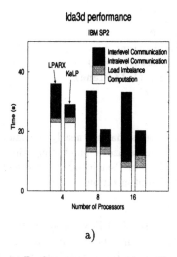
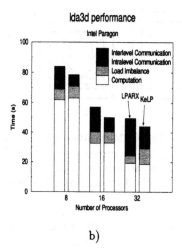

a)   b)

Fig. 4. Performance comparison for adaptive multigrid eigenvalue solver on a) IBM SP2 and b) Intel Paragon.

ghost cells on each face of its local partition, and then performs local relaxation independently.

Since the Jacobi algorithm is relatively simple, it was possible to write an optimized hand-coded version. Some communication optimizations performed in the hand-coded version are:

- Receive messages asynchronously in the order they arrive.
- Send contiguous faces in place to avoid buffer packing.
- Prepost messages one iteration in advance.

We developed three KeLP versions of the `jacobi3d` application. All three versions reuse the MotionPlan. The first version uses the `fillpatch` routine listed in Fig. 3 to generate the MotionPlan. Note that this generic fillpatch pattern fills in all ghost cells, communicating with up to 26 neighbors. However, for the `jacobi3d` relaxation, we only need ghost cells from the 6 Manhattan neighbors (no corners or edges). The second KeLP version builds a MotionPlan which only fills in ghost regions from Manhattan neighbors.

When communicating faces of a 3D array, user-level buffer packing and unpacking contribute substantially to communication overheads. However, note that two of the six faces generated by the Manhattan pattern are nearly contiguous. By growing these face Regions by one cell, they represent faces that are stored contiguously in a processor's memory and the KeLP run-time system is able to avoid buffer-packing and unpacking (see Fig. 5). Thus, we considered a third KeLP version which obtains the Manhattan pattern from version 2, and then directly modifies the MotionPlan to create contiguous faces wherever possible. The pseudocode for this direct schedule modification is shown in Fig. 5c [6].

---

[6] For the 4x4x2 processor arrangement used here, the buffer-packing optimization reduces the volume of user-level copying by a factor of 2.

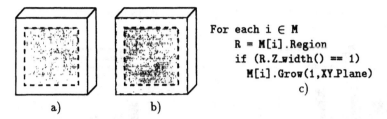

```
For each i ∈ M
    R = M[i].Region
    if (R.Z_width() == 1)
        M[i].Grow(1,XY_Plane)
                        c)
```

a)   b)

Fig. 5. a) The 3D Manhattan pattern transmits ghost faces that are nearly contiguous in memory. b) By growing these faces by one cell, we realize a block copy that is contiguous in memory and can avoid user-level copying. c) Pseudocode that directly modifies the Manhattan MotionPlan M to perform this optimization.

Fig. 6a compares the running times of these three KeLP versions with the LPARX version and the hand-coded version. The Figure shows that the KeLP implementation with a naive MotionPlan (version 1) reduces absolute communication time by a factor of two over the LPARX implementation, which does not employ data orchestration. Versions 2 and 3 tailor the MotionPlan for better efficiency and version 3 achieves performance within 15% of the hand-coded version. The communication overhead in KeLP version 3 is reduced by a factor of 2.1 compared to version 1. Fig. 6b shows the library overheads for the best KeLP version compared to the asynchronous LPARX version for both strip and block decompositions on the Intel Paragon and IBM SP2. In all cases KeLP achieves performance within 15% of the hand-coded version. The 15% overhead is due mostly to the fact that the hand-coded version exploits the repetitive communication pattern to pre-post asynchronous message receives well in advance. A future version of KeLP may support this type of optimization.

We note that the hand coded version we developed for this study is substantially more efficient than a naive message-passing code using blocking message primitives and extraneous user-level buffer-packing. We speculate that the optimized KeLP implementation would be at least as efficient as the hand-coded version in such cases.

4   Related work

Data orchestration is based on the inspector/executor paradigm, which was employed in the CHAOS [3], CHAOS++ [5] and Multiblock PARTI [4] run time systems. Our work is most similar to Multiblock PARTI, which provides coarse-grain block transfers over structured data decompositions. Multiblock PARTI supports regular block distributions for dynamic arrays, but does not directly support irregular block decompositions as in systems like KeLP. Multiblock PARTI provides two common communication patterns, one to fill in ghost regions and one that moves data over regular sections. KeLP differs from Multiblock PARTI in that KeLP exposes communication management to the programmer, who can then describe arbitrary communication patterns with high-level geometric operations. The Multiblock PARTI communication schedule is an opaque

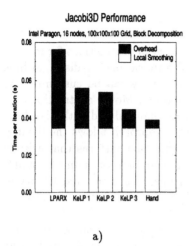
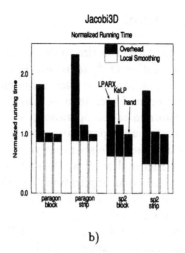

a)   b)

Fig. 6. a) Comparison of several jacobi3d implementations on the Intel Paragon. The first KeLP version uses the naive fillpatch schedule, the second uses a Manhattan neighbor pattern, and the third version is optimized to avoid buffer packing. b) Comparison of library overheads for jacobi3d implementation with 16-processor strip and block decompositions on the Intel Paragon and IBM SP2. In each case, the results are normalized so the hand-coded running time is 1.0.

object over which the user has limited control. In contrast, KeLP exposes the schedule to the programmer as a first class mutable object, which may be manipulated, modified and interpreted according to the programmer's needs.

LPARX introduced *structural abstraction*, a set of high-level geometric abstractions used to describe data layout and data motion in irregular dynamic structured applications [2]. LPARX uses an asynchronous communication model which is most appropriate for applications where run-time preprocessing of the communication pattern is impossible. However, when communication dependences can be computed beforehand, run-time preprocessing can significantly reduce communication overheads and synchronization.

Structural abstraction is employed in other adaptive finite difference solvers. Rendleman *et al.* have developed BOXLIB, a library for implementing Adaptive Mesh Refinement on single processor computers [11]. Parashar and Browne employ it in a novel implementation technique called DAGH [12].

Scheduled communication mechanisms have proven useful in several other contexts. The STANCE system [6] uses inspector/executor mechanisms to manage data-parallel applications on adaptive, non-uniform environments. The PASSION [13] and Jovian [14] systems pre-process communication patterns to optimize parallel I/O. Communication schedules have traditionally been considered for message-passing architectures. However, recent work [15, 16] has shown that inspector/executor techniques may be necessary to achieve good performance on distributed shared-memory architectures as well.

5 Conclusion

We have introduced run-time *data orchestration*, a set of abstractions for managing communication in dynamic block-structured applications. A distinguishing feature of our approach is that communication activity can be customized to the application and architecture. The MotionPlan and Mover abstractions expose the communication operations, which can be manipulated with high-level abstractions to suit a particular application. This approach allows the flexibility needed to describe elaborate dynamic communication patterns that arise in multilevel structured applications and to optimize common communication patterns for a particular application. To our knowledge, this is the first library to apply run-time communication scheduling techniques to a dynamic multilevel structured application.

Performance results show that KeLP's relaxed synchronization requirements can reduce communication times by a factor of two or more compared to an implementation relying on one-sided communication techniques. KeLP's flexible mechanisms give the programmer an intuitive methodology for describing irregular block-structured communication, which simplifies implementation of dynamic structured applications. For a simple regular static application, application-specific communication optimizations realized a further two-fold reduction in communication overhead.

We have shown that the ability to represent and interpret complex dynamic data motion patterns using data orchestration is vital in applications that employ computational adaptivity. We are currently investigating applications of data orchestration to hierarchical parallel architectures and to massive data analysis.

References

1. High Performance Fortran Forum, "High performance fortran language specification," Rice Univeristy, Houston, Texas, May 1993.
2. S. R. Kohn, *A Parallel Software Infrastructure for Dynamic Block-Irregular Scientific Calculations.* PhD thesis, University of California at San Diego, 1995.
3. R. Das, M. Uysal, J. Saltz, and Y.-S. Hwang, "Communication optimizations for irregular scientific computations on distributed memory architectures," *Journal of Parallel and Distributed Computing*, vol. 22, no. 3, pp. 462–479, 1994.
4. G. Agrawal, A. Sussman, and J. Saltz, "An integrated runtime and compile-time approach for parallelizing structured and block structured applications," *IEEE Transactions on Parallel and Distributed Systems*, to appear.
5. C. Chang, A. Sussman, and J. Saltz, "Support for distributed dynamic data structures in C++," Tech. Rep. CS-TR-3266, University of Maryland, 1995.
6. M. Kaddoura and S. Ranka, "Runtime support for data parallel applications for adaptive and non-uniform computational environments." Preliminary Version, February 1995.
7. S. R. Kohn and S. B. Baden, "Irregular coarse-grain data parallelism under LPARX," *J. Scientific Programming*, vol. 5, no. 3, 1996.
8. E. J. Bylaska, S. R. Kohn, S. B. Baden, A. Edelman, R. Kawai, M. E. G. Ong, and J. H. Weare, "Scalable parallel numerical methods and software tools for material

design," in *Proceedings of the Seventh SIAM Conference on Parallel Processing for Scientific Computing*, (San Francisco, CA), February 1995.

9. Message-Passing Interface Standard, "MPI: A message-passing interface standard," University of Tennessee, Knoxville, TN, June 1995.

10. G. M. Amdahl, "Validity of the single processor approach to achieving large scale computing capabilities," in *Proceedings of the AFIPS Spring Joint Computer Conference*, (Atlantic City, NJ), pp. 483–485, April 1967.

11. C. Rendleman, V. B. J. Bell, B. Crutchfield, L. Howell, and M. Welcome, "Boxlib users guide and manual: A library for managing rectangular domains. edition 1.99," tech. rep., Center for Computational Science and Engineering, Lawrence Livermore National Laboratory, 1995.

12. M. Parashar and J. C. Browne, "Dagh: A data-management infrastructure for parallel adaptive mesh refinement techniques," tech. rep., Department of Computer Science, University of Texas at Austin, 1995.

13. A. Choudhary, R. Bordawekar, M. Harry, R. Krishnaiyer, R. Ponnusamy, T. Singh, and R. Thakur, "PASSION:parallel and scalable software for I/O," Tech. Rep. SCCS-636, NPAC, September 1994.

14. R.Bennett, K. Bryant, A. Sussman, R. Das, and J. Saltz, "A framework for optimizing parallel I/O," Tech. Rep. CS-TR-3417, University of Maryland: Department of Computer Science, January 1995.

15. S. S. Mukherjee, S. D. Sharman, M. D. Hill, J. R. Larus, A. Rogers, and J. Saltz, "Efficient support for irregular applications on distributed memory machines," in *PPoPP 95*, 1995.

16. B. Falsafi, A. R. Lebeck, S. K. Reinhardt, I. Schoinas, M. D. Hill, J. R. Larus, A. Rogers, and D. A. Wood, "Application-specific protocols for user-level shared memory," in *Proceedings of Supercomputing '94*, November 1994.

Multi-Message Multicasting

Teofilo F. Gonzalez

Department of Computer Science,
University of California, Santa Barbara, CA, 93106, USA

Abstract. We consider the Multi-Message Multicasting problem for the n processor fully connected static network. We present an efficient algorithm to construct a communication schedule with total communication time at most d^2, where d is the maximum number of messages a processor may send (receive). We present an algorithm to construct for any problem instance of degree d and fan-out k (maximum number of processors that may receive a given message) a communication schedule with total communication time at most $qd + k^{\frac{1}{q}}(d-1)$, for any integer $q \geq 2$. The time complexity bound for our algorithm is $O(n(d(q + k^{\frac{1}{q}}))^q)$. Our main result is a linear time approximation algorithm with a smaller approximation bound for small values of k (< 100). We discuss applications and show how to adapt our algorithms to dynamic networks such as the Benes network, the interconnection network used in the Meiko CS-2.

1 Introduction

The Multi-Message Multicasting (MM_C) problem over an n processor static network consists of finding a communication schedule with least total communication time for multicasting a set of messages. Specifically, there are n processors, $P = \{P_1, P_2, \ldots, P_n\}$, interconnected via a network N. Each processor is executing processes, and these processes are exchanging messages that are routed through the links of N. The objective is to determine when each of these messages is to be transmitted so that all of the communications can be carried in the least total amount of time.

Routing in the complete static network (there are bidirectional links between every pair of processors), is the simplest and most flexible, when compared to other static networks with restricted structure like rings, mesh, star, binary trees, hypercube, cube connected cycles, shuffle exchange, etc., and dynamic networks, like Omega Networks, Benes Networks, Fat Trees, etc. The minimum total communication time for the MM_C problem is an obvious lower bound for the total communication time of the corresponding problem on any restricted communication network. But, most interesting, the MM_C for dynamic networks that can realize all permutations and replicate data (e.g., n by n Benes network based on 2 by 2 switches that can also act as replicators) is not that different, in the sense that the number of communication phases in these dynamic networks is twice of that in the complete network. This is because each communication phase in the complete network can be translated into two communication phases. In the first phase data is replicated and transmitted to other processors, and in the second phase data is distributed to the appropriate processors ([13], [14], and [16]). One may reduce the translation process to a single step, by increasing the number of network switches about 50% ([13], [14], and [16]). Multiprocessor systems based on Benes networks include the IBM GF11 machine [1], and the Meiko CS-2. The two stage translation process can be used in the Meiko CS-2 computer system and any multimessage multicasting schedule can be realized by using basic synchronization primitives. In what follows we concentrate on the MM_C problem because it has a simple structure, and, as we mentioned before, results for this network can be easily translated to a variety of dynamic networks.

Formally, processor P_i needs to multicast s_i messages, each requiring one time unit to reach any of its destinations. The jth message of processor P_i has to be sent to the set of processors $T_{i,j} \subseteq P - \{P_i\}$. Let r_i be the number of distinct messages that processor P_i may receive. We define the *degree* of a problem instance as $d = \mathbf{max}\{s_i, r_i\}$, i.e., the maximum number of messages that any processor sends or receives. We define the *fan-out* of a problem instance as $k = \mathbf{max}\{ \mid T_{i,j} \mid \}$, i.e., the maximum number of different processors that must receive any given message. Consider the following example.

Example 1. There are three processors ($n = 3$). Processors P_1, P_2, and P_3 must transmit 3, 4 and 2 messages, respectively (i.e., $s_1 = 3, s_2 = 4$, and $s_3 = 2$). The destinations of all of these messages is: $T_{1,1} = \{2\}, T_{1,2} = \{3\}, T_{1,3} = \{2,3\}, T_{2,1} = \{1\}, T_{2,2} = \{1\}, T_{2,3} = \{3\}, T_{2,4} = \{1,3\}, T_{3,1} = \{1,2\}, T_{3,2} = \{2\}$. In this case $r_1 = 4, r_2 = 4$, and $r_3 = 4$.

It is convenient to represent problem instances by directed multigraphs. Each processor P_i is represented by the vertex labeled i, and there is a directed edge (or branch) from vertex i to vertex j for each message that processor P_i has to transmit to processor P_j. The $|T_{i,j}|$ directed edges or branches associated with each message are *bundled* together. The problem instance given in Example 1 is shown in Figure 1 as a directed multi-graph.

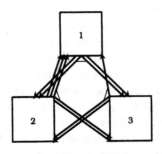

Fig. 1. Directed Multi-Graph Representation for Example 1. The thin line joins all the edges (branches) in the same bundle

The communications allowed must satisfy two restrictions:

1.- During each time unit each processor may transmit one message, but such message can be multicast to a set of processors; and
2.- During each time unit each processor may receive at most one message.

Our communication model allows us to transmit each message in one or more stages. I.e., each set $T_{i,j}$ can be partitioned into subsets, and each of these subsets is transmitted at a different time. Of course, this does not prevent one from sending a message to all its destinations at the same time. Restricting each message to be transmitted to all of its destinations at the same time increases the total communication time, and in some cases all feasible communication schedules have a total communication time that cannot be bounded (above) by any function $f(d)$. This is why it is important to send each message at different times.

A *communication mode* C is a collection of subsets of branches from a subset of the bundles that obey the following communications rules:

1.- Branches may emanate from at most one of the bundles in each processor; and
2.- All of the branches end at different processors.

A *communication schedule* S for a problem instance I is a sequence of communication modes such that each branch in each message is in exactly one of the communication modes. The *total communication time* is the latest time at which there is a communication which is equal to the number of communication modes in schedule S, and our problem consists of constructing a communication schedule with least total communication time. From the communication rules we know that a degree d problem instance has at least one processor that requires d time units to send, and/or receive all its messages. Therefore, d is a trivial lower bound for the total communication time. To simplify the analysis of our approximation bound we use this simple measure. Another reason for this is that load balancing procedures executed prior to the multicasting require a simple objective function in terms of the problem instance it generates.

Using our multigraph representation one can visualize the MM_C problem as a generalized edge coloring directed multigraph (GECG) problem. This problem consists of coloring the edges with the least number of colors (positive integers) so that the communication rules (now restated in the appropriate format) imposed by our network are satisfied: (1) every pair of edges from different bundles emanating from the same vertex must be colored differently; and (2) all incoming edges to each vertex must be colored differently. The colors correspond to different time periods. In what follows we corrupt our notation by using interchangeably colors and time periods; vertices and processors; and bundles, branches or edges, and messages.

In Section 2 we present an efficient algorithm to construct for any degree d problem instance a communication schedule with total communication time at most d^2. Gonzalez [7] has found problem instances for which this upper bound on the communication time is best possible, i.e. the upper bound is also a lower bound. One observes that the lower bound applies when the fan-out and the number of processors is huge. Since this environment is not likely in the near future, we study in subsequent sections important subproblems of the MM_C problems that are likely to arise in practice.

The *basic multicasting problem* (BM_C) is the degree $d = 1$ MM_C problem. The BM_C problem can be trivially solved by sending all the messages at time zero. There will be no conflicts because $d = 1$, i.e., each processor must send at most one message and receive at most one message. When a set of processors is connected via a dynamic network whose basic switches allow replication (input lines may be replicated to several output lines), the basic multicast problem can again be solved in two stages: the replication step followed by the distribution step ([13], [16], [14]).

Let us now consider the case when each message has fixed fan-out k. When $k = 1$ (multimessage unicasting problem MU_C), our problem has been reduced to the Openshop Preemptive Scheduling problem [7] which can be solved in polynomial time [8]. In this case, each degree d problem instance has a d color optimal coloration. The interesting point is that each communication mode translates into a single communication step for processors interconnected via permutation networks (e.g., Benes Network, Meiko CS-2, etc.), because in these networks all possible one-to-one communications can be performed in one step.

It is not surprising that several authors have studied the MU_C problem as well as several interesting variations for which NP-completeness has been established, subproblems have been shown to be polynomially solvable, and approximation algorithms and heuristics have been developed. Coffman, Garey, Johnson and LaPaugh [2] studied a version of the multi-message unicasting problem when messages have different lengths, each processor can send (receive) $\alpha(P_i) \geq 1$ $(\beta(P_i) \geq 1)$ messages simultaneously, and messages are transmitted without interruption (nonpreemptive mode). Whitehead [18] considered the case when messages can be sent indirectly. The preemptive version of these problems as well as other generalizations were studied by Choi and Hakimi ([4], [5], [3]), Hajek and Sasaki [11], Gopal, Bongiovanni, Bonuccelli, Tang, and Wong [9]. Some of these papers considered the case when the input and output units are interchangeable (can send or receive messages). Rivera-Vega, Varadarajan and Navathe [15] studied, the file transferring problem, a version the multi-message unicasting problem for the complete network when every vertex can send (receive) as many messages as the number of outgoing (incoming) links, all messages have the same length and take one unit of time to move along any link. Our MM_C problem is closest to the Meiko CS-2 communication model, and it involves multicasting rather than just unicasting.

The MM_C problem is significantly harder than the MU_C. Even when $k = 2$ the decision version of the MM_C problem is NP-complete [7]. Gonzalez [7] developed an $O(nd^{2.5})$ time algorithm to construct a communication schedule with total communication time at most $2d - 1$ for every n processor instance of the MM_C with fan-out $k = 2$.

In section 3 we present an algorithm to construct for any problem instance of degree d and fan-out k a communication schedule with total communication time at most $qd + k^{\frac{1}{q}}(d-1)$, for any integer $q \geq 2$. The time complexity bound for our algorithm is $O(n(d(q + k^{\frac{1}{q}}))^q)$. Our main result is a linear time approximation algorithm with a smaller approximation bound for small values of k (< 100), these are the problem instances most likely to arise in practice.

Multimessage multicasting arises in many applications. Suppose that we have a sparse system of linear equations to be solved via an iterative method (e.g., a Jacobi-like procedure). We are given the vector $X(0)$ and we need to evaluate $X(t)$ for $t = 1, 2, \ldots$, using the iteration $x_i(t+1) = f_i(X(t))$. But since the system is sparse every f_i depends on very few terms. A placement procedure assigns the x_is and $f_i()$s to the processors. Effective placement procedures assign a large number of $f_i()$s to the processor where the vector components it requires are being computed, and therefore can be computed locally. However, the remaining $f_i()$s need vector components computed by other processors. So at each iteration these components have to be multicasted to the set of processors that need them. The strategy is to compute $X(1)$, then perform the multimessage multicasting, then compute $X(2)$, and so on. The same communication schedule can be used at each iteration. Our approximation bounds are in terms of the lower bound d. This facilitates the placement procedure since it seeks a placement that induces a multimessage multicasting problem with minimum density d and small fan-out. Other applications include solution of non-linear equations, and most dynamic programming procedures, since all of the multicasting information depends only on the initial placement, which is determined a priori.

2 General Approximation Bound for the MM_C Problem

We show how to construct a communication schedule with total communication time at most d^2 for every degree d problem instance. Gonzalez [7] has shown that the bound of d^2 is tight in the sense that there are degree d problem instances such that all their communication schedules have total communication time at least d^2. For brevity we do not include this lower bound. It is important to note that the bound of d^2 arises in problem instances with huge fan-out and a huge number of processors. This is why we study in subsequent sections approximation algorithms for problem instances with restricted fan-out, which are the problem instances that are likely to arise in practice.

Let P be any n processor instance of the MM_C problem of degree d. The set of d^2 colors is $\{(i,j)|1 \leq i \leq d$ and $1 \leq j \leq d\}$. Now order the incoming edges to each vertex, and order all the bundles emanating from each vertex. Assign color (i,j) to edge $e = \{p,q\}$ if e belongs to the ith bundle emanating form vertex p, and e is the jth incoming edge to vertex q.

Theorem 1. *The informal algorithm described above generates a communication schedule with total communication time at most d^2 for every degree d instance of the MM_C problem. Furthermore, the algorithm can be implemented to take linear time with respect to the number of edges in the multi-graph.*

Proof. The proof follows from the observation that edges emanating from the same processor belonging to different bundles are colored with different colors, and all the incoming edges to a node are colored with different colors. The total number of colors is d^2. It is simple to show that the time complexity bound for the algorithm is linear with respect to the input size.

3 Approximating the MM_C with Fan-Out $k \geq 3$

Problem instances of degree $d = 1$ can always be colored with one color; the ones of degree $d = 2$ and $k = 3$ can always be colored with four colors; and similar results can be obtained for problems with fixed degree d and fan-out k. For brevity we do not prove these special cases.

3.1 Crude Approximations

Let us now consider some simple approximation algorithms for our problem. The algorithms color all edges emanating from $P_1, P_2, \ldots P_{j-1}$. With respect to this partial recoloration we define the following terms. Each branch emanating from P_j leads to a processor with at most $d - 1$ other edges incident to it, some of which have already been colored. These colors are called t_{j-1}-*forbidden* with respect to a given branch emanating from P_j.

A coloration in which every message is colored with exactly one color may require as many as $d + k(d - 1)$ colors. The reason is that each branch has $d - 1$ t_{j-1}-forbidden colors, and none of the t_{j-1}-forbidden colors in a branch can be used to color the corresponding bundle. Therefore, there can be $k(d - 1)$ t_{j-1}-forbidden colors that cannot be used in the bundle. Since there are at most d bundles emanating from a processor P_j, and every bundle is assigned one color, then $d + k(d - 1)$ colors are sufficient to color all the bundles emanating from processor P_j, and hence the multigraph.

The above upper bound can be decreased substantially by assigning up to two colors per message (bundle). Again, each branch has $d - 1$ t_{j-1}-forbidden colors. But, two colors that are not t_{j-1}-forbidden in the same branch of a bundle can be used to color that bundle. For example, if the forbidden colors in the branches are $\{1,2,3\}$, $\{2,3,4\}$ and $\{2,3,4\}$, respectively, one can color the first branch with color four, and the other two with color one. So the question is: What is the largest number of t_{j-1}-forbidden colors in a bundle such that no two of them can be used to color the bundle? For $k = 3$ and $d = 7$ it is nine. The t_{j-1}-forbidden colors in the three branches are: $\{1, 2, 4, 5, 7, 8\}$, $\{1, 3, 4, 6, 7, 9\}$, and $\{2, 3, 5, 6, 8, 9\}$. Note that no two of the nine colors can color completely the bundle. We have established that the largest number of t_{j-1}-forbidden colors in a bundle such that no two of them can color completely the bundle is $d - 1$ for $k = 2$, about $1.5(d - 1)$ for $k = 3$, etc.

We can restate this problem in graph theoretic terms as follows. Find the complete graph with the largest number of vertices such that all its edges are covered by k cliques of size $d - 1$. The vertices represent the colors, the cliques the $t_{j-1} - forbidden$ colors, and the number of cliques represent k. By simple counting arguments, the maximum number is less than $\sqrt{k}(d-1)$. Therefore, all the bundles emanating from processor P_j (and therefore the multigraph) can be colored with $2d + \sqrt{k}(d-1)$ colors, the $\sqrt{k}(d-1)$ colors are the t_{j-1}-forbidden colors, and the $2d$ colors are the one used in the coloration. One can easily prove smaller bounds, $3d - 1$ for $k = 2$; is about $3.5d - 1.5$ for $k = 3$; etc (see [7]).

The obvious generalization is to use q colors instead of two for each bundle. To find th number of colors needed in this case we need to generalize graphs to hypergraphs. A q-hypergraph consists of a set of vertices and a set of q-hyperedges, where a q-hyperedge is just a subset of q vertices. Clearly, a 2-hypergraph is just a graph. So the previous graph problem becomes, find the complete q-hypergraph with the largest number of vertices such that all its q-hyperedges are covered by k q-hypercliques of size $d - 1$. By simple counting arguments, the maximum number of vertices is less than $k^{\frac{1}{q}}(d - 1)$. Therefore, all the bundles emanating from processor P_j (and therefore the multigraph) can be colored with $qd + k^{\frac{1}{q}}(d - 1)$ colors. The time complexity bound in this case is $O(n(d(q + k^{\frac{1}{q}}))^q)$, by trying all subsets of colors of size q. The algorithm will color with at most q colors all the bundles emanating from each processor. We now state our result without its proof.

Theorem 2. *For every instance of the MM_C problem with fan-out $k \geq 3$, the informal algorithm generates in $O(n(d(q + k^{\frac{1}{q}}))^q)$ time a schedule with total communication time $qd + k^{\frac{1}{q}}(d - 1)$.*

Gonzalez [7] has developed a linear time algorithm, with respect to the input length, to generate a valid coloration for the above case. For brevity we do not include these result in this paper.

In what follows we present another procedure and carry out a much **sharper** analysis. Table 1 has the coefficient for d for different methods. The ones labeled "simple" are for the "crude" methods. The "involved (2c)" is the method we discuss in the next subsections. The other methods appear in [7] and for brevity are not described in this paper.

3.2 Sharper Approximation

We present an approximation algorithm and carry out a much **sharper and involved** analysis of its performance. The input to our algorithm is a multigraph G, and integers h and l that restrict the color selection process ($k > l > h \geq 1$). Note that k and d can be extracted from the graph. The algorithm colors the edges emanating out of P_1, then P_2, and so on. When considering processor P_j, a color is selected from each bundle from the set C_i with smallest index, and then the existence of a second color for the remaining branches is guaranteed by just having enough colors available. Before we present our results we define some useful terms.

At the beginning of the jth iteration the algorithm has colored all the branches emanating from processors $P_1, P_2, \ldots, P_{j-1}$ and it is ready to begin coloring all

Table 1. Number of Colors For The Different Methods.

Method \ k	3	4	5	7	10	15	20	50	100
Simple (2 colors)	3.73	4.00	4.23	4.65	5.16	5.87	6.47	9.07	12.00
Involved (2c)		3.33	3.50	3.60	4.50	4.60	5.53	6.00	8.56	11.54
With Matching		2.67	3.00	3.50	4.29	4.50	5.47	6.00	8.54	11.53
Better Bound		2.50	3.00	3.50	4.14	4.40	5.40	5.75	8.52	11.52
Simple (3 colors)	–	–	4.00	4.55	4.81	5.27	5.60	6.67	7.62
Involved (3c)	–	3.56	4.00	4.26	4.67	5.00	5.20	6.23	7.24
Simple (4 colors)	–	–	5.50	5.63	5.78	5.97	6.11	6.66	7.16
Simple (5 colors)	–	–	–	6.48	6.58	6.72	6.82	7.19	7.51

the branches emanating from P_j. For $0 \leq i \leq k$, let C_i^J be the set of colors that are t_{j-1}-forbidden in exactly i branches of bundle J. Let $c_i^J = |C_i^J|$. (When the set J is understood, we will use c_i for c_i^J, and C_i for C_i^J.) Since there can be at most $d-1$ t_{j-1}-forbidden colors in each branch and there are at most k branches in each bundle, it then follows that $\sum_{i=1}^{k} iC_i^J \leq (d-1)k$ for each bundle J emanating from P_j. Clearly, all the branches of bundle J can be colored with any of the colors in C_0^J. Also, one can color all the branches of bundle J with two colors, $a \in C_i^J$ and $b \in C_j^J$ provided that colors a and b are not t_{j-1}-forbidden in the same branch of bundle J and have not been used to color another branch emanating from processor P_j. Just after coloring a subset of branches of a bundle emanating from processor P_j, we say that a color is s_j-*free* if such color has not yet been used to color any of the branches emanating from processor P_j.

The input to the algorithm consists of G (the multi-graph), and h and l (to restrict the selection of colors). Note that k (the fan out), and d (the degree) can be computed from G. Later on give the specific values for which the algorithm is defined.

To simplify our notation we define the expressions L and R as follows

$$L = \frac{h^2+h+2}{2} + \frac{l}{d-1} - \frac{h^2+h-2}{2(d-1)}, \text{ and } R = (h+1)^2 + \frac{(h+1)(h^2+3h)}{2(l-h)} + \frac{-2lh^2+h^3+h}{2(d-1)(l-h)}$$

Our algorithm requires that $d \geq \frac{2l+2h^2}{h^2+3h-2}$, $k \geq L$, $k > l > h \geq 1$ and $d > 4$, which we will show later on is not a limiting factor. We begin by establishing in Lemma 3 that $L \leq R$, which we state without its proof. This fact will be used to partition in two cases the set of values for which our algorithm is defined.

Lemma 3. *If* $d \geq \frac{2l+2h^2}{h(h+3)}$ *then* $L \leq R$.

In Table 2 we define equations eq.(0), ..., eq.($h + 1$) that are used by the algorithm and are necessary for the correctness proof.

Procedure Coloring, whose input consists of the multi-graph G, and integers h and l, is given below. For the set of valid inputs, defined above, procedure

Table 2. Equations eq.(0), $\ldots$, eq.$(h+1)$

	$c_0 \geq d;$	eq.(0)
for $1 \leq j \leq h$	$\sum_{i=0}^{j} c_i \geq (j+2)d - 2j;$ or	eq.(j)
	$\sum_{i=0}^{l} c_i \geq (h+2)d - 2h.$	eq.$(h+1)$

computes the maximum number of colors needed (Δ) and a coloration for G with at most Δ colors.

Procedure Coloring (G, h, l)
/* Note that k, d, L, and R can be easily computed from G */
/* Procedure is defined for $d \geq \frac{2l+2h^2}{h(h+3)}$, $k \geq L$, $k > l > h \geq 1$, and $d \geq 4$ */
case
  :$R \leq k$: $\Delta = \frac{d(k+h+1)-(k+h)}{h+1};$
  :$L \leq k < R$: $\Delta = \frac{((2d-4)h+4d-2)l+2(d-1)k+(2-d)h^2+(d-2)h+2d}{2(l+1)};$
endcase
for each processor P_j **do**
  for each bundle J emanating from processor P_j **do**
    compute $C_0^J, C_1^J, C_2^J, \ldots C_k^J;$
    let p_J be the smallest integer such that equation eq.(p_J) holds;
    let $q_J = \min\{p_J, h\};$
    let $r_J = p_J$ if $0 \leq p_J \leq h$ and $r_J = l$ otherwise;
  endfor
  /* Color a subset of edges emanating from each bundle of P_j */
  for each uncolored bundle J of P_j **do**;
    color as many branches of bundle J with an s_j-free color in $C_0^J, C_1^J, \ldots, C_{q_J}^J;$
  /* Color the remaining uncolored edges emanating from P_j */
  for each partially colored bundle J of P_j with uncolored branches **do**;
    color all uncolored branches of J with an s_j-free color in $C_0^J, C_1^J, \ldots, C_{r_J}^J;$
  endfor;
end of Procedure Coloring

To establish that Procedure Coloration generates a valid coloration for the cases it is defined is difficult. At this point the readers might feel there are a large number of cases for which our algorithm is not defined, but we have established that these cases can be ignored because the corresponding graph G with other values for h and l that are valid for our algorithm and requires a smaller Δ.

In other words, the cases that are omitted by our algorithm do not enhance the overall performance of our algorithm. In Theorem 8 we establish that our algorithm generates valid colorations and that it takes linear time with respect to the input length. The proof of this theorem is based on Lemmas 6 and 7 that are used to establish that two colors can always be selected from the appropriate sets to color all the branches from the bundles that could not be colored with exactly one color. Lemma 5 is used in the proof of Lemmas 6 and 7, and requires Lemma 4. For brevity we just list the lemmas without their involved proofs. The proof of Theorem 8 shows the need for the lemmas.

Lemma 4. *If $d \geq \frac{2l+2h^2}{h(h+3)}$ then $(h+1)^2 - \frac{h^2}{d-1} + \frac{h+1}{d-1} \leq R$*

Lemma 5. *If $d \geq \frac{2l+2h^2}{h(h+3)}$ and $k \geq L$, then the value for Δ defined by Procedure Coloration is at greater than or equal to $(h+2)d - 2h$.*

Lemma 6. *If $k \geq L$ and $d \geq \frac{2l+2h^2}{h(h+3)}$, then at the beginning of the jth iteration of Procedure Coloring each bundle J emanating from processor P_j satisfies $\sum_{i=0}^{h} c_i^J \geq d$.*

Lemma 7. *If $d \geq \frac{2l+2h^2}{h(h+3)}$ and $L \leq k$, then at the beginning of the jth iteration of Procedure Coloring each bundle J emanating from processor P_j satisfies at least one of the inequalities eq.(j), for $0 \leq j \leq h+1$, holds.*

Theorem 8. *For every instance of the MM_C problem with fan-out $k \geq 2$, $d \geq \frac{2l+2h^2}{h(h^2+3)}$ and $L \leq k$, Procedure Coloring generates a communication schedule with total communication equal to the value of Δ computed by the algorithm. The time complexity of the procedure is linear with respect to the input size.*

Proof. First we prove that Procedure Coloration colors all the edges in the graph with a number of colors equal to Δ, as computed by the algorithm. Then we establish the time complexity bound.

Consider now the iteration for P_j for any $1 \leq j \leq n$. By Lemma 7 we know that at least one of the equations eq.(i) for $0 \leq i \leq h+1$ holds for each bundle emanating from P_j. Therefore, all the p_J values are integers in the range $[0,h+1]$, and all the q_J values are integers in the range $[0,h]$.

We now claim that one can color a nonempty subset of branches from each bundle with a distinct s-free color in $C_0^J, C_1^J, \ldots C_{q_j}^J$. We prove this by showing that $\sum_{i=0}^{q_J} c_i^J \geq d$, since this fact guarantees that one unique s-free color in $C_0^J, C_1^J, \ldots C_{q_j}^J$ for each bundle J can be selected in the first loop to color a nonempty subset of edges emanating out of each bundle. As we established before, $q_J \leq h$. If $q_J = h$ then by Lemma 6 it follows that $\sum_{i=0}^{q_J} c_i^J \geq d$. On the other hand, if $q_J < h$ then by definition of q_J and Lemma 7 we know that eq.(q_J) holds. This implies that either $c_0 \geq d$ or $\sum_{i=0}^{q_J} c_i \geq (q_J+2)d - 2q_J$. Since $d > 2$, it then follows that $\sum_{i=0}^{q_J} c_i^J \geq d$. Therefore, in the first loop one can select unique s-free color in $C_0^J, C_1^J, \ldots C_{q_j}^J$ for each bundle J to color a nonempty subset of edges emanating out of each bundle.

We now claim that at each iteration in the second loop one can select unique colors to color the remaining uncolored branches of each bundle. Remember that $\sum_{i=0}^{r_J} c_i \geq (r_J + 2)d - 2r_J$. The number of colors that were t_{j-1}-forbidden in the same branch as the color selected in the previous loop is at most $(d-2) \cdot q_J$, and the maximum number of colors used during both loops is at most $2d - 1$. It follows that the colors that one can use to color the remaining branches are at least $(r_J + 2)d - 2r_J - (d-2) \cdot q_J - 2d + 1$. This is equivalent to $(d-2)(r_J - q_J) + 1$. Since $d > 2$ and $r_J \geq q_J$, we know that there is at least one color left with which we can color all the remaining uncolored branches. This completes the correctness proof.

It is simple to see that all the steps take time $O(ndk)$, and can be implemented to take linear time with respect to the input length.

4 Discussion

For the case of $k = 3$ the approximation bound can be shown to be $\frac{5d-4}{2}$ and one can establish that any algorithm that colors the bundles emanating form each vertex at a time without recoloration must use at least $\frac{7d-3}{3}$ colors. As we mentioned before, for brevity we just presented some of the simpler approximation algorithms we have developed. It is worth noting that the proofs of all the lemmas in the previous subsection can be proved by a Symbolic Manipulator System such as Mathematica after adding several macros and functions. The need to use symbolic manipulators arose from the complexity of the expressions that need to be handled.

The MM_C problem can be viewed as the generalization of the multigraph edge coloration (EC) problem [17], where the edges are directed, and bundled in groups. Vizing's [17] approximation algorithm for the EC problem colors the edges one at a time with one of the $1.5d$ available colors, where d is the degree of the multigraph. If necessary the algorithm recolors some edges in order to color an edge. But, the necessary backtracking is limited. Recoloration in our problem is harder, because at each node there may be many edges that need to be recolored, rather than just two as in Vizing's algorithm. Our currently best approximation algorithm allows limited recoloration.

References

1. G. S. Almasi, and A. Gottlieb, *Highly Parallel Computing*, The Benjamin/Cummings Publishing Co., Inc., New York, 1994.
2. E. G. Coffman, Jr, M. R. Garey, D. S. Johnson, and A. S. LaPaugh, Scheduling File Transfers in Distributed Networks, *SIAM Journal on Computing*, 14(3) (1985), pp. 744 – 780.
3. H.-A. Choi, and S. L. Hakimi, Data Transfers in Networks, *Algorithmica*, Vol. 3, (1988), pp. 223 – 245.
4. H.-A. Choi, and S. L. Hakimi, Scheduling File Transfers for Trees and Odd Cycles, *SIAM Journal on Computing*, Vol. 16, No. 1, February 1987, pp. 162 – 168.

5. H.-A. Choi, and S. L. Hakimi, "Data Transfers in Networks with Transceivers," *Networks*, Vol. 17, (1987), pp. 393 – 421.
6. T. F. Gonzalez, "Unit Execution Time Shop Problems," *Mathematics of Operations Research,*" Vol. 7, No. 1, February 1982, pp. 57 - 66.
7. T. F. Gonzalez, "Multimessage Multicasting in Networks," UCSB Technical Report, (in preparation).
8. T. F. Gonzalez, and S. Sahni, Open Shop Scheduling to Minimize Finish Time, *Journal of the Association for Computing Machinery*, Vol. 23, No. 4, October 1976, pp. 665 – 679.
9. I. S. Gopal, G. Bongiovanni, M. A. Bonuccelli, D. T. Tang, and C. K. Wong, An Optimal Switching Algorithm for Multibean Satellite Systems with Variable Bandwidth Beams, *IEEE Transactions on Communications*, COM-30, 11 (1982) pp. 2475 – 2481.
10. A J. Hopcroft, and R. M. Karp, An $n^{2.5}$ Algorithm for Maximum Matchings in Bipartite Graphs, *SIAM J. Computing*, (1973), pp. 225 – 231.
11. B. Hajek, and G. Sasaki, Link Scheduling in Polynomial Time, *IEEE Transactions on Information Theory*, Vol. 34, No. 5, Sept. 1988, pp. 910 – 917.
12. I. Holyer, The NP-completeness of Edge-Coloring, *SIAM J. Comput.*, 11 (1982), pp. 117 – 129.
13. T. T. Lee, Non-blocking Copy Networks for Multicast Packet Switching, *IEEE J. Selected Areas of Communication*, Vol. 6, No 9, Dec. 1988, pp. 1455 – 1467.
14. S. C. Liew, A General Packet Replication Scheme for Multicasting in Interconnection Networks, *Proceedings IEEE INFOCOM '95*, Vol.1 (1995), pp. 394 – 401.
15. P. I. Rivera-Vega, R, Varadarajan, and S. B. Navathe, "Scheduling File Transfers in Fully Connected Networks," *Networks*, Vol. 22, (1992), pp. 563 – 588.
16. J. S. Turner, A Practical Version of Lee's Multicast Switch Architecture, *IEEE Transactions on Communications*, Vol. 41, No 8, Aug. 1993, pp. 1166 – 1169.
17. V. G. Vizing, On an Estimate of the Chromatic Class of a p-graph, *Diskret. Analiz.*, 3 (1964), pp. 25 – 30 (In Russian).
18. J. Whitehead, The Complexity of File Transfer Scheduling with Forwarding, *SIAM Journal on Computing* Vol. 19, No 2, April 1990, pp. 222 – 245.

Synchronization as a Strategy for Designing Efficient Parallel Algorithms

Claude G. Diderich[1]* and Marc Gengler[2]

[1] Swiss Federal Institute of Technology – Lausanne, Computer Science Department,
CH-1015 Lausanne, Switzerland, E-mail: diderich@di.epfl.ch
[2] Ecole Normale Supérieure de Lyon, Laboratoire de l'Informatique du Parallélisme,
F-69364 Lyon, France, E-mail: Marc.Gengler@lip.ens-lyon.fr

Abstract. This paper presents a simple to use and general approach for designing efficient parallel algorithms for distributed memory machines. This approach is well suited for solving both regular and irregular problems using dynamic data. It is based on the notion of *synchronized iterative algorithms*. The idea is to alternate between computation and macro-communication steps, where a macro-communication step is composed of synchronization and load balancing or data redistribution operations. The simplicity and generality of this approach is shown on a theoretical example by proving non trivial lower and upper bounds for the efficiency. Experimental results certify the validity of the approach by parallelizing the best-first branch and bound algorithm for solving traveling salesman problems on a Cray T3D machine.

1 Introduction

In recent years large efforts have been put into developing parallel algorithms for distributed memory machines. Various very efficient algorithms have been proposed. But most of them are very problem dependent and the basic ideas used cannot easily be applied to other algorithms. To develop a simple, but nevertheless efficient method for designing parallel algorithms for distributed memory massively parallel machines, we generalize the concept of synchronized iterative algorithms. The approach presented is based on the idea of alternating computation and synchronization or load balancing steps. This concept, although often used implicitly, is well known in the area of parallel numerical algorithms [6]. We generalize the concept for irregular algorithms that use dynamically generated data, like tree search algorithms or enumeration techniques. Although our approach is very simple and intuitive, we argue that it has not received enough attention when solving irregular problems. Most of the time, people use complicated approaches and load balancing techniques, based on active messages, which are very difficult to control, maintain, or prove correct. To this we oppose a very regular approach of the SIMD kind, combining the simplicity of such a scheme with the efficiency of solving irregular problems.

* Research supported by the Swiss National Science Foundation grants SPP-IF 5003-034349 and SPP-IF 5003-034349/2.

2   Extracting parallelism from sequential algorithms

In this paper we are interested in extracting the maximal possible parallelism from sequential algorithms. We look for sets of operations that are independent from each other and that can be executed in parallel.

The machine model. We consider multiple instruction, multiple data, distributed memory (MIMD-DM) massively parallel machines using the single program, multiple data (SPMD) paradigm as underlying computation model. Most of the currently available parallel computers, like the SP-2, the Paragon or the T3D are MIMD-DM machines. The SPMD approach is, together with the virtual shared memory model, the most common programming model used to develop parallel algorithms. We show the importance of making a clear distinction between computation and communication operations.

Irregular problems and dynamic data. In parallel as well as in sequential algorithmics, there exist regular as well as irregular problems. The regularity of a problem depends on the regularity of the data it uses. Furthermore, the data structures may be static, like vectors or matrices, or may be dynamically generated, like lists or trees. The strategy for designing efficient parallel algorithms described in this paper has initially been developed for parallelizing irregular algorithms using dynamic data structures. Nevertheless, it is also valid for parallelizing regular algorithms and/or algorithms using static data structures, but which show irregular and unpredictable behavior in their computation times.

The correctness guarantee. The most important requirement in designing parallel algorithms is to *guarantee correctness*. Guaranteeing correctness can be seen as verifying that all dependences that exist in the sequential algorithm are verified in the parallelized one. We are only interested in dependences and not in other correctness conditions, like numerical stability conditions for instance. In fact, the latter ones can be modeled as additional dependences. Various techniques exist for extracting dependences from a program. They usually depend on the availability of the data. If the data used is dynamically generated, static data dependence analysis techniques usually fail. One possible technique for extracting dependences is to use an axiomatic description of the sequential algorithm [5]. The goal is to find equivalent sets of problems or data items that can be solved or worked on in parallel.

Idle time. Another important aspect to be addressed when designing efficient parallel algorithms is *minimizing idle time* of any processor. This can be achieved by introducing data redistribution and load balancing operations. These operations may be implicit or explicit and may concern all processors or only a subset of them (local vs. global). But, as these operations are not for free, the overhead due to load balancing and related communication operations has to be minimized in order to obtain good efficiencies. There is hence a tradeoff between the possible reduction of the computation time due to load balancing and the cost introduced to realize it. Classical approaches are based on local load balancing or load sharing strategies [4] and use different informations.

True and efficiency dependences. When analyzing the dependences existing in a sequential algorithm, one can distinguish between two classes. The first class, which we call *true dependences*, contains all the dependences that must be verified in order to obtain correct results. The second class of dependences, which we call *efficiency dependences*, guarantees an efficient execution of the sequential algorithm. Efficiency dependences impose an order in which a set of operations are to be performed. However, different efficiency dependences, that is, computation orders, lead to the same result. Usually parallelism is introduced in sequential algorithms by removing some or all of the efficiency dependences. Removing efficiency dependences may increase the amount of work done. Therefore it is important to find a good tradeoff between relaxing efficiency dependences and limiting or avoiding useless work. This may either be done by using a reduced parallelization scheme or by providing a run-time control of the parallelism exploited. The notion of efficiency dependence is fundamentally global. Except for rare cases, it is impossible to verify all efficiency dependences using only partial information. This gives a big handicap to local load balancing or scheduling techniques. The global knowledge allows to optimally balance the load, verify efficiency dependences or drop a minimal number of such dependences in order to obtain precisely the parallelism needed. Controlling the frequency of the synchronizations additionally allows to bound the amount of useless work and, hence, guarantee a minimal efficiency. The only important remaining point is the one of the cost of the synchronizations and their frequency. This question boils in fact down to a tradeoff between the cost of a synchronization and the part of the computations that risk to be useless.

3 Synchronized parallel algorithms

3.1 General structure

In the previous section, we discussed the most important basic requirements a parallel algorithm has to fulfill so as to be efficient. We now propose a general structure of an efficient parallel algorithm. It is based on the idea of alternating computation and so called global synchronization steps. This general structure or strategy, denoted by *synchronized parallel algorithm* (SPA), can be described by the following pseudo-code.

---

repeat
    ⟨computation step⟩
    ⟨synchronization step⟩
until ⟨the problem has been solved⟩

During the computation step, part of the problem is solved. Previously determined independent operations are performed in parallel. All processors should finish their computation step approximately at the same time. This is usually a hard task to achieve and heavily depends on the specific problem to be solved.

One of the goals of the synchronization step is to assure that all of the true data dependences are satisfied. This is a global operation in the sense that all the processors participate in it. Therefore, each processor executes exactly the same number of synchronization steps. Another important function of the synchronization step is to redistribute the data such that 1) the load during the next computation step is evenly balanced, 2) the data used by any processor is local to it and 3) the efficiency dependences are all verified as much as desired. It is important to conceive the synchronization step such that

$$T(\text{synchronization}) \ll T(\text{computation}) \tag{1}$$

where T represents the execution time or the complexity.

Most of the irregular algorithms dealing with dynamic data use some kind of global information in order to generate new data. In the branch and bound algorithm lower and upper bounds represent such global information. Although these global informations may not be necessary for correctness, their knowledge by each processor represents an efficiency dependence.

The fundamental justification for using a load balancing scheme based on a global state is the fact that the parallelization of an algorithm which dynamically generates interdependent data can, in principle, not be scheduled efficiently (or even not at all) by having the processors take local decisions.

3.2 Breath-first tree traversal

In this section we will briefly illustrate the SPA strategy by developing an algorithm for traversing trees in a breath-first way using that structure. Let us consider a general tree having 2^i nodes at level or depth i, the exact number of sons per father node being an unspecified random variable. We want to solve the problem of finding a node in the tree which satisfies a given property. We suppose that the generation of nodes at level i depends on all the nodes generated at level $i - 1$. There exists a true dependence between the different levels of the tree. Nodes at a given level form a set of equivalent and independent problems.

This problem can be efficiently solved using a SPA. Each processor has a global information which represents the dependences between levels and a set of nodes at each iteration which it has to expand. The synchronization step checks if the problem has been solved and computes the global information for the next computation step.

3.3 Some ideas about complexity and efficiency issues

Most of the previous work on complexity and efficiency issues has focused on using statistical models. Our main idea is to separate the complexity of computing from the complexity of the synchronization and the load balancing.

In our model n is the problem size and p the number of processors. The execution time $T(n,p)$ of a SPA, is given by $T(n,p) = C \cdot \sum_i c_i(n,p) + S \cdot \sum_i s_i(n,p)$. The function $c_i(n,p)$ denotes the computational complexity of one computation step i in model C. The model C may be expressed in terms of RAM operations, or any other sequential model. The function $s_i(n,p)$ expresses the complexity of synchronization phase i in model S. S may consider as a basic unit the number of messages sent by any processor or any other relevant quantity for expressing communication costs. In this model we do not take into account computations made during the synchronization phase. C and S are constants which express the execution time of one computation and one communication operation respectively. In order to minimize the overhead due to synchronization steps, we maximize the ratio $(C \cdot \sum_i c_i(n,p))/(S \cdot \sum_i s_i(n,p))$ under the constraint that the correctness of the parallel algorithm is guaranteed.

Our model differs from other suggested models for parallel computing by two basic facts: 1) the number of processes is an explicit parameter — this allows to express the scalability, and 2) there is a clear distinction between computation and communication — this allows to consider, for example, the topology of the underlying hardware.

3.4 Complexity of parallel synchronized breath-first tree traversal

We now analyze the efficiency of the parallel synchronized algorithm for breath-first tree traversal of Sec. 3.2. Without loss of generality, we assume that the node verifying the given property, is found at depth k in the tree. Furthermore, in order to simplify the analysis, we suppose that the numbers of nodes generated by any two processors at level i differ by at most i. Finally, we suppose a hypercube connected MIMD-DM machine network topology.

Let T_S, resp. T_P, denote the sequential, resp. parallel, execution times. For the sake of simplicity, we define a basic computation operation as generating all the sons of one node and suppose that one communication operation equals to sending one message. With these assumptions $(2^k - 1) \cdot C \le T_S \le (2^{k+1} - 1) \cdot C$.

As we suppose that the load is evenly balanced at the beginning of each computation step, we have $2^i/p \le c_i \le 2^i/p + 1$. One load balancing step is made up of a gossiping operation, which require $O(\log p)$ time as we consider that any message takes unit cost. The load balancing operation sends, by hypothesis, at most i nodes, which requires at most $O(i \cdot \log p)$ time.

By these considerations and the definition of efficiency [1], for sufficiently large problems, we can guarantee a worst-case efficiency of 0.5 for any number of processors. In fact, for $k \gg \log p$, $1/2 \le \text{Eff} \le 1$.

3.5 General considerations about the efficiency and scalability

Two main questions have to be considered. The first one concerns the relative cost of the synchronizations. Reasonable efficiencies can be expected in a large number of cases. The second question is about the scalability of the SPA. Our major motivation for proposing the SPA did not come from the need of keeping all processors busy, but from the wish to respect as far as possible all efficiency dependences. As a consequence, we have to verify that massive parallel algorithms can be employed without dropping necessarily all efficiency dependences. If the contrary were always the case, the SPA would only present minor advantages.

Concerning the first aspect, let us assume that the resolution of a problem (tree search for instances) produces n subproblems (nodes in the tree). Note that

n is not known in general. Hence, a discussion on the efficiency will only be valid for a formula which does not refer to n. We suppose that during each computation step, every processors computes d subproblems. Let the diameter of the underlying network topology be δ. There is some constant S taking into account the speed of the message passing. The parallel time is obtained by observing that 1) all processors (up to some constant) are active during a computation step and that 2) the number of synchronization steps can be bounded by $n/(d\,p)$, where p is the number of processors. It is reasonable to suppose that the complexity of a synchronization depends linearly on the diameter of the network and less than linearly on the number of problems treated per processor during the previous computation step. We can derive the efficiency as $\text{Eff} = 1/(1 + S/C\ \delta/(d^{1-\epsilon}))$. The ratio S/C compares the relative speed of the network to the time used for solving one subproblem. The ratio $\delta/d^{1-\epsilon}$ can be chosen so as to produce a good efficiency. Assuming, for instance, that $\epsilon = 0.5$ and that the network is a hypercube, $\delta = \log p$, one observes that it is sufficient to choose d such that $\log p \ll d^{1-\epsilon}$, while still guaranteeing good efficiencies on large number of processors. Similar results can be derived for many configuration. The concept of synchronization and the SPA should thus produce excellent results for a large number of configurations.

Due to lack of space, the question of scalability is not treated in detail here. Let us assume that the efficiency dependences are expressed trough values, called precedences, such that the order of the naturals corresponds to the the order in which the problems should be considered for maximal efficiency. In this setting, the question of scalability reduces to know whether there are reasonable problems for which the number of subproblems with the same value associated to them is large. A direct correspondence can also be established with the lower bound values associated to the subproblems of a branch and bound search. The basic assumptions of the models developed in [3, 7] say that the precedences of a problem and its subproblems are linked. It can be shown that these hypotheses lead, with high probability, to large sets of equivalent problems. As a consequence, there are sufficiently many problems that need to be solved more or less simultaneously. Using massively parallel algorithms does hence not force us to drop all efficiency dependences. For such problems the SPA is very well adapted and produces excellent speedups, particularly when compared to other approaches based on local decisions.

4 A real world example — The branch and bound algorithm

The sequential best-first branch and bound algorithm is a method for solving combinatorial optimization problems optimally. It proceeds by traversing a tree in which each node is a subproblem of the initial problem in order to find a feasible leaf node with optimal value. For each non leaf node, the solution of at least one of its sons corresponds to the solution of that node. The nodes in the search tree are explored in increasing order according to their lower bounds. This traversal order, also called best-first traversal order, guarantees that a minimal number of nodes are explored. As one can easily show, traversing the search tree in any order will yield the optimal solution. But, depending on the traversal order, more or less nodes will be explored. Therefore the best-first traversal order represents an efficiency dependence.

When formally analyzing the best-first branch traversal order [5], it is possible to define the notion of fringes, or equivalent subproblems, within a branch and bound search tree. At any time of the computation, a fringe consists in the subset of unexpanded problems that have the same lower bound. All problems belonging to the best fringe, that is, the fringe with the smallest lower bound associated, can therefore be processed in parallel and independently one from the other. This processing yields one parallel computation step without violating any efficiency dependences. It is followed by a synchronization step which determines the next best fringe and evenly redistributes all the problems belonging to it on the processors.

4.1 Experimental results

To show the efficiency of the SPA applied to the best-first branch and bound algorithm, we have implemented heuristics for solving *symmetric traveling salesman problems* (STSP) (see [2] for further details on solving STSPs by using the branch and bound algorithm). We applied the algorithm to various problems from the TSPLIB on a 256 processor Cray T3D.

There exists an upper limit on the number of processors that can efficiently be used in order to solve problems. Increasing the number of processors will still reduce the computation times, but the synchronization time becomes too important compared to the computation time and relation (1) is no longer verified. This observation is similar to the efficiency dropping to zero. To show the relation between the total time spent in computation, resp. communication, we have represented the values $\sum c_i$, resp. $\sum s_i$, on Fig. 1, when solving the problem ts45 on 32, 64, 128 and 256 processors. The ratio between computation and communication is large as required by relation (1). For the 64 processor example about 15% of the time is spent in synchronization and waiting. When moving from 32 to 64 processors, the effective computation time is approximately reduced by 50% whereas the time spent in synchronization steps increases slightly. This shows that the SPA strategy can be successfully applied to parallelize the best-first branch and bound algorithm.

5 Conclusion and further work

We have presented a simple and general approach for designing efficient parallel algorithms called SPA structure. We have generalized the well known concept of synchronized iterative algorithms to irregular problems and dynamic data. The SPA structure has been applied to a theoretical as well as a practical problem. For the theoretical example of best-first tree search, we have shown that, for any

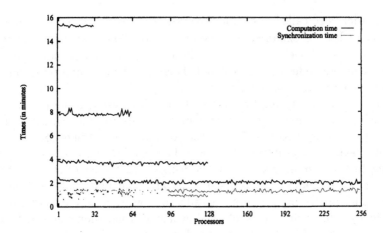

Fig. 1. Computation versus synchronization time for the problem `ts45` solved on 32, 64, 128 and 256 processors on a Cray T3D.

number of processors, there exists a sufficiently large problem instance which guarantees an efficiency of at least 50%. On the other hand, we have shown experimental results of an actual implementation of a parallelization of the best-first branch and bound algorithm according to the SPA structure. We have observed that, for large enough problem, the resulting algorithm spends more than 80% of its time on actual computations.

References

1. S. G. Akl. *The Design and Analysis of Parallel Algorithms*. Prentice-Hall International, Englewood Cliffs, NJ, 1989.
2. C. G. Diderich and M. Gengler. Solving traveling salesman problems using a parallel synchronized branch and bound algorithm. In *Proc. HPCN Europe '96*, Brussels, Belgium, April 1996.
3. M. Dion, M. Gengler, and S. Ubéda. Comparing two probabilistic models of the computational complexity of the branch and bound algorithm. In *Proc. CONPAR '94 – VAPP VI*, volume 854 of *LNCS*, pages 359–370. Springer-Verlag, 1994.
4. D. L. Eager, E. D. Lazowska, and J. Zahorjan. Adaptive load sharing in homogeneous distributed system. *IEEE Trans. Software Engrg.*, 12(5):662–675, 1986.
5. M. Gengler and G. Coray. A parallel best-first b&b algorithm and its axiomatization. *Parallel Algo. and Appl.*, 2:60–80, 1994.
6. K. Hwang and F. A. Briggs. *Computer Architectures and Parallel Processing*, chapter 8 – Multiprocessing Control and Algorithms, pages 613–636. McGraw-Hill, New York, NY, 1984.
7. B. W. Wah and C. F. Yu. Probabilistic modeling of branch and bound algorithms. In *Proc. COMPSAC*, pages 647–653, 1982.

Supporting Dynamic Data and Processor Repartitioning for Irregular Applications

José E. Moreira   Kalluri Eswar   Ravi B. Konuru   Vijay K. Naik

{*moreira,eswar,ravik,vkn*}*@watson.ibm.com*

IBM T. J. Watson Research Center
P. O. Box 218
Yorktown Heights, NY 10598-0218

Abstract. Recent research has shown that dynamic reconfiguration of resources allocated to parallel applications can improve both system utilization and application throughput. Distributed Resource Management System (DRMS) is a parallel programming environment that supports development and execution of reconfigurable applications on a dynamically varying set of resources. This paper describes DRMS support for developing reconfigurable irregular applications, using a sparse Cholesky factorization as a model application. We present performance levels achieved by DRMS redistribution primitives, which show that the cost of dynamic data redistribution between different processor configurations for irregular data are comparable to those for regular data.

Keywords: Irregular applications, dynamic data distribution, reconfigurable partitions, DRMS

1   Introduction

Dynamic manipulation of resources among competing parallel applications can result in substantial performance benefits [12, 14, 10]. In reconfigurable environments, resources available to an executing job are dynamically altered and applications must adapt to the resource changes at run-time. To make this promise of better performance through resource reconfiguration into a reality, we have designed and implemented the Distributed Resource Management System (DRMS) [10].

Traditionally, support for irregular applications on new programming paradigms has always lagged behind support for regular applications. For example, HPF provides data distribution directives for regular cases only [7]. Nevertheless, irregular problems are common to many computational science and engineering disciplines. In DRMS, we have included support for both regular and irregular applications and, in this paper, we describe support for the latter in some detail. In particular, we describe data distribution constructs for irregular data structures such as those for representing sparse matrices. As a model problem, we use a parallel version of the Cholesky factorization of sparse matrices. Our performance results show that the cost of dynamic data redistribution between different processor configurations for irregular data are comparable to those for regular data.

This paper is organized as follows. Section 2 describes DRMS support for developing and executing applications that adapt to reconfigurable processor partitions. The Cholesky factorization algorithm and the augmented DRMS version are discussed in

Section 3. Section 4 presents the techniques we use to perform the redistribution of irregular data in DRMS. Section 5 analyzes the results from our performance studies. Related work and conclusions are presented in Section 6 and Section 7, respectively. The full version of this paper is available as IBM Research Report RC20426, at `http://www.watson.ibm.com:8080/main-cgi-bin/search_paper.pl/entry_ids=8049`.

2   DRMS

DRMS provides (i) support for reconfigurable application development and (ii) the resource management infrastructure to perform dynamic data redistribution and partition reconfiguration. The resource management infrastructure consists of a job scheduler and analyzer (JSA), a resource coordinator (RC) and several slave coordinators, and a run-time system (RTS). The JSA, RC, and RTS coordinate to achieve dynamic data and processor reconfiguration. For more details refer to [10]. To take full advantage of these dynamic allocation facilities at the system level, applications must be *reconfigurable*; *i.e.*, they must execute under a dynamically varying resource pool. DRMS provides a set of *language extensions* and *library functions* for Fortran that enable and facilitate the development of reconfigurable applications. These extensions and functions implement the *DRMS programming model*, derived from the SPMD model.

Programming model: In the SPMD programming model, a fixed group of processors execute the same code, but each processor operates on a different section of the global data set. In the DRMS model, a parallel program execution consists of the consecutive execution of SPMD stages, where each stage specifies its own resource requirements, data distribution, and execution code. The boundary between two stages identifies a *schedulable and observable point* (SOP). An application's processor partition can be reconfigured at an SOP, either at its own initiative or in response to a decision by the job scheduler. The more SOPs an application provides, the quicker it can respond to changes in both its internal requirements and the system state. In our model, a stage consists of four sections:

$$stage = \{ \ resource \ section; \ data \ section; \ control \ section; \ computation \ section; \ \}$$

The *resource section* specifies the type and quantity of each resource necessary for execution of the stage. Upon entering a stage, resources are acquired or released by the application, always in accordance with the requirements. The *data section* specifies how the data structures are to be distributed among the processors executing the stage. The data distribution among processors can change from one stage to next because of a change in resources (processors) or because the new stage needs a different form of distribution. Whenever there is a change of distribution, the RTS moves data across processors to comply with the new specification. The *control section* specifies values for variables that control the execution of code inside a stage. Usually, the flow of this execution depends on resource allocation and data partitioning. The *computation section* specifies the computations to be performed in each processor, as well as the interprocessor communication. Each of the above sections can, in general, be parameterized on the actual resource availability and other problem specific factors, such as data size, numerical conditioning, etc. In this paper we show that it is possible to efficiently decompose sparse matrix operations, such as factorization, into stages.

Language extensions: DRMS language extensions are in the form of *annotations*, source level comments that are ignored by a regular Fortran compiler. The DRMS compiler, built using Sage++ [6], translates these annotations into executable Fortran code in a preprocessing phase. The output of the preprocessor is then compiled by a regular Fortran compiler and linked with the DRMS run-time library, thus generating a DRMS executable. Some DRMS annotations are illustrated in Section 3. Of particular relevance to this paper is the annotation for arbitrary data distribution. The arbitrary data distribution in DRMS is designed to be used in irregular problems. It allows a completely arbitrary partitioning of an array axis. It is specified as ARBITRARY (n, l, m) where n is an integer scalar and l and m are integer vectors of length (at least) n. The specification of such distribution for an array axis with N elements, on a processor grid axis of P elements, causes the axis to be divided into n blocks, numbered $1, \ldots, n$. The length of block i is l_i. It is a requirement that $\sum_{i=1}^{n} l_i = N$. Finally, block i is mapped to processor m_i, where $1 \leq m_i \leq P$ is the index in the corresponding processor grid axis.

3   Cholesky Algorithm

We use a sparse Cholesky factorization algorithm to evaluate the suitability and efficiency of our arbitrary data distribution support. In this section, we present an SPMD parallel version of *column-oriented* sparse Cholesky factorization and then we augment this algorithm with DRMS annotations that allow it to execute on reconfigurable processor partitions.

For an $n \times n$ matrix A, let $A_{i,j}$ denote the element at row i and column j, $A_{i,:}$ the i-th row of A, $A_{:,j}$ the j-th column of A, and $A_{i:k,j:l}$ the array section formed by the intersection of rows i through k with columns j through l. For a vector v, let v_i denote its i-th element. An SPMD version of parallel sparse Cholesky algorithm for factoring matrix A is shown in Figure 1(a). The first step of the algorithm is the partitioning of matrix A (procedure *RecursivePartitioning*()) where a vector w is computed such that w_j is the processor owning column j, $j = 1, \ldots, n$. We use the heuristic described in [16] for partitioning the matrix. After partitioning the matrix A, a vector r is computed (procedure *NumberAggregates*()) such that r_j holds the number of aggregates that the owner of column j will receive. An aggregate is a partial update vector in computing column j of the factor. It is computed only by the processors that do not own column j, but are the owners of one or more columns that update column j. The 'for $j \leftarrow 1$ to n' loop, computes the Cholesky factor. In iteration j, the owner processor first updates column j with all owned columns k that affect column j. It then receives aggregates for column j from other processors, updating column j in the process, and finally normalizes the column. If a processor does not own column j, it computes the aggregate of all updates on column j by the columns it owns, and then sends the aggregate to the owner of column j.

If processors pause after iteration j', $1 \leq j' \leq n$, then we obtain a complete factorization of columns 1 to j' with no updates of the remaining columns ($j' + 1$ through n).

```
procedure SPMDCholesky(A, n) {
    ! Set # of processors and processor id
    GetEnvironment(p,me)
    ! Compute column owners and # of update aggregates
    w ← RecursivePartitioning(A, n, p)
    r ← NumberAggregates(A, n, p, w)
    for j ← 1 to n {
        if w_j = me { ! Column j owner
            for k ← 1 to j − 1 | (w_k = me ∧ A_{j,k} ≠ 0) {
                A_{:,j} ← A_{:,j} − A_{j:n,k} A_{j,k}
            } ! local updates
            while r_j ≠ 0 {
                receive(x,k)
                A_{:,k} ← A_{:,k} − x
                r_k ← r_k − 1
            } ! updates with remote aggregates
            A_{:,j} ← A_{:,j} / √(A_{j,j})  ! normalize col j
        } else { ! non-owner of col j
            x ← 0
            for k ← 1 to j − 1 | (w_k = me ∧ A_{j,k} ≠ 0) {
                x ← x + A_{j:n,k} A_{j,k}
            } ! aggregate contribution to remote col j
            send(x,j,w_j) ! send aggregate to col j owner
        }
    }
}
```

(a)

```
procedure DRMSCholesky(A, n) {
    GetEnvironment(p,me)
    w ← RecursivePartitioning(A, n, p)
    r ← NumberAggregates(A, n, p, w)
    l_j ← length of column j, j = 1, ..., n
    ! Initial distribution for matrix A
    PROCESSORS, DIMENSION(p)  ::  P
    DIMENSION(nnz), DISTRIBUTE(
    ARBITRARY(n,l,w)) ONTO P :: A
    for j ← 1 to n {
        ! Specify processor range
        RESIZE 4:32:*2
        GetEnvironment(p,me)
        ! New column owners and update aggregates
        w ← RecursivePartitioning(A, n, p)
        r ← NumberAggregates(A, n, p, w)
        ! New data distribution
        PROCESSORS, DIMENSION(p)  ::  P
        DIMENSION(nnz), DISTRIBUTE(
        ARBITRARY(n,l,w)) ONTO P :: A
        ! The rest same as in SPMDCholesky
        if w_j = me {
            . . .
        } else {
            . . .
        }
    }
}
```

(b)

Fig. 1. (a) SPMD and (b) DRMS versions of parallel Cholesky factorization of sparse matrix A.

Thus, a well-defined intermediate state can be obtained by synchronizing processors at the beginning of any iteration of the SPMD Cholesky algorithm. This forms the basis for the DRMS version of Cholesky factorization. The annotated DRMS version of the algorithm is shown in Figure 1(b). In procedure *DRMSCholesky*(), an initial distribution is declared for matrix A. Similar to HPF, the data distribution is accomplished, using DRMS annotations PROCESSORS and DISTRIBUTE, by first defining a virtual processor grid and then distributing data onto that grid. The SOP (Section 2) is placed at the beginning of each iteration. Thus, each iteration of the factorization constitutes a stage in the DRMS programming model. The RESIZE annotation declares a range of valid processors from 4 to 32 in multiplicative steps of 2. When the partition size changes, the application reinitializes so that a new column to processor mapping is defined, the new number of aggregates to be received is computed, and a new distribution of matrix A is specified.

4 Arbitrary Distribution Support in the DRMS Run-Time System

In this section, we describe our data distribution framework in three parts: (i) the conceptual representation of array distributions, (ii) our general redistribution algorithm, and (iii) some specifics of the implementation of redistribution of irregular data.

Representation of array distributions: We start with the *range* and *slice* concepts. A range $r = (r_1, \ldots, r_n)$ is an ordered set of integers, in increasing order. Let $|r|$ be the number of elements (size) of range r. A range can be used to represent a set of indices along an axis of an array. A slice $s = (s_1, \ldots, s_d)$ is an ordered set of ranges. Let $|s|$ be the number of ranges (rank) of slice s. A slice of rank d can be used to represent the indices of a d-dimensional array section, where s_i is the range of indices along the i-th axis. We define two operations on ranges: intersection and normalization. The intersection of two ranges q and r, denoted by $q * r$, is a range given by the ordered set of all elements that belong to both ranges:

$$q * r = \{x \mid (x \in q) \wedge (x \in r)\}. \tag{1}$$

The normalization of a range q with respect to a range r, denoted by q/r, is a range given by the ordered set of indices that give the location of each element of q in r. It is required that $q \subseteq r$:

$$q/r = \{i \mid r_i = q_j, \ j = 1, \ldots, q_{|q|}\}. \tag{2}$$

The intersection and normalization operations can be extended to slices s and t of the same rank by performing the operations between corresponding pairs of ranges.

Redistribution algorithm: An array element can be referenced both by global and local indices. A global index refers to the location in the array distributed over processors. A local index refers to the location in the local section of a distributed array. In general, the shapes (extents along each dimension) of the local section and the global array are different. Let $S(p, \mathcal{D}_A)$ be the slice of global indices of the section of an array A that is mapped onto processor p in a particular distribution $\mathcal{D}_A$. Also, let x be the slice of global indices of some array section of A. The slice $y = (x * S(p, A))/S(p, A)$ contains the local indices for all elements of x that are mapped onto p.

The algorithm in Figure 2 performs redistribution of an array from a current source distribution $\mathcal{D}_A$ on a processor grid P to a new target distribution $\mathcal{D}'_A$ on a processor grid Q. We use the notation $A(y)$ to represent that section of array A whose elements are given by slice y. Redistribution involves computing the old and new slices that define the sections and then performing pair-wise intersection of those slices for each pair of old and new processors. This determines the data that has to be exchanged between each pair of processors in terms of the global indices. Then the global indices are transformed into local indices (normalization) which are then used in actual data exchange.

DRMS implementation: For arbitrary distributions in DRMS, each range of indices is represented as an ordered list of segments, each segment represented by a 3-tuple $< a, d, n >$, where a is the starting index, d is the stride and n is the number of elements in that segment. When an ARBITRARY (n, l, m) distribution is specified, a list of n segments is created. Each segment defines one block in the distribution and the strides are always 1.

The algorithm for computing the intersection of two segment lists is shown in Figure 3(a). Note the intersection operator ζ that returns an intersection of the given ranges and a *tail*. This operator is defined as follows:

$$\zeta(q, r) = \{\{q * r\}, \{x \mid (x \in q) \wedge (x > y, \forall y \in r)\}\} \tag{3}$$

```
procedure Redistribute(D_A, D'_A) {
    P ← processor grid of D_A
    Q ← processor grid of D'_A
    for every processor p ∈ P {                    for every processor q ∈ Q {
        for every processor q ∈ Q {                    for every processor p ∈ P {
            x ← S(q, D'_A) * S(p, D_A)                     x ← S(q, D'_A) * S(p, D_A)
            y ← x/S(p, D_A)                                y ← x/S(q, D'_A)
            processor p sends A(y) to q                    processor q receives A(y) from p
        }                                              }
    }                                              }
}                                              }
```

Fig. 2. Algorithm for redistributing from A to B.

where $q * r$ is the intersection of two ranges as given by Equation (1). Consider two segment lists Q and R that contain segments q_i and r_i respectively. We define the intersection operator ζ on segments q_i and r_i that returns the intersection and also a *tail* with the elements in q_i that are greater than all elements in r_i. This *tail* is then used in computing the rest of intersection of the segment list R with q_i. This process repeats until either of the lists is exhausted. It can be verified that this algorithm executes in $O(n)$ time where n is the number of segments in the lists.

```
SegmentList Operator *(Q, R) {              SegmentList Operator /(Q, R) {
    SegmentList ilist ← NULL                    SegmentList nlist ← NULL
    Segment isegment ← NULL                     Segment nsegment ← NULL
    Segment q ← head(Q)                         Segment q ← head(Q)
    Segment r ← head(R)                         Segment r ← head(R)
    while (q ≠ ∅) ∧ (r ≠ ∅) {                   offset ← 0
        Segment tail ← q                        while (q ≠ ∅) ∧ (r ≠ ∅) {
        while (tail ≠ ∅) ∧ (r ≠ ∅) {                Segment tail ← q
            [isegment, tail] ← ζ(tail, r)           while (tail ≠ ∅) ∧ (r ≠ ∅) {
            if isegment ≠ ∅ {                           [nsegment, tail] ← η(tail, r, offset)
                ilist ← ilist + isegment                if nsegment ≠ ∅ {
            }                                               nlist ← nlist + nsegment
            if tail ≠ ∅ {                               }
                r ← next(R)                             if tail ≠ ∅ {
            }                                               r ← next(R)
        }                                                   offset ← offset + r.n
        q ← next(Q)                                     }
    }                                               }
    return ilist                                    q ← next(Q)
}                                               }
                                                return nlist
                                            }

            (a)                                         (b)
```

Fig. 3. Algorithms for (a) intersection and (b) normalization of two ranges.

The algorithm for normalization is given in Figure 3(b). It differs from the intersection algorithm in the use of the normalization operator η. This operator is defined as:

$$\eta(q, r, z) = \{\{q/r\} + z, \{x \mid (x \in q) \wedge (x > y, \forall y \in r)\}\} \tag{4}$$

where q/r is the normalization of two ranges as given by Equation 2. An offset z, equal to the displacement of the first element of r from the beginning of the corresponding segment list, has to be added to each element of q/r. Note that the *offset* in Figure 3(b) is incremented with the number of elements in *r2*. Again, the *tail* segment from a previous segment normalization is used in computing the rest of the normalization on the segment lists. Again this algorithm executes in $O(n)$ time, where n is the total number of segments.

5   Performance Evaluation

In this section, we analyze the performance of reconfiguring the Cholesky application by changing the processor partition size while the factorization is in progress. We measure two types of overheads: (i) the computation overhead of the DRMS program compared to the original SPMD version, and (ii) the actual cost of performing a reconfiguration operation to change the number of processors. The computation overhead is originated by our compiler transformations that add the necessary code to create a reconfigurable application. A program with DRMS annotations always incurs the computation overhead regardless of the number of reconfigurations it encounters. We measure this computation overhead by comparing the time for factoring large sparse matrices using the SPMD and DRMS versions on the same number of processors. We define the *reconfigure time* for a reconfiguration operation as the elapsed time between an application finding out that its number of processors will change until the point where the application is ready to continue on the new number of processors. This reconfigure time has four main components: (i) the time to acquire or release processors, (ii) the time to reconfigure the new processor partition, (iii) the time to restart the application on the new set of processors, and (iv) the *redistribute time* — the time it takes to move the data from one distribution configuration to another. The first three components are system related and independent of the of data distributions used. We report these costs elsewhere. In this paper, we present the cost of the fourth component. We also compare the redistribute time of arbitrary distributions to that of more regular distributions (block and cyclic).

Experimental environment: We conducted our experiments on a 32-processor partition of an IBM SP2 with wide nodes at NASA Ames Research Center. We refer to [1] for information on the software and hardware architecture of the SP2. In our experiments we used the MPL message passing protocol. We measured the elapsed time for the execution of operations by using a real time clock with resolution better than $1\mu s$.

Benchmark matrices: Listed in Table 1 are five sparse matrices from the Harwell-Boeing collection [3] that we used as input to our SPMD and DRMS factorization programs. Column "matrix" gives the identifier for each matrix, the "description" column gives a brief description of the structural problem corresponding to the matrix, column "n" is the number of columns (order) in each matrix, and "nnz" is the number of nonzeros in the lower triangular factor (L) of the matrix. The "sparsity" index of the matrix is the ratio of nonzeros to the total number of elements in the matrix (n^2). Finally, "operations" is the number of floating point operations ($+, -, \times, \div, and \sqrt{}$ count as 1 operation) necessary to compute L on 1 processor. Fur purpose of arbitrary distribution, the matrices are divided into blocks. A block is a maximal set of contiguous columns that are owned by the same processor.

Table 1. Characteristics of the sparse matrices used in our study.

Matrix	Description	n	nnz	Sparsity	Operations
STK29	Boeing 767 bulkhead	13992	1,694,796	0.0087	393×10^6
STK30	Off-shore generator platform	28924	3,843,435	0.0046	928×10^6
STK31	Automobile component	35588	5,308,247	0.0042	2551×10^6
STK32	Automobile chassis	44609	5,246,353	0.0026	1109×10^6
STK33	Pin boss (automobile steering)	8738	2,546,802	0.0334	1204×10^6

Table 2. Comparison of SPMD and DRMS performance for Cholesky factorization.

Matrix	Factorization Time (s)											
	4 PEs			8 PEs			16 PEs			32 PEs		
	t_{SPMD}	t_{DRMS}	%	t_{SPMD}	t_{DRMS}	%	t_{SPMD}	t_{DRMS}	%	t_{SPMD}	t_{DRMS}	%
STK29	13.6	14.1	4	10.9	11.3	4	7.8	8.1	4	5.3	5.5	5
STK30	37.7	39.1	3	26.2	27.0	3	19.9	20.7	4	13.7	14.4	5
STK31	59.2	60.3	2	33.6	34.3	2	20.3	20.8	2	12.5	12.9	3
STK32	31.9	33.1	4	21.7	22.6	4	18.0	18.8	4	13.3	13.9	5
STK33	21.1	21.6	2	14.0	14.3	2	8.4	8.7	3	5.1	5.3	4

Results for DRMS *vs* SPMD: We ran both the SPMD and the DRMS versions on partitions with 4, 8, 16, and 32 PEs. The DRMS version ran without any reconfigurations (the same number of processors from begin to end). The execution times (in seconds) are tabulated for the two cases in Table 2. Each reported measurement is a mean of 10 runs. The largest coefficient of variation observed for any data point was 0.02, indicating that the factorization time varies little around the observed mean. The "%" column is computed as $100 \times (t_{DRMS} - t_{SPMD})/t_{SPMD}$. We note that, in the worst case, the DRMS version is only 5% slower than the corresponding SPMD version. This computation overhead of DRMS has several components: changes in memory layout and access patterns caused by the DRMS compiler, run-time tests inserted by the compiler, change in the code organization, etc.

Results for reconfiguration time: Table 3 summarizes the total reconfiguration time for each of the five matrices and each possible reconfiguration among the valid partition sizes we selected. The notation $P_1 \rightarrow P_2$ denotes a resize from P_1 to P_2 processors. Each entry in the table shows the mean and variance ($\mu \pm \sigma$) of all the samples for that particular reconfiguration. We first note that each entry displays a large variance. The coefficients of variation range from 0.06 to 0.48. This large variance in the cost of a reconfiguration operation is expected because of all the external factors that influence the operation. The SP2 that we used for our measurements operates in a multiprogrammed environment. Even though nodes are assigned exclusively to one application, other resources are shared. For example, the partition manager, which reconfigures the partition tables of the SP2 when there is a change in the number of processors, is shared with all other jobs.

Also, the time to restart an application on a new node is highly variable, depending on how fast the node can access the text of the application.

Table 3. Total reconfiguration time for the five sparse matrices.

resize	time(s)				
$P_1 \rightarrow P_2$	STK29	STK30	STK31	STK32	STK33
$4 \rightarrow 8$	3.90 ± 0.56	4.93 ± 1.80	4.90 ± 1.01	5.13 ± 0.68	4.97 ± 0.33
$4 \rightarrow 16$	4.93 ± 1.42	7.07 ± 2.35	7.64 ± 2.53	6.61 ± 2.03	4.99 ± 0.81
$4 \rightarrow 32$	7.44 ± 2.12	8.85 ± 2.43	9.39 ± 2.32	8.30 ± 2.01	8.41 ± 2.23
$8 \rightarrow 4$	4.28 ± 1.57	5.38 ± 0.62	7.22 ± 2.30	6.16 ± 0.59	4.94 ± 1.26
$8 \rightarrow 16$	5.17 ± 1.81	6.54 ± 2.52	7.20 ± 2.42	6.77 ± 2.24	6.78 ± 2.74
$8 \rightarrow 32$	8.29 ± 2.85	9.07 ± 2.94	7.88 ± 2.34	8.34 ± 2.18	9.37 ± 2.59
$16 \rightarrow 4$	4.39 ± 2.03	5.36 ± 1.04	6.23 ± 0.73	6.07 ± 0.44	4.84 ± 0.81
$16 \rightarrow 8$	7.17 ± 2.96	5.72 ± 1.26	7.08 ± 1.88	6.45 ± 0.90	5.96 ± 2.16
$16 \rightarrow 32$	8.34 ± 2.85	8.61 ± 2.51	9.94 ± 2.71	9.05 ± 2.48	10.37 ± 2.98
$32 \rightarrow 4$	5.95 ± 2.17	6.50 ± 1.83	6.47 ± 0.88	7.10 ± 1.32	6.72 ± 2.68
$32 \rightarrow 8$	6.50 ± 3.09	7.47 ± 2.56	6.79 ± 1.41	8.22 ± 2.42	7.12 ± 2.88
$32 \rightarrow 16$	11.59 ± 0.73	9.28 ± 2.71	11.06 ± 2.99	11.20 ± 2.74	8.85 ± 2.89

Results for redistribution time: We now present the performance of the data redistribution operations for arbitrarily distributed arrays. To get a better feel for the cost of these redistributions we present their absolute performance and compare them with respect to more regular, HPF style, block and cyclic distributions. For these comparisons, we define for each of our sparse matrices a corresponding dense rectangular matrix with the same number of columns (n) and same number (within 1%) of elements (nnz). In all cases, the matrices are distributed along their column dimension. In the block case, processor 1 gets columns 1 through n/p, while in the cyclic case processor 1 gets columns $1, p + 1, 2p + 1, \ldots$, where p is the number of processors.

Our results are summarized in Table 4. For each test matrix, and reconfiguration operation, we present the redistribution time for arbitrary, block, and cyclic distributions. Each data point presented is the average of many samples (between 18 and 64). The maximum observed coefficient of variation for the samples was 0.10, indicating that redistribution has a much smaller relative variation than resize. This is expected because the redistribution operation involves only those processors that, at the moment, are assigned exclusively to the application. We note that the redistribution times are a small fraction of the total resize times, presented in Table 3. For the arbitrary distributions, redistribution costs are almost always on the order of $0.5s$ or less, while resize costs are on the order of 4 to $12s$. We should note that the redistribution cost grows with the size of the data set, while the other costs are fixed. Therefore we can expect the share of redistribution in resize to increase for larger problem sizes. For matrix STK29, redistribution for arbitrary is significantly slower than for regular (block and cyclic) distributions. For the other matrices the redistribution times are comparable for all three distributions. We observed that the arbitrary distributions of STK29 use a much larger number of blocks than the other matrices. This large number of blocks has a negative impact on the performance of the intersection and normalization algorithms discussed in Section 4.

Table 4. Time for different redistributions.

matrix	distribution	Redistribution time (*ms*)												MB/*s*/PE	
		4↓8	4↓16	4↓32	8↓4	8↓16	8↓32	16↓4	16↓8	16↓32	32↓4	32↓8	32↓16	min	max
STK29	arbitrary	304	372	556	296	368	569	369	366	628	662	646	657	1.2	10.9
	block	176	155	169	166	104	106	146	97	82	191	107	89	9.1	22.2
	cyclic	144	161	180	151	119	132	155	119	128	176	137	123	6.3	22.4
STK30	arbitrary	379	378	437	385	280	347	368	291	343	415	379	349	5.3	19.9
	block	370	320	329	349	201	195	299	189	130	387	198	147	12.4	24.5
	cyclic	299	328	355	295	235	248	320	234	226	351	258	215	8.1	24.8
STK31	arbitrary	518	454	484	486	324	336	470	308	291	483	381	289	8.7	22.3
	block	514	437	443	471	269	255	408	251	168	525	259	188	13.4	24.8
	cyclic	392	437	468	390	296	311	423	295	278	466	330	262	9.1	26.0
STK32	arbitrary	502	477	514	471	311	360	502	318	322	530	402	354	7.1	21.2
	block	511	442	448	467	271	257	408	250	166	524	259	190	13.2	24.5
	cyclic	435	471	497	429	341	346	454	338	321	497	364	306	7.8	23.3
STK33	arbitrary	255	257	299	247	180	230	272	187	236	315	261	243	5.0	19.6
	block	248	214	222	234	140	136	199	128	100	264	142	110	11.1	24.4
	cyclic	154	186	210	163	112	138	180	114	118	211	147	112	10.3	31.5

The last two columns of Table 4 list the *redistribution rate* for the redistribution operations. Only the minimum and maximum observed for each of the 12 individual operations are listed. The rate is computed as the total problem data size (the number of nonzeros, *nnz*, times the size of an element, 8 bytes) divided by the time to perform the redistribution divided by the number of processors in the smaller of the two partitions (source and target). We observe a large variation between minimum and maximum for all problems and distribution forms. We also observe that very high redistribution rates, between 20 and 30 MB/*s*/PE are achieved in many cases.

6 Related Work

The Chaos run-time system [17] supports dynamic data redistribution for irregular applications, which is an essential step in creating dynamically reconfigurable applications. In contrast, DRMS supports primitives not only for dynamic data redistribution but also for dynamic changes in the allocated set of processors. The Adaptive Multiblock PARTI (AMP) library [4] supports dynamic reconfigurable applications by defining *remap points*. In AMP an application is spawned on the maximum number of processors it can run on and at each remap point a different subset of these processors can be chosen to actually execute the application (but the application keeps hold of all processors). Such an approach results in performance degradation not only for the application but also interferes with the execution of other applications in multi-user environments. In DRMS, in contrast, the overhead occurs only at SOPs for the processors executing the application, since we spawn new processes on demand. The LPARX run-time system [8] provides dynamic distribution for block irregular data structures. Different from DRMS, it does not provide any language extensions or compiler support, and it does not support reconfigurable programs.

Many extensions to the Fortran language, and corresponding compilers, exist that support irregular data distribution. The PST compiler [13] extends HPF by including directives for irregular distribution, but they apply directly only to one-dimensional arrays (multi-dimensional arrays are linearized). Both Fortran D [5] and Vienna Fortran [2] support irregular distributions that can map each element of an array axis individually. None of those languages are used in the context of reconfigurable processor partitions. Efficient redistribution of irregularly distributed data for the PARADIGM compiler is described in [11].

Systems like UPVM [9] and Minos [12] decompose a parallel application into a number of light-weight virtual processors greater than the number of actual processors. The system then provides dynamic reconfiguration via application-transparent migration of these light-weight VPs. In DRMS there is always a single thread of execution per physical processor. This is important for using optimized message passing on the SP2. It also avoid thread switching overhead and allows more controlled memory access patterns. Finally, we note that our research is related to work that combines the simultaneous exploitation of task and data parallelism in the same application, such as in PARADIGM [15].

7 Conclusions

Development of reconfigurable applications is an important step towards achieving dynamic allocation of resources. A fundamental component in making an application reconfigurable is the ability to dynamically redistribute its data structures. The programming model for DRMS includes language extensions and run-time system support for distributing both regular and irregular data structures. For irregular data structures, the DRMS ARBITRARY annotation can be used to partition an array axis into an arbitrary number of blocks, each with its own length and owner processor specification. Using the example of sparse Cholesky factorization, in this paper, we have shown that the redistribution of irregular data in DRMS can be done with efficiency comparable to that of regular distributions. We have also shown that we can achieve a high redistribution rate. We note here that although we have considered data redistribution exclusively in the context of supporting processor partition reconfigurations, the DRMS programming model is rich enough to support run-time changes in other resources, including those arising from computational changes within the application itself.

Acknowledgments: This work is partially supported by NASA under the HPCCPT-1 Cooperative Research Agreement No. NCC2-9000.

References

1. Agerwala, T., Martin, J. L., Mirza, J. H., Sadler, D. C., Dias, D. M., and Snir, M. SP2 system architecture. *IBM Systems Journal*, 34(2):152–184, 1995.

2. Chapman, B., Mehrotra, P., and Zima, H. User defined mappings in Vienna Fortran. *SIGPLAN Notices*, 28(1), 1993.

3. Duff, I. S., Grimes, R. G., and Lewis, J. G. Sparse matrix test problems. *ACM Transactions on Mathematical Software*, 15:1–14, 1989.

4. Edjlali, E., Agrawal, G., Sussman, A., and Saltz, J. Data parallel programming in an adaptive environment. In *Proceedings of 9th International Parallel Processing Symposium*, Santa Barbara, CA, April 1995.

5. Fox, G., Hiranandani, S., Kennedy, K., Koelbel, C., Kremer, U., Tseng, C., and Wu, M. Fortran D language specification. Technical Report COMP TR90-141, Department of Computer Science, Rice University, December 1990.

6. Indiana University. *Sage++, A Class library for Building Fortran 90 and C++ Restructuring Tools*, May 1995.

7. Koelbel, C. H., Loveman, D. B., Schreiber, R. S., Steele Jr., G. L., and Zosel, M. E. *The High Performance Fortran Handbook*. The MIT Press, 1994.

8. Kohn, S. R., and Baden, S. B. A robust parallel programming model for dynamic non-uniform scientific computations. In *Proceedings of Scalable High-Performance Computing Conference*, pages 509–517, Knoxville, TN, May 1994.

9. Konuru, R., Casas, J., Otto, S. W., Prouty, R., and Walpole, J. A user-level process package for PVM. In *Proceedings of the Scalable High Performance Computing Conference*, pages 48–55, Knoxville, TN, May 1994.

10. Konuru, R. B., Moreira, J. E., and Naik, V. K. Application-assisted dynamic scheduling on large-scale multi-computer systems. Technical Report RC 20390, IBM Research Division, February 1996. To appear in Euro-Par'96, Lyon, France, August 27-29, 1996.

11. Lain, A. and Banerjee, P. Exploiting spatial regularity in irregular iterative applications. In *Proceedings of the 9th International Parallel Processing Symposium*, pages 820–827, Santa Barbara, CA, April 1995.

12. McCann, C., Vaswami, R., and Zahorjan, J. A dynamic processor allocation policy for multiprogrammed shared-memory multiprocessors. *ACM Transactions on Computer Systems*, 11(2):146–178, May 1993.

13. Müller, A. and Rühl, R. Extending High Performance Fortran for the support of unstructured computations. In *Proceedings of the 1995 International Conference on Supercomputing*, pages 127–136, July 3-7 1995.

14. Naik, V. K., Setia, S. K., and Squillante, M. S. Processor allocation in multiprogrammed, distributed-memory parallel computer systems. Technical Report RC 20239, IBM Research Division, October 1995. Submitted to Journal of Parallel and Distributed Computing.

15. Ramaswamy, S. and Banerjee, P. Processor allocation and scheduling of macro dataflow graphs on distributed memory multicomputers by the PARADIGM compiler. In *Proceedings of the International Conference on Parallel Processing*, pages II:134–138, August 1993.

16. Sadayappan, P. and Visvanathan, V. Distributed sparse factorization of circuit matrices via recursive e-tree partitioning. In *SIAM Symposium on Sparse Matrices, Gleneden Beach, OR*, 1989.

17. Sharma, S. D., Ponnusamy, R., Moon, B., Hwang, Y., Das, R., and Saltz, J. Run-time and compile-time support for adaptive irregular problems. In *Proceedings of Supercomputing '94*, pages 97–106, November 1994.

Simple *Quantitative* Experiments with a Sparse Compiler *

Aart J.C. Bik and Harry A.G. Wijshoff

High Performance Computing Division
Department of Computer Science,
Leiden University
P.O. Box 9512, 2300 RA Leiden,
The Netherlands

ajcbik@cs.leidenuniv.nl

Abstract. The complexity of writing sparse codes can be simplified enormously if the sparsity of matrices is dealt with at compilation level rather than at programming level. In this approach, a compiler automatically transforms a program operating 2-dimensional arrays into code that operates on sparse storage schemes.

These ideas have resulted in the implementation of a prototype compiler that is capable of automatically transforming a dense program into semantically equivalent sparse code. In this paper, we present some simple quantitative experiments that have been conducted with this sparse compiler.

1 Introduction

Because the development and maintenance of sparse applications requires a lot of programming effort, in earlier work we proposed an alternative approach to the generation of such applications [1, 3]. Instead of dealing with the sparsity of matrices at programming level to reduce the storage requirements and computational time of an application, as done traditionally (see e.g. [5, 6, 7, 10]), this exploitation is done at compilation level.

These ideas have resulted in the implementation of a special kind of restructuring compiler, which we refer to as a **sparse compiler**. This compiler expects a FORTRAN program in which 2-dimensional arrays are used as enveloping data structures for all implicitly sparse matrices, i.e. matrices of which the sparsity is not dealt with explicitly by the programmer. Annotations are used to supply the compiler with information that cannot be expressed in the dense program. Thereafter, the compiler applies conventional program transformation to enable the automatic conversion into efficient sparse code. Information about the nonzero structure of each implicitly sparse matrix, obtained by annotations or automatic analysis of files is used to control these transformations. The compiler tries to isolate regions in a matrix having certain properties and to enforce a uniform access direction through

---

* Support was provided by the Foundation for Computer Science (SION) of the Dutch Organization for Scientific Research (NWO) and the EC Esprit Agency DG XIII under Grant No. APPARC 6634 BRA III.

each region. Operations on zero elements are eliminated. Moreover, the sparse compiler can select a hybrid sparse storage scheme for each implicitly sparse matrix, where *static* and *dynamic* storage are used to store the dense and sparse regions in a matrix respectively. Thereafter, the program is converted accordingly and a sparse program results. This resulting program together with a library containing some useful primitives that may be used in the sparse code are supplied to a conventional FORTRAN compiler for the desired target architecture.

Automatically generating sparse codes has a number of advantages. It simplifies the task of the programmer substantially and enables regular data dependence analysis and standard optimizations to be applied to the original dense code. Moreover, since characteristics of both the nonzero structure as well as the target machine can be accounted for by the compiler, one dense program can be converted into many sparse versions, each of which is tailored for one particular instance of the same problem. Especially this last advantage makes it worthwhile to consider this new approach, since a simple implementation of an algorithm can be converted into a range of algorithms, varying from algorithms for band matrices to algorithms that exploit all nonzero elements in the sparse matrices and that allow for fill-in (the creation of new nonzero elements) at arbitrary positions.

In this paper, we present some simple quantitative experiments that have been conducted with the first implementation of a sparse compiler. Although some remarks about the way the sparse compiler works will be made in the discussion of these experiments, space constraints enforce us to refer to [1, 2, 3, 4] for a detailed discussion of the methods used by the sparse compiler.

2 Quantitative Experiments

The experiments have been conducted on one CPU of a Cray C98/4256, where all programs are compiled with the native FORTRAN compiler having default vectorization enabled. All experiments have been conducted with sparse matrices of the $E(n, c)$-class of [10], which are $n \times n$ matrices A having the following nonzero elements:

$$\begin{cases} a_{ii} & = +4.0 & i = 1, \ldots, n \\ a_{i,i+1} = a_{i+1,i} = -1.0 & i = 1, \ldots, n-1 \\ a_{i,i+c} = a_{i+c,i} = -1.0 & i = 1, \ldots, n-c \end{cases}$$

In figure 1, the nonzero structure of $E(20, 5)$ is given. Although this matrix has a very simple nonzero structure, it enable us to test the generated sparse program for varying matrix sizes. Moreover, since for each n, at most 5 nonzero elements appear in each row, the execution time of an algorithm that fully exploits the sparsity of the matrix is expected to depend linearly on the order of the matrix. For a number of dense programs and varying values of n, a version for (i) a general sparse row-wise matrix and for (ii) the matrix having the specific nonzero structure of matrices of the $E(n, 5)$-class are generated. Subsequently, the execution time of each version is measured using the appropriate matrix of the $E(n, 5)$-class. Since general sparse row-wise versions can also be used for sparse matrices having an arbitrary nonzero structure, these versions probably trade some performance for generality with respect to versions tailored for the specific nonzero structure of matrices of the $E(n, 5)$-class.

Fig. 1. Nonzero Structure of $E(20, 5)$

We can enforce the sparse compiler to select general sparse row-wise for an implicitly $n \times n$ sparse matrix A with enveloping data structure A by adding the following annotation to the declaration of this array, which simply states that the region consisting of the whole matrix is sparse and the preferred access direction of this region is $(0, 1)^T$:

```
REAL     A(N,N)
C_SPARSE(A : SPARSE()(0,1))
```

Likewise, we can supply the specific nonzero structure of a matrix of the $E(n, 5)$-class to the sparse compiler by replacing the previous annotation with the following annotations, in which the index set of each region is described in terms of a simple section, and where the preferred access direction of each region is $(1, 1)^T$:

```
C_SPARSE(A : _ZERO  (1-N <= I-J <=  -6)(1,1))
C_SPARSE(A : _DENSE( -5 <= I-J <=  -5)(1,1))
C_SPARSE(A : _ZERO ( -4 <= I-J <=  -2)(1,1))
C_SPARSE(A : _DENSE( -1 <= I-J <=   1)(1,1))
C_SPARSE(A : _ZERO (  2 <= I-J <=   4)(1,1))
C_SPARSE(A : _DENSE(  5 <= I-J <=   5)(1,1))
C_SPARSE(A : _ZERO (  6 <= I-J <= N-1)(1,1))
```

In fact, this information can also be obtained automatically by the nonzero structure analyzer of the sparse compiler if, at compile-time, each specific matrix of the $E(n, 5)$-class is available on file.

2.1 Matrix times Vector

Computing the product of a matrix and a vector forms the basic computation of many iterative methods. Below, we present a dense implementation of $\mathbf{b} = A\mathbf{x}$, where the I-loop is placed innermost to enhance data locality or vector performance:

```
DO J = 1, N
  DO I = 1, N
    B(I) = B(I) + A(I,J) * X(J)
  ENDDO
ENDDO
```

Depending on whether the annotations enforcing the selection of (i) general sparse row-wise or (ii) static dense storage of nonzero diagonals are used, the sparse compiler automatically converts the double loop shown above into one of the following fragments, where NP_A=N and SZ_A provides sufficient space for all entries:

```
Sparse:                          Diagonals:

REAL    VAL_A(1:SZ_A)            REAL DN1_A(6:N), DN2_A(1:N-5), DN3_A(1:N,-1:1)
INTEGER LOW_A(1:NP_A), HGH_A(1:NP_A)  ...
INTEGER IND_A(1:SZ_A), LST_A     DO I = 6, N
...                                B(I) = B(I) + DN2_A(I-5) * X(I-5)
DO I = 1, N                      ENDDO
  DO J_ = LOW_A(I), HGH_A(I)     DO J = -1, 1
    J = IND_A(J_)                  DO I = MAXO(1, 1-J), MINO(100, 100-J)
    B(I) = B(I) + VAL_A(J_) * X(J)   B(I) = B(I) + DN3_A(J+I,-J) * X(J+I)
  ENDDO                           ENDDO
ENDDO                           ENDDO
                                DO I = 1, N - 5
                                  B(I) = B(I) + DN1_A(I+5) * X(I+5)
                                ENDDO
```

The first fragment results after loop interchanging has been applied by a reshaping method to enforce row-wise access patterns for the occurrence of the enveloping data structure A.

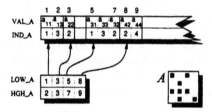

Fig. 2. General Sparse Row-wise Storage

Thereafter, general sparse row-wise storage is selected (illustrated for a small sparse matrix in figure 2 and discussed in more detail in [1]), and a construct iterating over all entries in each Ith row is generated.

To obtain the second fragment, first a unimodular loop transformation is applied to enforce regular diagonal-wise access patterns. Thereafter, iteration space partitioning is used to separate operations on zero diagonals from the operations on nonzero diagonals. Finally, occurrences of A in the resulting loops are either replaced by a zero constant or an appropriate occurrence of the static dense storage that has been selected for the nonzero diagonals, after which useless assignment statements and DO-loops are eliminated at compile-time.

In figure 3, the execution times on the Cray of the original dense fragment, the general sparse code and the diagonal code are shown (labeled Dense, Sparse, and Diagonals respectively). Exploiting the sparsity decreases the execution time (and storage requirements) of the algorithm substantially, which has now become linearly dependent on the order of the sparse matrix. This reduction becomes more profound if the specific characteristics of the nonzero structure of the sparse matrices of the $E(n, 5)$-class are exploited. The execution time of the general sparse code applied to a dense matrix is also shown (labeled Sparse(D)).

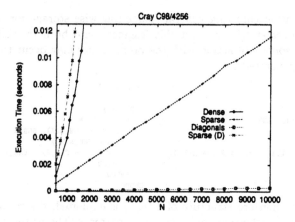

Fig. 3. Computation of $b \leftarrow Ax$

2.2 Matrix times Matrix

Although the product of two matrices can be computed by repetitively calling a
subroutine that computes the product of a matrix and a vector, we can also compute
$C \leftarrow C + AB$ directly using the following dense implementation:

```
DO I = 1, N
  DO J = 1, N
    DO K = 1, N
      C(I,J) = C(I,J) + A(I,K) * B(K,J)
    ENDDO
  ENDDO
ENDDO
```

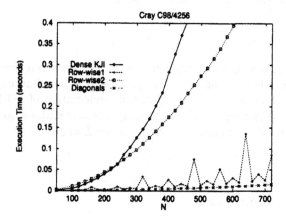

Fig. 4. Computation of $C \leftarrow C + AB$

If the annotation enforcing general sparse-row wise storage for A is used, the compiler can automatically convert this fragment into both the following sparse fragments (and some interaction with the programmer may occur to decide which one is actually generated):

Row-wise1:

```
DO I = 1, N
  DO K_ = LOW_A(I), HGH_A(I)
    K = IND_A(K_)
    DO J = 1, N
      C(I,J) = C(I,J) + VAL_A(K_) * B(K,J)
    ENDDO
  ENDDO
ENDDO
```

Row-wise2:

```
DO I = 1, N
  DO J = 1, N
    DO K_ = LOW_A(I), HGH_A(I)
      K = IND_A(K_)
      C(I,J) = C(I,J) + VAL_A(K_) * B(K,J)
    ENDDO
  ENDDO
ENDDO
```

If the specific nonzero structure of $E(n,5)$ is exploited, the reshaping method is used to enforce regular diagonal-wise access patterns. Thereafter, iteration space partitioning is used to separate operations on zero elements for operations on entries. Finally, useless assignment statements and DO-loops are eliminated at compile-time and static dense storage is selected:

```
DO I = 1, N
  DO K = 1, N-5
    C(K+5,I) = C(K+5,I) + DN2_A(K) * B(K,I)
  ENDDO
  DO J = -1, 1
    DO K = MAXO(1, J+1), MINO(N, J+N)
      C(K-J,I) = C(K-J,I) + DN3_A(K,-J) * B(K,I)
    ENDDO
  ENDDO
  DO K = 6, N
    C(K-5,I) = C(K-5,I) + DN1_A(K) * B(K,I)
  ENDDO
ENDDO
```

In figure 4, the execution times on the Cray of these fragments are shown, where the dense version with the best performance is used (the KJI-version). Again, exploiting sparsity reduces the execution time substantially. In [1], we show that the sparse compiler can also generate efficient sparse code for the more realistic situation in which all three matrices A, B, and C are sparse.

2.3   LU-Factorization

An important step in solving a linear system of equations $Ax = b$ is the factorization of a square matrix A into a unit lower triangular matrix L and an upper triangular matrix U according to $A = LU$. A dense implementation of LU-factorization without pivoting is shown below, where the array A that is initially used to store A becomes overwritten with the elements of the factors L and U:

```
DO K = 1, N-1
  DO I = K+1, N
    A(I,K) = A(I,K) / A(K,K)
    DO J = K+1, N
      A(I,J) = A(I,J) - A(I,K) * A(K,J)
    ENDDO
  ENDDO
ENDDO
```

Because matrices of the $E(n, 5)$-class are positive definite, factorization without pivoting is stable. A straightforward way to exploit the sparsity of the matrix to reduce the computational time of the algorithm is to guard the loop-body of the I-loop with the test 'A(I,K).NE.0.0)'. However, in this manner, the storage requirements of the algorithm are not reduced.

Note that if the sparse compiler converts this fragment into sparse code, it must account for the fact that **fill-in** [5, 6, 7, 10] may occur, because the nonzero structure of the sparse matrix changes into the nonzero structure of the filled matrix, i.e. $L+U$. In figure 5, the nonzero structure of the matrix $E(20, 5)$ and the nonzero structure of the filled matrix arising after the factorization are shown.

If we use an annotation enforce the selection of general sparse row-wise storage for the implicitly sparse matrix A with enveloping data structure A, the sparse compiler interchanges the I- and J-loop to obtain row-wise access patterns for the three occurrences A(I,K) after the programmer has indicated that the access patterns of occurrence A(K,K) may be ignored during the reshaping. Thereafter, the following sparse code is generated:

```
DO I = 2, N
   CALL SSCT_(VAL_A1, IND_A, LOW_A(I), HGH_A(I), SAP_10, SWT_10)
   DO K = 1, I-1
      IF (SWT_10(K)) THEN
         SAP_10(K) = SAP_10(K) / VAL_A(LKP_(IND_A, LOW_A(K), HGH_A(K), K))
         LEN_J = HGH_A(K) - LOW_A(K)
         DO J_ = 0, LEN_J
            J = IND_A(LOW_A(K)+J_)
            IF (K+1.LE.J) THEN
               IF (.NOT.SWT_10(J)) THEN
                  SWT_10(J) = .TRUE.
                  CALL SINS_(VAL_A, IND_A, LOW_A, HGH_A, I, N, SZ_A, LST_A, L_, J)
               END IF
               SAP_10(J) = SAP_10(J) - SAP_10(K) * VAL_A(LOW_A(K+J_))
            END IF
         ENDDO
      END IF
   ENDDO
   CALL SGTH_(VAL_A1, IND_A, LOW_A(I), HGH_A(I), SAP_10, SWT_10)
ENDDO
```

In the resulting fragment, each Ith row is expanded into a 1-dimensional array SAP_10 before operated upon using the primitive 'SSCT_'. This primitive also constructs a so-called switch-array SWT_10 [7] to record the position of the entries within the expanded row. If fill-in occurs (detected by the test '.NOT.SWT_10(J)'), then the primitive 'SINS_' is called to insert a new entry in the *dynamic* general sparse row-wise storage at run-time. After the Ith row has been fully processed, it is gathered back into dynamic sparse storage using the primitive 'SGTH_'. The primitives are discussed in more detail in [1].

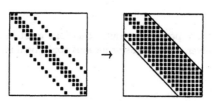

Fig. 5. Nonzero Structure of $E(20, 5)$ and the Filled Matrix

However, in this automatically generated version, the size of the execution set of the K-loop has not been reduced using so-called 'guard encapsulation' (i.e. the technique that has been applied to the J-loop). Therefore, we expect that the execution still grows at least quadratically in the order of the sparse matrix, which makes solving large sparse systems infeasible.

One step towards solving this problem is observing that in the original fragment the strict lower triangular part is mainly accessed along columns, whereas the strict upper triangular part is only accessed along rows. Moreover, because the elements along the main diagonal are used as pivots, these elements must be nonzero. Hence, we can help the sparse compiler by supplying this information by means of the following annotations:

```
C_SPARSE(A : _SPARSE(1-N <= I-J <= -1)(0,1))
C_SPARSE(A : _DENSE ( 0 <= I-J <= 0)(1,1))
C_SPARSE(A : _SPARSE( 1 <= I-J <= N-1)(1,0))
```

Thereafter, the sparse compiler performs iteration space partitioning to isolate operations on the strict lower and upper triangular part and the main diagonal:

```
                                  ...
                                  DO J = K+1, I-1
                                    A(I,J) = A(I,J) - A(I,K) * A(K,J)
...                               ENDDO
DO J = K+1, N                                  A(I,I) = A(I,I) - A(I,K) * A(K,I)
  A(I,J) = A(I,J) - A(I,K) * A(K,J)   I ≤ J ≤ I   DO J = I+1, N
ENDDO                             →     A(I,J) = A(I,J) - A(I,K) * A(K,J)
...                               ENDDO
                                  ...
```

Thereafter, loop distribution is applied to the I-loop, after which loop interchanging is applied to the first resulting loop in order obtain column-wise access of the strict lower triangular part.[2] Finally, the compiler selects a sparse storage scheme in which the entries in the strict lower and upper triangular part of A are stored in separate sparse vectors, whereas static dense storage is used for the main diagonal of A. We refer to this storage scheme as the LDU-scheme (illustrated in figure 6).

First, applying guard encapsulation to the first I-loop is done as shown below, because all entries in column K below the main diagonal are stored in the K+N-1th sparse vector of the pool:

```
DO K = 1, N-1
  DO I_ = LOW_A(K+N-1), HGH_A(K+N-1)
    I = IND_A(I_)
    VAL_A(I_) = VAL_A(I_) / DN1_A(K)
  ENDDO
```

---

[2] In the current prototype, these particular transformations must be guided by the programmer. In principle, however, these transformations could be done automatically in a future implementation.

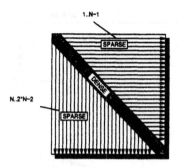

Fig. 6. LDU-scheme

Subsequently, the double loop performing the updates on the strict lower triangular part of A is converted into a construct that iterates over entries in the strict upper triangular part of the Kth row (stored in the Kth sparse vector) and entries in the strict lower triangular part of the Kth column (stored in the N-K+1th sparse vector), where relative addressing is used to account for possible data movement. The Jth column below the main diagonal is expanded before operated upon:

```
LEN_J = HGH_A(K) - LOW_A(K)
DO J_ = 0, LEN_J
  J = IND_A(LOW_A(K)+J_)
  CALL SSCT__(VAL_A, IND_A, LOW_A(J+N-1), HGH_A(J+N-1), SAP_20, SWT_20)
  IF (J+1.LE.100) THEN
    LEN_I = HGH_A(K+N-1) - LOW_A(K+N-1)
    DO I_ = 0, LEN_I, 1
      I = IND_A((LOW_A(K+N-1)+I_))
      IF (J+1.LE.I) THEN
        IF (.NOT.SWT_20(I)) THEN
          SWT_20(I) = .TRUE.
          CALL SINS__(VAL_A, IND_A, LOW_A, HGH_A, J+N-1, N, SZ_A, LST_A, L_, I)
        ENDIF
        SAP_20(I) = SAP_20(I) - VAL_A((LOW_A(K+N-1)+I_)) * VAL_A((LOW_A(K)+J_))
      ENDIF
    ENDDO
  ENDIF
  CALL SGTH__(VAL_A, IND_A, LOW_A(J+N-1), HGH_A(J+N-1), SAP_20, SWT_20)
ENDDO
```

Updating the elements along the main diagonal is implemented as follows:

```
CALL SSCT_(VAL_A, IND_A, LOW_A(K), HGH_A(K), SAP_10, SWT_10)
DO I_ = LOW_A(K+N-1), HGH_A(K+N-1)
  I = IND_A(I_)
  IF (SWT_10(I)) THEN
    DN1_A(I) = DN1_A(I) - VAL_A(I_) * SAP_10(I)
  ENDIF
ENDDO
CALL SGTH_(VAL_A, IND_A, LOW_A(K), HGH_A(K), SAP_10, SWT_10)
```

Because the sparse code generated for the double loop that performs the updating of elements in the strict upper triangular part is very similar to the code that updates the strict lower triangular part, this code is not shown completely:

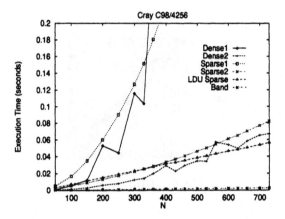

Fig. 7. LU-Factorization

```
LEN_I = HGH_A(K+N-1) - LOW_A(K+N-1)
DO I_ = 0, LEN_I
   I = IND_A(LOW_A(K)+N-1+I_)
   ...
      ...
   ...
ENDDO
ENDDO     ! main K-loop
```

As a final example, if we account for the specific nonzero structure of matrices of the $E(n, 5)$-class, then we can inform the compiler about the fact that the implicitly sparse matrix A eventually becomes a band matrix with semi-bandwidths 5 using the following annotations (note that the zero regions outside the band will be preserved at run-time):

```
C_SPARSE(A : _ZERO (1-N <= I-J <=  -6))
C_SPARSE(A : _DENSE( -5 <= I-J <=   5))
C_SPARSE(A : _ZERO (  6 <= I-J <= N-1))
```

In this case, the sparse compiler automatically converts the original implementation of LU-factorization into the following band formulation of LU-factorization using iteration space partitioning and the compile-time elimination of useless assignment statements and DO-loops. Fill-in is simply accounted for by allocating *static* dense storage for the complete band in advance:

```
REAL DN1_A(1:N,-5:5)
...
DO K = 1, N-1
  DO I = K+1, MINO(N, K+5)
    DN1_A(K,I-K) = DN1_A(K,I-K) / DN1_A(K,0)
    DO J = K+1, MINO(N, K+5)
      DN1_A(J,I-J) = DN1_A(J,I-J) - DN1_A(K,I-K) * DN1_A(J,K-J)
    ENDDO
  ENDDO
ENDDO
```

In figure 7, we present the execution times of these fragments (Dense1 and Dense2 denote the original dense implementation and the dense implementation with a conditional statement respectively, while Sparse 1 and Sparse 2 denote a preliminary version presented in [1, 3] and the first sparse LU-version presented in this paper). Although none of the general sparse versions convincingly outperforms the dense implementation using a conditional statement for small matrices, in figure 8 we see that the true run-time behavior of each implementation becomes clear for larger matrices.

2.4   Forward and Back Substitution

After a matrix A has been factorized into $A = LU$, a system $Ax = b$ is solved by forward substitution of the system $Lc = b$, followed by back substitution of $Ux = c$.

Dense implementations of forward and back substitution, where an in-place conversion of the vector **b** into **x** is performed, are shown below:

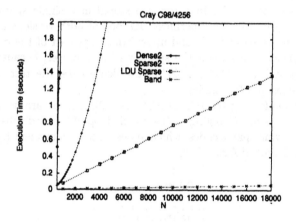

Fig. 8. LU-Factorization

Forward Substitution:

```
DO I = 2, N
  DO J = 1, I-1
    B(I) = B(I) - A(I,J) * B(J)
  ENDDO
ENDDO
```

Back Substitution:

```
DO I = N, 1, -1
  DO J = I+1, N
    B(I) = B(I) - A(I,J) * B(J)
  ENDDO
  B(I) = B(I) / A(I,I)
ENDDO
```

If an annotation enforcing general sparse row-wise storage of A is used, the sparse compiler converts these fragments into the following sparse codes:

Sparse Forward:

```
DO I = 2, N
   DO J_ = LOW_A(I), HGH_A(I)
      J = IND_A(J_)
      IF (J.LE.I-1) THEN
         B(I) = B(I) - VAL_A(J_) * B(J)
      END IF
   ENDDO
ENDDO
```

Sparse Back:

```
DO I = N, 1, -1
   IF (I+1.LE.N) THEN
      DO J_ = LOW_A(I), HGH_A(I)
         J = IND_A(J_)
         IF ((I+1.LE.J) THEN
            B(I) = B(I) - VAL_A(J_) * B(J)
         END IF
      ENDDO
   ENDIF
   B(I) = B(I) / VAL_A( LKP_(IND_A, LOW_A(I),
  +                             HGH_A(I), I) )
ENDDO
```

Note that although the resulting fragments strongly resemble the code generated for the product of a sparse matrix with a vector, there are some differences. First, a lookup is required in the back substitution, because the access patterns of $A(I,I)$ are inconsistent with the way in which the entries of A are stored. Moreover, because the execution set of the J-loop is empty for I=N, the generated J_-loop is protected by the test '(I+1.LE.N)' to prevent erroneous accesses to entries in the Nth row of the sparse matrix (although the test could be safely omitted for this particular example).

Finally, because *all* entries in a row are stored in a single sparse vector, an IF-statement is required in the innermost DO-loop of both versions to distinguish between entries in the strict lower and upper triangular part of the matrix respectively. The fragments still exploit the sparsity of A, however, because in contrast with using the test '(A(I,J).NE.0.0)' in the dense case, the test in the sparse versions is only executed for entries.

If annotations enforcing the selection of the LDU-scheme are used, the sparse compiler applies loop interchanging to the double loop of forward substitution, and generates the following sparse codes, which are essentially equivalent to codes found in e.g. SPARSKIT and SPARK [8, 9]:

LDU Forward:

```
DO J = 1, N-1
   DO I_ = LOW_A(J+N-1), HGH_A(J+N-1)
      I = IND_A(I_)
      B(I) = B(I) - VAL_A(I_) * B(J)
   ENDDO
ENDDO
```

LDU Back:

```
DO I = N, 1, -1
   IF (I+1.LT.N) THEN
      DO J_ = LOW_A(I), HGH_A(I)
         J = IND_A(J_)
         B(I) = B(I) - VAL_A(J_) * B(J)
      ENDDO
   ENDIF
   B(I) = B(I) / DN1_A(I)
ENDDO
```

Loop interchanging has, in fact, converted the inner product formulation of forward substitution into an outer product formulation [6, p.25-28]. No IF-statements are required in the body of the J_-loops because entries in the strict lower and upper triangular part of A are stored in separate sparse vectors. Moreover, because static dense storage is used for the main diagonal of A, the lookup in back substitution vanishes. However, in this case it is essential to protect the J_-loop of back substitution with the test '(I+1.LE.N)', because otherwise the the N sparse vector would be erroneously be accessed, which is used to store entries in the first column of A (alternatively, we can peel one iteration of the I-loop to prevent this test).

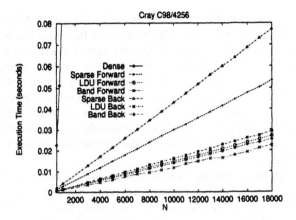

Fig. 9. Forward and Back Substitution

Finally, if we inform the sparse compiler about the specific band characteristics of matrices of the $E(n, 5)$-class after the factorization, the following band versions are generated automatically:

Band Forward:

```
DO I = 2, N
  DO J = MAXO(1, I-5), I-1
    B(I) = B(I) - DN1_A(J,I-J) * B(J)
  ENDDO
ENDDO
```

Band Back:

```
DO I = N, 1, -1
  DO J = I+1, MINO(N, I+5)
    B(I) = B(I) - DN1_A(J,I-J) * B(J)
  ENDDO
  B(I) = B(I) / DN1_A(I,0)
ENDDO
```

Due to data dependences, none of the access patterns can be reshaped along the diagonals. However, iteration space partitioning and the compile-time elimination of useless assignment statements and DO-loops is applicable to the innermost DO-loop, which reduces the amount of operations that must be executed.

In figure 9, the execution times of all versions of forward and back substitution are presented (dense forward and back substitution have almost identical execution times). Because for general sparse row-wise storage a lookup remains in the code of back substitution, this version has the largest execution time of all sparse versions. Nevertheless, it is clear that all sparse versions fully exploit sparsity.

3 Conclusions

In this paper, we have presented a few simple quantitative experiments that have been conducted with a prototype sparse compiler. These experiments indicate that a sparse compiler is capable of transforming a dense algorithm into efficient sparse code, where the generated sparse code becomes more efficient if more peculiarities of the nonzero structures of the sparse matrices can be accounted for during this transformation.

Although the results of the experiments in the first place motivate the use of sparse algorithms rather than dense algorithms, the fact a simple dense implementation can be converted into a range of efficient sparse algorithms seems to justify the use of a sparse compiler, because the automatic conversion requires less programming effort and is less error-prone. Although more experiments and probably the development of more advanced strategies are required to determine whether a successful conversion is also feasible for large programs, the experiments indicate that in principle the complexity of writing sparse codes can be reduced substantially by dealing with the sparsity of matrices at the compilation level rather than at the programming level.

Before this approach can be truly competitive with hand-coded sparse codes in which fill-in occurs for general sparse matrices, however, the sparse compiler must be able to automatically incorporate so-called sparsity reordering methods (see e.g. [5, 6, 7, 10]). Future research should be aimed at this issue.

References

1. Aart J.C. Bik. *Compiler Support for Sparse Matrix Computations*. PhD thesis, Department of Computer Science, Leiden University, 1996. ISBN 90-9009442-3.
2. Aart J.C. Bik and Harry A.G. Wijshoff. Advanced compiler optimizations for sparse computations. *Journal of Parallel and Distributed Computing*, 31:14–24, 1995.
3. Aart J.C. Bik and Harry A.G. Wijshoff. Automatic data structure selection and transformation for sparse matrix computations. *IEEE Transactions on Parallel and Distributed Systems*, 7(2):109–126, 1996.
4. Aart J.C. Bik and Harry A.G. Wijshoff. The use of iteration space partitioning to construct representative simple sections. *Journal of Parallel and Distributed Computing*, 34:95–110, 1996.
5. Iain S. Duff, A.M. Erisman, and J.K. Reid. *Direct Methods for Sparse Matrices*. Oxford Science Publications, Oxford, 1990.
6. Alan George and Joseph W.H. Liu. *Computer Solution of Large Sparse Positive Definite Systems*. Prentice-Hall, Englewood Cliffs, New York, 1981.
7. Sergio Pissanetsky. *Sparse Matrix Technology*. Academic Press, London, 1984.
8. Youcef Saad. SPARSKIT: a basic tool kit for sparse matrix computations. CSRD/RIACS, 1990.
9. Youcef Saad and Harry A.G. Wijshoff. Spark: A benchmark package for sparse computations. In *Proceedings of the International Conference on Supercomputing*, pages 239–253, 1990.
10. Zahari Zlatev. *Computational Methods for General Sparse Matrices*. Kluwer, Dordrecht, 1991.

Using Algorithmic Skeletons with Dynamic Data Structures

George Horatiu Botorog*   Herbert Kuchen

Aachen University of Technology, Lehrstuhl für Informatik II
Ahornstr. 55, D-52074 Aachen, Germany
{botorog,herbert}@i2.informatik.rwth-aachen.de

Abstract. Algorithmic skeletons are polymorphic higher-order functions representing common parallelization patterns. A special category are data-parallel skeletons, which perform operations on a distributed data structure. In this paper, we consider the case of distributed data structures with dynamic elements. We present the enhancements necessary in order to cope with these data structures, both on the language level and in the implementation of the skeletons. Further, we show that these enhancements practically do not affect the user, who merely has to supply two additional functional arguments to the communication skeletons. We then implement a parallel sorting algorithm using dynamic data with the enhanced skeletons on a MIMD distributed memory machine. Run-time measurements show that the speedups of the skeleton-based implementation are comparable to those obtained for a direct C implementation.

1   Introduction

Algorithmic skeletons represent an approach to parallel programming which combines the advantages of high-level (declarative) languages, and those of efficient (imperative) ones. The aim is to obtain languages that allow easy parallel programming, such that the user does not need to explicitly handle low-level features, like communication and synchronization, and does not have to fight with problems like deadlocks or non-deterministic program runs. At the same time, skeleton-based programs should be efficiently implementable, coming close to the performance of low-level approaches, such as message-passing on MIMD machines with distributed memory.

A *skeleton* is an algorithmic abstraction common to a series of applications, which can be implemented in parallel [9]. Skeletons are embedded into a sequential host language, thus being the only source of parallelism in a program. Classical examples include **map**, which applies a given function to all elements of a data structure, **farm**, which models master-slave parallelism and **divide&conquer**, which solves a problem be recursive splitting [10].

---

* The work of this author is supported by the "Graduiertenkolleg Informatik und Technik" at the Aachen University of Technology.

Depending on the kind of parallelism used, skeletons can be classified into *process parallel* and *data parallel* ones. In the first case, the skeleton (dynamically) creates processes, which run concurrently. Some examples are **pipe**, **farm** and **divide&conquer** [1, 9, 10]. In the second case, the skeleton works on a distributed data structure, performing the same operations on some or all elements of this structure. Data parallel skeletons, like **map**, **fold** or **rotate** are used in [1, 5, 6, 7, 10, 11, 13, 17].

In this paper, we place the emphasis on the second category. More exactly, we address here the issue of skeletons working with dynamic distributed data structures. We present the additional features that are necessary in order to cope with dynamic data, both in the language and in the implementation of skeletons. We then show how a parallel algorithm that uses dynamic data can be implemented with skeletons, and that the speedups of this implementation are comparable to those of its direct (low-level) implementation.

The rest of the paper is organized as follows. Section 2 gives an overview of the host language and the features needed to integrate the skeletons. Section 3 addresses the additional problems that arise when using dynamic data structures, as well as how they can be dealt with in the implementation of skeletons. Section 4 then presents some skeletons working on arrays with dynamic components. Section 5 shows how a parallel sorting algorithm (PSRS) can be implemented with these skeletons. It further gives run-time results and a comparison with results obtained for a direct implementation in parallel C. Section 6 compares our approach with some related work and the last section draws conclusions.

2 The Language

An important characteristic of skeletons is their *generality*, i.e. the possibility to use them in different applications. For this, most skeletons have functional arguments and a polymorphic type. Hence, most languages with skeletons are built upon a *functional* host [10, 13]. The main drawback is that the efficiency of these implementations lags behind that of low-level languages [13].

To obtain a better performance, we have used an imperative language, namely C[1], as the basis of our host, which we have called *Skil*, as an acronym for *Sk*eleton *I*mperative *L*anguage. However, in order to allow skeletons to be integrated in their full generality, we have provided Skil with some functional features as well as with a polymorphic type system. These additional features are described in [6], we give here only a brief overview:

- Since most skeletons are higher-order functions, i.e. functions with functional arguments and/or return type, we need *higher-order functions* in Skil. For example, the skeleton **map** applies a given function to all elements of data structure:

$$\text{map } (f, [x_1, \ldots, x_n]) = [f(x_1), \ldots, f(x_n)]$$

---

[1] This is however only a pragmatic choice, other imperative languages can equally well be used instead.

- Closely related to higher-order functions is *partial function application*, i.e. the application of an *n*-ary function to $k \leq n$ arguments. Partial applications are useful in generating new functions at run-time and in supplying additional parameters to functions [5, 6, 7].
- Another feature is the *conversion of operators to functions*, which allows passing operators as functional arguments to skeletons, as well as partial applications of operators. This conversion is done by enclosing the operator between brackets, e.g. '(+)'.
- Skil has a *polymorphic type system*, which allows skeletons to be (re-)used in solving similar or related problems. Polymorphism is achieved by using *type variables*, which can be instantiated with arbitrary types. Syntactically, a type variable is an identifier which begins with a $, e.g. '$t'.
- Skil allows the definition of *distributed data structures*, as long as they are 'homogeneous', in the sense that they are composed of identical data structures placed on each processor. This is done by means of the '**pardata**' construct [6]. As an example, consider the data structure "distributed array". The 'header' of this data structure is:

```
pardata array <$t> ;
```

where the type parameter **$t** denotes the type of the elements of the array. A distributed array of double precision reals can then be declared as:

```
typedef array <double> realarray ;
```

The type arguments of a pardata can be instantiated with arbitrary types. However, some additional problems appear if *dynamic* (pointer-based) data types are used. In this case, special care has to be taken in the implementation of skeletons that move elements of the pardata from one processor to another, since one should not move the pointer as such, but the data pointed to by it. This issue is addressed in the next section.

3 Coping with Dynamic Data Structures

A distributed data structure defined by the **pardata** construct can be dynamic in its entirety, like for instance an adaptively refined grid, or it can have an overall regular structure, but be parameterized by a dynamic data structure, like for example an array with arrays of variable length as elements. The first case was considered in [5]. We showed there, that the irregularity of the data structure is dealt with on a high level, by defining special skeletons which implement 'irregular' operations such as grid refinement or load balancing. We shall focus here on the second case, where a handling on the language and skeleton implementation level is necessary.

Consider the following type definition of an array with variable length of integers:

```
typedef struct {int *fields; int cnt;} VarArr ;
```

where **fields** is a pointer[2] to the array elements and **cnt** gives the number of elements. Based on this data structure, a distributed array with **VarArr**'s as elements can be defined[3]:

```
typedef array <VarArr> vararray ;
```

While some skeletons working on distributed arrays, such as **map**, are not affected by this instantiation, a problem arises in the case of communication skeletons, which move array elements from one processor to another. Since moving pointers between processors obviously leads to incorrect results, pointer-based (and hence dynamic) data structures have to be 'flattened' before sending and 'unflattened' at the destination.

The next question is whether this packing/unpacking can be done automatically by the skeleton. The main problem is here the fact that a pointer of type t can point to a memory area containing several data structures of the type t, like in the **VarArr** example above, where **fields** points to a block of **cnt** integers. Void pointers and casts blur the entire issue even more, so that automatic packing and unpacking are hard to achieve.

The solution is based on the functional features of Skil, which allow passing argument functions to skeletons. Communication skeletons, like **fold** or **permute** (see Section 4) get two additional functional parameters, **pack_f** and **unpack_f**, where the user can supply the appropriate routines for the type with which he has instantiated the distributed data structure. These functions have the types:

```
void pack_f ($t, Buff) ;
void unpack_f (Buff, $t *) ;
```

where **$t** is the type of the array elements[4] and **Buff** is a predefined buffer structure, containing a string and its length.

A further problem in sending an element with variable size is the length of the resulting message. In most message-passing systems, the receiver has to know the size of the incoming message beforehand, in order to allocate the receive buffer. Consequently, the size of the element that will be sent must first be communicated to the destination processor. This is illustrated by the following pseudo-code fragment:

(Sender)	*(Receiver)*
`pack_f (a[i], buf) ;`	`Recv (src, buf->len, 1) ;`
`Send (dest, buf->len, 1) ;`	`Recv (src, buf->buf, buf->len);`
`Send (dest, buf->buf, buf->len);`	`unpack_f (buf, &a[j]) ;`

---

[2] We regard here pointer-based structures, since this is the way dynamic data structures can be defined in C and also in Skil.

[3] Such data structures can be used, for instance, to represent sparse matrices.

[4] In case of other distributed data structures, which are parameterized by a different number of type variables, the arity of **pack_f**/**unpack_f** changes appropriately.

However, this packing/unpacking becomes inefficient, if the elements of the data structure have a static type. On the one hand, these elements do not have to be 'flattened', but can be copied directly into the output buffer. On the other hand, their size is known, thus making the first message superfluous. In order to avoid this overhead, the internal function **$$dyn** was defined. This function tests if a data type is dynamic and can be used in the implementation of skeletons. Since **$$dyn** is evaluated by the Skil compiler *after* the instantiation of polymorphism, it can also be applied to polymorphic types, as shown below.

```
skel (array <$t> a, ..., void pack_f (), void unpack_f ())
   { ...
   if (! $$dyn ($t))
      Send (dest, a[i], sizeof (a[i])) ;
   else { pack_f (a[i], buf) ;
          Send (dest, buf->len, 1) ;
          Send (dest, buf->buf, buf->len) ; }
   ... }
```

4 The Skeletons

We shall now briefly present some skeletons for the distributed data structure **array**. Since most of these skeletons are described in [6] and [7] for arrays with static elements, we shall focus here on the dynamic case. For each skeleton, we give its syntax, informal semantics and complexity (i.e. the actual computation time $t(n)$; the overall complexity can be derived as $c(n) = t(n) \cdot p$). Note that the complexity of some skeletons increases if the elements of the array have a dynamic type, because of the packing/unpacking and additional messages.

Let p be the number of processors (and, hence, of array partitions) and d the dimension of the array. We assume that our arrays have the same size n in each dimension. This condition is not necessary, but serves to simplify the expressions obtained for the complexity. For simplicity, we assume that both a local operation on a processor and the sending of one array element from one processor to one of his neighbors equally take one time unit.

4.1 The *create* and *destroy* Skeletons

The skeleton **array_create** creates a new, block-wise distributed array and initializes it using a given function. The skeleton has the following syntax:

```
array <$t> array_create (int dim, Size size, Size blocksize, Index
                         lowerbd, $t init_elem (Index), int distr);
```

where **dim** is the number of dimensions of the array, the types **Size** and **Index** are (classical) arrays with **dim** components, **size** contains the global sizes of the array, **blocksize** contains the sizes of a partition, **lowerbd** is the lowest index of a partition, **init_elem** is a user-defined function that initializes each element of the array depending on its index and `distr` gives the virtual (software) topology onto which the array is mapped [7]. In the example in the following section, the array is mapped directly onto the hardware topology (`DISTR_DEFAULT`).

If we notate the complexity of the initialization function with t_i, then the complexity of the skeleton is $t(n) \in \mathcal{O}\left(t_i \cdot n^d/p\right)$, since we have to call `init_elem` for each element of a partition and all partitions are processed in parallel.

The skeleton `array_destroy` deallocates an existing array. The argument function `destr_elem` is called only in case of dynamic elements. The complexity is thus $t(n) \in \mathcal{O}(1)$ in the static case, and $t(n) \in \mathcal{O}\left(t_d \cdot n^d/p\right)$ in the dynamic case, where t_d is the complexity of the element deallocation function.

```
void array_destroy (array <$t> a, void destr_elem ($t)) ;
```

4.2 The *map* Skeleton

`array_map` applies a given function to all elements of an array, and puts the results into another array. However, the two arrays can be identical; in this case the skeleton does an in-situ replacement. The syntax is:

```
void array_map ($t2 map_f ($t1, Index), array <$t1> from,
                array <$t2> to) ;
```

The complexity of this skeleton is similar to that of `array_create`: $t(n) \in \mathcal{O}\left(t_m \cdot n^d/p\right)$, where t_m is the complexity of the applied function `map_f`.

4.3 The *fold* Skeleton

`array_fold` composes ("folds together") all elements of an array.

```
$t2 array_fold ($t2 fold_f ($t2, $t2), array <$t1> a, void
                pack_f ($t2, Buff), void unpack_f (Buff, $t2 *)) ;
```

First, each processor composes all elements of its partition using the folding function `fold_f`. After that, the results from all partitions are folded together. Since the order of composition is non-deterministic, the user should provide an associative and commutative folding function, otherwise the result is non-deterministic. In our implementation, the second step is performed along the edges of a software tree topology, with the result finally collected at the root. In order to make the result known to all processors, it is broadcasted from the root along the tree edges to all other processors.

If t_f is the complexity of the folding function, then the complexity of the skeleton is given by the local (sequential) folding, by the folding of the single results from each processor, and by the broadcasting of the final results and amounts to $t(n) \in \mathcal{O}\left(t_f \cdot \left(n^d/p + \log_2 p\right)\right)$[5] for static elements, and to $t(n) \in \mathcal{O}\left(t_f \cdot \left(n^d/p + \log_2 p\right) + (t_p + t_u) \cdot \log_2 p\right)$ for dynamic elements, where t_p and t_u are the complexities of the packing and unpacking functions, respectively.

---

[5] Actually, if the hardware topology is not a tree, then this complexity becomes $t(n) \in \mathcal{O}\left(t_f \cdot \left(n^d/p + \delta \cdot \log_2 p\right)\right)$, where δ is the dilation of embedding the tree into the hardware topology [16].

4.4 The *permute* Skeleton

`array_permute_parts` switches the partitions of an array using a given permutation function (`perm_f`). This function takes the index of an element of the partition placed on the source processor and returns the index of an element placed on the target processor. This apparently complicated procedure is done in order to maintain the transparency of the mapping of array partitions onto processors. The user must provide a bijective function on $\{0, \ldots, p-1\}$, otherwise a run-time error occurs.

```
void array_permute_parts (array <$t> from, Index perm_f (Index),
                          array <$t> to, void pack_f ($t, Buff),
                          void unpack_f (Buff, $t *)) ;
```

The complexity of this skeleton is given by the complexity of evaluating the permutation function t_f and by that of sending a partition (comprising n^d/p elements) to another processor. The distance on the network between the source and the target processor is determined by `perm_f` and is at most equal to the diameter of the topology. In case of a mesh, this diameter is $\mathcal{O}\left(\sqrt{p}\right)$. The complexity of the skeleton is thus $t(n) \in \mathcal{O}\left(n^d/p \cdot \sqrt{p} + t_f\right) = \mathcal{O}\left(n^d/\sqrt{p} + t_f\right)$ in the static case, and $t(n) \in \mathcal{O}\left((t_p + t_u) \cdot n^d/\sqrt{p} + t_f\right)$ in the dynamic case, where t_p and t_u are the complexities of the packing and unpacking functions, respectively.

5 An Application: Parallel Sorting by Regular Sampling

We shall now present the Parallel Sorting by Regular Sampling[6] (PSRS) algorithm [14], and show how it can be implemented on the basis of skeletons. The algorithm internally uses array blocks of variable size, as well as dynamically growing blocks during an accumulation phase, thus being an appropriate application of the previously discussed features for dynamic data structures[7]. We then give some run-time results and compare the achieved speedups with those obtained by the authors of the algorithm for a direct (C) implementation.

5.1 The PSRS Algorithm

PSRS is a combination of a local (sequential) sort, a load balancing phase, a data exchange and a parallel merge [14]. We assume that we have to sort a distributed array with n keys on p processors (the example in Fig. 1 taken from [15] illustrates this for $n = 27$ and $p = 3$). The algorithm consists of four phases:

---

[6] The term 'regular' refers here to the fact that the distance between the indices of the selected samples is constant.

[7] Of course, variable-sized arrays could be implemented as arrays with fixed size, by estimating the maximal size. We wanted to give a simple example for a technique that can be used with arbitrarily complicated dynamic data structures.

1. Each processor, in parallel, sorts its partition of n/p elements of the array using a sequential algorithm, for instance quicksort. Each processor then selects its *regular samples* as the 1st, $w + 1^{st}$, ..., $(p - 1) \cdot w + 1^{st}$ elements of his partition, where $w = n/p^2$. In Fig. 1, each processor selects its 1st, 4th and 7th elements as local samples.

2. One processor gathers all local samples and sorts them. Then, it selects $p - 1$ pivots, as the samples with indices $p + \rho$, $2p + \rho$, ..., $(p - 1)p + \rho$, where $\rho = \lfloor p/2 \rfloor$. In Fig. 1, the 4th and 7th samples (33 and 69) are chosen as pivots. The pivots are then broadcasted to all processors.

3. Upon receiving the pivots, each processor spilts its array partition into p disjoint blocks, containing the elements whose values are situated between the values of neighboring pivots. Then, in parallel, each processor i keeps the ith block for itself and sends the jth block to processor j. Thus, each processor keeps one block and re-assigns $p - 1$ blocks. In Fig. 1, processor 1 receives the first blocks from processors 2 and 3, and sends the second and third blocks to processors 2 and 3, respectively. At the end of this phase, each processor i hold those elements of the initial array, whose value is between that of the $i - 1^{st}$ and i^{th} pivots.

4. Each processor, in parallel, merges its blocks into a single partition. The concatenation of the single partitions is the final sorted array.

5.2 Implementation with Skeletons

We shall now describe the skeleton-based implementation of PSRS. While the first and second phases remain more or less unchanged, the third and fourth ones are partly interleaved. The skeleton program is given in Fig. 2. The pre-defined variables **procId** and **netSize** denote the own processor number and the total number of processors (p), respectively.

The first two lines contain the declarations of two distributed arrays, the first having **VarArr**'s as elements (see Section 3), the second **MultArr**'s (arrays of **VarArr**'s), which are used to store the blocks in the third and fourth phase.

The initial array **a** is represented as an array with p elements, each partition thus being one **VarArr** with n/p elements. The first phase is implemented by using a **map** skeleton, which applies a (sequential) sorting function to each element (i.e. to each **VarArr**), and puts the results back into the initial array. Then, the array **s** is created to hold the samples. The partitions of this array also consist of one element, which is a **VarArr** with p components. The selection of the samples is done by again using the **map** skeleton, this time with the argument function **sample_f**. This function selects from a **VarArr** the elements with indices 1, $w+1$, ..., $(p - 1) \cdot w + 1$. For that, **sample_f** is applied to all elements of **a**, which it leaves unchanged, storing the result as a side-effect in the array **s**. Note that the additional parameters **s** and **w** are supplied by *partial application*, whereas the last two arguments come from the **map** skeleton (see [5, 7] for further details). The type of this function is thus:

```
VarArr sample_f (vararray s, int w, VarArr v, Index ix) ;
```

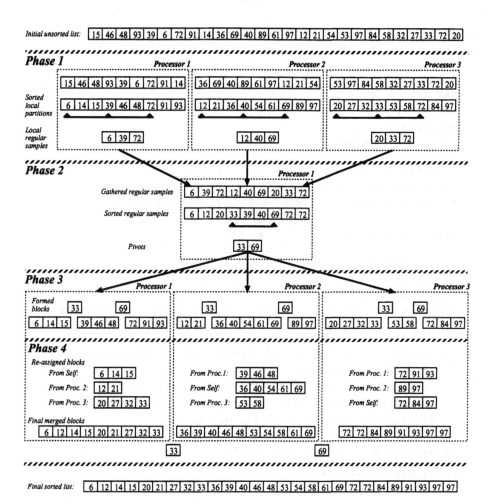

Fig. 1. A PSRS example

In the second phase, the samples from each processor are gathered by the `fold` skeleton. Since the `VarArr` holding the samples grows in each inter-processor folding step, the skeleton must apply the techniques described in Section 3 for handling dynamic data. This complication is however hidden from the user, whose only additional task is to supply the packing and unpacking argument functions. After gathering the samples, the 'root' processor broadcasts them back to all other processors. Thus, the samples are known on all processors after the folding, so that each processor can compute the pivots by itself[8].

---

[8] This is a slight deviation from the algorithm, but it is more efficient to take advantage of the broadcast done anyway by the skeleton, than to first compute the pivots on the root processor, and then use an extra broadcast to spread them to all processors.

```
typedef array <VarArr>  vararray  ;
typedef array <MultArr> multarray ;

void psrs (vararray a) {
   vararray s, q, r ;
   multarray m ;
   VarArr v ;
   int i, j, *pivots ;

   /* Phase 1: */
   array_map (sort_f, a, a) ;
   s = array_create (1, {netSize,0}⁹, {1,0}, {procId,0}, init_f,
                     DISTR_DEFAULT) ;
   array_map (sample_f (s, w), a, a) ;

   /* Phase 2: */
   v = array_fold (append_f, s, pck_f, upck_f) ;
   sort_f (v, {0,0}) ;
   copy each wᵗʰ element from the sample array s into the vector pivots ;

   /* Phases 3 and 4, partly interleaved: */
   create q, r and m with the same dimensions and distribution as s ;
   for (i = 0 ; i < netSize ; i++) {
      array_map (get_ith_block ((i + procId) q), a, a) ;
      array_permute_parts (q, perm_f (i), r, pck_f, upck_f) ;
      array_map (copy_ith_block (i, m), r, r) ;
   }
   array_map (merge_blocks (a), m, m) ;

   array_destroy (s, destroy_f) ;
   destroy q, r and m ;
}
```

Fig. 2. Skeleton-based implementation of the PSRS algorithm

As already mentioned, phases 3 and 4 are partly interleaved. Thus, instead of first splitting the partitions into blocks and then performing an all-to-all communication, we proceed in i steps ($0 \le i \le p - 1$) as follows. Each processor $procId$ determines the $i + procId^{th}$ block of his partition. These blocks are stored into a temporary array q, which then undergoes a permutation operation, such that the $i + procId^{th}$ block goes to the $i + procId^{th}$ processor. This permutation is actually a cyclic shift with i positions, whereas the new position (destination partition) is computed by the user-defined function **perm_f**. Further, since the sizes

---

[9] For simplicity, we have used the pseudo-code notation {a,b} for the (classic) array with elements a and b.

of the blocks may vary, the skeleton uses the packing and unpacking functions, similarly to **fold**. After that, the permuted blocks (now stored in the temporary array **r**) are copied into elements of the **multarray m**. This is done by mapping a copying function to all elements of **r**, with a side-effect to **m**. Finally, after all blocks are on the 'right' processors, they can be merged together. This is done by mapping a merging function to all elements of **m** and putting the result in the array **a**, which then contains the sorted overall array.

5.3 Run-time Results

We have implemented the PSRS algorithm with skeletons on a Parsytec SC 320 distributed memory machine with T800 transputers and 4 MB per node. The run-time results for 1 to 32 processors and 100,000 to 800,000 array elements are summarized below.

p \ n	100.000	200.000	400.000	800.000
1	23.72	50.03	105.36	221.36
4	7.11	14.81	30.89	–
8	4.26	8.69	17.89	36.91
16	3.18	6.02	11.83	23.91
32	4.04	6.76	11.43	20.46

Table 1. Run-time results for the skeleton implementation of the PSRS algorithm

Based on these values, we have studied the speedup behavior of our implementation. We have considered speedups rather than absolute run-times, since our parallel computer was different than the ones used by the authors of the algorithm (see below).

The results are depicted in the first graphic in Fig. 3. One can see that the speedup curves become flat for more than 16 processors. The main reason is that the problem size gets too small for the network size. This is clearly visible in the results presented by the authors of the algorithm, which show good speedups (i.e. an efficiency of more than 50%) for array sizes between 2,000,000 and 8,000,000 elements [14]. Unfortunately, we could not test these cases, since we only had 4 MB memory per node.

We have then compared our results with those presented in [14], for the array sizes we could deal with. In [14] results are given for the Intel iPSC/860, iPSC/2-386, the BBN TC2000, as well as for a LAN of workstations. Since the TC2000 has both distributed and shared memory, thus allowing simple and very efficient implementation of operations like broadcasting and folding, and since the workstation cluster has a different architecture than the one we used, we have chosen the iPSC/860 results as reference for our comparison. The speedups for the direct implementation are given in the second graphic in Fig. 3.

Notice that the curves in the two graphics resemble each other, whereas the speedups of the direct implementation are slightly better (e.g. 14 compared to 11 on 32 processors). This is no surprise, since the iPSC's hypercube topology is 'richer' than the SC's topology of degree 4, thus allowing more efficient implementation of some operations. For instance, a broadcast can be done on the hypercube in $\mathcal{O}(\log p)$ steps, since a hypercube has for each node a spanning tree rooted at that node, whereas for a general topology a broadcast requires $\mathcal{O}(\delta \cdot \log p)$ steps, where δ is the dilation of embedding a tree into that topology.

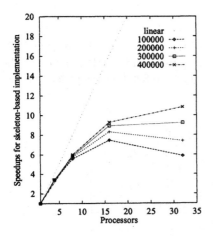 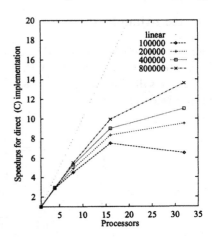

Fig. 3. Speedups for PSRS: skeleton-based implementation (left) and C implementation (right)

6 Related Work

High-level features are the basis of several approaches that aim to simplify the task of parallel programming. Without trying to be exhaustive, we shall compare Skil with some of them.

HPF [12] extends Fortran-90 by constructs for declaring distributed arrays, for mapping them onto processors and for specifying parallel loops. However, no arbitrary distributed data structures, like those defined by the **pardata** construct, nor task-parallel operations are supported.

NESL [3] is a first-order functional, polymorphic, data parallel language, which supports nested parallelism. The latter is only partly supported by Skil, which allows nesting of skeleton calls, but not of **pardata** declarations. On the other hand, due to the fact that they are higher-order, skeletons are more powerful than NESL's parallel constructs. For example, NESL's operations **sum**, **count**, **max_index** and **min_index** can be implemented in Skil as instances of the **fold** skeleton.

Numerous parallel languages are based on C++. One could mention here pC++ [4], which supports data parallelism, CC++ [8], supporting task parallelism, or HPC++ [2], which integrates both paradigms. These languages are related to Skil as far as the type system is concerned, i.e. the Skil polymorphism could be expressed by C++ templates. However, the main difference lies in the functional features, which cannot be expressed in any of these languages. This can very well be seen in the case of P^3L [1], which is a C++-based language with algorithmic skeletons. In order to cope with higher-order functionality, the language was enhanced by special syntactic constructs [1].

However, enhancing C++ with functional features (yielding "Skil++") would be a further, very promising step. Apart from polymorphism, which would come for free, the more important gain would lie in the use of C++'s object-oriented mechanisms, such as encapsulation of data. This would allow to extend the concept of skeleton to that of a *parallel abstract data type* [5], consisting of a distributed data structure, and a set of higher-order, powerful functions operating on this data structure.

Finally, we consider some languages with skeletons. Most of these take a functional approach [10, 13], however some use an imperative host, e.g. P^3L [1], or even a two-layer language – functional for the application and imperative for the skeletons – as in the case of SPP(X) [11]. We have done some comparisons with DPFL, a data parallel functional language with skeletons [13], for a series of matrix applications. The results showed that the Skil implementation was about 6 times faster than the DPFL one, while approaching the performance of message-passing C [7].

7 Conclusions and Future Work

In this paper, we have described a technique that allows the use of algorithmic skeletons on distributed data structures with dynamic or variable-sized components. For that, we have enhanced the communication inside the skeletons with additional messages, packing/unpacking of data elements and, for reasons of efficiency, with a test on dynamic data types.

From the point of view of the user, handling dynamic data structures amounts to the task of specifying two functions for each such structure, which are passed as additional arguments to the skeletons that move data elements between processors. Note that this view is consistent with the philosophy of data parallel skeletons, which aims at reducing the description of a distributed data structure and its functionality to local descriptions of its elements and their functionality.

We have then shown how a parallel algorithm that uses dynamic data can be implemented on the basis of skeletons. The results we have obtained support the idea that the use of skeletons leads to efficient parallel programs, with small losses in performance relative to direct low-level implementations. On the whole, this is a small price to pay for the considerable rise in programming convenience, safety and portability.

Future plans include the handling of 'overall' dynamic data structures, in particular the implementation of adaptive multigrid methods based on the skeletons presented in [5].

References

1. B. Bacci, M. Danelutto, S. Orlando, S. Pelagatti, M. Vanneschi: P^3L : a Structured High-level Parallel Language and its Structured Support, Technical Report HPL-PSC-93-55, Pisa Science Center, Hewlett-Packard Laboratories, 1993.

2. P. Beckman, D. Gannon, E. Johnson: Portable Parallel Programming in HPC++, to appear in Proceedings of ICPP '96, 1996.

3. G. Blelloch: NESL: A Nested Data-Parallel Language (3.1), Technical Report CMU-CS-95-170, Carnegie-Mellon University, 1995.

4. F. Bodin, P. Beckman, D. Gannon, S. Narayana, S. X. Yang: Distributed pC++: Basic Ideas for an Object-Oriented Parallel Language, in Scientific Programming, Vol. 2, Nr. 3, 1993.

5. G. H. Botorog, H. Kuchen: Algorithmic Skeletons for Adaptive Multigrid Methods, in Proceedings of IRREGULAR '95, LNCS 980, Springer, 1995.

6. G. H. Botorog, H. Kuchen: Skil: An Imperative Language with Algorithmic Skeletons for Efficient Distributed Programming, to appear in Proceedings of the Fifth International Symposium on High Performance Distributed Computing (HPDC-5), IEEE Computer Society Press, 1996.

7. G. H. Botorog, H. Kuchen: Parallel Programming in an Imperative Language with Algorithmic Skeletons, to appear in Proceedings of EURO-PAR '96, LNCS, Springer, 1996.

8. M. Chandi, C. Kesselman: CC++: A Declarative Concurrent Object Oriented Programming Notation, in Research Directions in Concurrent Object-Oriented Programming, MIT Press, 1993.

9. M. I. Cole: Algorithmic Skeletons: Structured Management of Parallel Computation, MIT Press, 1989.

10. J. Darlington, A. J. Field, P. G. Harrison et al: Parallel Programming Using Skeleton Functions, in Proceedings of PARLE '93, LNCS 694, Springer, 1993.

11. J. Darlington, Y. Guo, H. W. To, J. Yang: Functional Skeletons for Parallel Coordination, in Proceedings of EURO-PAR '95, LNCS 966, Springer, 1995.

12. High Performance Fortran Language Specification, in Scientific Programming, Vol. 2, No. 1, 1993.

13. H. Kuchen, R. Plasmeijer, H. Stoltze: Efficient Distributed Memory Implementation of a Data Parallel Functional Language, in Proceedings of PARLE '94, LNCS 817, Springer, 1994.

14. X. Li, P. Lu, J. Schaeffer et al.: On the Versatility of Parallel Sorting by Regular Sampling, Parallel Computing, Vol. 19, North-Holland, 1993.

15. M. J. Quinn: Parallel Computing: Theory and Practice, McGraw-Hill, 1994.

16. M. Röttger, U. P. Schroeder, J. Simon: Virtual Topology Library for Parix, Technical Report 148, University of Paderborn, 1994.

17. D. Skillicorn: Foundations of Parallel Programming, Cambridge University Press, 1994.

An Interface Design for General Parallel Branch-and-Bound Algorithms

Yuji Shinano*, Masahiro Higaki and Ryuichi Hirabayashi

Science University of Tokyo 1-3, Kagurazaka, Shinjuku-ku, Tokyo 162, Japan
E-mail:shinano@ms.kagu.sut.ac.jp

Abstract. Branch-and-Bound algorithms are general methods applicable to various combinatorial optimization problems. There are two hopeful methods to improve the algorithms. One is development of the algorithms which exploit the structure of each problem. The other is parallelization of the algorithms. These two methods have been studied by different research communities independently. If a well-designed interface separating the two kinds of implementation of the methods clearly could be constructed, it would enable us to adapt latest algorithms or technology easily. In this paper, we propose a small and simple interface design of a generalized system for parallel branch-and-bound algorithms.
Key words: parallel processing, combinatorial optimization problem, branch-and-bound algorithms.

1   Introduction

Branch-and-bound algorithms are general methods applicable to various combinatorial optimization problems. These algorithms are search-based techniques that enumerate the entire solution space implicitly. In order to perform this enumeration efficiently, it is necessary to limit the number of feasible solutions that need to be explicitly produced. This process can be accomplished by clever algorithms, which exploit the structure of each problem, and many complicated algorithms have been proposed for each problem. We call implementations of such algorithms *problem depending implementation*. Unfortunately, even if such procedures are applied, some instances of the problems cannot be solved in a reasonable amount of time.

Parallelization is one of the most hopeful methods to accelerate the enumeration speed. We consider high-level parallelism of such algorithms. In such kinds of applications of parallelism, generality of the branch-and-bound algorithm framework should be maintained. Therefore, it is reasonable to develop a *generalized system* that provides the general framework of the parallel branch-and-bound algorithms and some facilities to make use of it. There are several architectures of parallel computers and several ways to map the framework on a architecture of them. Therefore, many implementations of high-level parallelism should be considered. We call an implementation of the parallelism *parallelization architecture depending implementation*.

---

* Supported by JSPS Research Fellowships for Young Scientists.

We consider all parallelization architecture depending implementations to be embedded into the generalized system. Then an *interface* of the generalized system is not only a boundary of the general framework of the parallel branch-and-bound algorithms and their applications, but also a boundary of the two kinds of implementations. These two kinds have been studied by different research communities. Therefore, if the two kinds of implementations are separated completely in the generalized system, it would enable latest algorithms or technology to be applied easily. Hence, the interface design is very important.

There are two approaches to make such a generalized system. One is to develop a generalized system from general formulations [1, 6]. The other is to generalize techniques derived from specific problem implementations [10]. The first approach usually provides a good sophisticated interface design but has problems in implementation. That is, the implementation does not always achieve sufficient efficiency. The second approach is quite successful (in terms of efficiency) for some problems but it is usually not so sophisticated as the first.

On the development of the generalized system, data types used in the problem depending implementation are unspecified. In order to maintain the generality of the system and to provide an interface that separates the two kinds completely, abstract data type is necessary. In this paper, we provide a model of a generalized system based on an object-oriented paradigm and an interface design using the object-oriented programming language C++ which is widespread and accessible to many researchers.

2 General branch-and-bound algorithms

We assume, without loss of generality, that the combinatorial optimization problem we wish to solve is posed as the minimization problem:

$$\mathbf{P_0}: \left| \begin{array}{l} \text{minimize } f(\boldsymbol{x}) \\ \text{subject to } \boldsymbol{x} \in X_0 \end{array} \right.$$

where X_0 is a discrete set. A general branch and bound algorithm for solving $\mathbf{P_0}$ is presented as follows. In the algorithm, $\tilde{z}$ maintains the latest found upper bound of z_0 and is called an *incumbent value* of $\mathbf{P_0}$, while $\tilde{\boldsymbol{x}}$ (a solution corresponding to $\tilde{z}$) is an *incumbent solution* of $\mathbf{P_0}$.

```
1  procedure General branch and bound algorithm(GBBA) ;
2  begin
3      z̃ := +∞; L := {P₀}; {initialization}
4      while L ≠ ∅ do
5      begin
6          Select a subproblem Pᵢ from L;
7          L := L \ {Pᵢ};
8          Solve Pᵢ's relaxation problem RPᵢ;
9          if an optimal solution of RPᵢ exists then
10             {Let zᵢᴿ be the optimal value of RPᵢ
                and xᵢᴿ be an optimal solution of RPᵢ}
11             if zᵢᴿ < z̃ then
12                 if xᵢᴿ ∈ Xᵢ then
13                     begin
14                         z̃ := zᵢᴿ; x̃ := xᵢᴿ;
```

```
15                   L := L \ {P_j : P_j with z_j^R ≥ z̃}
16              end
17          else
18              begin
19                  Let {X_ij}_{j=1}^k be a division of X_i;
20                  L := L ∪ {P_ij}_{j=1}^k where z_ij^R := z_i^R   for j = 1,...,k
21              end
22      end
23      if z̃ = +∞ then
24          P_0 has no feasible solution
25      else
26          x̃ is an optimal solution of P_0, and z̃ is the optimal value of P_0
27  end
```

When this is implemented on a single processor, this becomes the sequential branch-and-bound algorithm.

3 A model of generalized system based on an object-oriented paradigm

We propose a model of a generalized system for parallel branch-and-bound algorithms based on an object-oriented paradigm. We consider the preparation of base classes for general branch-and-bound algorithms and the preparation of a skeleton for using the base classes as a generalized system. The parts of classes that depend on solving algorithm of each specific problem, are written as derived classes. This relation is showed in Figure 1.

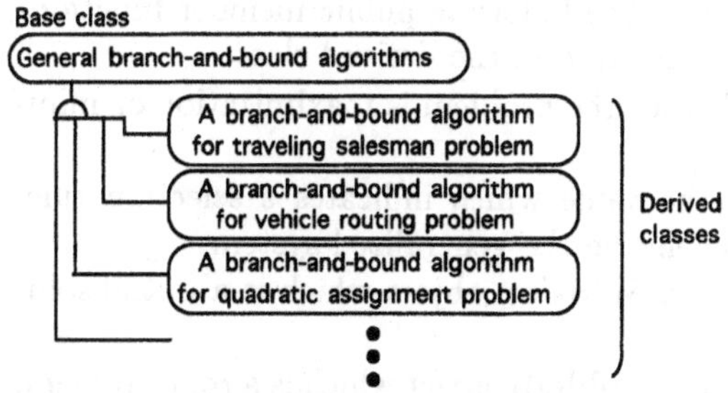

Fig. 1. The relation between a base class and derived classes

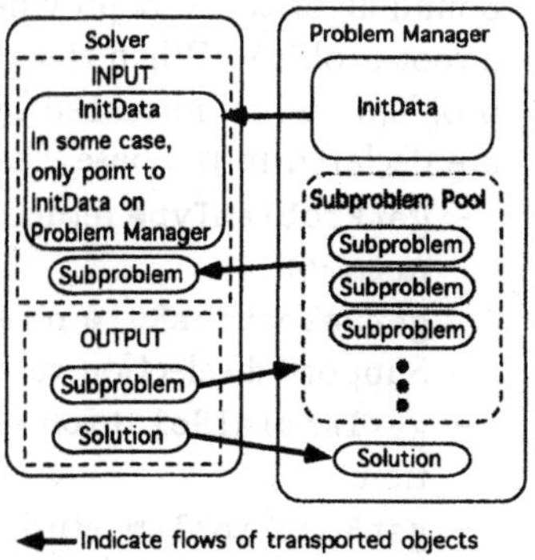

Fig. 2. The relation of objects for general branch-and-bound algorithms

The model is composed of the following five objects. All objects are created from derived classes for solving algorithm of each specific problem. Figure 2 shows the relation of these objects.

Problem Manager This object is an abstraction of the manager for solving problems with branch-and-bound algorithms and has all knowledge produced by the algorithms. Therefore, this object determines the rule by which the subproblem next to be solved should be selected. The rule is called *selection rule*. In this object, *elimination rule* that recognizes and eliminates subproblems that cannot yield an optimal solution to the original problem, is also applied, when an improvement of a solution value is notified. The following public member functions are realized by the base class.

- **getIncumbentValue** returns the incumbent value. In the parallelization, the incumbent value should remain globally best in the **Problem Manager**.
- **getSubproblem** returns a **Subproblem** to evaluate.
- **putSubproblem** puts a created **Subproblem** into the **Problem Manager**.
- **putSolution** puts a created **Solution** into the **Problem Manager**.
- **removeSubproblemBySolved** removes an evaluated **Subproblem** from the **Problem Manager**.
- **printSolution** outputs a solution by calling **print** member function of **InitData**.

Solver This object is an abstraction of the solving algorithms for a subproblem. The algorithms include *bounding rule* that computes a bound value on the optimal solution of a subproblem, *branching rule* that determines how to divide a subproblem into subproblems, and elimination rule. We call the procedure performed by the algorithms an *evaluation of a subproblem*. The following public member function is declared in the base class and realized in the derived class.

- **solve** performs sequential branch-and-bound algorithm.

InitData This object is an abstraction of all initialization data for branch-and-bound algorithms. It provides problem instance data, an initial solution and a root problem. When this object is constructed, it reads data for the target problem and is initialized by them. The following public member functions are declared in the base class and realized in the derived class.

- **getProblemType** returns whether the problem is maximization or minimization.
- **getSelectionRule** returns the value which indicates a selection rule. Supported selection rules depend on the generalized system.
- **getInitialSolution** returns a **Solution** object which is a initial solution.
- **getRootProblem** returns a **Subproblem** object which is a root problem.

Solution This object is an abstraction of the solution. With the help of the **InitData** object, this object represents the solution. When this object is constructed, an objective value is passed as an argument of a base class constructor and is set in this object. The following public member function is realized in the base class.

- **getObjectiveValue** returns the objective value of this object.

The following public member function is declared in the base class and realized in the derived class.

- **print** displays a solution by editing the contents of this object.

Subproblem This object is an abstraction of the subproblem. With the help of the **InitData** object, this object represents the subproblem. When this object is constructed, a bound value is passed as an argument of a base class constructor and is set in this object. The following public member functions are realized by the base class.

- **getBound** returns the bound value of this object.
- **setSelectionCriterion** sets a *selection criterion value* on this object. The value can be used by the **Problem Manager** when a **Subproblem** next to be solved is selected.
- **getSelectionCriterion** returns the selection criterion value.
- **shallIUseInternalVariables** returns whether this object is a direct son of the **Subproblem** evaluated in previous calculation of the same **Solver** or not.

We define *transported objects* as the generic name for **InitData, Solution, Subproblem**. In parallelized implementation, since several **Solver** objects should exist on a system, transported objects may be transferred between processors.

4 Skeleton for general branch-and-bound algorithms in the model

Now, we provide a skeleton. Any branch-and-bound algorithm which has the GBBA framework described in Section 2 can be implemented in the skeleton. In order to describe the skeleton, we show the interface related program codes of derived classes for TSP as an example. For presentation of the skeleton, we prepare the **main** function and the derived class of the **Problem Manager** for sequential branch-and-bond algorithms temporarily in Figure 3. The derived class for **Solver** is presented in Figure 4.

```
1    class TspProblemManager : public ProblemManagerBase {
2    public:
3        TspProblemManager(char *pcInputFileName, ... )
4            { pInitData = new TspInitData(pcInputFileName);
5              pBestSolution = pInitData->getInitialSolution();
6              pRootProblem = pInitData->getRootProblem();  }
7    };
8    int main(
9        int argc, char* argv
10   ) {
11       TspProblemManager* pPm = new TspProblemManager( ... );
12       TspSolver* pSolver = new TspSolver();
13       pSolver->solve( pPm );
14       pPm->printSolution();
15       delete pSolver;
16       delete pPm;
17       return 0;
18   }
```

Fig. 3. The main function and the definition of TspProblemManager

The initialization procedure in GBBA(line 3) corresponds to the construction of the **Problem Manager**(line 11 and line 3-6) and the result output procedure in GBBA(line 23-26) corresponds to the **printSolution** call of the **Problem Manager**(line 14). Other parts of GBBA correspond to the codes of the **solve** function of the **Solver**. The skeleton in the **solve** member function has much flexibility, because it has small interfaces and less restriction on the usage of the member functions of the **Problem Manager**. The only restrictions are that `getSubproblem` needs to be called at the beginning of an evaluation (line 13) and `removeSubproblemBySolved` (line 21) to be called at the end of an evaluation. The number of calls of `putSubproblem` is the number of branches from the **Subproblem** obtained from the **Problem Manager** at the beginning of an evaluation. Some low-level parallelism can be implemented here (line 20).

```
1    class TspSolver : public SolverBase {
2    public:
3        void solve(ProblemManagerBase*);
4    private:
5    };
6    void TspSolver::solve(
7        ProblemManagerBase* pPmBase
8    ){
9        TspProblemManager* pPm
10           = (TspProblemManager*)pPmBase;
11       TspInitData* pIDat
12           = (TspInitData*)pPm->getInitData();
13       while( TspSubproblem* pSpb = (TspSubproblem*)pPm->getSubproblem() ){
14           if ( pSpb->shallIUseInternalVariables()
15                  == SubproblemBase::YOU_SHOULD_NOT_USE_IT ){
16               // Initialize internal variables
17           } else {
18               // Use internal variables of the previous calculation
19           }
20           // Routines for an evaluation
                 :
21           pPm->removeSubproblemBySolved( pSpb );
22       }
23   }
```

Fig. 4. The definition of TspSolver

5   On the development of a generalized system

Implementations of the **Problem Manager** are the greater part of a generalized system development. The **Problem Manager** can handle transported objects as abstract data types and also its internal architecture (single-pool or multiple-pools, synchronous or asynchronous) is hidden from the **Solver**. Hence program codes for problem depending implementations can exchange from one parallelization architecture depending implementation to another without any modification. In this context, a sequential architecture is considered as a special case of parallelization architecture. Therefore, program codes for the problem depending implementation presented in the skeleton of the previous section can translate to parallel platforms without being changed them.

In some parallelization architecture, it may be necessary that **Problem Manager** maps on several processors and all of its functions are realized by several modules. In such a case, the designer of a generalized system needs to make a kind of other classes which are derived from the base class of the **Problem Manager** with respect to the mapping. Even if such a mapping changes internal architecture of the **Problem Manager**, all services provided in the base class can be inherited. The **main** functions should be provided by the generalized systems, because the number of main functions and the codes written in it need to be changed depending on the architecture. For example, when the **Problem Manager** is composed of several modules, the module on which procedures of data input and results output are performed depends on the architecture. The derived class of the **Problem Manager** is closely related to the parallelization architecture used and it should be written mechanically. Therefore, the main functions and the derived class of the **Problem Manager** should be generated by the system.

A synchronization paradigm is realized as an implementation of the member function getSubproblem in the **Problem Manager**. In a synchronized implementation, the function waits to return a **Subproblem** until an evaluation calculated in all **Solvers** has finished. In a asynchronous implementation, the function returns a **Subproblem** immediately as long as the subproblem pools are not empty.

6 Discussion

We checked if our proposed interface did not lose generality of branch-and-algorithms by comparing with several general formulations [1, 4, 5, 8]. As a result, we found out that our implementation does not support pruning by *dominance test*[3]. However, it can be supported only by adding a declaration of the public member function dominated(IntDataBase*, SubproblemBase*) on the base class of the **Subproblem** and realized in the derived class. This member function returns true when the **Subproblem** is dominated by the **Subproblem** that is given by the argument. If this member function is implemented in the base class, it would be possible for the **Problem Manager** to perform the dominance test.

In our model, the representations of a subproblem (and solution) force the programmer to divide the **Subproblem** and the **InitData** (the **Solution** and the **InitData**) explicitly. The **InitData** should have all fixed parts of transported objects, because it is usually transmitted only once throughout the calculation. While the **Subproblem** (and the **Solution**) has variable parts, it may be transmitted many times. In order to reduce the amount of transmission data, the size of the data members in the **Subproblem** (and the **Solution**) should be as small as possible. The transmission costs heavily depend on the data structure to represent them. It is good for the programmer to be conscious of this division without being concerned about the way of parallelization, because the method of making the **Subproblem** (and the **Solution**) small is the parts problem depending implementation.

7 Concluding remarks

In this paper, we proposed an interface design of a generalized system based on an object-oriented paradigm for parallel branch-and-bound algorithms. It separates the problem depending implementation and parallelization architecture depending implementation clearly with small interfaces, so that it is flexible on both sides. We provided a skeleton in problem depending implementation and showed a guideline of how to make a generalized system using our model. Furthermore, a generalized system using our model has been already realized on renewed PUBB(Parallelization Utility for Branch-and-Bound algorithms)[9], though the precise specification of member functions were not presented in this paper, due to space restrictions.

Many implementations for parallel branch-and-bound algorithms have appeared [2]. However, the situation is confused when we try to compare them with each other, because the two kinds of implementations are usually mixed. Therefore, we need a standard interface. If a standard interface could be provided, it would enable us not only to use the latest algorithms and technology easily but also to compare the implementations accurately. It would give more clear insight into the effectiveness of parallelization of the algorithms.

Acknowledgments

We would like to thank Yoshiko Ikebe for reading the draft so many times and the anonymous referees for the helpful suggestions.

References

1. R.Corrêa. A Parallel Formulation for General Branch-and-Bound Algorithms. *Parallel Algorithms for Irregularly Structured Problems*, A.Ferreira and J.Rolim(eds.), LNCS **980**, 395-409, Springer, 1995.
2. B.Gendron and T.G.Crainic. Parallel Branch-and-Bound Algorithms: Survey and Synthesis. *Operations Research*, 42(6):1042-1066, 1994.
3. T.Ibaraki. The Power of Dominance Relations in Branch-and-Bound Algorithms. *Journal of the ACM*, 24(2):264-279, 1977.
4. T.Ibaraki. Branch-and-Bound Procedure and State-Space Representation of Combinatorial Optimization Problems. *Information and Control*, 36:1-27, 1978.
5. V.Kumar and L.N.Kanal. A General Branch and Bound Formulation for Understanding and Synthesizing And/Or Tree Search Procedures. *Artificial Intelligence*, 21:179-198, 1983.
6. G.P.McKeown, V.J.Rayward-Smith and H.J.Turpin. Branch-and-Bound as a Higher-Order Function. *Annals of Operations Research*, 33:379-402, 1991.
7. G.P.McKeown, V.J.Rayward-Smith and S.A.Rush. Parallel Branch-and-Bound. *Advances in Parallel Algorithms*, L.Kronsjö and D.Shumsheruddin(eds.), Advanced topics in computer science, 111-150, Blackwell, 1992.
8. D.S.Nau, V.Kumar and L.Kanal. General Branch and Bound, and Its Relation to A* and AO*. *Artificial Intelligence*, 23:29-58, 1984.
9. Y.Shinano, M.Higaki and R.Hirabayashi. A Genearlized Utility for Parallel Branch and Bound Algorithms. *Proc. of the 7th IEEE Symposium on Parallel and Distributed Processing*, 392-401, IEEE Computer Society Press, 1995.
10. S.Tchöke, R.Lüling and B.Monien. Solving the Traveling Salesman Problem with a Distributed Branch-and-Bound Algorithm on a 1024 Processor Network. *Proc. of the 9th International Parallel Processing Symposium*, Santa Barbara, CA , April 1995. To appear.

Support for Irregular Computation in High Performance Fortran

Rob Schreiber

Hewlett Packard
schreibr@hp.com

Abstract. High Performance Fortran is an extension of the Fortran 95 language designed for data-parallel computing. It was designed to address the need for a vendor-independent, high-level programming language for parallel machines with distributed memory. The array language of Fortran 95 naturally allows parallel programs where the principal parallel idiom is evaluation of a scalar function for every element of a Fortran array.

Algorithms based on irregular meshes, graphs, sets, ensembles of particles (in N-body models of molecules, galaxies, etc.) and other irregular structures, while they may be data-parallel, do not naturally fit the array parallel style. HPF version 2.0, due to be released in December 1996, addresses some of these issues. It does so without enlarging the underlying Fortran language. I will discuss the proposed language extensions, and some alternatives that were not included, for irregular data mapping, user-specified computation mapping, reductions in parallel loops, and multiple process (or task) parallelism.

Efficient Dynamic Embedding
of Arbitrary Binary Trees into Hypercubes

Volker Heun   Ernst W. Mayr

Institut für Informatik der Technischen Universität München
D-80290 München, Germany
{heun|mayr}@informatik.tu-muenchen.de
http://wwwmayr.informatik.tu-muenchen.de/

Abstract. In this paper, a deterministic algorithm for dynamically embedding binary trees into next to optimal hypercubes is presented. Due to a known lower bound, any such algorithm must use either randomization or migration, i.e., remapping of tree vertices, to obtain an embedding of trees into hypercubes with small dilation, load, and expansion simultaneously. The algorithm presented here uses migration of previously mapped tree vertices and achieves dilation 9, unit load, expansion <4 and constant node-congestion. Moreover, the embedding can be computed on the hypercube. The amortized time for each new vertex is constant, if in each step one new leaf is spawned. If in each step a group of M new leaves is added, the amortized cost for each new group of leaves is bounded by $O(\log^2(M))$.

1   Introduction

Hypercubes are a very popular model for parallel computation because of their regularity and their relatively small number of interprocessor connections. Another important property of an interconnection network is its ability to simulate efficiently the communication of parallel algorithms. Thus, it is desirable to find suitable embeddings of graphs representing the communication structure of parallel algorithms into hypercubes representing the interconnection network of a parallel computer.

Embeddings of graphs with a regular structure, like rings, (multidimensional) grids, complete trees, binomial trees, pyramids, X-trees, meshes of trees and so on, have been investigated by numerous researchers, see, e.g., [4, 5, 6, 7, 8, 20, 19, 21, 22]. Unfortunately, the communication structure of a parallel algorithm can often be very irregular. Embeddings of such irregular graphs, like binary tree, caterpillars, graphs with bounded treewidth, have also been studied in, e.g., [1, 3, 10, 11, 12, 13, 14, 16, 18]. For arbitrary binary trees, one-to-one embeddings into their optimal hypercubes with constant dilation and constant node-congestion have been constructed in [3, 13, 18]. The embedding given in [13] yields dilation 8 and constant node-congestion. This is the best known bound on the dilation. Furthermore, this embedding can be efficiently computed on the hypercube itself. In [10], Havel has conjectured that every binary tree has a one-to-one embedding into its optimal hypercube with dilation at most 2. This conjecture is still open. In terms of lower bounds, a simple parity argument shows that the complete binary tree of size $2^d - 1$ cannot be a subgraph of the d-dimensional hypercube, see [4, 19, 22].

All these embeddings are constructed as *static* embeddings, which means that the whole information about the structure of the guest graph is known in advance. Since the guest graph represents the communication structure of a parallel algorithm, the guest graph may vary during the execution of the algorithm. Thus, it is important to investigate *dynamic* embeddings of graphs. Static embeddings are usually much easier to construct than dynamic embeddings. Moreover, it might be impossible to construct dynamic embeddings deterministically with high quality. For arbitrary binary trees, it has been proved that dynamic embeddings cannot be constructed with high quality if neither randomization nor migration, i.e., remapping of tree vertices, is allowed [17].

For embedding complete binary trees into optimal hypercubes, optimal deterministic algorithms have been presented in [9, 15]. These embeddings achieve dilation 2, unit load, and unit congestion, whereas the running time is constant for each new level of leaves. A first challenge of dynamically embedding arbitrary binary trees into hypercubes was the work in [2]. It presents a randomized algorithm for embedding binary trees into hypercubes with dilation $O(\log\log(n))$ and, with high probability, constant load. This was improved in [17], where a randomized algorithm for embedding binary trees into hypercubes with dilation 8 and, with high probability, constant load was explored. The edge-congestion of the embedding is constant, whereas node-congestion was not considered. These algorithms do not permit migration of mapped tree vertices.

In this paper, we will consider a deterministic algorithm using migration for embedding binary trees into hypercubes. It will be shown that a binary tree can be dynamically embedded into its next to optimal hypercube with dilation at most 9, unit load and constant node-congestion. The quality of our dynamic embedding improves the previous results. Moreover, the embedding can be computed on the hypercube itself. The amortized time for each new vertex is constant if in each step at most one new leaf is spawned. If in each step a group of M new leaves gets spawned, the amortized cost for each new group of leaves is bounded by $O(\log^2(M))$.

The remainder of this paper is organized as follows. First, we recall some basic definitions and notations which we will use later. In the third section, we review a lower bound on dynamic embeddings of binary trees into hypercubes. We recall the basic results on statically embedding binary trees into hypercubes in the fourth section and introduce our main tool for dynamic embeddings, the (h, o, τ)-tree. In the fifth section, we present the deterministic algorithm for dynamic embedding and analyze its complexity. Finally, we give some concluding remarks.

2 Preliminaries

An *embedding* of a graph $G=(V_G, E_G)$, called *guest graph*, into a graph $H=(V_H, E_H)$, called *host graph*, is a mapping $\varphi:G \to H$ consisting of two mappings $\varphi_V:V_G \to V_H$ and $\varphi_E:E_G \to \mathcal{P}(H)$. Here, $\mathcal{P}(G)$ denotes the set of paths in the graph $G=(V, E)$. The mapping φ_E maps each edge $\{v, w\} \in E_G$ to a path $p \in \mathcal{P}(H)$ connecting $\varphi_V(v)$ and $\varphi_V(w)$. We call an embedding *one-to-one* if the mapping φ_V is 1-1.

The *dilation* of an edge $e \in E_G$ under an embedding φ is the length of the path $\varphi_E(e)$. Here, the length of a path p is the number of its edges. The *dilation of an embedding* φ is the maximal dilation of an edge in G. The number of vertices of a guest graph which are mapped onto a vertex v in the host graph, is called the *load* of the vertex v. The *load of an embedding* φ is the maximal load of a vertex in the host graph. The ratio $|V_H|/|V_G|$ is called the *expansion* of the embedding φ. The *congestion* of an edge

$e' \in E_H$ is the number of paths in $\{\varphi_E(e) \mid e \in E_G\}$ that contain e'. The *edge-congestion* is the maximal congestion over all edges in H. The *congestion* of a vertex $v \in V_H$ is the number of paths in $\{\varphi_E(e) \mid e \in E_G\}$ containing v. Again, the *node-congestion* is the maximal congestion over all vertices in H. In the following, we initially restrict our attention to finding a suitable mapping φ_V, and we will use shortest paths in the hypercube for the mapping φ_E. Nevertheless, it is still important to decide which paths we choose, since we are interested in obtaining an embedding with small node-congestion.

A *hypercube of dimension d* is a graph with 2^d vertices, labeled 1-1 with the strings in $\{0,1\}^d$. Two vertices are connected iff their labels differ in exactly one position. The smallest hypercube into which we can embed a given graph $G=(V,E)$ with load one is called its *optimal* hypercube. Thus, the dimension of the optimal hypercube is $\lceil \log(|V|) \rceil$. The next larger hypercube of dimension $\lceil \log(|V|) \rceil + 1$ is called its *next to optimal hypercube*. Hence, an embedding of a graph G into its optimal hypercube (resp,. next to optimal hypercube) has expansion less than two (resp., four).

The *level* of a vertex v in a tree is the number of vertices on the path from the root to v. Hence, the level of the root is 1. The *height* of a tree T is the maximum level of a vertex in T. Given a vertex v in a tree, a vertex w is called a *descendant* of v if it lies on a path from v to a leaf of the tree. A subtree rooted at a vertex v is the induced subgraph of all descendants of v in the tree. We call a vertex of a tree an *internal* vertex if it is not a leaf of the tree.

3 Lower Bounds

In this section, we briefly review that any deterministic algorithm for dynamically embedding binary trees cannot achieve constant load, dilation and expansion without migration. This was first proved in [17] for embeddings with load greater than one:

Theorem 1. *Any deterministic algorithm for dynamically embedding binary trees of size M into a hypercube of size $N \leq M$ that achieves load cM/N and does not use migration must have average dilation $\Omega((\log(N))^{\frac{1}{2}}/c^2)$.*

In fact, the proof was given for caterpillars with maximal degree 3. Using the same technique as in [17], the following theorem concerning one-to-one embeddings into hypercubes can be proved.

Theorem 2. *Any deterministic algorithm for dynamically embedding binary trees of size M into a hypercube of size $N \geq M$ that achieves unit load and does not use migration must have average dilation $\Omega(\alpha^2(\log(N))^{\frac{1}{2}})$, where $\alpha = \frac{M}{N}$.*

4 Review of Static Embeddings

In this section, we review the main results stated in [13] which we will need for our construction of a dynamic embedding. The details of the embedding are slightly different from [13], in order to obtain a presentation more suitable for our purposes.

4.1 Definition of an (h, o, τ)-Tree

To construct our embedding, we use the data structure of an (h, o, τ)-tree. The (h, o, τ)-tree is a complete quadtree of height h with integer node weights, also called the *capacities* of the nodes. The capacities depend on the level of a vertex, and on the parameters o

and τ, with $o \in \mathbb{N}$ and $\tau \in \{0, 1\}$. We also distinguish between a *full* and a *partial* (h, o, τ)-tree, which differ only in the capacities of the root. A node at level ℓ of a full (resp., partial) (h, o, τ)-tree has a capacity of $2^o(6(h-\ell+1)-5+3\tau)+\delta_{1,\ell}2^o(2h+1+\tau)$. (resp, $2^o(6(h-\ell+1)-5+3\tau)$). Here, $\delta_{i,j}$ denotes the Kronecker symbol. In the following, we call vertices of an (h, o, τ)-tree *nodes*, and we denote the capacity of a node at level ℓ by $c(\ell)$. Unless stated otherwise, we mean by an (h, o, τ)-tree a full (h, o, τ)-tree. Note that given a node v at level ℓ of the (h, o, τ)-tree, the subtree rooted at v is itself a partial $(h-\ell+1, o, \tau)$-tree.

Lemma 3. *The overall capacity of a full (h, o, τ)-tree is $2^{2h+o+\tau}$ and of a partial (h, o, τ)-tree is $2^{2h+o+\tau} - 2^o(2h+1+\tau)$.*

4.2 Embeddings Using the (h, o, τ)-Tree

We now describe a mapping of an (h, o, τ)-tree into its optimal hypercube such that each node of the (h, o, τ)-tree occupies as many vertices of the hypercube as given by its capacity. Each node in an (h, o, τ)-tree can be represented by a string in $(\{0, 1\}^2)^*$ as follows. The empty string ε represents the root of the (h, o, τ)-tree. If α represents a node v of the (h, o, τ)-tree, then the strings $\alpha 00$, $\alpha 01$, $\alpha 10$, and $\alpha 11$ represent the four children of v from left to right. We define the following sets of hypercube locations, where α represents some arbitrary node in an (h, o, τ)-tree:

$$S_\alpha := \{\alpha\beta\gamma\delta \in \{0,1\}^{2h+o+\tau} : \beta \in (0+1)^*1 \wedge |\beta| \leq 2 \wedge \gamma \in 0^*10^* \wedge \delta \in \{0,1\}^o\}$$
$$R := \{\gamma\delta \in \{0,1\}^{2h+o+\tau} : \gamma \in (0^*10^*+0^*) \wedge \delta \in \{0,1\}^o\}$$

We also define the set $S := \bigcup_\alpha S_\alpha$. The vertices of the given graph mapped to the node of a full (h, o, τ)-tree represented by α, will finally be mapped to hypercube locations in the set $L_\alpha := S_\alpha$ if $\alpha \neq \varepsilon$, and $L_\varepsilon := S_\varepsilon \cup R$ otherwise. In case of a partial (h, o, τ)-tree, we define $L_\varepsilon := S_\varepsilon$. It can easily be verified that the capacity of a node in the (h, o, τ)-tree is equal to the cardinality of the set of vertices in the hypercube to which it is mapped.

Lemma 4. *Let v be a node at level ℓ of a (h, o, τ)-tree represented by α, then we have $|S_\alpha| = 2^o(6(h-\ell+1)-5+3\tau)$. Furthermore, $|R| = 2^o(2h+1+\tau)$ and $|L_\alpha| = c(\ell)$.*

Furthermore, it can easily be verified that for every $\alpha \neq \alpha' \in (\{0,1\}^2)^*$, $S_\alpha \cap S_{\alpha'} = \emptyset$ and $S_\alpha \cap R = \emptyset$, and hence $L_\alpha \cap L_{\alpha'} = \emptyset$ for every $\alpha \neq \alpha' \in (\{0,1\}^2)^*$. Hence, for each string $s \in S \cup R$ there is a unique decomposition $s = \alpha\beta\gamma\delta$ as used in the definition of S_α and R. Given a hypercube location u, we call the node α of the (h, o, τ)-tree such that $u \in L_\alpha$ its *corresponding* node. The following theorem was proved in [13].

Lemma 5. *Let v and w be two nodes in an (h, o, τ)-tree such that their lowest common ancestor is at distance $\leq \Delta$ from both v and w. The labels of any pair of corresponding vertices in the hypercube to which v and w are mapped differ in at most $2\Delta + o + 4$ positions.*

4.3 Outline of the Static Embedding

Our embedding of binary trees into hypercubes is achieved in two steps. First, we embed the binary tree into an (h, o, τ)-tree. Then, we use the mapping presented in the previous subsection to complete the embedding. To obtain a small dilation, adjacent vertices of the binary tree are mapped to locations which are close in the (h, o, τ)-tree. Our goal is to obtain an embedding of the binary tree into an (h, o, τ)-tree such that adjacent tree vertices are mapped to two nodes of the (h, o, τ)-tree with distance ≤ 1 from their lowest common ancestor of the (h, o, τ)-tree. It can be shown that this goal can be reached, except for tree vertices that get mapped to (h, o, τ)-tree nodes close to the leaves, where distance ≤ 2 can be obtained. Our method leads to an embedding of the binary tree into the hypercube with dilation $8+o$. The number o can be chosen as 3. Using local modifications of the mapping, we can then reduce the dilation to 9. The dilation given here is greater than in [13], where we achieve dilation 8, but it yields a simpler description for our dynamic embedding. To embed the binary tree into the (h, o, τ)-tree such that the load of each node is bounded by its capacity, we will need the following lemma (for a proof see [13]).

Lemma 6. *Let $F=(V, E)$ be a forest of binary trees containing marked vertices, and let V' be the set of marked vertices. Removing at most $6\lfloor \log(|V|) \rfloor - 2$ edges, F can be decomposed into four forests F_1, F_2, F_3, and F_4 such that the size of each forest is $\lfloor |V|/4 \rfloor$ or $\lceil |V|/4 \rceil$. Furthermore, the number of partition vertices and marked vertices in each F_k is at most $\lceil |V'|/4 \rceil + 3\lfloor \log(|V|) \rfloor$ and the number of marked vertices in each F_k is at most $\lceil |V'|/4 \rceil + \lfloor \log(|V|) \rfloor$.*

The algorithm for the embedding proceeds in $h = \Theta(\log(n))$ stages. Each stage is associated with a level of the (h, o, τ)-tree. At the first stage, we fill up the root of the (h, o, τ)-tree with vertices and mark all unmapped neighbors of the mapped vertices. Then, we decompose the tree into four parts using Lemma 6 and associate the four parts with the four children of the root. In the subsequent stages, we map the partition vertices and the marked vertices to the corresponding child node in the (h, o, τ)-tree. Then, we fill up each child node with arbitrary vertices from the binary tree in such a way that each mapped vertex has at most two unmapped neighbors. Again, we mark all unmapped neighbors of mapped vertices and decompose the forest into four 'balanced' forests as above. This procedure will be iterated in parallel until the leaves of the (h, o, τ)-tree are reached.

4.4 Complexity of the Static Embedding
In [13], the following theorem has been proved.

Theorem 7. *Let $F=(V, E)$ be a forest of binary trees of size n. There exists a one-to-one embedding of F into its optimal hypercube with dilation at most 9 and constant node-congestion. This embedding can be computed in time $O(\log^2(n) \log\log\log(n) \log^*(n))$ on the optimal hypercube provided that the forest is stored one vertex per processor.*

Provided that the forest of binary trees is stored in the hypercube in a more suitable way, the running time of this algorithm can be improved. A tree vertex is called a *left* (resp., *right*) *vertex*, if it is the left (resp., right) child of its parent. For simplicity, the root is a left vertex. We assume that for any left (resp., right) vertex the size of its left (resp., right) subtree is at least as big as the size of its right (resp., left) subtree. If the forest is ordered in this way and stored in inorder one vertex per processor, we obtain a faster algorithm for embedding forests of binary trees.

Theorem 8. *Let $F=(V, E)$ be a forest of binary trees of size n. There exists a one-to-one embedding of F into its optimal hypercube with dilation at most 9 and constant* *node-congestion. This embedding can be computed in time $O(\log^2(n))$ on the optimal hypercube provided that the forest is stored as described above.*

5 Dynamic Embedding

5.1 Outline of the Dynamic Embedding

Our model of growing trees is as follows. We distinguish between spawning and migration steps which alternate. In a spawning step, each tree vertex with fewer than two children can spawn a new child or not. In the subsequent migration step, the new leaves are mapped to the leaves of the (h, o, τ)-tree, and possibly some of the tree vertices will be remapped. This will ensure that the embedding achieves unit load. For our embedding, we use a next to optimal hypercube for our one-to-one embedding. This implies that between a quarter and a half of the hypercube locations are images of tree vertices. We will describe the embedding of a binary tree into the (h, o, τ)-tree. The extension to an embedding into hypercubes follows immediately.

After a spawning step, the embedded tree is remapped such that the load of each (h, o, τ)-tree node is less than or equal its capacity. We will not recompute the embedding of the whole binary tree, because this would be to expensive. Instead, we only recompute the embedding into the smallest subtrees of the (h, o, τ)-tree such that the load does not exceed the capacity. Our main observation is that we can find a one-to-one mapping of hypercube locations corresponding to the internal (h, o, τ)-tree nodes to hypercube locations corresponding to the leaves of the (h, o, τ)-subtree. Moreover, the Hamming distance of such a pair of hypercube locations is at most 3. In the first phase of the remapping, the newly created leaves at internal (h, o, τ)-tree nodes will be mapped to the leaves given by the mapping above. Now all newly created leaves are mapped to the leaves in the (h, o, τ)-tree implying that the load of an internal node of the (h, o, τ)-tree is less than or equal to its capacity. In the second phase, we first determine the subtrees of the (h, o, τ)-tree for which the embedding has to be recomputed. Then we recompute the embedding for all these subtrees in parallel using our algorithm for static embedding given in the previous section.

During a recomputation of the embedding into a subtree T of the (h, o, τ)-tree, there exist tree vertices which are mapped to T whose parents are not mapped to T. It is necessary to ensure that such tree vertices are mapped close to their parents in the hypercube. To maintain this condition, it is sufficient, as we shall see later, to map these tree vertices to the children of the root of T.

5.2 Additional Properties of the (h, o, τ)-Tree

We now will show how to assign each hypercube location whose corresponding node is an internal vertex , to a hypercube location whose corresponding node is a leaf of the (h, o, τ)-tree. Let v be a hypercube location which corresponds to an internal vertex of the $(h, 0, 1)$-tree. We denote by $\lambda(v)$ the assigned hypercube location corresponding to a leaf of the $(h, 0, 1)$-tree. Without loss of generality, we consider in the following a $(h, 0, \tau)$-tree, since the extension to an (h, o, τ)-tree is straightforward.

We first consider a $(h, 0, 1)$-tree. It has by definition 4^{h-1} leaves, and each leaf has a capacity of 4. Thus, the capacities of all leaves is 2^{2h} which is one half of the overall capacity of the tree. We will construct the mapping such that λ is one-to-one. The mapping

a)
u		α	β'	$0\cdots\cdots010\cdots\cdots0$	00
$\lambda(u)$		α	β'	$0\cdots\cdots010\cdots\cdots0$	11

b)
u	α	β'	$0\cdots\cdots\cdots\cdots0$	00	10
$\lambda(u)$	α	β'	$0\cdots\cdots\cdots\cdots0$	11	00

c)
u	α	β'	$0\cdots\cdots\cdots0$	00	01
$\lambda(u)$	α	β'	$0\cdots\cdots\cdots0$	11	11

d)
u	α	11	$0\cdots\cdots\cdots0$	00	00
$\lambda(u)$	α	11	$0\cdots\cdots\cdots0$	00	11

Left part:

a)
u	α	β'	$0\cdots\cdots010\cdots\cdots0$	000
$\lambda(u)$	α	β'	$0\cdots\cdots010\cdots\cdots0$	011

b)
u	α	β'	$0\cdots\cdots\cdots\cdots0$	001
$\lambda(u)$	α	β'	$0\cdots\cdots\cdots\cdots0$	101

c)
u	α	β'	$0\cdots\cdots\cdots\cdots0$	100
$\lambda(u)$	α	β'	$0\cdots\cdots\cdots\cdots0$	111

d)
u	α	β'	$0\cdots\cdots\cdots\cdots0$	010
$\lambda(u)$	α	β'	$0\cdots\cdots\cdots\cdots0$	110

e)
u	α	11	$0\cdots\cdots\cdots\cdots0$	000
$\lambda(u)$	α	11	$0\cdots\cdots\cdots\cdots0$	011

f)
u	$0\cdots\cdots\cdots010\cdots\cdots\cdots0$	000
$\lambda(u)$	$0\cdots\cdots\cdots010\cdots\cdots\cdots0$	011

g)
u	$0\cdots\cdots\cdots\cdots\cdots0$	100
$\lambda(u)$	$0\cdots\cdots\cdots\cdots\cdots0$	101

h)
u	$0\cdots\cdots\cdots\cdots\cdots0$	010
$\lambda(u)$	$0\cdots\cdots\cdots\cdots\cdots0$	110

i)
u	$0\cdots\cdots\cdots\cdots\cdots0$	001
$\lambda(u)$	$0\cdots\cdots\cdots\cdots\cdots0$	111

j)
u	$0\cdots\cdots\cdots\cdots\cdots0$	000
$\lambda(u)$	$0\cdots\cdots\cdots\cdots\cdots0$	011

Right part:

e)
u	α	10	01
$\lambda(u)$	α	10	10

f)
u	α	01	01
$\lambda(u)$	α	01	10

g)
u	α	11	01
$\lambda(u)$	α	11	10

h)
u	$0\cdots\cdots\cdots010\cdots\cdots\cdots0$	00
$\lambda(u)$	$0\cdots\cdots\cdots010\cdots\cdots\cdots0$	11

i)
u	$0\cdots\cdots\cdots\cdots0$	00	10
$\lambda(u)$	$0\cdots\cdots\cdots\cdots0$	00	11

j)
u	$0\cdots\cdots\cdots\cdots0$	00	01
$\lambda(u)$	$0\cdots\cdots\cdots\cdots0$	11	11

k)
u	$0\cdots\cdots\cdots\cdots0$	00	00
$\lambda(u)$	$0\cdots\cdots\cdots\cdots0$	11	00

Fig. 1. Label of an Internal Vertex and Corresponding labels of a Leaf in a $(h, 0, \tau)$-Tree

λ is illustrated in the left part of Figure 1, where $\alpha \in (\{0,1\}^2)^*$ and $\beta' \in \{01, 10, 11\}$. The mapping λ for hypercube locations corresponding to a $(h, 0, 1)$-tree node represented by α is given in rows a) through e). In rows f) through j), the mapping λ for hypercube locations in the additional set R belonging to the root of the $(h, 0, 1)$-tree is given.

We now consider a $(h, 0, 0)$-tree. As follows from the definition, it has 4^{h-1} leaves and each leaf has a capacity of 1, which altogether is 2^{2h-2}. Since this is not one half of the capacity of the $(h, 0, 0)$-tree, we will also use some of the hypercube locations corresponding to the parents of the leaves as images of our mapping λ. Of course, such hypercube locations corresponding to parents of leaves will be removed from the domain of λ. Since $2^{2h-1} = 4^{h-1} + 4 \cdot 4^{h-2}$, we need from each parent of a leaf an additional 4 (of $c(h-1)=7$) corresponding hypercube locations. The hypercube locations corresponding to parents of leaves with 01 in the final two position of its label belongs to the domain of the mapping λ, the other hypercube locations (ending with 10 and 00) will be used in the image of λ. This is illustrated in the right part Figure 1, where $\alpha \in (\{0,1\}^2)^*$ and $\beta' \in \{01, 10, 11\}$. First we consider hypercube locations corresponding to a node at level $\ell \geq h-2$ of a $(h, 0, 0)$-tree. For a hypercube location whose corresponding node is represented by α the mapping λ is illustrated in rows a) through d). Next we consider hypercube locations corresponding to parents of leaves. Recall that for each node only three of seven hypercube locations remain in the domain of λ. The images of such hypercube locations also correspond to parents of leaves. The mapping λ for these parents of leaves is given in row e) through g). In rows h) through k) the mapping λ for hypercube locations in the additional set R belonging to the root of the $(h, 0, 0)$-tree is given.

As mentioned in the previous subsection, during a recomputation of the embedding into a subtree of the (h, o, τ)-tree, there exist tree vertices mapped to the subtree whose parents are not mapped to it. Consider a fixed subtree T of the (h, o, τ)-tree. A tree vertex mapped to T is called a *sprout in T*, if its parent is not mapped to T. If it is clear which subtree is involved, we call such a tree vertex simply a sprout. All other tree vertices which are not sprouts are called *wooden vertices in T*.

Consider a subtree T of height $h-\ell+1$ rooted at a node at level ℓ. We will count the sprouts mapped to T whose number is denoted by $t(\ell)$. As mentioned earlier, each such subtree is itself a $(h-\ell+1, o, \tau)$-tree except that the additional set R of hypercube locations is not assigned to the root of that subtree. Exactly these hypercube locations in the set $\lambda(R)$ (of the subtree T) are the hypercube locations containing children spawned form vertices which do not belong to this subtree, i.e., sprouts will only be grown at hypercube locations in $\lambda(R)$. Since each tree vertex can spawn at most two leaves, the number of sprouts mapped to a subtree is at most $t(\ell)=2|R|$. It remains to investigate what happens when the mapping is recomputed. We first assume that the parent of a sprout is not involved in the remapping. In this case, the sprouts could be remapped but their parents (which are mapped to a node outside the subtree) remain at their hypercube locations. It follows that the hypercube locations in the set $\lambda(R)$ cannot be images of new sprouts. Otherwise, the parent of a sprout is also remapped. This means that we recompute a new embedding corresponding to a subtree of the (h, o, τ)-tree also containing the image of the parent of the sprout is mapped. But this implies that the sprout becomes a wooden vertex of T. Altogether, we have proved the following lemma.

Lemma 9. *Let T be a complete subtree of height h' of the (h, o, τ)-tree. The number of sprouts in T is bounded by $2^{o+1}(2h' + 1 + \tau)$.*

Finally, it remains to show that the dilation of the edge joining a sprout and its parent is at most 9. This can be observed from the following diagram.

Here, v denotes the hypercube location of a remapped sprout and u denotes the hypercube location of its parent. We assume that v is remapped during a recomputation of the embedding into the subtree T rooted at the node represented by α'. This implies that v is a sprout in the subtree T. Due to our construction, α' is a prefix of the hypercube location to which the vertex u is mapped.

5.3 Dilation of the Dynamic Embedding

In order to compute the number of tree vertices mapped to a single node in the (h, o, τ)-tree let $n(\ell)$ be the maximum number of marked vertices and partition vertices mapped to a single node of the (h, o, τ)-tree at level ℓ, and let $f(\ell)$ be the size of the associated forest which is partitioned at a node of the (h, o, τ)-tree at level ℓ. An obvious upper bound for $f(\ell)$ is $\lfloor \frac{2^{2h+2+\tau} - c(1)}{4^{\ell-1}} \rfloor$. Recall that $c(\ell)$ denotes the capacity of a node in the (h, o, τ)-tree at level ℓ. The number of marked vertices in a forest corresponding to a node at level ℓ before the partitioning is at most $2c(\ell)$, since each mapped vertex has at most two unmapped neighbors. Also note that the spouts are distributed evenly. Hence, we obtain for $\ell \geq 2$:

$$n(\ell) \leq 3 \lfloor \log\left(f(\ell - 1)\right) \rfloor + \left\lceil \frac{1}{4}\left[2c(\ell - 1) + t(\ell)\right] \right\rceil$$

$$\leq 3\left\lfloor \log\left(\frac{2^{2h+2+\tau}-1}{4^{\ell-2}}\right)\right\rfloor + \frac{8}{2}\left(6(h-(\ell-1)+1)-5+3\tau\right) + \frac{16}{4}\left(2(h-\ell+1)+1+\tau\right)$$

$$= 3\,(2h-2\ell+5+\tau) + 32\,(h-\ell+1) + 8 + 16\tau \quad = \quad 38(h-\ell+1)+17+19\tau$$

Since the capacity of a node on level ℓ of a $(h,3,\tau)$-tree is $48(h-\ell+1)-40+24\tau$, $n(\ell)$ should be less than this expression. This is the case for $\ell \leq h-5$. For the lower levels, the excess at a node will be distributed evenly among its children by shifting downward some tree vertices. If we do not care which vertices will be shifted, we obtain an embedding with dilation at most 11. Using a more sophisticated strategy, the dilation of the embedding can be bounded by 9. The details are omitted due to space limitations.

5.4 Complexity of the Dynamic Embedding

In this subsection, we will bound the amortized cost for each new spawned leaf. For the analysis of the time complexity of our algorithm, we first assume that in each spawning step exactly one new leaf is grown. We will later generalize our results assuming that in each step at most M new children get spawned.

We consider the growing period of the binary tree in which its size increases from $2^{2h+1+\tau}$ to $2^{2h+2+\tau}$. Thus, the tree grows in a $2h+3+\tau$-dimensional hypercube or, equivalently, in an $(h,3,\tau)$-tree. Without loss of generality, we consider the embedding into an $(h,3,1)$-tree. The following argument is similar for an $(h,3,0)$-tree. The *load of a subtree T* of an (h,o,τ)-tree, denoted by $\mathrm{load}(T)$, is the sum of the loads over all vertices in T. Remember, that a subtree of an (h,o,τ)-tree is itself an (h,o,τ)-tree. The *slack of a subtree T* of an (h,o,τ)-tree is defined as the overall capacity of T minus the load of T. Consider a subtree T of the (h,o,τ)-tree rooted at node v and let T_i $(i\in[1:4])$ be the four subtrees rooted at the children of T. We denote by $\mathrm{imb}(T)=\sum_{i=1}^{4}\mathrm{load}(T_i)-4\min_{i\in[1:4]}(\mathrm{load}(T_i))$ the *imbalance* of the subtree T. Note that the imbalance of a subtree T implies that after the last rebalancing in which the whole tree was involved at least $\mathrm{imb}(T)-3$ tree vertices have been mapped to T. If the load of a subtree T is greater than its overall capacity then the imbalance of T is bounded by the number of new leaves spawned in a single spawning step.

We now give a more detailed description of the migration step. Let v be a node of the (h,o,τ)-tree. We recursively define a procedure rebalance(v) which computes the new embedding into the subtree rooted at the node v. If the load of this subtree is greater than its capacity or the imbalance of this subtree is less than $\alpha(h')^5$ then we call the procedure rebalance recursively with the parent of v as its argument. Here, α is a constant to be defined later. Otherwise we compute the embedding for the subtree as mentioned in the previous section.

After the migration step, we have to ensure that the load of each subtree is at most its overall capacity. Since we only use the embedding algorithm for a subtree of the (h,o,τ)-tree whose load is at most its overall capacity, we achieve an embedding of the binary tree into the hypercube with unit load. It remains to show that if we call the procedure rebalance at the parent of the root of the (h,o,τ)-tree that the load of the (h,o,τ)-tree is at least one half of its overall capacity. Suppose the procedure rebalance is invoked at the parent of the root. This implies that either the load of the (h,o,τ)-tree is greater than its overall capacity or the imbalance at the root is less than $\alpha\cdot h^5$. In the first case we are done. Now assume that the imbalance of the (h,o,τ)-tree is less than $\alpha\cdot h^5$.

We will count the slack of the (h, o, τ)-tree. The first call to the procedure rebalance during this rebalancing was made by a leaf of the (h, o, τ)-tree with zero slack. At each node v on the path from the leaf to the root the imbalance of the subtree rooted at v is less than $\alpha(h-\ell+1)^5$, where ℓ is the level of v in the (h, o, τ)-tree. Thus we get the following recurrence for the slack $S(\ell)$ of the subtree rooted at a vertex at level ℓ on that path:

$$S(h) = 0; \qquad S(\ell) \le 4S(\ell + 1) + \alpha(h - \ell + 1)^5.$$

It can easily be verified that $S(\ell) \le \sum_{i=\ell}^{h-1} 4^{i-\ell}\alpha(h-i+1)^5$ is a solution of this recurrence.

$$S(1) \le \sum_{i=1}^{h-1} 4^{i-1}\alpha(h - i + 1)^5 = \alpha \sum_{i=2}^{h} i^5 4^{h-i} \le \alpha 4^h \sum_{i=2}^{\infty} \frac{i^5}{4^i} \le 17\alpha 2^{2h} \le 2^{2h+2+\tau},$$

if we choose $\alpha = \frac{4}{17} \le \frac{2^{2+\tau}}{17}$. Hence, the slack of the (h, o, τ)-tree is at most one half of its overall capacity, implying that the load of the (h, o, τ)-tree is at least one half of its overall capacity. Whenever the procedure rebalance is invoked at the parent of the root, we can increase the dimension of the hypercube by one while maintaining the invariant that the load of the (h, o, τ)-tree ranges between one fourth and one half of its total capacity.

We will now compute the amortized cost for embedding a new leaf. As mentioned earlier, the imbalance of a subtree T implies that since the last rebalancing in which the whole tree was involved at least $\max\{\text{imb}(T)-3, 0\}$ tree vertices have been mapped to T. Suppose the procedure rebalance is invoked at node v and assume that the level of v in the (h, o, τ)-tree is ℓ. As stated in the previous section the recomputation of the embedding can be done in time $O((h-\ell+1)^3)$. Since the imbalance of the subtree rooted at v is at least $\alpha \cdot (h-\ell+1)^5$, we charge to each of these tree vertices an amount of $1/(h-\ell+1)^2$. Note further that each tree vertex can contribute at most once to the imbalance of a subtree rooted at a node v at some fixed level, since after the rebalancing of the subtree rooted at v the imbalance of that tree is at most 3. Hence, we charge to each vertex an amount of at most $\sum_{i=1}^{h} 1/(h-\ell+1)^2 \le \pi^2/6$. Thus, the amortized cost for embedding a newly spawned tree vertex is constant.

Theorem 10. *An arbitrary binary tree can be dynamically embedded into its next to optimal hypercube with unit load, dilation at most 9, and constant node-congestion. The embedding can be computed on the hypercube in constant amortized time provided that in each step at most one new leaf is spawned.*

We now consider the case that in each spawning step at most M new leaves are grown. It is possible that all these leaves are spawned from tree vertices which are mapped to a subtree of the (h, o, τ)-tree of height $\Theta(\log_4(M))$. Due to our construction they cannot be mapped into a subtree of height $o(\log_4(M))$. So we modify our rebalancing procedure as follows. The procedure rebalance will now be invoked from a node v at level ℓ if the imbalance of the subtree rooted at v is at least $\alpha M(h-\ell+1)^5$. Again, this implies that between two invocations of rebalance from the node v at least $\alpha \cdot (h-\ell+1)^5$ spawning steps have been made. After each spawning step, we recompute the embedding in a subtree of the (h, o, τ)-tree of height $2\log_4(M)$ implying that the forest of binary trees mapped to this subtree is stored in inorder. Thus, the remapping can be done in time $O(\log^2(M))$. Now the amount of $1/(h-\ell+1)^2$ is charged to the spawning step.

As before, each spawning step is thus charged a constant amount. It remains to show that the load of the (h, o, τ)-tree is at least half of its overall capacity if the procedure rebalance is called from the parent of the root. Again, we will count the slack of the (h, o, τ)-tree. Since we rebalance each subtree of height $2 \log_4(M)$ after the spawning step, we now obtain the following recurrence:

$$S(h - 2\log_4(M)) = 0; \qquad S(\ell) \leq 4S(\ell+1) + \alpha M(h - \ell + 1)^5.$$

Since $S(\ell) \leq \displaystyle\sum_{i=\ell}^{h-2\log_4(M)-1} 4^{i-\ell}\alpha(h-i+1)^5$ is a solution, it can be shown that the slack $S(1)$ of the whole (h, o, τ)-tree is bounded by $2^{2h+2+\tau}$ if α is chosen as $1/680$. Again, the load of the (h, o, τ)-tree is at least one half of its overall capacity.

Theorem 11. *An arbitrary binary tree can be dynamically embedded into its next to optimal hypercube with unit load, dilation at most 9, and constant node-congestion. If in each step at most M leaves are spawned, the embedding can computed on the hypercube in amortized time $O(\log^2(M))$ per spawning step.*

5.5 Remarks on the Implementation

Recall that we have assumed that there exist spawning steps and migration steps which alternate. This assumption is not correct. Consider two small subtrees of the (h, o, τ)-tree which have decided to remap their embeddings. The distance of these two subtree in the hypercube might be larger than the computation needed for the remapping of both subtrees. Thus, it is in general not possible to broadcast to the whole (h, o, τ)-tree that there is a migration step. So in general, some parts of the binary tree will spawn new leaves while some other parts of the binary tree are involved in a remapping phase. Fortunately, this will not effect our algorithm. Since different subtrees of a (h, o, τ)-tree are stored in different subcubes of the hypercube, a remapping in one subcube cannot interact with a spawning or remapping step in another subcube.

Another problem which may arise is that in one subtree of a (h, o, τ)-tree the rebalancing procedure will climb the (h, o, τ)-tree upwards while another subtree whose root is descendant of a vertex in the rebalancing path is already involved in a remapping phase. Thus, the remapping phase of two subtrees might overlap. Also this problem can easily be resolved. First a message is broadcasted to the whole subtree of the (h, o, τ)-tree when a remapping is necessary. A vertex of a subtree which receives this message and which is itself involved in a remapping interrupts the current remapping. Clearly, the time for broadcasting is negligible against the time for the remapping.

6 Conclusion

We have presented a deterministic algorithm for dynamically embedding arbitrary binary trees into their next to optimal hypercubes with unit load, dilation at most 9, and constant node-congestion. The algorithm can be implemented on the hypercube itself spending amortized time $O(\log^2(M))$ if in each step at most M new children are inserted. The necessity of the migration of tree vertices follows from a simple adaptation of a lower bound given in [17]. Our algorithm presents an alternative way for embedding dynamically binary trees into hypercubes. Moreover, our algorithm has the advantage that simultaneous growing of new leaves is permitted. It is also possible to lower the expansion of our embedding to $2+\varepsilon$, but doing do increases the amortized time spent for embedding new groups of leaves by $O(1/\varepsilon)$. Using an appropriate model of growing graphs, our algorithm can be extended to grow graphs with bounded treewidth into hypercubes.

References

1. S. Bezrukov, B. Monien, W. Unger, G. Wechsung: Embedding Ladders and Caterpillars into the Hypercube, Preprint, GH-Univ. Paderborn, 1993, *to appear in Disc. Appl. Math.*.
2. S. Bhatt, J.-Y. Cai: Taking Random Walks to Grow Trees in Hypercubes, *J. ACM*, **40**(1993), 741-764.
3. S. Bhatt, F. Chung, T. Leighton, A. Rosenberg: Efficient Embeddings of Trees in Hypercubes, *SIAM J. Comput.*, **21**(1992), 151–162.
4. S. Bhatt, I. Ipsen: How to embed trees in hypercubes, *Yale University Research Report* RR-443, 1985.
5. M.Y. Chan: Embedding of d-Dimensional Grids into Optimal Hypercubes, *Proc. of the 1989 Symp. on Parallel Algorithms and Architectures*, 52–57.
6. M.Y. Chan: Embedding of Grids into Optimal Hypercubes, *SIAM J. Comput.*, **20**(1991), 834–864.
7. M. Chan, F. Chin, C. Chu, W. Mak: Dilation-5 Embedding of 3-Dimensional Grids into Hypercubes, *J. Parallel Distrib. Comput.*, **33**(1996), 98-106.
8. K. Efe: Embedding Mesh of Trees in the Hypercube, *J. Parallel Distrib. Comput.*, **11**(1991), 222–230.
9. T. Feder, E. Mayr: An Efficient Algorithm for Embedding Complete Binary Trees in the Hypercube, *Stanford University*, 1987.
10. I. Havel: On Hamiltonian Circuits and Spanning Trees of Hypercubes (in Czech.), *Časopis. Pěst. Mat.*, **109**(1984), 145–152.
11. I. Havel, P. Liebl: Embedding the Polytomic Tree into the n-Cube, *Časopis. Pěst. Mat.*, **98**(1973), 307–314.
12. I. Havel, P. Liebl: One-Legged Caterpillars Span Hypercubes, *J. Graph Theory*, **10** (1986), 69–76.
13. V. Heun, E. Mayr: A New Efficient Algorithm for Embedding an Arbitrary Binary Tree into Its Optimal Hypercube, *J. Algorithms*, **20**(1996), 375–199.
14. V. Heun, E. Mayr: Embedding Graphs with Bounded Treewidth into Optimal Hypercubes, *Proc. of the 13th Symp. on Theoretical Aspects of Computer Science*, LNCS 1046, 157–168.
15. V. Heun, E. Mayr: Optimal Dynamic Edge-Disjoint Embeddings of Complete Binary Trees into Hypercubes, (to appear in *Proc. of the 4th Workshop on Parallel Systems and Algorithms*).
16. V. Heun, E. Mayr: A General Method for Efficient Embeddings of Graphs into Optimal Hypercubes, (to appear in *Proc. of the* EURO-PAR'96).
17. T. Leighton, M. Newman, A. Ranade, W. Schwabe: Dynamic Tree Embeddings in Butterflies and Hypercubes, *SIAM J. Comput.*, **21**(1992), 639–654.
18. B. Monien, H. Sudborough: Simulating Binary Trees on Hypercubes, *Proc. of the 3rd Aegean Workshop on Computing*, LNCS 319, 170–180.
19. Y. Saad, M. Schulz: Topological Properties of the Hypercube, *Yale University Research Report* RR-389, 1985.
20. X. Sheen, Q. Hu, W. Liang: Embedding k-ary Complete Trees into Hypercubes, *J. Parallel Distrib. Comput.*, **24**(1995), 100–106.
21. Q. Stout: Hypercubes and Pyramids, *Proc. of the NATO Advanced Research Workshop on Pyramidal Systems for Computer Vision 1986*, 75–89.
22. A. Wu: Embedding of tree networks into hypercubes, *J. Parallel Distrib. Comput.*, **2**(1985), 238-249.

Practical Dynamic Load Balancing
for Irregular Problems *

Jerrell Watts, Marc Rieffel and Stephen Taylor

California Institute of Technology, Pasadena CA 91125, USA

Abstract. In this paper, we present a cohesive, practical load balancing framework that addresses many shortcomings of existing strategies. These techniques are portable to a broad range of prevalent architectures, including massively parallel machines such as the Cray T3D and Intel Paragon, shared memory systems such as the SGI Power Challenge, and networks of workstations. This scheme improves on earlier work in this area and can be analyzed using well-understood techniques. The algorithm operates using nearest-neighbor communication and inherently maintains existing locality in the application. A simple software interface allows the programmer to use load balancing with very little effort. Unlike many previous efforts in this arena, the techniques have been applied to large-scale industrial applications, one of which is described herein.

1 Introduction

A number of trends in computational science and engineering have increased the need for effective dynamic load balancing techniques. In particular, particle/plasma simulations, which have recently become common, generally have much less favorable load distribution characteristics than continuum calculations, such as Navier-Stokes flow solvers. Even for continuum problems, the use of dynamically adapted grids for moving boundaries and solution resolution necessitates runtime load balancing to maintain efficiency. In the past ten years, researchers have proposed a number of strategies for dynamic load balancing [2, 3, 4, 6, 7, 9, 11, 12]. Unfortunately, the majority of these techniques have (at least) one of these deficiencies: A few are unscalable, and those that are scalable cannot always be analyzed theoretically. Some are application-specific, while others have only been applied to unrealistic "toy" problems on small numbers of processors. Many are too complex to reasonably implement. Finally, the methods may fail to consider communication locality, or they may be inherently synchronous in their operation.

The goal of this work was thus to address the limitations of current load balancing strategies. The techniques are designed to be highly portable and easy-to-use. Improvements over existing algorithms include a more accurate diffusive scheme that retains the properties of scalability and correctness. Mechanisms for

---

* This research is sponsored by subcontract OSP-95-11-437-001 under NASA NAG 1-1760. The first author is partially supported by a NSF fellowship.

selecting and transferring tasks are introduced. All of the techniques maintain the communication locality of the underlying application. Finally, the framework is applied to a high-end application running on hundreds of processors. The success of the methods for this application demonstrates their utility.

2 Methodology

The abstract goal of load balancing can be stated as follows:

Given a collection of tasks comprising a computation and a set of computers on which these tasks can be executed, find the mapping of tasks to computers that minimizes the runtime of the computation.

In considering the load balancing problem it is important to distinguish between *problem decomposition* and *task mapping*. Problem decomposition involves the exploitation of parallelism in the control and data access of an algorithm. The result of this decomposition is a set of communicating tasks that solve the problem in parallel. These tasks can then be mapped to computers in a way that best fits the problem. One goal in task mapping is that each computer have a roughly equal workload. This is the load balancing problem, as stated above. The computation time associated with a given task can, in come cases, be determined a priori. In such circumstances one can perform the task mapping before beginning the computation; this is called *static* load balancing. For an important and increasingly common class of applications, the workload for a particular task may change over the course of a computation and cannot be estimated beforehand. For these applications the mapping of tasks to computers must change *dynamically*, at runtime.

A practical solution to the dynamic load balancing problem involves five distinct phases [12]:[2]

1. **Load Evaluation:** Some estimate of a computer's load must be provided to determine whether or not a load imbalance exists. Estimates of the work loads associated with individual tasks must also be maintained to determine which tasks should be transferred to best balance the computation.
2. **Profitability Determination:** Once the loads of the computers have been measured, the presence of a load imbalance can be detected. If the cost of the imbalance exceeds the cost of load balancing, then load balancing should be performed.
3. **Work Transfer Vector Calculation:** Based on the measurements taken in the first phase, the ideal work transfers necessary to balance the computation are calculated.
4. **Task Selection:** Tasks are selected for transfer or *exchange* to best fulfill the vectors provided by the previous step. Task selection is typically constrained by communication locality and storage requirement considerations.

---

[2] Actually, the authors of [12] divided the problem into four phases, merging "task selection" and "task migration" into a single step.

5. **Task Migration:** Once selected, tasks are transferred from one computer to another; state and communications channel integrity must be maintained to ensure algorithmic correctness.

By decomposing the load balancing process into distinct phases, one can easily experiment with different strategies at each of the above steps, allowing the space of techniques to be more fully and readily explored. Few strategies in the literature provide this capability. Indeed, many of the current load balancing algorithms fail to address several of the above concerns altogether. Most provide only the work transfer vectors in step three, above. While this is certainly an important contribution, it does not comprise a complete solution to the load balancing problem.

3 Implementation

As outlined in the previous section, there are five steps in a practical load balancing approach. These steps were implemented in the context of the Concurrent Graph Library, an applications framework which has been successfully applied to a number of large-scale irregular problems [10]. This section first presents a brief overview of the functionality of the Concurrent Graph Library, then gives details on the specific instantiations of the load balancing phases outlined above.

The Concurrent Graph Library. The Concurrent Graph Library (hereafter referred to simply as the Graph Library) provides an ideal framework in which to implement a practical load balancing algorithm. In the Graph Library, the computational entities (tasks) are called "nodes." Nodes communicate with one another over unidirectional channels. The mapping of nodes to computers is controlled by the Graph Library and is hidden from the user by these communication channels. Thus, because the mapping of work to computers is not explicit, it is possible to dynamically change this mapping, so long as the user provides some mechanism for packing/unpacking the context of a node (i.e., the node's state) into/from a buffer. Fig.1 shows an example computational graph and its mapping to a set of computers, as well as a schematic representation of the software structure of an individual node.

The above functionality is layered on top of a small set of routines that are easily realizable using standard message passing libraries, such as NX on the Intel Paragon, remote memory operations on the Cray T3D, and MPI or PVM on networks of workstations. Once these low-level routines have been implemented on a particular machine, the rest of the library is immediately portable. As a result, the time to port an application under the Graph Library is typically a matter of hours.

Load Evaluation. Empirical load measurement provides an accurate, simple way in which to ascertain the relative amounts of computation time associated with various tasks. Typical machines provide clocks with milli- to microsecond level accuracy. One can use these timing facilities to time each task, providing

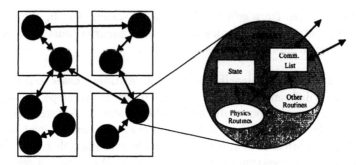

Fig. 1. A computational graph of nine nodes mapped onto four computers, and the internal software structure of one of those nodes.

accurate measurements in the categories of execution time, idle time and communication overhead. In fact, the user need not manually time the code at all. These timings are easily taken at the Graph Library level: Any time between communication operations is labeled as runtime, any time actually sending or receiving data is tagged as communication time, and any time waiting to receive a message is accumulated as idle time.

The Graph Library provides a basic set of task load functions which may be supplied to the load balancing routines. Once the loads for all of the tasks on a computer have been calculated, those loads can be totaled to give the aggregate load for that computer, which will serve as input to the next two phases of load balancing.

Load Balance Initiation. For load balancing to be useful, one must first determine *when* to load balance. Doing so is comprised of two phases: detecting that a load imbalance exists and determining if the cost of load balancing exceeds its possible benefits.

Most scientific codes have inherent synchronization points. In particular, global norm calculations and other determination detection mechanisms typically involve a global sum or similar reduction operation. These provide a natural, clean point at which to initiate load balancing. When a global operation is initiated, the average load of all of the computers is determined. If the aggregate efficiency is below some user-specified limit, the workload is considered to be imbalanced. If the cost of the imbalance (in terms of unnecessary runtime prior to the next load balancing opportunity) exceeds the expected cost of load balancing (based on previous load balancing runs), then load balancing is performed.

Work Transfer Vector Calculation. Heat diffusion provides an intuitive, correct and scalable mechanism for determining where work should be migrated in an unbalanced computation. Diffusion was first presented as a method for load balancing in [2]. Diffusion was also explored in [12] and was found to be superior to other load balancing strategies. A more general diffusive strategy is given in [4]. This method uses a fully implicit differencing scheme to solve the heat equation on a multi-dimensional mesh to a specified accuracy.

The basic diffusion algorithm presented in [4] has a number of weaknesses in terms of its compatibility with our methodology as well as its performance relative to the desired accuracy. To remedy these shortcomings, a second-order accurate, unconditionally stable differencing scheme was used to improve the convergence rate by allowing larger time steps to be taken without adding substantial complexity. The algorithm in [4] also made no mention of task selection, considering work to be essentially a continuous quantity. Therefore, work migration and selection were moved out of the algorithm to the appropriate phases in the broader framework presented here. Like the algorithm in [4], the new algorithm is guaranteed to converge, employs a body of theory that allows its rate of convergence to be quantified and maintains existing communication locality through its nearest-neighbor approach. Unlike the algorithm in [4], which was only analyzed theoretically and simulated, the algorithm in this paper has been applied to large-scale simulations. Pseudocode for the resulting algorithm is given in [10].

Task Selection. Once work transfer vectors between computers have been calculated, it is necessary to determine which tasks should be moved to meet those vectors. There are two options in satisfying a transfer vector between two computers. One can attempt to move tasks unidirectionally from one computer to another, or one can exchange tasks between the two computers, resulting in a net transfer of work. If the average task's workload is high relative to the magnitude of the transfer vectors, it may be very difficult to find tasks that fit the vectors. On the other hand, by exchanging tasks one can potentially satisfy small transfer vectors by swapping sets of tasks with close to the same load.

The problem of selecting which tasks to move to satisfy a particular transfer vector is **NP**-complete, since it is simply the subset sum problem. Thus, exhaustive searches are necessary to determine the optimal solution, but much cheaper approximation algorithms can often be used to great efficacy. In our implementation, we use an exhaustive, best-fit search when the number of tasks per computer is small (e.g., less than 20) and a faster, first-fit search when the number of tasks per computer is large (e.g., more than 20). In practice, this has proven to be very effective, since transfer vectors are hardest to satisfy for a small number of tasks; hence, exhaustive searches are necessary in such cases.

It is important to note that other concerns may constrain task transfer options. In particular, transferring certain tasks may exceed the available memory on the computers involved. One way to avoid this is to keep track of the size of data structures allocated by a particular task via an intermediate memory allocation layer. Only those tasks which would fit on the destination computer should be considered for transfer. Also, arbitrary movement of nodes, even between neighboring computers, may eventually disrupt communications locality. Thus, the Graph Library keeps track of the distance between a node and its neighbors in the graph, and does not move nodes in such a way that this distance exceeds a fixed limit.

Task Migration. The Graph Library provides a routine to move a task from one computer to another. This routine requires only that the user provide procedures for packing the task's state at the old computer, unpacking it at the new computer and freeing the original on the old computer. Task movement itself is a completely local interaction. Only the computers from and to which the task is being moved as well as those computers containing tasks with which the task in question communicates are informed of the transfer. Communication channels are automatically reoriented by this protocol. A fault-tolerant mechanism covers cases of memory allocation failure on the destination computer.

4 Experiments

The load balancing implementation described above was applied to a large-scale Direct Simulation Monte Carlo (DSMC) application running under the Graph Library. This application exhibits very poor load distribution properties on relevant problems. This section gives a brief overview of the application, including the algorithm and the specific problems to which it was applied. It also presents performance numbers before and after load balancing, demonstrating the practical efficacy of the methods described in the previous section.

DSMC Technique. DSMC is a method for the simulation of collisional plasmas and rarefied gases [8]. It is applied to particle flows in which the density is too low for continuum methods such as Navier-Stokes and too high for collisionless methods such as Particle-in-Cell. Like other gas and fluid modeling techniques, the DSMC method is based on a spatial gridding of the physical problem domain. At each time step particles may interact (collide) only with other particles in the same grid cell. DSMC techniques, as the name implies, simulate the collision of particles using a stochastic model, rather than calculating actual path intersections. When a collision occurs, depending on the species of particles involved, they may simply rebound off of one another or react chemically. Based on particle distribution, macroscopic properties such as pressure, temperature and average velocity can be calculated.

Application Description. Hawk is a three-dimensional concurrent DSMC application based on techniques developed by Bird [8, 10]. It was written in conjunction with researchers from the Intel Corporation and the Philips Laboratory at Edwards Air Force Base. Hawk is currently being applied to plasma reactor simulations for the Intel and Tegal Corporations.

Under the graph abstraction, each node represents a contiguous partition of physical space and executes the DSMC algorithm. The *state* of a node consists of the grid cells and particles contained in a region. As stated in the description of the DSMC technique, collisions within each partition (and grid cell therein) are calculated independently. In the process of particle movement, any particles that have exited from a grid cell are migrated to their new cells, which may reside in different partitions; in the latter case, communication is required.

Problem of Interest. Plasma reactors are prominent in many stages of microprocessor fabrication. Specifically, they are involved in the etching of and

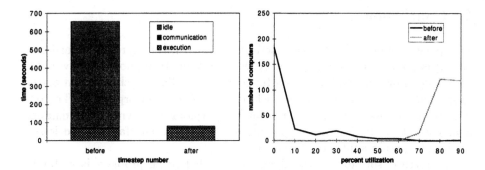

Fig. 2. (Left) run time breakdowns and (right) utilization distributions for 100 time steps of the DSMC code before and after load balancing.

deposition onto a wafer substrate. Improvements in reactor design could greatly impact the cost, quality and efficiency of microelectronics fabrication.

The Gaseous Electronics Conference (GEC) reference cell is a standard reactor design that is being studied extensively. As such, it is a perfect target for parametric studies. The Hawk code described above has been used to study the GEC reactor. Simulations of up to 2.8 million particles have been conducted using a 580,000-cell grid of the GEC geometry. In these simulations, ambient conditions such as the port inflow and surface temperatures are specified.

Results. The particle density in the GEC reactor can vary by up to an order of magnitude. Consequently, one would expect that a standard spatial decomposition and mapping of the grid would result in a very inefficient computation. This is indeed the case. The GEC grid was divided into 2,560 partitions and naively mapped onto 256 processors of an Intel Paragon. Because of the wide variance in particle density for each partition, the overall efficiency of the computation was quite low, at approximately 11 percent. As shown in Fig. 2, this efficiency was improved to 86 percent by load balancing. This resulted in an 88 percent reduction in the run time. Fig. 2 also shows the corresponding improvement in workload distribution. Load balancing required only a few percent of the runtime.

5   Related Work

Two other libraries that provide support for parallel programming and load balancing, CHAOS [5] and Cilk [1], are particularly interesting. CHAOS provides a framework for data and control decomposition of irregular, adaptive array-based codes via index translation and communication scheduling. It differs from our approach in that it is appropriate only for FORTRAN-style regular data structures and in that the communication structure is determined implicitly by the reference patterns in the code. Cilk provides a multithreaded environment with integrated load balancing. It is best applied to tree-structured computations, however, and does not fit the SPMD style typical of scientific applications.

6 Conclusion

This paper demonstrates that a practical, comprehensive approach to load balancing is possible and effective. More work remains to be done, however. Algorithmic improvements such as faster-converging diffusion schemes and better approximation algorithms for task selection need to be incorporated. The option of an asynchronous implementation begs exploration. Dynamic granularity management via task adaption and improved software interfaces would lessen the burden on the application developer.

A practical solution to the dynamic load balancing problem is certainly within reach. This work takes important steps toward that solution, and prepares the way for strategies that better support current and future applications.

References

1. Blufome, R., et al.: Cilk: an efficient multithreaded runtime system. Proc. Fifth ACM SIGPLAN Sym. on Principles & Practice of Parallel Programming (1995) 207–216
2. Cybenko, G.: Dynamic load balancing for distributed memory multiprocessors. J. Parallel and Distributed Computing **7** (1989) 279–301
3. Evans, D., Butt, W.: Dynamic load balancing using task-transfer probabilities. Parallel Computing **19** (1993) 897–916
4. Heirich, A., Taylor, S.: A parabolic load balancing algorithm. Proc. 24th Int'l Conf. on Parallel Programming **3** (1995) 192–202
5. Hwang, Y.-S., et al.: Runtime and language support for compiling adaptive irregular problems on distributed-memory machines. Software: Practice and Experience **25** (1995) 597–621
6. Kohring, G.: Dynamic load balancing for parallelized particle simulations on MIMD computers. Parallel Computing **21** (1995) 683–693
7. Muniz, F., Zaluska, E.: Parallel load-balancing: an extension to the gradient model. Parallel Computing **21** (1995) 287–301
8. Rieffel, M.: Concurrent simulations of plasma reactors for VLSI manufacturing. CITCSTR95-012 (1995)
9. Song, J.: A partially asynchronous and iterative algorithm for distributed load balancing. Parallel Computing **20** (1994) 853–868
10. Taylor, S., Watts, J., Rieffel, M., Palmer, M.: The concurrent graph: basic technology for irregular problems. IEEE Parallel and Distributed Technology **4** (1996) 15–25
11. Van Driessche, R., Roose, D.: An improved spectral bisection algorithm and its application to dynamic load balancing. Parallel Computing **21** (1995) 29–48
12. Willebeek-LeMair, M., Reeves, A.: Strategies for dynamic load balancing on highly parallel computers. IEEE Trans. on Parallel and Distributed Systems **4** (1993) 979–993

The Module Allocation Problem:
An Average Case Analysis

M. LAMARI AND W. FERNANDEZ DE LA VEGA

ABSTRACT.. In the module allocation problem we are given n tasks
to be executed by m processors, subject to both execution and communication costs. The problem is to find an assignment of the tasks to
the processors which minimizes the overall cost. We consider various
random versions of this problem In particular:

- When the communication graph GC has an edge probability
independent of n we obtain asymptotically optimal (as $n \to \infty$)
allocation algorithms.

- When GC is regular with a fixed degree r, we give a simple
algorithm with an uniformly bounded approximation ratio.

1 Introduction

We present here an average case analysis of the problem of assigning tasks to
processors in the case where two kinds of costs: inter-task communication costs
and execution costs, are considered. The problem is then to find an assignment
that minimizes the sum of these two kinds of costs. Thus, neither processor
capacity limitations nor precedence constraints or completion time are taken
into account in this model.

This problem has been proved to be $\mathcal{N}P$-hard by Magirou and Milis [6] using
results of Stone [8] and of Dalhaus et al. [7]. Exact polynomial algorithms are
known for the case of two processors (Stone [8]) and when the graph of the
communicating tasks is a tree (Bokhari [4]). Fernandez-Baca [5] has shown that
this problem has no polynomial approximation scheme.

Our analysis concerns vatious random models.

We consider two kinds of execution costs distributions: a bi-valued case in
which the execution cost e_{ij} of task i on processor j is equal to a fixed positive
number e_o with a given probability $q \in]0,1[$, or to 0 (with probability 1-q) and
a more practical continuous case. The bi-valued case is treated because it leads
to an explicit solution.

The communication costs distribution is defined via a random "communication graph" GC whose vertices are the tasks and whose edges indicate the

pairs of tasks with non-zero communication costs, and a common probability distribution for these non-zero costs. We consider two models for GC:

- Model 1: GC is the random graph $G(n, p)$ on n vertices with fixed edge probability $0 < p < 1$. It is convenient here (see proposition 1) to scale by $1/n$ the distribution of the non-zero communication costs. Thus, denoting by $E(G)$ the edge set of the graph G, we will take, with c_o a fixed positive number, $c_{ij} = 0$ if $\{t_i, t_j\} \notin E(GC)$ and $c_{ij} = \frac{c_o}{n}$ if $\{t_i, t_j\} \in E(GC)$ Note that this scaling in which the individual execution costs tend to 0 as the size of the problem tends to infinity does not lead to the same solution as the one obtained by ignoring this costs.

- Model 2: GC is distributed as the random r-regular graph $G(n, r - reg)$ on n vertices with fixed degree r, $r \geq 3$, and all non-zero communication costs are equal to a fixed $c_o \in R^+$.

For model 1, we shall assume for simplicity that the number m of processors is potentially infinite. It will be seen that for each system of values of the parameters, the number of processors involved in an asymptotically optimum solution does not depend on n. Observe that there is no loss of generality in choosing execution costs independent of n. The following proposition whose proof is omitted disposes of the "trivial" cases.

Proposition 1 *Assume an execution costs distribution as defined above with e_o and q fixed (independent of n) and assume that the communication costs are distributed as follows:*

$$\Pr[c_{ij} = c(n)] = p(n), \ \Pr[c_{ij} = 0] = 1 - p(n), \ 0 < p(n) < 1, \ 1 \leq i < j \leq n,$$

where $c(.)$ and $p(.)$ are arbitrary positive functions. Then:

i) If the product ncp tends to infinity with n and the number m of processors satisfies $m \leq 2^{n^\alpha}$, then there exists an asymptotically optimal solution using only one processor,

ii) Assume that the product ncp tends to 0, and that the number m of processors is fixed. There exists then an asymptotically optimum solution with negligible communication cost.

Let us now fix some notation. We let $T = \{t_1, \cdots, t_n\}$ denote the set of tasks and $\mathcal{P} = \{P_1, \cdots, P_m\}$ the set of processors. An assignment is a mapping $A : T \to \mathcal{P}$. We shall write $Exec(A)$ for the execution cost of the assignment A on a generic instance ω and $Com(A)$ for the corresponding execution cost. We write $Cost(A)$ for the total cost: $Cost(A) = Exec(A) + Com(A)$, and $Opt = \min Cost(A)$ where for each ω, the min is taken over all assignments. Finally, we write $A_{opt} = A_{opt}(\omega)$ for any optimal assignment.

2 Dense communication Graph: Model 1

Let $\pi = \{T_1, ..., T_l\}$ be a partition of the set of tasks and let γ_{ij} denote the number of edges of the communication graph GC with one end point in T_i and the other in T_j. Define $Cut(\pi) = \sum_{1 \leq i < j \leq l} \gamma_{ij}$ and $Com(\pi) = \frac{c_o}{n} \sum_{1 \leq i < j \leq l} \gamma_{ij}$.

If $A : T \to \mathcal{P}$ is any assignment inducing the partition π, then we have $Com(\pi) = Com(A)$. Accordingly, we shall also write $S(A)$ for $S(\pi)$. Our proofs depend on the three following lemmas whose proofs are omitted in this extended abstact.

Lemma 1 *Let GC and the functions $S(.)$ and $Com(.)$ be defined as above. Assume that the integer $s = s(n)$ satisfies $s \geq n^{1+\delta}$ for some positive constant δ. We have then, for any positive ϵ and for sufficiently large n,*

$$\Pr[(1 - \epsilon)ps \leq \min Cut(\pi) \leq \max Cut(\pi) \leq (1 + \epsilon)ps] \geq 1 - \exp(-\tfrac{\epsilon^2 ps}{13})$$

and

$$\Pr[(1 - \epsilon)pc_o sn^{-1} \leq \min Com(\pi) \leq \max Com(\pi) \leq (1 + \epsilon)pc_o sn^{-1}] \geq 1 - \exp(-\tfrac{\epsilon^2 ps}{13})$$

where the min and the max are taken over all partitions π of the set T having $S(\pi) = s$.

Lemma 2 *Assume that the number m of processors satisfies $m(n) \leq 2^{n^{\alpha}}$, for some fixed $\alpha < 1$. and let k be a fixed integer with $1 \leq k \leq m$. For any sequence $L = (P_{\rho(1)}, ..., P_{\rho(k)})$ of k distinct processors let $f(L)$ denote the number of tasks with execution cost c_o on each of the processors $P_{\rho(1)}, ..., P_{\rho(k-1)}$ and cost 0 on $P_{\rho(k)}$. We have then, for every $\epsilon > 0$,*

$$\Pr[nq(1 - q)^{k-1} - n^{1/2+\epsilon} \leq \min f(L) \leq \max f(L) \leq nq(1 - q)^{k-1} + n^{1/2+\epsilon}]$$
$$= 1 - o(1),$$

where the max and the min are taken over all sequences of $k + 1$ processors.

Lemma 3 *Assume our communication costs model with parameter $p \in]0, 1[$:*

$$\Pr[e_{ij} = e_o] = p, \quad \Pr[e_{ij} = 0] = 1 - p,$$

and assume that the number m of processors satisfies $m \leq 2^{n^{\beta}}$ with $\beta < 1$. Let α satisfy $0 \leq \alpha \leq 1$. We have then, with probability $1\text{-}o(1)$,

$$Exec(A) \leq \alpha e_o np \Rightarrow Cut(A) \geq p(1 - p)(1 - \alpha)n^2(1 - o(1)).$$

We turn now to model 1.

Theorem 1 *In model 1 with parameters e_o, q, c_o and p, the minimum cost is asymptotically equivalent to the min of the products $nC(l)$, where l ranges over the set $\mathbf{N}^* \cup \{\{+\infty\}\}$ and $C(l)$ is given by*

$$C(l) = e_o(1 - q)^l + \frac{pc_o}{2}\left(1 - 2q^l(1 - q) - q^{2l} - \frac{(1 - q)(1 - q^{2l})}{1 + q}\right), \quad l = 1, 2, ...$$

Sketch proof Let A be some assignment and let π_A be the partition of the set of tasks induced by A. We have $S(A) = \sum_{1 \leq i < j \leq m} m_i m_j$ where, for $1 \leq i \leq m$, m_i is the load of processor P_i in the assignment A. Lemma 2 implies that the communication cost of A satisfies $nCom(A) = c_o pS(A)(1+o(1))$ in probability, as $n \to \infty$. This shows that we can replace the objective function by the functional

$Cost^*(A) = Exec(A) + c_o p n^{-1} S(A)$. Observe that $S(A)$ decreases when we move any task from a processor P to another processor whose load is not smaller than that of P. This implies with lemma 2 that, if we fix the number, say n_o, of tasks executed with cost 0 and define l

$$n - n_o = (q^l - \delta)n ,$$

then, there is an asymptotically optimal solution of the following form, for some sequence of $l + 1$ processors which we denote $P_{\rho(1)}, ..., P_{\rho(l+1)}$:

• For $1 \leq j \leq l$ execute on processor $P_{\rho(j)}$ all the tasks with cost 0 on this processor and cost e_o on the preceding processors.

• Execute δn tasks with cost 0 on $P_{\rho(l+1)}$

• Execute (with individual costs e_o) the remaining tasks on $P_{\rho(1)}$.

We can then easily compute the asymptotic loads of the processors $P_{\rho(1)}, ..., P_{\rho(l+1)}$ in this assignment and the theorem is obtained by minimizing the resulting cost relatively to n_o. □

3 The Case of a Regular Communication Graph

We denote by $G(n, r - reg)$ the random regular graph of degree r on n vertices. **Theorem 2** *Let us consider model 2 with $GC \sim G(n, r - reg)$, $r \geq 3$ fixed, and let us assume that the number of processors tends to infinity with n. Let ω be any entry and let us define the functionals $Cost_{exec}(.)$ and $Cost_{com}(.)$ by $Cost_{exec}(\omega) = \min\{Cost(A) : A \text{ minimizes } Exec(\omega)\}$, and $Cost_{com}(\omega) = \min\{Cost(A) : A \text{ minimizes } Com(\omega)\}$. Let us define moreover*

$$\overline{Opt}(\omega) = \min\{Cost_{exec}(\omega), Cost_{com}(\omega)\} .$$

Then there exists a strictly positive constant γ_r such that

$$\frac{\overline{Opt}(\omega)}{Opt(\omega)} \leq \gamma_r$$

with probability tending to 1 as $n \to \infty$ and uniformly in the whole ranges of the parameters e, q and c.

Proof of Theorem 2 The proof is based on the following "expansion" lemma (see Lubotzky [2] for analogous results))

Lemma 3 *Let $r \geq 3$. There exists a strictly positive constant β_r such that, with probability tending to 1 as n tends to infinity, every cut $\delta(S)$ of $G(n, r - reg)$ defined by a set of vertices S of cardinality $|S| \leq n/2$ has size $|\delta(S)| \geq r\beta_r|S|$.*

For the proof of theorem 2, we need first bounds for the values of the functionals $Cost_{exec}$ and $Cost_{com}$.

i) Bounding of $Cost_{exec}$. Let A denote the assignment in which the tasks which have non-zero execution costs on all the processors are assigned to P_1 and each of the other tasks is assigned to the processor with smallest index on which it has cost 0. Clearly, A has minimum execution cost and we have thus $Cost_{exec} \leq Cost(A)$ for every ω. Writing $Int(A) = |Cut(A) \cap E(GC)|$, we have of course $Com(A) = c_o n^{-1} Int(A)$. For $1 \leq i < j \leq \infty$. It can then be proved that we have

$$Int(A) = (1 + o(1)) \frac{nrq}{1+q}$$

The communication cost of A will thus satisfy, for a.e. entry,

$$Cost_{exec} \leq \frac{(1 + o(1))nrqc}{1+q}$$

ii) Bounding of $Cost_{com}$. In order to obtain a minimum communication cost, we must assign $n(1 - o(1))$ tasks to the same processor. This gives

$$Cost_{com} = qne(1 + o(1)) \, .$$

We claim now that we have, almost always, for any assignment A,

(1) $$Exec(A) \leq \frac{qne}{2} \longrightarrow Com(A) \geq \frac{0.49\lambda_r nqc}{1+q},$$

which implies obviously

$$Opt \geq \min\{(1/2)qne, 0.49\lambda_r nqc(1+q)^{-1}\} \, .$$

Since by i) and ii) we have at our disposal solutions with costs $(1+o(1))nrqc/(1+q)$ and $qne(1 + o(1))$, the theorem follows with any $\gamma_r > \frac{1}{0.49\lambda_r}$. It remains only to prove the claim. Assume $Exec(A) \leq (1/2)qne$, which means of course that at least $(1 - q/2)n$ tasks are executed with cost 0. By lemma 3, if α is any constant strictly smaller than $1/2$, there is necessarily a set of processors which executes a total number of tasks lying in the interval $I = [\alpha nq, (1 - \alpha q)n]$. Fix now $\alpha = 0.49$. The size of the cut of the communication graph corresponding to A is with probability 1-o(1) at least $0.49\lambda_r nrq$, giving a communication cost $Com(A) \geq 0.49\lambda_r nrqc$, as was to be proved. □

It can be checked that Lemma 3 holds with constants $\lambda_r \geq 0.08$ for each $r \geq 3$. Theorem 2 provides thus an allocation algorithm with approximation ratio $\gamma \leq 26$ on almost all entry in model 2, for each r.

4 The Case of Continuous Costs Distributions

We assume now the following:
- Each execution cost is uniformly distributed in an interval $[0, e_o]$, for some $e_o \in N^+\backslash\{0\}$.
- The communication costs are uniformly distributed in an interval $[0, c]$ where $c = c(n) \in N^+\backslash\{0\}$.

We shall assume for simplicity that the number m of processors is fixed. The proof of lemma 2 carries over to this case without difficulty. We can thus, similarly as in section 3, restate the problem as that of finding an assignment A which minimises the functional $\overline{Cost}$ defined by $\overline{Cost}(A) = Exec(A) + \frac{pc_o}{2n}S(A)$.

Consider only the assignments which give non-increasing loads $|A^{-1}P_1| \geq |A^{-1}P_2| \geq .... \geq |A^{-1}P_m|$ to $P_1, ..., P_m$. It is then eassy to show that there are non-increasing constants $\gamma_1 \geq \gamma_2 \geq ..... \geq \gamma_m$ such that the assignment A defined by

$$
\begin{aligned}
A^{-1}(P_1) &= \{t : e(t, P_1) \leq \gamma_1 e_o\} \\
A^{-1}(P_2) &= \{t : e(t, P_2) \leq \gamma_2 e_o\} \backslash A^{-1}(P_1)
\end{aligned}
$$

$$
A^{-1}(P_m) = \{t : e(t, P_m) \leq \gamma_m e_o\} \backslash \cup_{j=1}^{m-1} A^{-1}(P_m)
$$

is optimal with respect to the functional $\overline{Cost}(.)$ (and thus also asymptotically optimal with respect to $Cost(.)$). Using simple algebra, we can then show that, setting $\pi_o = 1$ and $\pi_i = \Pi_{j=1}^{i}(1 - \gamma_j)$, in order to minimize the overall cost corresponding to the strategy just defined, we have to minimize the function

$$
f(\gamma_1, ..., \gamma_m) = \frac{e_o}{2} \sum_{i=1}^{m} \frac{(\pi_{i-1} - \pi_i)^2}{\pi_{i-1}} + \frac{c_o}{4}\left(1 - \sum_{i=1}^{m}(\pi_{i-1} - \pi_i)^2\right).
$$

Clearly f can be minimised by using dynamic programming. $\qquad\square$

References

1. B. Bollobás, Random Graphs, Academic Press, London 1985.
2. A. Lubotzky, Discrete Groups, Expanding Graphs and Invariant Measures, Birkhäuser, 1994.
3. Billonnet A., Costa M.C., Sutter A., An Efficient Algorithm for the Task Allocation Problem, *Journal of the Association for Computing Machinary*, Vol. 39, No. 3, pp. 502-518, 1992.
4. Bokhari S.H., A Shortest Tree Algorithm for Optimal Assignments Across Space and Time in a Distributed Processor System, *IEEE Trans. Softw. Eng.*, Vol. SE-7, No. 6, 1981.
5. Fernandez-Baca D., Allocating Modules to Processors in a Distributed System, *IEEE Trans. Softw. Eng.*, Vol. 15, No. 11, 1989.
6. Magirou V.F., Milis J.Z., An Algorithm for the Multiprocessor Assignment Problem, *Operation Research Letters* 8, 1989, 351-356.
7. Dalhaus E., Johnson D. S., Papadimitriou C. H., Seymour P., and Yannakakis M., The Complexity of Multiway Cut, *In Proc. 24th ACM STOC 1992*, 241-251.
8. Stone H. S., Multiprocessor Scheduling with the Aid of Network Flow Algorithms, *IEEE Trans. Softw. Eng.*, Vol. SE-3, No. 1, 1977.

UNIVERSITÉ DE PARIS SUD, L.R.I, CNRS, UA 410, CENTRE D'ORSAY, 91405 ORSAY, FRANCE

Dynamically Adapting the Degree of Parallelism with Reflexive Programs

Niels Reimer (`reimer@ira.uka.de`) *
Stefan U. Hänßgen (`haenssgen@ira.uka.de`)
Walter F. Tichy (`tichy@ira.uka.de`)

IPD, Fakultät für Informatik, Universität Karlsruhe, Germany

Abstract. In this paper we present a new method for achieving a higher cost–efficiency on parallel computers. We insert routines into a program which detect the amount of computational work without using problem–specific parameters and adapt the number of used CPUs at runtime under given speedup/efficiency constraints. Several user–tunable strategies for selecting the number of processors are presented and compared. The modularity of this approach and its application–independence permit a general use on parallel computers with a scalable degree of parallelism.

1 Introduction

Programs on parallel computers usually use all available processors. This is a waste of resources if the load is not evenly distributed or the amount of work is too small to justify a further partitioning. Our goal is to reduce the costs[1] by adapting the number of used processors dynamically according to the current load. In order to do so, the program observes its parallel routines and controls the degree of parallelism individually at runtime. This leads to an implicit load balancing because the load is automatically distributed evenly with each call of the parallel routines. In this paper we therefore do not deal with load balancing algorithms which are described e.g. in [1]. The search for related work in the area of reflexive programs or adapting the amount of parallel resources showed no exploitable references.

In our work we improved the cost–efficiency of a parallelised molecular dynamics (MD) simulation program, but any application with frequent calls of parallel subroutines can benefit from this method. We define the cost–efficiency as the sequential-to-parallel cost ratio.

2 Molecular Dynamics as an Irregular Problem

The importance of MD in the area of biological, chemical and medical research is increasing. Simulations with larger molecules require a computational performance which necessiates the use of parallel computers. We first introduce the principles of MD briefly and show that it is an example of an irregular problem.

---

* This research was performed at the EMBL (European Molecular Biology Laboratory) Heidelberg in co-operation with the University of Karlsruhe.
[1] The cost is the sum of all used CPU seconds over all used processors.

MD simulations calculate the interactions of particles (molecules/atoms) in order to derive geometrical and structural properties of molecules. For simulation purpose, the timescale is split into regular steps. At each timestep, the interactions of the particles are calculated and used to determine the position of each particle in the next timestep. To be physically accurate, ideally the interaction of each pair of particles has to be considered. Since the forces decay at least with the square of the particles' distance, one can speed up calculation by ignoring the interactions to particles beyond a certain cutoff radius from a particle. However, the relevant particle pairs then have to be managed in addition to the force calculations. Most MD–programs perform the following cycle of steps:

1. **Generate pairlist** with all relevant pairs of particles.
2. **Calculate forces** according to the pairlists and the particle data.
3. **Update particle data** by applying the forces to the particles.

Parallelisation approaches of MD–programs usually associate particle data to processors. The movement of the particles then leads to unpredictable irregular communication patterns among the processors, hence parallel MD is an irregular problem. The corresponding pairlist routine shows an increase of work load with the square of the number of particles. The work load of the force calculation routines increases only linearily with the number of particles because the maximum number of particles inside a cutoff radius sphere is limited. Further information about MD can be found in [3].

To allow the use of more specialised force calculation routines, the MD–program ARGOS [8] distinguishes between two classes of particles:

1. **Solvent particles** which are all equal (generally water molecules).
2. **Solute particles** which are normally the atoms of the examined chemical compounds, e.g., proteins.

As a result, there are three pairlist and three force calculation routines, each with its individual amount of work. For the pairlist routines this depends on the number of particles, which is constant within each simulation. The work load for the force calculation depends on the density of particles, which can vary to a large extent during simulation. Therefore, the most cost–efficient number of processors to use for each routine is different and variable.

Different approaches of the parallelisation of a MD–program are described in the work of Hanxleden [2]. As part of our work, we parallelised the sequential MD–program "ARGOS" [7], [8] on a SGI Power Challenge, a shared memory machine with 16 R8000 processors [6].

3 Dynamically Adapting the Degree of Parallelism

Traditional load balancing methods redistribute the amount of work among all processors of the parallel computer at certain time intervals or on demand in order to reduce the number of idle processors. This leads to a higher cost–efficiency and a shorter runtime, provided that there is sufficient work for each processor. However, with powerful processors suitable for coarse–grained parallelisation this is often not the case since larger pieces of work cannot be distributed evenly. It is then advantageous to adapt the number of used processors to the program's resource consumption to offer each processor a suitable amount of work. The unused processors of this parallel machine (or of a cluster of workstations) are not wasted since they are available to all other users. The cost function therefore only takes the CPU–seconds of the used processors into account.

If the parallelised program contains sequential parts and several parallel routines, each of these routines is likely to require a different number of processors to reach an appropriate load level. Furthermore, this number can change during runtime. All of these problems occur in the parallelised version of ARGOS. Most computation time is consumed by the pairlist generation and the force calculation, hence it is sufficient to parallelise only these particular routines.

The idea is to estimate the load produced by each parallel routine and adapt the number of assigned processors accordingly. Thus, the program observes its own behaviour, which is why we call it reflexive. The load determination should be problem– and machine–independent. The convincing approach is to measure the time spent inside the parallel part. The requirement of adapting each parallel routine individually can be satisfied using a separate adaptation for each routine. This also leads to more modular code. Each parallel routine is therefore encaspulated in a preroutine which sequentially executes the following tasks:

1. Set the number of processors for the parallel routine
2. Start the timing
3. Invoke the parallel routine
4. Stop the timing
5. Calculate data for the setting of the number at the next invocation

The determination of the number of processors at the next invocation is based upon calculations of the timings, and is done according to a strategy described later. Figure 1 represents the encapsulation and the structure of a preroutine.

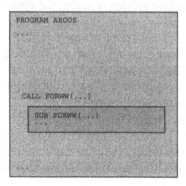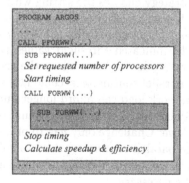

Fig. 1. Structure of the program with and without preroutine. The force calculation routine FORWW is executed in parallel.

With this approach, we gain a dynamic adaptation at runtime and a reflexive behaviour of the program without using problem–specific data. This implies the possibility to combine this approach with any parallel application.

4 Adaptation Strategies

In this paper we will consider three strategies in detail[2]. The *speedup–driven incremental search strategy (SISS)* works in the following way. The initial setting is one processor to determine the "sequential" execution time of the controlled routine. On return from the parallel routine call, the timing is taken and speedup and efficiency are calculated. With every subsequent invocation, the number of processors is increased by one if the measured efficiency rate is above and not too close to a fixed threshold (e.g. the rate is 5% above the threshold EFFTHR = 50%). If it is inside this region, the number remains fixed to minimise the number of threshold violations. If it is below the threshold, the number is decreased by one. The next timing results in a new efficiency rate and so on. After a certain number of invocations, the strategy calibrates itself by repeating the one-processor run to keep the "sequential" execution time up-to-date for the next calculations. Once the optimum is reached, the number of processors oscillates or remains temporarily fixed, which guarantees that the average efficiency is close to the threshold. An oscillation itself causes no additional costs since the number has to be set anyway at each invocation of the parallel routine.

An incremental search runs the risk of finding only a local mimimum. This problem was not encountered in the parallel version of ARGOS, but may occur with other applications.

To avoid this, a global search strategy can be used which splits the adaptation process into three phases: 1) a global search over all possible processor numbers is performed, 2) the best setting with the highest speedup is chosen under the restriction that the efficiency has to be above the threshold value. This feature gives the strategy its name: *speedup–driven global search strategy (SGSS)*. 3) this setting is kept fixed for a certain number of invocations. After this, the strategy starts again with the first phase (calibration) to gather the data.

A variation of this strategy is derived by changing the optimisation goal. This last strategy chooses the setting with the highest efficiency under the constraint that it must guarantee a speedup of at least a certain threshold value. This strategy is therefore called *efficiency–driven global search strategy (EGSS)*.

The indicated threshold values of the strategies are user-adjustable parameters. Modularity also allows the use of different parameters and strategies for each parallel routine to accomodate special requirements, e.g., routines with a stable work load can afford longer durations of the third phase.

Global searches for the optimum processor number are not prohibitive since the Power Challenge only has 16 processors. That means the first 16 invocations of the parallel routine are used to collect the timing data for each setting. On parallel computers with significantly more processors other scanning approaches will be necessary.

5 Results

Simulations of scenarios in which the pairlist lengths change, especially all denaturation simulations, challenge the adaptation algorithms with a dynamically

---

[2] For a closer study of more strategies we refer the reader to [5].

changing work load. Figure 2 shows the evolution of the pairlist lengths obtained from a denaturation simulation of a large protein (*myoglobin*) in water.

To reduce the comparison of the strategies to the highlights, we here present only the results for the force calculation of the solvent–solvent interactions because their work load changes most dramatically. The adaptation of routines with a more stable work load are equally accurate for all strategies. Figures 3 and 4 show the numbers of processors used for the force calculation of the solvent–solvent interactions using the SISS and the SGSS.

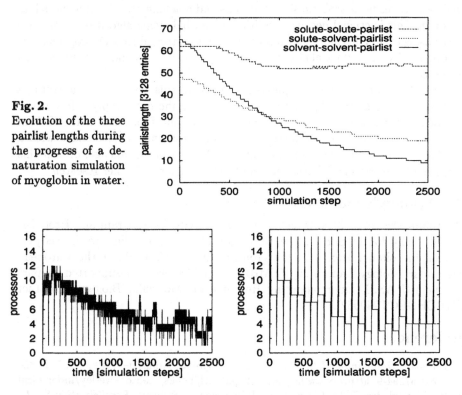

Fig. 2.
Evolution of the three pairlist lengths during the progress of a denaturation simulation of myoglobin in water.

Fig. 3. Assigned processors for the force calculation of the solvent–solvent interactions using SISS

Fig. 4. Assigned processors for the force calculation of the solvent–solvent interactions using SGSS

The requested numbers of processors follow ideally the same trend as the pairlist lengths. The comparision of the curves in figure 3 and 4 shows that the results of the incremental search correspond to those of the global search, which demonstrates that local minima have no effect here.

Table 1 shows the runtimes and the costs obtained from the denaturation simulation to compare the different strategies with the commonly used alternative (*16 P*) which is to use always the maximum available number of processors (here 16).

These numbers demonstrate the potential of self–adapting reflexive programs to reduce the costs while maintaining a reasonable speedup.

	SISS	SGSS	EGSS	16 P
Runtime [sec]	3831	3436	4220	2886
Cost [CPUsec]	20817	23038	18626	40508

Table 1. Runtimes and costs of the different strategies and the 16–processor alternative

6 Conclusion and Future Work

Reflexive programs that dynamically adapt their degree of parallelism show that a problem–independent self–control mechanism can be used to achieve a higher cost–efficiency. The mechanism presented considers runtimes and thus automatically takes both problem size variations and machine–specific influences into account. This is crucial because traditional load balancing algorithms disregard these aspects. Furthermore, our approach is not restricted to MD–programs but can be used with any parallelised application that allows timings of the parallel executed parts.

Still, there are many open questions related to this work. What advantages and disadvantages would the use of problem–specific data imply? How can a compiler for parallel machines automatically benefit from this method? Will (heterogenous) workstation clusters of a PVM environment [4] behave with a similar "linear" and smooth scaling like the SGI Power Challenge, or will this require other strategies? These questions are a matter of further research.

7 Acknowledgements

We thank Dr. T. P. Straatsma for use of the ARGOS program and Prof. Dr. W. F. Tichy for support at the University of Karlsruhe. This work was performed in collaboration with the group of Dr. R. C. Wade at the European Molecular Biology Laboratory (EMBL) at Heidelberg and supported in part by the EU ASLI Supercomputing Resource for Molecular Biology (Contract ERBCHGECT940062).

References

1. I. Foster, *Designing and Building Parallel Programs*, Addison–Wesley, 1995, ISBN: 0-201-57594-9, http://www.hensa.ac.uk/parallel/books/addison–wesley/index.html
2. R. v. Hanxleden, T. W. Clark, J. A. McCammon, L. R. Scott, *Parallelization Strategies for a Molecular Dynamics Program*, Intel Technology Focus Conf. Proc., 1992
3. J. A. McCammon und S. C. Harvey, *Dynamics of proteins and nucleic acids*, Cambridge University Press 1987, ISBN: 0-521-35654-0
4. A. Geist, A. Beguelin, J. Dongarra, W. Jiang, R. Manchek and V. S. Sunderam, *A Users' Guide and Tutorial for Network Parallel Computing*, MIT Press, November 1994, ISBN: 0-262-57108-0, http://www.hensa.ac.uk/parallel/books/mit/pvm
5. N. Reimer, *Dynamische Einstellung des Parallelitätsgrades mit reflexiven Programmen*, reimer@ira.uka.de, University of Karlsruhe, January 1996
6. Silicon Graphics Inc., *Power Challenge Technical Report*, SGI 2011 Northern Shoreline Boulevard, Mountain View, CA 94039-7311, 1994
7. T. P. Straatsma, *ARGOS Reference Manual*, tp_straatsma@pnl.gov, 1994
8. T. P. Straatsma, J. A. McCammon, *ARGOS, a vectorized general molecular dynamics program*, Journal of Computational Chemistry II(8): 943-951, 1990

On the Complexity of the Generalized Block Distribution

Michelangelo Grigni[1] and Fredrik Manne[2]

[1] Department of Mathematics and Computer Science, Emory University,
Atlanta, Georgia 30322, USA
[2] Department of Informatics, University of Bergen,
N-5020 Bergen, Norway

Abstract. We consider the problem of mapping an array onto a mesh of processors in such a way that locality is preserved. When the computational work associated with the array is distributed in an unstructured way the generalized block distribution has been recognized as an efficient way of achieving an even load balance while at the same time imposing a simple communication pattern.

In this paper we consider the problem of computing an optimal generalized block distribution. We show that this problem is NP-complete even for very simple cost functions. We also classify a number of variants of the general problem.

Keywords: Load balancing, parallel data structures, scheduling and mapping

1 Introduction

A basic task in parallel computing is the partitioning and subsequent distribution of data among processors. The problem one faces in this operation is how to balance two often contradictory aims; finding an equal distribution of the computational work and at the same time minimizing the imposed communication.

For data stored in an array several high performance computing languages allow the user to specify a partitioning and distribution of data onto a logical set of processors. The compiler then maps the data onto the physical processors and determines the communication pattern. An example of such a scheme is the block distribution found in languages such as Vienna Fortran [1] and HPF [7]. This mapping results in equal size blocks and therefore cannot adapt to any load imbalance which might be present.

More general partitioning schemes which have been proposed for these kinds of problems include the generalized and semi-generalized block distribution [2, 12, 13, 14]. The generalized block distribution preserves the array-structured communication of the block distribution while at the same time allowing for different sized blocks.

In [10] a number of algorithms were described for computing a well-balanced generalized block distribution. These were compared with other distribution schemes which showed that in many cases the generalized block distribution can give a good load balance while at the same time maintaining a simple communication pattern.

In this paper we show that the problem of computing a generalized block distribution of cost less than some constant K is NP-complete, even for very simple cost functions. This implies that one cannot generally expect to compute an optimal generalized block distribution.

The outline of this paper is as follows: In Section 2 we give a formal definition of the problem, in Section 3 we show that the problem of determining whether there exists a solution of cost less than K is NP-complete, and finally in Section 4 we discuss variants of this problem and point to some open problems.

2 The Generalized Block Distribution

For integers a and b, let $[a, b]$ denote the interval of integers $\{a, a + 1, \ldots, b\}$ (empty if $a > b$). Let $[a]$ denote $[1, a]$.

Given $A \in \Re^{m \times n}$ and integers p and q such that $p \in [m]$ and $q \in [n]$. Let $R = (r_0, r_1, \ldots, r_p)$ be a sequence of integers such that $1 = r_0 \leq r_1 \leq \ldots \leq r_p = m + 1$. Then R defines a *partition* of $[m]$ into the p intervals $[r_i, r_{i+1} - 1]$, for i in $[0, p - 1]$. We denote each interval by R_i. Note that some intervals may be the empty interval.

Definition 1 General Block Distribution. Given A, p and q as above, a *generalized block distribution* consists of a partition of $[m]$ into p intervals and of $[n]$ into q intervals, so that A partitions into $p \times q$ contiguous blocks. For $i \in [p]$ and $j \in [q]$, we denote the ijth block by A_{ij}.

See Fig. 1 for an example of the generalized block distribution.

The generalized block distribution was first discussed by Fox *et al.* [4] and implemented as part of Superb environment [14] and later in Vienna Fortran [3]. It is also a candidate to be included as part of the ongoing HPF2 effort [8]. See [2] and [9] for examples of how the generalized block distribution can be used in areas such as sparse-matrix and particle-in-cell computations.

In a parallel environment the time spent on a computation is determined by the processor taking the longest time. To estimate the time needed to process each block we define a non-negative cost function ϕ on contiguous blocks of A. We assume that if a and b are blocks of A such that a is contained in b then $\phi(a) \leq \phi(b)$, and that $\phi(a) = 0$ if and only if a is the empty block. For reasonable functions ϕ we also expect that if the value of $\phi(a)$ (or $\phi(b)$) is known then the value of $\phi(b)$ (or $\phi(a)$) can be computed in $O(|b| - |a|)$ time. An example of ϕ might be the number of non-zero elements, or the sum of the absolute values of the elements in a block.

Then the natural optimization problem is to find a generalized block distribution that minimizes the maximum ϕ over all blocks. The equivalent decision problem is the following:

(GBD) Instance: A, p, q and ϕ as above, and an integer K.
Question: Does there exist a generalized block distribution on A such that

$$\max_{i \in [p], j \in [q]} \phi(A_{ij}) \leq K .$$

8	1	3	7	1	1
3	3	1	2	0	1
1	2	0	0	1	1
2	4	2	3	1	2
3	1	0	3	1	2
6	6	2	2	3	1

Fig. 1. An example of the generalized block distribution

3   GBD is NP-Complete

In this section we show that GBD is NP-complete. First we note that a solution to GBD can be verified efficiently, so GBD is in NP. To show that GBD is NP-complete we will reduce the NP-complete problem "Balanced Complete Bipartite Subgraph" [5, GT24] to GBD.

[Problem GT24] Balanced Complete Bipartite Subgraph (BCBS)
Instance: Given a bipartite graph $G = (V_1, V_2, E)$, and a positive integer K.

Question: Are there subsets $U_1 \subseteq V_1$ and $U_2 \subseteq V_2$ such that $|U_1| = |U_2| = K$, and such that $u \in U_1$ and $v \in U_2$ imply $(u, v) \in E$ (that is, $U_1 \times U_2 \subseteq E$)?

Note that we may add isolated vertices above to assure that $|V_1| = |V_2|$. We now transform BCBS to a problem on the bipartite complement of G. That is, graph G' has the same vertex sets and the edge set $E' = V_1 \times V_2 - E$. Also let $K' = |V_1| - K$. We now have a problem equivalent to BCBS:

Balanced Bipartite Cover (**BBC**)
Instance: Given a bipartite graph $G' = (V_1, V_2, E')$ with $|V_1| = |V_2|$ and a positive integer K'.
Question: Are there subsets $U_1 \subseteq V_1$ and $U_2 \subseteq V_2$ such that $|U_1| = |U_2| = K'$, and such that each edge $(u, v) \in E'$ has either $u \in U_1$ or $v \in U_2$?

It is clear from the construction of G' that BBC is NP-complete. Note that a solution for BBC leaves no "uncovered" edges between $V_1 - U_1$ and $V_2 - U_2$. Thus BBC may be formulated in terms of the adjacency matrix of G':

Is it possible to choose K rows and K columns of a matrix so that these rows and columns contain all the non-zero entries?

We now show how to reduce an instance (G', K') of BBC to a particular instance (A, p, q, K, ϕ) of GBD. In fact we will have $K = 1$ and ϕ equal to the number of non-zero elements in a block.

Let $n = |V_1| = |V_2|$ in the given instance of BBC. We construct a $2(n + 1) \times 2(n+1)$ zero-one matrix A as part of the GBD instance. The rows of A are labeled (in order) $\{s_{0,0}, s_{0,1}, s_{1,0}, s_{1,1}, \ldots s_{n,0}, s_{n,1}\}$, and similarly the columns are labeled $\{t_{0,0}, t_{0,1}, t_{1,0}, t_{1,1}, \ldots t_{n,0}, t_{n,1}\}$. The following entries of A are set to one:

1. $(s_{0,0}, t_{0,0})$
2. $(s_{0,0}, t_{2i,1})$ and $(s_{0,0}, t_{2i+1,0})$ for $0 \leq i < \lceil n/2 \rceil$
3. $(s_{0,1}, t_{2i+1,1})$ and $(s_{0,1}, t_{2i+2,0})$ for $0 \leq i < \lfloor n/2 \rfloor$
4. $(s_{2i,1}, t_{0,0})$ and $(s_{2i+1,0}, t_{0,0})$ for $0 \leq i < \lceil m/2 \rceil$
5. $(s_{2i+1,1}, t_{0,1})$ and $(s_{2i+2,0}, t_{0,1})$ for $0 \leq i < \lfloor m/2 \rfloor$
6. $(s_{i,0}, t_{j,0})$ and $(s_{i,1}, t_{j,1})$, for all $(i, j) \in E'$.

All other entries of A are set to zero. The first two rows and columns of the matrix in Fig. 2 illustrate how rules 1 through 5 effect A. If we are to find a solution to GBD with $K = 1$, these elements force us to at least place $n + 1$ horizontal and $n + 1$ vertical delimiters as shown by the dotted lines. Setting $p = q = n + K' + 2$, this leaves us with K' horizontal delimiters and K' vertical delimiters to partition the remaining matrix. For each edge in G', rule 6 constructs a 2×2 block in A with ones on the diagonal as shown in Fig. 2. Each such block must be split by either a horizontal or a vertical line (or both) if we are to achieve a cost of at most 1. Splitting such a block with a horizontal delimiter corresponds to choosing a vertex from V_1 in BBC, and splitting it with a vertical delimiter corresponds to choosing a vertex in V_2. It is clear from the construction of this matrix that there exists a solution to this GBD problem if and only if the corresponding BBC problem has a solution. Thus we can state our main result:

Theorem 2. *GBD is NP-Complete.*

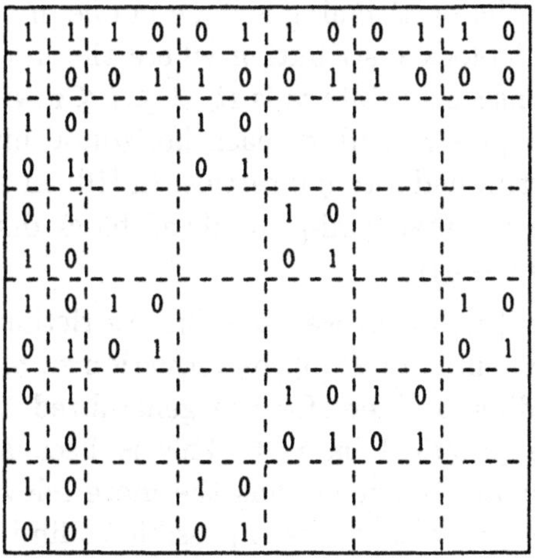

```
1 1 1 0 0 1 1 0 0 1 1 0
1 0 0 1 1 0 0 1 1 0 0 0
1 0     1 0
0 1     0 1
0 1         1 0
1 0         0 1
1 0 1 0             1 0
0 1 0 1             0 1
0 1         1 0 1 0
1 0         0 1 0 1
1 0     1 0
0 0     0 1
```

Fig. 2. Forcing the delimiters to create 2×2 squares

4 Conclusion

We have shown that GBD is NP-complete with ϕ equal to the number of elements in a block. This implies that GBD remains NP-complete for any derived cost function such as the sum of the elements in a block. Thus we have to settle for approximation algorithms to achieve an even load balance for this distribution. In a recent development [6] it has been shown that if $p = q$ with ϕ equal to the sum of the elements in a block then one of the algorithms in [10] gives a solution that is guaranteed to be within a bound of $4\sqrt{p}$ of the optimal.

We note that the following three variants of GBD can be solved in polynomial time:

- $n = q = 1$. The problem now becomes to partition a vector of length m into p segments. This problem has been studied extensively and the current fastest algorithm for computing an optimal solution runs in time $O(p(m - p))$ [11].
- p is fixed. Assume that we are given a fixed horizontal partition. The cost of a vertical interval is now defined to be the maximum cost of the p blocks inside this interval. Using this cost function this problem becomes equivalent to the one dimensional case. Since there are only polynomial many placements of the $p - 1$ horizontal delimiters this problem is also solvable in polynomial time.
- If we relax how the partitioning is done in one dimension we get the semi-generalized block distribution where the interval $[m]$ is partitioned into p consecutive intervals R_i, $1 \le i \le p$ without restrictions on the size of $r_{i+1} - r_i$ and for each horizontal interval R_i, the interval $[n]$ is partitioned into q intervals. In [10] an algorithm is given to computes an optimal semi-generalized block distribution in time $O(pqm(m - p)(n - q))$.

If, instead of $|V_1| = |V_2| = K$, we have the restriction $|V_1| + |V_2| = K$ then the BCBS problem is in P [5], by reduction to matching. We note that the corresponding problem for the generalized block distribution is of no immediate practical interest. This is because the number of processors $p \times q$ usually is fixed. Thus the more relevant question is if given the number of processors r, is it possible to find a factorization of $r = p \times q$ that solves the GBD problem. However, as the following shows this problem still remains NP-complete. Given an instance of GBD with cost matrix A, $K = 1$, and ϕ equal to the number of elements in a block. Let g be the smallest prime such that $g > \max\{p, q\}$ and let $r = g^2$. We construct a new matrix C with A and a matrix B on the diagonal where B consists of a $(g - p) \times (g - q)$ block of all ones. In addition we set $c_{g,n} = c_{m,g} = 1$. All other elements of C are set to zero. Any solution to this problem requires that B is separated from A and that B is completely partitioned using $g - p$ horizontal delimiters and $g - q$ vertical ones. Since the only factorizations of r are $r = 1 \times g^2$, $r = g^2 \times 1$, and $r = g \times g$ it follows that r must be factored into $g \times g$ if we are to obtain a positive solution. This leaves $p - 1$ horizontal delimiters and $q - 1$ vertical ones to partition A. Thus this problem can be solved if and only if we can solve the corresponding GBD problem as well.

Another case of interested is the symmetric generalized block distribution. Here we assume that $m = n$ and $p = q$ and we add the extra restriction to any solution that $p_i = q_i$ for $1 \leq i \leq p$. This means that the diagonal blocks will be square and the diagonal elements of the matrix will lie on the diagonal processors. This is very convenient if one wants to gather a vector along the rows and then distribute the result along the columns. This is a typical situation in iterative linear solvers where one is performing series of matrix-vector multiplications. This problem appears simpler than the general problem since the number of possible solutions is reduces from $\binom{m}{p} \times \binom{n}{q}$ to $\binom{m}{p}$. However, we do not know the complexity of this problem.

References

1. B. Chapman, P. Mehrotra, and H. Zima, *Programming in Vienna Fortran*, Sci. Prog., 1 (1992), pp. 31–50.

2. ———, *High performance Fortran languages: Advanced applications and their implementation*, Future Generation Computer Systems, (1995), pp. 401–407.

3. ———, *Extending HPF for advanced data parallel applications*, IEEE Trans. Par. Dist. Syst., (Fall 1994), pp. 59–70.

4. G. Fox, M. Johnson, G. Lyzenga, S. Otto, J. Salmon, and D. Walker, *Solving Problems on Concurrent Processors*, vol. 1, Prentice-Hall, Englewood Cliffs, NJ, 1988.

5. M. R. Garey and D. S. Johnson, *Computers and Intractability*, Freeman, 1979.

6. M. Halldorsson and F. Manne. Private communications.

7. High Performance Fortran Forum, *High performance language specification. Version 1.0*, Sci. Prog., 1–2 (1993), pp. 1–170.

8. *High Performance Fortran Forum Home Page.* http://www.crpc.rice.edu/HPFF/home.html.

9. F. Manne, *Load Balancing in Parallel Sparse Matrix Computations*, PhD thesis, University of Bergen, Norway, 1993.

10. F. Manne and T. Sørevik, *Structured partitioning of arrays*, Tech. Rep. CS-96-119, Department of Informatics, University of Bergen, Norway, 1996.

11. B. Olstad and F. Manne, *Efficient partitioning of sequences*, IEEE Trans. Comput., 44 (1995), pp. 1322–1326.

12. M. UJALDON, S. D. SHARMA, J. SALTZ, AND E. ZAPATA, *Run-time techniques for parallelizing sparse matrix problems*, in Proceedings of 1995 Workshop on Irregular Problems, 1995.

13. M. UJALDON, E. L. ZAPATA, B. M. CHAPMAN, AND H. P. ZIMA, *Vienna-Fortran/HPF extensions for sparse and irregular problems and their compilation*. Submitted to IEEE Trans. Par. Dist. Syst.

14. H. ZIMA, H. BAST, AND M. GERNDT, *Superb: A tool for semi-automatic MIMD/SIMD parallelization*, Parallel Comput., (1986), pp. 1–18.

Adaptive Load Balancing of Irregular Applications
A Case Study: IDA* Applied to the 15-Puzzle Problem

N. Melab, N. Devesa[†], M.P. Lecouffe, B. Toursel[†]
Laboratoire d'Informatique Fondamentale de Lille (CNRS URA 369)
Université des Sciences et Technologies de Lille1
59655 Villeneuve d'Ascq cedex -France
E-mail: melab@lifl.lifl.fr - Tel 20 43 45 39 - fax (33) 20 43 65 66
[†]EUDIL(Ecole Universitaire D'Ingénieurs de Lille)

Abstract

This paper describes an adaptive algorithm called ALBA (Adaptive Load Balancing Algorithm) for load balancing of irregular applications on parallel and distributed architectures. ALBA uses an adaptive centralized load information collection policy to maintain a global current load state in the machine. The transfer and location decisions are taken locally on each node of the architecture. A thread-based approach is used to implement ALBA on a farm of DEC/ALPHA processors. An application to a multithreaded IDA* program applied to the 15-puzzle problem is presented. An average speed-up of 14.8 has been obtained on the longest instances of the problem on a farm of 16 processors.

1 Introduction

The performance of an application execution on a distributed architecture depends strongly on the policy used to distribute the processes composing the application among the nodes of the architecture (a node consists of a processor with its local memory and its communication interface). A distribution policy can be either statical or dynamical. For irregular problems a dynamic load balancing algorithm is rather better than a static one because the former takes in account the current load state of the machine. This load state can be obtained by exchanging information between the different nodes of the architecture. On this information basis the load balancing algorithm takes transfer and location decisions. The main purpose of a dynamic load balancing algorithm is to improve the performance of an application execution by redistributing its workload among the nodes of the machine. This can be done, on the one hand, by providing an accurate and current information without inducing excessive computation and communication overheads. So, a good choice of the load information collection frequency is needed and the best choice is to adjust the frequency to the load variation in the machine. On the other hand, the algorithm must dynamically take transfer and location decisions which do not lead to a flood or a laziness of nodes. In order to overlap the communications involved in the collection of the load information and the transfers of processes a multithreaded environment is well suited to implement the algorithm.

Within the framework of the PARALF[1] project of the PALOMA[2] team, our objective is to provide a thread-based adaptive load balancing algorithm which satisfies the purposes quoted above. Moreover, we aim at evaluating the performance of our algorithm on some irregular applications. In this paper, we focus on one combinatorial problem. It is about the IDA* algorithm applied to the 15-puzzle problem [6]. A thread-based version of this application is presented with some performance measurements on a farm of DEC/ALPHA processors and under a multithreaded and distributed programming environment called PM^2[9].

Section 2 briefly summarizes the related work on the load balancing area. The proposed dynamic load balancing algorithm is detailed in section 3. Section 4 presents the architecture and environment underlying to our algorithm implementation. Before the conclusion is drawn, section 5 briefly describes the IDA* algorithm and the 15-puzzle problem, and some results are also presented.

2 Dynamic load balancing

When executing a program on a distributed architecture it is possible for some nodes to be *heavily loaded* while others are *idle*, resulting in a poor overall system performance[3]. The main purpose of a dynamic load balancing algorithm is to improve the efficiency of the execution by attempting to redistribute at best the workload among the nodes during the execution. The algorithm is generally composed of three agents : an information agent, a transfer agent and a location agent. The information agent includes a *computation function of the load* of any node and a *load information collection policy* which maintains a current load state (partial or global) of the machine. The load computation function can combine several load indications : the length of the CPU queue, the rate of the memory occupancy, the rate of the CPU utilization, the rate of communications in the network, and so on. The load information collection policy has a structure which can be either centralized, hierarchical or distributed. In the centralized case, the global load indication can be saved on a single node, the server (master). It can also be broadcast to all the other nodes (the slaves). The exchange of load information between nodes can be either continue, relative, explicit or periodical [11].

The transfer agent decides on transfers of processes. It is generally based on a threshold. A node exports load if its local load is over a certain threshold. The problem is how to choose the value of this latter.

The location agent determines the node where to transfer or create processes. It can be either blind or intelligent. Distribution methods with a blind location agent such as cyclic and random ones do not use load information [2]. An intelligent location agent chooses the node where an activity has to be created

---

[1] **PARAll**élisme et **L**angages **F**onctionnels
[2] **PA**rallélisme **LO**giciel et **MA**tériel
[3] The overall system performance is often measured as the average response time of the nodes of the machine and the variance of the individual time responses of the latter

or transferred depending on the load information provided by the information agent. The least loaded node is generally chosen. More precisions about load balancing can be found in [7, 11].

Within the framework of the load balancing of distributed irregular applications, our main purpose is to propose an algorithm with an information agent which produces a current load information without inducing too much communication overhead. We also aim at including in our algorithm a location agent which prevents taking decisions which may lead to a flood of nodes. The information agent of our scheme uses a combination of relative and periodic information exchange protocol. Unlike the most load balancing algorithms using periodic information exchange policies, the period we use is adaptive and its initial and lower values are determined in accordance with the execution target architecture and the underlying programming environment. Our location agent includes a technique which inhibits the flood of nodes. To minimize the overhead induced by the load balancing system, we use a thread-based implementation of the algorithm. The next section describes our load balancing policy for distributed irregular applications.

3 ALBA : An Adaptive Load Balancing Algorithm

3.1 The information agent

3.1.1 The load computation function

An analysis of the influence of the load indications on an application execution performance is done in [1]. It is shown that the length of the CPU queue has a big influence on the load balancing performance. However, it can be revealed a bad indication for very irregular applications because processes are generally of important duration of life range. If the processes are lightweight (threads) then this range is not high, and then the number of threads in the CPU queue is more accurate and so a good load information is guaranteed. The choice of the load indication depends on the nature of the application and the used environment. For the IDA* applied to the 15-puzzle problem (presented in section 6) and executed in a multithreaded context, we used the number of active (ready to be executed) threads to estimate the load of any node. We did not consider the waiting threads because their resumption in the application does not require a long time and so they do not reveal a good future indication load.

3.1.2 An adaptive load information collection policy

The load information collection policy [8] is composed of two types of processes $S\_PROCESS$ and $M\_PROCESS$ which cooperate according to a master/slave scheme (see figure 1). One process of the first type is delegated to each node to compute the local load indication (lli) and then sends it to the $M\_PROCESS$ process. One process of the second process type is created on a single node, the one which starts the application. This process uses the global **load** indication (gli), composed by all the local load indications sent up by the $S\_PROCESS$ processes, in order to compute the global **load state** indication (*glsi*) of the machine. This information is then broadcast to all the nodes. *glsi* is a table of all the *lightly loaded* nodes of the machine. A lightly loaded node is a node with a local load indication under a certain threshold. We fixed this threshold equal to 5 empirically using IDA* applied to the 15-puzzle problem.

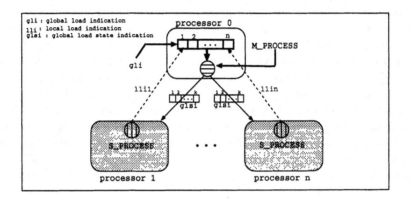

Fig. 1. The information agent of *ALBA*

The load information collection policy *periodically* computes the local loads and consults the global load. The used periods are *adaptive*. Moreover, the load information exchange is *relative*. Firstly, the local load computation is periodical because each *S_PROCESS* calculates its own *lli* at intervals of time named *L_DELAY*. The global load consultation is periodical because it is done by the *M_PROCESS* at intervals of time called *G_DELAY*. Secondly, the periods are adaptive because both the above delays are continually updated during the application execution according to the variation of the load (local or global) in the machine. The next section presents the mathematical formulation of these delays. Thirdly, the information exchange is relative because on the one hand, each *S_PROCESS* sends up its *lli* only if this information has changed[4] in comparison with the last computed value. On the other hand, the brodcast of *glsi* is done only in the case when there exists at least one node in which *lli* has varied in comparison with the last time when a broadcast or a broadcast attempt has been carried out.

3.1.3 Calculation of the delays

Before giving the formulæ we must define two concepts : *the factor r_l of local load variation* and *the factor r_g of global load variation*.

Definition 1 : the factor of local load variation in the processor j between two adjacent moments of *lli* measurement t_i and t_{i+1} is expressed as follows :

$$r_l(j) = \frac{|lli_j(t_{i+1}) - lli_j(t_i)|}{Max(lli_j(t_i), lli_j(t_{i+1}))}$$

---

[4] of two active threads for example in the IDA* applied to the 15-puzzle problem.

Definition 2 : **the factor of global load variation** in a machine of n nodes between two adjacent moments of gli consultation t_i and t_{i+1} is expressed as follows :

$$r_g = \frac{1}{n} \sum_{j=1}^{n} \frac{|gli[j](t_{i+1}) - gli[j](t_i)|}{Max(gli[j](t_i), gli[j](t_{i+1}))} \tag{1}$$

These two factors belong to $[0,1]$. They are used for the computation of the delays, this is why these delays are adaptive. Their interest is to reveal the load variations in the machine. If the factor of local (respectively global) load variation of a given node is null then there is no load variation in that node (respectively machine). On the contrary, if these factors are not null then they measure the load variation. The formulæ expressing the delays are given below, they are recurrent. In these expressions, t_i and t_{i+1} are two successive moments of the execution, t_0 is the moment when the execution of the load balancing algorithm is started, $r_l(j)$ and r_g designate the factors defined above and r_1 and r_2 are two constants empirically fixed and respectively equal to 0.01 and 0.1. *INIT_DELAY* is a parameter computed in section 3.1.4.

a) Expression of L_DELAY in a given node j

    ●$L\_DELAY(t_0) = INIT\_DELAY$

$$\bullet \ L\_DELAY(t_{i+1}) = \begin{cases} (1 - r_l(j)).L\_DELAY(t_i) & if \ \ r_1 \leq r_l(j) \leq r_2 \\ (1 - r_2).L\_DELAY(t_i) & if \ \ r_l > r_2 \\ (1 + r_1).L\_DELAY(t_i) & if \ \ r_l < r_1 \end{cases}$$

b) Expression of G_DELAY

    ● $G\_DELAY(t_0) = INIT\_DELAY$

$$\bullet \ G\_DELAY(t_{i+1}) = \begin{cases} (1 - r_g).G\_DELAY(t_i) & if \ \ r_1 \leq r_g \leq r_2 \\ (1 - r_2).G\_DELAY(t_i) & if \ \ r_g > r_2 \\ (1 + r_1).G\_DELAY(t_i) & if \ \ r_g < r_1 \end{cases}$$

A similar expression of G_DELAY is used in [12] with a difference in the computation of r_g. A comparison between the two expressions is done in [8]. It is shown with help of an example that our formula is more reliable.

Let us now explain the interest of the boundaries r_1 and r_2 of the factors of load variation. The two parameters are very necessary to control the update frequency of the delays. Indeed, when the system is stable (r_l, $r_g \rightarrow 0$), the delays increase with a rate equal to r_1, which makes it possible to avoid an unfruitful information exchange. On the other hand, if the system is very fluctuating, the factors of the load variation grow rapidly. Therefore, the delays decrease with an important slope which allows to get a current state but induces too much communication overhead. That is why we have introduced the parameter r_2, in order to lower the decreasing slope of the delays. Nevertheless, this solution is not sufficient. Indeed, when the fluctuation of the system lasts a long time, the delays inevitably tend to 0 leading to a collapse of the system. We have observed this phenomenon on a farm of DEC/ALPHA nodes. To overcome this problem, we must lower the sequence of delays. Let us call the limit *LOW_DELAY*. The question to be answered is how to fix this value? The answer is given in the next section. The computation of the initial value of the delays is also presented.

3.1.4 Calculation of LOW_DELAY and INIT_DELAY

Before giving the computation formulæ, let us introduce the concept of the *session of load information*.

Definition 3 : a **session of load information** is the period of time going from the moment when all the *S_PROCESS* send up their local loads to the moment when they receive the global load state indication *glsi* broadcat by the *M_PROCESS*.

Let us name d_{si} the duration of one session of load information. In section 4.2 we give the values of d_{si} obtained on a farm of DEC/ALPHA nodes under the PM^2 programming environment (it uses the PVM[3] communication interface). These values are functions of the number n of the nodes in the machine. We can express *LOW_DELAY* and *INIT_DELAY* as follows :

$$LOW\_DELAY = \alpha . d_{si} \text{ and } INIT\_DELAY = \beta . d_{si}$$

The values of α and β used in our implementation are given in the section 4.2.

3.2 The transfer and location agents

The question of process transfer rises at the process creation. No process transfer decision passes by the master node. Therefore, the transfer agent is totally distributed. Two criteria are considered : the granularity of the processes and the load conditions of the machine. The granularity criterion is expressed in section 6.3. The load conditions of the machine are supplied by the information agent. A process transfer is decided on a given node when this latter is not lightly loaded and the version of *glsi* in that node is not empty (i.e. there is no lightly loaded node).

If a process transfer is decided by the transfer agent, the location agent uses the *glsi* table to select the target node of the transfer. Because nodes receive the same *glsi*, it is possible for several nodes to select the same transfer target node from their local versions of *glsi*. This leads to a flood of the selected node. To alleviate this problem each node uses a pointer called *next* to indicate the next transfer target node. The initial value of *next* in each node is *numNode + 1 modulo ll*, where *numNode* is the index of the node and *ll* is the number of the lightly loaded nodes in *glsi*. After each process transfer the location agent increases *next* and decreases *ll*. Consequently, a node selected between two broadcasts of *glsi* can not be selected another time.

4 Implementation of ALBA

4.1 The underlying architecture

The underlying architecture to our algorithm implementation is a farm of 16 DEC/ALPHA processors (133 MHz clock, 64 MegaByte RAM and 1 GigaByte Disc) interconnected by an Ethernet network (10 Mbps). The farm operates under OSF/1 operating system.

4.2 The underlying programming environment

We firstly investigated a task-based approach using the PVM environment. With this approach we have seen the necessity of the thread-based approach. We used PM^2 for this latter. The two following sections present the two approaches and the corresponding used environments.

4.2.1 The PVM environment for a task-based approach

With this approach, the *M_PROCESS* and *S_PROCESS* are tasks (heavyweight processes). The *M_PROCESS* holds in its local memory the *gli* table. The sending up of the local loads *lli* by the *S_PROCESS* to the *M_PROCESS* is done by message passing. The processing of the messages is an update of the *gli* table. On the other hand, the broadcast of the *glsi* table to all the *S_PROCESS* is also done by using message passing. The processing of the messages is an update of the local version of the *glsi* table. All these communications are done with the respect of the above delays *L_DELAY* and *G_DELAY*. For managing both delays two other heavyweight processes called *alarms* are used, one for each of *M_PROCESS* and *S_PROCESS*. The communications between the two processes and their alarms are done by using signals. After each *L_DELAY* (respectively *G_DELAY*) delay, the alarm associated with *S_PROCESS* (respectively *M_PROCESS*) sends a signal to the latter. The handler of the signal executed by each *S_PROCESS* consists of computing the local load and eventually sending it up to the *M_PROCESS*. The handler of the signal executed by the *M_PROCESS* consists of computing the *glsi* table and eventually broadcasting it to the *S_PROCESS*. Consequently, PVM primitives may be called in handling the signals. In addition to the problems of a task-based approach quoted in section 4, we have been confronted in this solution to the problem of signal handling : PVM is neither signal-safe nor reentrant, so using signals under PVM is a "gas works". Therefore, a thread-based approach is necessary to avoid such problems.

4.2.2 The PM^2 environment for a thread-based approach

We used the PM^2 environment defined in [9] for the implementation with a thread-based approach. PM^2 is a layer above PVM which integrates a set of functionnalities (remote creation of threads, migration, etc) which allow programming with distributed threads. The main primitive of this platform is the

"Lightweight Remote Procedure Call" (LRPC) which can be synchronous, asynchronous or asynchronous with deferred waiting. The latter enables a thread to do local processing while it is waiting for results from other threads.

Our load balancing algorithm is implemented using asynchronous LRPC. The M_PROCESS and S_PROCESS, the global load indication (gli) update and the global load state indication ($glsi$) update are asynchronous LRPC. Under these implementation considerations, the curve of the duration d_{si} of one session of load information obtained with a series of measures is shown in figure 2. According to this figure, d_{si} can be expressed by linear interpolation as follows :

$$d_{si} = 2.7.n + 0.3$$

Let us remember that the interest of computing d_{si} is to calculate the values of LOW_DELAY and INIT_DELAY expressed in section 3.1. For the IDA* applied to the 15-puzzle problem, we fixed α and β as follows : α=2 and β=10. So, the expressions of LOW_DELAY and INIT_DELAY become the following ones :

$$LOW\_DELAY\,(in\ ms) = 5.4.n + 0.6 \quad and \quad INIT\_DELAY\,(in\ ms) = 27.n + 3$$

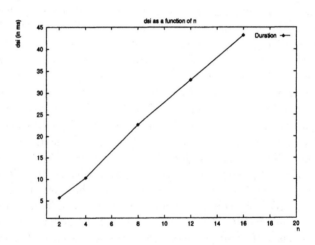

Fig. 2. d_{si} as a function of the number of nodes

5 Application : IDA* applied to the 15-puzzle problem

5.1 The IDA* algorithm

IDA*(Iterative-Deepening A*) [6] is a depth-first search algorithm used in artificial intelligence. IDA* performs repeated cost-bounded search over a search space using two functions g and h. For a node n of the space, $g(n)$ is the cost of searching n from the initial node and $h(n)$ is the estimated cost of searching a nearest goal node from n. In each iteration the algorithm expands nodes until the total cost $g(n)+h(n)$ of a selected node exceeds a given threshold. For the first iteration this threshold is equal to the cost of the initial node. For a new iteration, the threshold is equal to the minimum of all the minimum node costs that exceed the threshold of the previous iteration. The search continues until a goal node is found. Parallelism can be considered in exploring the search space.

5.2 The 15-puzzle problem

The 15-puzzle [6] is a 4x4 square tray containing 15 square tiles, each of these carries a number between 1 and 15. The sixteenth tile is uncovered and called the *blank*. The problem consists of transforming an initial configuration of the square into a final one[5] by sliding step by step the tiles adjacent to the *blank* into the space occupied by this latter. For example, the figure (3.a) shows the initial configuration of the 15-puzzle problem number 12 given in [6][6]. The final configuration of the 15-puzzle problem is shown in figure (3.b). The configuration obtained at each step represents a node of the search space. IDA* is used to explore all the generated nodes.

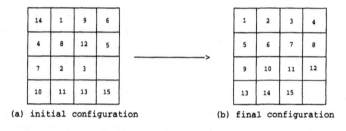

(a) initial configuration   (b) final configuration

Fig. 3. The configuration number 12 of the 15-puzzle problem

5.3 IDA* applied to the 15-puzzle problem

We have implemented a multithreaded version of IDA* applied to the 15-puzzle problem on a farm of DEC/ALPHA processors under PM^2. For the 15-puzzle problem, the function h(n) of IDA* designates the sum of the Manhattan distances [10] of the node n, this means the sum of the differences of the lines and columns between the configuration associated with the node n and the final one. The exploration of the search space of the problem is done by using asynchronous LRPC with deferred waiting. Initially, one thread is created to start the exploration at the root of the search space (tree). Then, this thread creates other threads to explore different sub-trees of the search tree. These threads in turn generate other threads and so on. Two kinds of threads are used : *fertile* threads and *sterile* (or sequential) ones. Unlike *fertile* threads, the *sterile* threads

---

[5] a configuration where the numbers in the tiles are ordered.
[6] 100 randomly generated configurations are presented in [6]

sequentially explore sub-trees without generating other ones, i.e. without calling the transfer and location agents of *ALBA*. The root n of the sub-tree explored by each *sterile* thread verifies the following condition :

$$|g(n) + h(n) - threshold\ of\ iteration| \leq 4$$

This condition determines the grain of the *sterile* threads, i.e. the size of the sub-tree to be explored by each *sterile* thread. The boundary 4 has been chosen after several tests with the values 2, 4, 6, 8, 10 and 12. The tests reveal that the value 4 gives the best results.

The load balancing problem concerns all the threads generated to explore the search tree. At the generation of each exploration thread, if the transfer agent of *ALBA* decides of its transfer the location agent is called to determine its target execution node on the basis of the load information supplied by the information agent. Therefore, the strategy of *ALBA* is *active* or *source-initiative*.

5.4 Preliminary results

The application has been experimented on some instances of the 15-puzzle problem presented in [6]. Before choosing the instances to be tested, we have classified the different problem instances. The classification criterion is the duration of the sequential search (the application execution on a single node) of the solutions corresponding to the instances. These durations are those given in [4] for the execution on the same machine i.e. a farm of DEC/ALPHA processors. Three classes are identified : *light*, *normal* and *heavy*. These classes contain the instances executing in about respectively few seconds, few minutes and few hours. Three configurations are selected from each class. The table 1 shows the configurations precisely chosen, they are given outside the brackets in the second column. They are those of about 10, 20 and 30 seconds for the *light* class and 10, 20 and 30 minutes for the *normal* class. For the *heavy* class, we have considered those of the longest duration of the sequential search on a single node according to [4]. The table 1 shows the average relative speed-up[7] and the efficiency[8] obtained with 16 processors for each class of configurations. These preliminary results point out that the speed-up and the efficiency are weak for *light* configurations. This is due to the time spent in the initial distribution of work, this is important relatively to the total duration of the search tree exploration. In this case, the nodes of the machine are not fully used and there is no overlapping between the space search exploration and the communications involved in load balancing. The results also show that the speed-up and efficiency grow with the growing of the total duration of the solution search. They become very important for the heavy configurations. For these configurations, the communications induced in the work distribution are overlapped by the search tree exploration thanks to the thread-based approach of the implementation.

---

[7] speed-up = The execution time on a single node/The parallel execution time on 16 nodes

[8] efficiency = The speed-up/The number of nodes of the machine.

We can conclude that the multithreaded parallel execution of IDA* applied to the 15-puzzle problem with *ALBA* is efficient. In the near future, we will experiment the performance of *ALBA* on the whole hundred configurations in order to compare our results to those obtained in [5].

Table 1. IDA* applied to the 15-puzzle problem : preliminary results

class	configurations with their sequential duration execution	average relative speed-up	efficiency
light	28(11.3s), 78(20.5s), 23(29.7s)	6.45	0.40
normal	27(9.2 min), 32(20.5 min), 63(29.6 min)	12.45	0.77
heavy	60(1h45), 82(2h52), 88(3h19)	14.83	0.92

6 Conclusions and future work

We proposed a dynamic load balancing algorithm called *ALBA*. This algorithm uses an adaptive load information collection policy. The calculation of the load information is relative but their exchange is periodical. The used periods are computed as functions of the load variation in the machine. For the implementation of *ALBA*, we used a thread-based approach in order to overlap the involved communications. The results obtained on a multithreaded version of the IDA* algorithm applied to some instances of the 15-puzzle problem are encouraging.

In the future, we will focus our work on the following points :

- improving the performance measurements by :
  - comparing the performances of *ALBA* with those of blind (random and cyclic) methods ;
  - experimenting *ALBA* on the whole hundred instances of the 15-puzzle problem in order to compare our work to others [5] ;
  - considering a broader range of test problems. The next application to be experimented is another kind of irregular problems, it is about the parallel evaluation of functional languages (PARALF project).
- enhancing the scalability of *ALBA* by extending it to a hierarchical algorithm. An outline of solution is to consider that the information agent is a recursive application of the one given above to the different layers of the hierarchical algorithm. The transfer and location agents are the same than the ones of *ALBA* with a difference in the considered load state. Indeed, the hierarchical algorithm will not maintain a global load state in the machine but a partial one. That is to say the load state of each cluster. Consequently, the target node of a load transfer is chosen between the lightly loaded nodes of the cluster.

Acknowledgments

Many thanks to Dr. E-G. Talbi and Z. Hafidi for all the discussions we had on respectively dynamic load balancing and the IDA* algorithm applied to the 15-puzzle problem.

References

1. S. Dowaji. *Contribution à l'étude des problèmes d'équilibrage de charge dans les environnements distribués.* PhD thesis, Université de Versailles, 1995.

2. D. Eager, E. Lazowska, and J. Zahorjan. Adaptive Load Sharing In Homogeneous Distributed Systems. *IEEE Transactions on Software Engeneering*, SE–12(No.5):662–675, 1986.

3. A. Geist, A. Beguelin, J. Dongarra, and al., editors. *PVM : Parallel Virtual Machine, A User's guide and tutorial for Networked Parallel Computing.* MIT Press, 1994.

4. Z. Hafidi. Parcours parallèle IDA* sous PVM. *Mémoire de DEA. Université de Lille I (LIFL)*, 1994.

5. Z. Hafidi, E.G. Talbi, and G. Goncalves. Load balancing and parallel tree search : The MPIDA* algorithm. *Parco'95 proc. Gent Belgium*, Sept 1995.

6. R. E. Korf. Depth-first iterative-deepening : An optimal admissible tree search. *Artificial Intelligence*, Vol. 32(No. 27):97–109, Feb 1985.

7. N. Melab. Synthèse des méthodes de distribution statique et dynamique de la charge sur architectures MIMD. Etude de cas : langages fonctionnels. *Publication interne. Univ. de Lille I, LIFL*, (AS–94–160), Oct 1994.

8. N. Melab, N. Devesa, M.P. Lecouffe, and B. Toursel. An Adaptive Load Information Collection Policy. *Int. Conf. on Parallel and Distributed Processing Techniques and Applications (PDPTA'96), Sunnyvale, California, USA*, 9–11 Aug 1996.

9. R. Namyst and J.F. Méhaut. PM^2 : Parallel Multithreaded Machine. A computing environment for distributed architectures. *Parco'95 proc. Gent Belgium*, Sept 1995.

10. N.J. Nilsson. Principles of artificial intelligence. *Palo Alto, CA:Tioga*, 1980.

11. E. G. Talbi. Allocation dynamique de processus dans les systèmes distribués et parallèles : Etat de l'art. *Publication interne. Univ. de Lille I, LIFL*, (AS–95–162), Jan 1995.

12. J. Xu and K. Hwang. Heuristic Methods for Dynamic Load Balancing in A Message-Passing Supercomputer. *IEEE*, pages 888–897, Apr 1991.

Manufacturing Progressive Addition Lenses using Distributed Parallel Processing

José M. Cela[1], Juan C. Dürsteler[2] and Jesús Labarta[1]

[1] European Center for Parallelism at Barcelona (CEPBA),
Universidad Politécnica de Cataluña, SPAIN, (cela@ac.upc.es)
[2] Research Department of INDO S.A., SPAIN, (Dus@indo.es)

Abstract. We describe a distributed parallel implementation of a Finite Element simulation used in the ophthalmic optics industry. We use non overlapped domain decomposition methods to perform the parallelization on a cluster of workstations. Different numerical techniques was implemented, and the code was tuned with performance analyzer for distributed parallel programs.

1 Introduction

In this article we describe how parallel computing was introduced to improve economically and technically the manufacture of a kind of ophthalmic lens, progressive addition lens (PAL). A PAL is a type of lens one of which faces is designed so that the focal distance varies continuously between the upper and the lower parts of it. This variation in the focal distance is due to the fact that the curvature of the lens variates continuously.

A new method to manufacturing a PAL was defined in [4]. In this method a pre-made spherical lens is deformed by thermo-moulding on a refractory mould. This mould is shaped with the surface obtained in design cycle. This process does not need a high accuracy, because small irregularities in the mould will not be copied. Once the refractory mould is made, a polished spherical lens blank is placed onto the mould. The ensemble is passed through a furnace, inside of which it suffers a temperature cycle that leads it to the softening point. As the lens reaches to this temperature, it slumps smoothly onto the mould. Then, the shape of the mould is copied to both sides of the lens blank. The outer surface, which is the important one, does not lose its polish in the process, it only copies the overall shape. Finally the inner surface of the lens is ground, lapped and polish spherically to the desired prescription. There is a drawback in the thermo-moulding process, as the lens blank has considerable thickness, the outer surface does not exactly reproduce the shape ground in the mould. This means that a correction has to be found for the shape of the mould in order to obtain the desired shape in the lens. This correction was found in the past with experimental measures on prototypes. This is a lengthy procedure, as between producing a prototype and modifying the design to restart the cycle, 3 to 4 days are required. Then, to obtain the desired correction by this way can last about

8 to 10 months. For this reason the introduction in this process of a computer simulation which reduces the number of prototypes is critical for its competitiveness. Moreover, the number of variations which must be analyzed require a short execution time for one simulation, then is natural to introduce the parallel computing technology. As in all industrial processes, economical requirements are fundamental. Lens manufacturers are medium enterprises which do not want to pay for expensive, non standard parallel machines. The parallel technology was introduced in these medium enterprises using clusters of workstations joint with a software environment which guarantees portability of the developed programs. In our case the hardware was a cluster of IBM workstations (R60000 processors) and the software platform selected was the Parallel Virtual Machine (PVM) [6].

2   Physical model and mathematical approach

The thermo-moulding process is considered as a non isothermal transient incompressible creeping flow of a Newtonian liquid. The characteristic of this flow is that the liquid domain vary with time and the boundary conditions have to be updated at each time instant. The basic set of modeling equations are the Navier-Stokes equations written with some creeping flow assumptions, i.e., non transport and incompressible flow, Newtonian isotropic fluid, heavy fluid (the gravity effects must be considered), the pressure is eliminated by a penalty method and the boundary conditions are linearized. After some mathematical manipulations two parabolic PDEs need to be solved, the first one models the temperature in the glass (T), and the second one models the velocity (v) of the glass particles under the gravity field.

$$\rho C_p \frac{\partial T}{\partial t} - \nabla(K \nabla T) = 0 \qquad (1)$$

$$\rho \frac{\partial v}{\partial t} - \nabla \sigma - \rho g = 0 \qquad (2)$$

where C_p is the specific heat, K is the diffusion coefficient of the heat in the liquid glass, ρ is the density, g the gravity field and σ is computed as:

$$\sigma = \lambda \nabla v I + \mu(\nabla v + \nabla v^t) \qquad (3)$$

where λ is the bulk viscosity, μ is the classical viscosity, and I is the identity matrix. The coupling between the thermal and the dynamic problem occurs with the dependence of the coefficients with T.

At each instant the boundary Γ of the computational domain is split into two non overlapped boundaries. A free boundary Γ_f and a contact boundary with the mould Γ_c. We define $\mathbf{n}$ as the normal to Γ_f or Γ_c. Γ_f is assumed to be unconstrained for the dynamic problem: $\sigma \mathbf{n} = 0$. On Γ_c there is a non slip contact condition: $v = 0$. Boundary conditions for the thermal problem are fitted to functions depending on the position and the time both in Γ_f and in Γ_c. During an initial phase only the thermal problem is analyzed, until a fraction of the lens volume reaches a fraction of the Littleton temperature, then the dynamic problems starts to be analyzed.

In our target problem explicit methods require a extremely small time step to be stable, for these reason we use an implicit method (Crank-Nicholson) for time integration. An unstructured finite elements mesh was used for the spatial discretization. Thus, the simulation program is a time loop where the following steps are performed in sequence: 1. Compute the new time step; 2. Compute T from equation (1); 3. Update the values of the coefficients; 4. Compute v from equation (2); 5. Modify the geometry of the mesh; 6. Update the boundary conditions.

3 Parallelization of the simulation

Points 1, 3, 5 and 6 in the simulation algorithm can be done in parallel without any communication between the parallel processes. The computational kernel of the simulation algorithm are points 2 and 4. In these points we must to assembly a matrix and then solve a large sparse linear system like the following in each time step:

$$Ax = b \qquad (4)$$

To solve (4) we consider preconditioned iterative Krylov subspace methods. In the following we describe the solvers for a generic non symmetric matrix, however other specific possibilities (symmetric positive defined) were considered in the developed code, but we omit details about them. The needed accuracy in terms of residual norm goes from 10^{-8} to 10^{-12} for the dynamic problem, and from 10^{-3} to 10^{-6} for the thermal problem.

Our target architecture is a cluster of workstations, those parallel computers require a coarse grain parallelization to obtain a good performance. Several data distributions were considered in the past to perform a coarse grain parallelization, but one of the most successful are those based on non overlapped Domain Decomposition methods. The problem of generating an *optimal* domain decomposition is in general NP-complete [5]. However, in some situations is possible to perform a quasi-optimal domain decomposition using simple partitioning methods. This is our case due to the simple geometry of a lens blank; it is a curved cylinder section without any hole.

If a domain decomposition has been performed, then ordering firstly internal unknowns and secondly boundary ones, a block arrow structured matrix like the following is obtained:

$$\begin{pmatrix} A_{ii}^{(1)} & & & A_{ib}^{(1)} \\ & \ddots & & \vdots \\ & & A_{ii}^{(P)} & A_{ib}^{(P)} \\ A_{bi}^{(1)} & \cdots & A_{bi}^{(P)} & A_{BB} \end{pmatrix} \begin{pmatrix} x_i^{(1)} \\ \vdots \\ x_i^{(P)} \\ x_B \end{pmatrix} = \begin{pmatrix} f_i^{(1)} \\ \vdots \\ f_i^{(P)} \\ f_B \end{pmatrix} \qquad (5)$$

The k-th process stores the $A_{ii}^{(k)}$, $A_{ib}^{(k)}$ and $A_{bi}^{(k)}$ sub-matrices. The sub-matrix A_{BB} is distributed by blocks of rows among the processes. The group of rows stored by one process are those associated with the boundary nodes assigned to this process/domain. We call $A_{bb}^{(k)}$ the sub-matrix of the same size that A_{BB} formed by the set of rows of A_{BB} assigned to the k-th process and zero somewhere else. All the sub-matrices ($A_{ii}^{(k)}$, $A_{ib}^{(k)}$, $A_{bi}^{(k)}$, $A_{bb}^{(k)}$) are stored in a sparse format to exploit their internal sparsity.

With respect to the storage of the vectors, each process stores the part associated with its internal unknowns. The part of the vectors associated with boundary unknowns is replicated among all the processes. Note that one process does not need all the boundary vector, it only needs those parts of the boundary vector associated with its neighbor domains. We use the following notation for the vectors: $y_i^{(k)}$ is the vector associated with the internal unknowns of the k-th process, $y_b^{(k)}$ the vector associated with the boundary unknowns of the k-th process, and $y_B^{(k)}$ is the set of y_b vectors stored by the k-th process, i.e., it is the union of $y_b^{(k)}$ with the vectors $y_b^{(i)}$ where $i \in Neigh(k)$. We denote by $Neigh(k)$ the set of neighbors of the k-th domain.

An iterative method to solve (5) can be applied directly to the matrix A using the Domain Decomposition data distribution to parallelize the algorithm. We call this option Whole Matrix Solvers (WMS). A second option to solve (5) is to apply an iterative method to the Schur complement system,

$$\left(A_{BB} - \sum_{k=1}^{P} A_{bi}^{(k)} A_{ii}^{(k)^{-1}} A_{ib}^{(k)} \right) x_B = f_B - \sum_{k=1}^{P} A_{bi}^{(k)} A_{ii}^{(k)^{-1}} f_i^{(k)} \qquad (6)$$

At the end of the iterative method only the boundary part of the solution is obtained. The internal unknowns can be computed in a parallel backward substitution. We call this option Schur Matrix Solvers (SMS).

3.1 Whole matrix solvers

All the iterative methods have four main operations: vector updates ($\mathbf{x} = \mathbf{x} + \alpha \mathbf{y}$), dot products ($\alpha = <\mathbf{x}, \mathbf{y}>$), matrix-vector multiplication ($\mathbf{y} = A\mathbf{x}$), and apply the preconditioner.

Vector updates can be done completely in parallel if the scalar α is replicated among all the processes. Dot products can be computed using a global communication algorithm which adds the contributions from all the process and broadcast the result to all the process is needed. It is well known that the best way to perform this global communication is with a binary tree algorithm which perform all the communications in $O(2\log_2 P)$ steps, where P is the number of processes. This kind of communications will be a bottleneck only if the number of processes is extremely large, in our case $P \leq 100$.

The following algorithm is executed by the k-th process to perform the matrix by vector product:

MATRIX-VECTOR PRODUCT: $\mathbf{y} = A\mathbf{x}$
$$y_i^{(k)} = A_{ii}^{(k)} x_i^{(k)} + A_{ib}^{(k)} x_B^{(k)}$$
$$y_B^{(k)} = A_{bi}^{(k)} x_i^{(k)} + A_{bb}^{(k)} x_B^{(k)}$$
For $i \in Neigh(k)$ /* Accumulate contributions */
    EXCHANGE: I send to my neighbor the proper part of my vector $y_B^{(k)}$. I
           receive from my neighbor the proper piece of its $y_B^{(i)}$ vector.
    Add the received vector to my $y_b^{(k)}$
EndFor
For $i \in Neigh(k)$ /* Replicate my part of boundary */
    EXCHANGE: I send to my neighbor my $y_b^{(k)}$ vector. I receive from my
           neighbor its $y_b^{(i)}$ vector.
EndFor

It is important to note that all the communications in this algorithm are between pairs of processes. A scheduling of these communications can be computed in the pre-processing phase of the application, in such a way that they are done in parallel as much as possible without deadlocks. Clearly, the performance of this scheduling depends on the decomposition, but for problems where a quasi-optimal decomposition is possible, this communications are not a bottleneck and a good scalability of the matrix-vector product is possible.

We have implemented a parallel incomplete factorization called PILUt as preconditioner. This preconditioner is based in the original idea of the ILUt preconditioner defined in [8]. The main difference between ILUt and PILUt is how the fill-in is controlled in the factorization process. By construction $A_{ib}^{(k)}$, $A_{bi}^{(k)}$ and $A_{bb}^{(k)}$ matrices have no null entries only in those rows/columns associated with the boundaries of the neighbors of the k-th domain. When the factorization algorithm is applied the block level fill-in is concentrate in the A_{BB} matrix, i.e., although there is fill-in also in the matrices A_{II}, A_{IB} and A_{BI}, the internal block structure of those matrices remains the same. The block fill-in in the A_{BB} matrix can be see as the addition of two consecutive block fill-ins, the first one originated by factorization of the A_{BI} matrix, and the second one due to the factorization of the A_{BB} matrix itself. Note that the first class of block fill-in is restricted by construction to the blocks of $A_{bb}^{(k)}$ associated with the boundaries of the neighbors of the neighbors of the k-th process.

Because the ILUt algorithm select a fill-in only as a function of its numerical value, there is not any control on the block structure of the L_{BB} and U_{BB} matrices. Note that a fill-in in a block which originally was a null block in the A_{BB} matrix means a communication between no neighbor processes when the triangular system must to be solve. We have introduce a new parameter **bfil** in the PILUt algorithm to select the allowed block fill-in. If **bfil** = 0 the block structure of the L_{BB} and U_{BB} matrices is the same that the block structure of the A_{BB} matrix. Then, the communications of the k-th process are restricted to its neighbors. If **bfil** = 1: The first block fill-in is allowed. Then, the k-th process has communications with its direct neighbors and with the neighbors of its neighbors. If **bfil** > 1: All the block fill-ins are allowed.

In [2] it was showed that for problems where the influence between two nodes in the mesh decreases when the distance between the nodes increases the block fill-in can be ignored without a significant reduction in the convergence of the iterative methods. Then in our target problem we select **bfil** = 0, i.e., the application of the preconditioner is a sparse triangular system solution, where the triangular factors are distributed among processors in the same way as the matrix A. Unfortunately these preconditioners limit the parallelization of the iterative method, because solving sparse triangular linear systems is a well known bottleneck. When triangular systems are solved the k-th process can not start to compute its piece of the boundary until all its previous neighbors have finished. To minimize the impact of this bottleneck a coloring technique can be applied. The coloring technique is main factor to obtain a reasonable speed-up with WMS using incomplete factorizations as preconditioner. Moreover, we have tried to reduced the critical chain when the solution vector from a color set is used to update the right hand side of the following color set. This is done by sorting the color sets by the number of connections with other color sets and the domains inside a color set by the number of connections with domains in other color sets. However, we observed that this factor does not introduce a significant improvement in the global speed-up ($\leq 15\%$).

We identified the existence of communications for which data was received much later than sent because of the fixed scheduling of receptions carried out at the source code level. In the first code structure a process does the loop on its *previous neighbors* in an specific sequence, receiving from one of them at a time and updating its local data. The order in which the receptions are done was computed at the beginning of the application and stored in a data structure. The possible imbalance of computations between the processes is not taken into account in this static scheduling decision. It is clear that never will be a perfect load balancing between processes. Then, the order in which a process receives the previously computed pieces is not the same order in which these pieces are available, and some idle time is spent by the process. Our second approach was to introduce a dynamic scheduling in which the receiver waits for a message which may come from any source process. The different updates will then be done in the order of message arrival.

3.2 Schur matrix solvers (SMS)

Working with the Schur complement instead of the whole matrix has the main advantage that for many problems the Schur matrix has a better condition number than the whole matrix. Because an iterative method requires only the product of the matrix by a vector, this can be computed using the implicit definition of S. Then, the k-th process executes the following algorithm to perform the product of the Schur matrix by a vector:

SCHUR MATRIX TIMES VECTOR: $\mathbf{y} = S\mathbf{x}$
$$q_i^{(k)} = A_{ib}^{(k)} x_B^{(k)}$$
Solve: $A_{ii}^{(k)} p_i^{(k)} = q_i^{(k)}$
$$y_B^{(k)} = A_{bi}^{(k)} p_i^{(k)} + A_{bb}^{(k)} x_B^{(k)}$$
Communications with the neighbor processes to accumulate contributions and to replicate the $y_b^{(k)}$ vector

As in the WMS the Schur matrix times vector algorithm has communications which can be scheduled in the pre-processor, overlapping a considerable number of them. The previous algorithm requires the solution of a local linear system within each domain for each iteration of the solver. The first approach is to perform a LU decomposition of the $A_{ii}^{(k)}$ matrices in the initial phase of the solver, and solve two triangular systems each time. This method has the drawback of requiring a significant amount of time at the start up of the solver. It also requires a significant amount of memory to store the $L_{ii}^{(k)}$ and $U_{ii}^{(k)}$ matrices. Although the use of local reordering techniques, like Minimum degree, may reduce these drawbacks it will not eliminate them. Another attempt may be solving the local linear systems through an iterative method. Different local iterative methods combined with different local preconditioners were tested. To ensure the convergence of the Schur method, the local iterative method must have more accuracy than the one required for the external iterative solver. Experimental results show that for the target problem the increase of accuracy goes from 2 to 4 orders of magnitude.

For SMS a preconditioner based on the diagonal blocks of the matrix A_{BB} was used. We call this preconditioner Block Diagonal (BD). The preconditioner is defined as a diagonal block matrix where each block is a block in the diagonal of the A_{BB} matrix, i.e, each block of the preconditioner is associated with the connections between the boundary nodes of a single domain. The entries in the A_{BB} matrix associated with connections between the boundaries of different domains are neglected. The justification of this preconditioner is based on the experimental observation that for many problems the reduced interface operator has a strong spatial local coupling and a weak global coupling. This observation was described by T. Chan and it was the base of the MSC(k) preconditioner [3]. Other related preconditioner was proposed by O. Axelsson [1]. He proposed to use the complete A_{BB} matrix as preconditioner, neglecting the contribution of the term $A_{BI} A_{II}^{-1} A_{IB}$. Because, in general the A_{BB} matrix will be not block diagonal, this preconditioner requires again to solve triangular systems.

Our preconditioner use the main information available in the A_{BB} matrix, neglecting the connections between different boundaries. Note that in 3-D meshes there are only two possible boundaries between domains. *Boundaries between only two domains* (surfaces), and *Boundaries between several domains*, (curves). Nodes on surfaces can be numbered in such a way that half of the surface is assigned to one domain a the other half to the other domain, then the connection between the boundary of the two domains is reduced to a line of nodes. The nodes in the curves can be number again in a strip decomposition which minimize the connections between the boundaries assigned to each domain touching the curve. We have observed that the improvement in the convergence when all the A_{BB} matrix is used as preconditioner does not compensate the communication cost needed to take into account all connections.

4   Performance experiments

In this section we present some results of the experiments carried out in order to analyze the performance of the solvers. The objective is to check the achieved parallelism and the factors that limit the performance. A large part of the results here presented have been obtained through a commercial tracing and simulation tool developed in the CEPBA [7]. Using this tool we can compare behaviors on system configurations which we have not available or which can not be devoted to performance measuring.

4.1   Performance of the matrix assembly and the matrix-vector multiplication

A previous step to solve the linear system is to assembly the sub-matrices $A_{ii}^{(k)}$, $A_{ib}^{(k)}$, $A_{bi}^{(k)}$ and $A_{bb}^{(k)}$. This algorithm has the same communication pattern that the matrix-vector multiplication. Then, we expect to obtain a high speed-up. In figure 1 the computational time in front of the communication time is showed for different number of parallel processes, the A matrix in this example has 50,000 rows. We can see that the communication time is a extremely small fraction of the total time to assembly the sub-matrices. Figure 2 shows the matrix-vector multiplication speed-up. We can see that it is quasi optimal. Then, we can conclude that both matrix assembly and matrix-vector multiplication are quasi perfectly parallelized with the domain decomposition scheme.

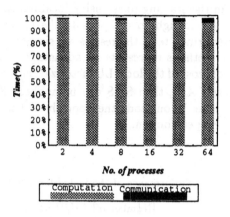

Fig. 1. Matrix assembly time

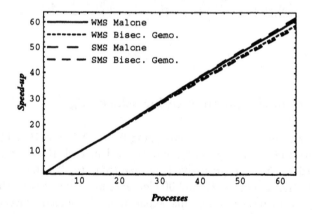

Fig. 2. Speed-up of the matrix-vector multiplication

4.2 Performance of the Schur matrix solvers

In our implementation of the SMS, the most sensitive parameter is the efficiency of the local solver in each domain. This is because our preconditioner for the Schur matrix has not any communication and the amount of extra computation has little significance. Table 1 shows the results for two test problems of 25,000 and 50,000 unknowns. The mesh was partitioned in 32 domains in both cases. The accuracy of the local iterative methods was 10^{-11} and the accuracy of the iterative method on the Schur matrix was 10^{-8}. We observe that in all the cases the time saved in the starting phase using local iterative methods is quite important, but it is not enough to compensate the increase in the time per iteration. In all the performed tests the results are similar. We conclude that to use the local iterative methods represents no advantage in our target problem. Moreover the computing cost of the local LU factorizations grows with the square of the size of the matrix $A_{ii}^{(k)}$, then SMS can be applied efficiently only if the domains are not too large. In our code the upper bound to use SMS is around 2,000 internal unknowns per domain.

Table 1. Performance of the tested local solvers

Size	Description	Number of ext. iter.	LU/ILUt comp. time	Time per iteration	Total Time
	LU	24	20.02	0.42	30.1
25000	BiCGstab+ILUt	26	2.01	3.2	85.21
	GMRES(32)+ILUt	26	2.01	2.71	72.47
	LU	35	70.65	0.46	86.75
50000	BiCGstab+ILUt	37	5.97	4.2	161.37
	GMRES(32)+ILUt	37	5.97	4.1	157.67

4.3   Influence of the communication scheduling

Several tests were done with problems going from 10,000 to 100,000 unknowns. Figure 3 shows the percentage of time decreased in each iteration of the solver when an unordered receive primitive (*"receive from any"*) is used instead of the usual ordered one. A mesh with 50,000 elements partitioned with the geometric bisection algorithm was used in this experiment. Geometric bisection was selected because it generates a relative large number of neighbors, then the results will be an upper bound of the improvement. It is clear that the improvement can be zero if the communication pattern of the triangular system solver is simple enough. For example, for the same test problem if a 1-D strip partitioning is made, the k-th parallel process has only two neighbors processes. The k-th process must receive only from one neighbor and must send only to one neighbor. Then, the time to solve the triangular system is the same for all the scheduling policies. Other experiments show us that the improvement in time used to go from 20% to 37%. Then, we conclude that the use of a *"receive from any"* communication primitive is important to obtain good speed-up with the WMS.

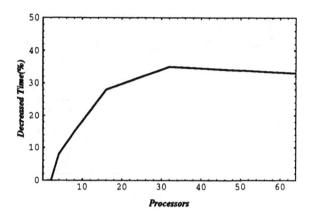

Fig. 3. Percentage of decreased time for an unordered receive primitive

4.4 WMS versus SMS

Our experiments show that SMS always converge faster than WMS both in iterations and in time. This is because the preconditioner for the Schur matrix is extremely good in our target problem. Figure 4 shows the convergence for a test problem with 50,000 unknowns partitioned in 32 domains. The iterative method was in all the cases the BiCGstab. The line marked with 1 corresponds to a WMS without preconditioner, the line marked with 2 corresponds to a WMS with a PILUt($0,10^{-}3,0$) preconditioner, the line marked with 3 corresponds to a SMS using the A_{BB} matrix as preconditioner, and the line marked with 4 corresponds to a SMS using the BD preconditioner.

About the scalability, SMS are again superior, because they have not any sequential bottleneck. However, it is also possible to obtain a good speed-up with WMS if more than one parallel task per processor is allocated. Our general conclusions are that SMS are limited by the time and memory spent computing the local LU, and WMS are limited by the performance of the triangular system solution, i.e., by the degree of parallelism achieved when coloring the domains. Due to their good convergence we have select SMS as working solvers.

4.5 Simulation results

The astigmatism measures obtained from the simulation differs from the experimental ones in about 0.25 diopters. The accuracy which allows to eliminate completely the prototypes would be about ±0.02 diopters. This is a very demanding goal, as changes in the order of microns in the surface of the lens produce changes of the order of hundredth of diopter. Nevertheless, being able to simulate our prototypes within 0.25 diopters of accuracy, enables us to distinguish between slightly different designs and reduces strongly the need to use

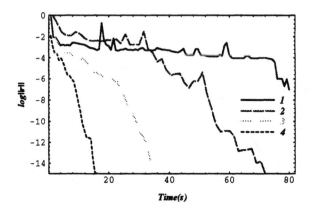

Fig. 4. Convergence of the solvers

prototypes. In fact we have reduced the work of making trials to 1/4 of what was needed when we did not have access to the computer simulations. Moreover we are now able to experience with lots of new designs that we could not have evaluated because of lack of time. This implies also a reduction in design costs, as there is possible to substitute a great deal of prototypes by computer simulations. It also implies a reduction of the overall time to market that can be estimated in about a 30% compared with the previous time of the adjusting and fine tuning of the production process.

References

1. O. Axelsson, *Iterative Solution Methods*, ISBN 0-521-44524-8, Cambridge University Press, 1994.
2. Cela, J. M.: PILUt: A parallelized incomplete factorization preconditioner. CEPBA/UPC Tech. Report No. RR-95/08, 1995.
3. Chan, T.: Boundary Probe Domain Decomposition Preconditioners for Fourth Order Problems. Proceedings of the Second International Symposium on Domain Decomposition Methods, published by SIAM, Los Angeles, January 1988.
4. Dürsteler, J. C.: Sistema de Diseño de Lentes Progresivas Asistido por Ordenador. Ph.D. Thesis, Universidad Politécnica de Cataluña, 1991.
5. Garey, M. R., Johnson, D. S.: Computers and Intractability, A guide to theory of NP-Completeness. San Francisco, CA Freeman, 1979.
6. Geist, A., Beguelin, A., Dongarra, J., Jiang, W.: PVM3 User's Guide and Reference Manual. Oak Ridge National Laboratory Technical Report ORNL/TM-12187, May 1993.
7. Labarta, J., Girona, S., Pillet, V., Cortes, T., Cela, J. M.: A Parallel Program Development Environment. CEPBA/UPC Tech. Report No. RR-95/02 (1995).
8. Saad, Y.: ILUT: a dual Threshold Incomplete LU factorization. Numerical Linear Algebra with applications, Vol. 1, No. 4, (1994) 387–402.

The Parallel Complexity of Randomized Fractals

Raymond Greenlaw[1] * and Jonathan Machta[2]**

[1] Department of Computer Science, University of New Hampshire, Durham, New Hampshire 03824, e-mail address: greenlaw@cs.unh.edu
[2] Department of Physics and Astronomy, University of Massachusetts, Amherst, Massachusetts 01003, e-mail address: machta@phast.umass.edu

Abstract. This interdisciplinary research examines several algorithms from statistical physics that generate random fractals. The algorithms are studied using parallel complexity theory. Decision problems based on diffusion limited aggregation and a number of widely used algorithms for equilibrating the Ising model are proved **P**-complete. This is in contrast to Mandelbrot percolation that is shown to be in (non-uniform) $\mathbf{AC}^0$. Our research helps shed light on the intrinsic complexity of these models relative to each other and to different growth processes that have recently been studied using complexity theory. The results may serve as a guide to simulation physics.

1 Introduction

Random fractals are an important branch of statistical physics. A number of models generate random fractals and they have been extensively studied by computer simulation methods. Often, the models are defined by the algorithms that are used to simulate them. In this paper we examine such defining algorithms from the viewpoint of parallel computation. Results in this paper are:

1. Mandelbrot percolation is in (non-uniform) $\mathbf{AC}^0$.
2. Diffusion limited aggregation (DLA) is **P**-complete.
3. Metropolis dynamics for the Ising model is **P**-complete.
4. Wolff dynamics for the Ising model is **P**-complete.
5. Swendsen-Wang dynamics for the Ising model is **P**-complete.

Motivation: First, computational complexity may serve as a guide to simulation physics. With the availability of massively parallel computers, it is important to investigate models from the perspective of parallel complexity. Another, perhaps more significant, motivation is to provide an alternative characterization of these models. An enormous amount of effort has gone into characterizing the

* This research partially supported by National Science Foundation grant CCR-9209184 and a Spanish Fellowship for Scientific and Technical Investigations 1996. Part of this research was conducted while Ray was on sabbatical at UPC in Barcelona and the department's hospitality is greatly appreciated.
** This research was partially funded by the National Science Foundation Grant DMR-9311580.

morphology of fractal patterns via critical exponents, fractal and multifractal dimensions, scaling functions, and so on. Such characterizations fail to adequately distinguish these models from the standpoint of what can be described intuitively as complexity. We believe that the intuitive notion of physical complexity is at least partially captured by the computational complexity measure of parallel time (with the number of processors appropriately restricted). This idea, in a slightly different form, has been previously proposed by Bennett [1].

In brief the idea is that simple objects can be generated quickly while complex objects require a long history for their formation. We illustrate this by comparing two fractals. On the one hand, Mandelbrot percolation [7] can be generated in (non-uniform) $\mathbf{AC}^0$. Though they are fractals, there is very little interesting morphology; the structure on each length scale is independent of the structure on other length scales. In contrast DLA [9] generates dendritic fractal patterns. DLA patterns are produced by a highly sequential algorithm that seems to require polynomial parallel time; they reflect a subtle interplay of randomness and structure on many length scales. Whether or not one accepts a definition of physical complexity in terms of computational complexity, it is interesting that a variety of models in statistical physics can be sharply separated from one another by using parallel complexity theory as a yardstick.

Our research extends a study of the complexity of a number of growth models. Ref. [4] is concerned with a fluid invasion model that generates clusters with the same statistics as DLA. This model is $\mathbf{P}$-complete. Here we show that the original random walk dynamics for generating DLA clusters is also inherently sequential. In Ref. [5] we considered a number of other growth models—invasion percolation, Eden growth, ballistic deposition and solid-on-solid growth—and showed that all of these models are in $\mathbf{NC}$. Although each of these models is less complex than DLA, each is more complex than Mandelbrot percolation.

All proofs have been omitted due to space constraints (see [6]). For many notions in complexity theory relevant to this work see [3].

2 Sampling Methods and Their Complexity

Computer scientists study decision problems whereas computational statistical physicists are usually concerned with sampling problems—generating states from some equilibrium or nonequilibrium distribution. Sampling algorithms require a supply of random numbers and produce as output a system configuration. This configuration is described by m bits representing the degrees of freedom of the system expressed in binary. One can extend the ideas of complexity theory to sampling methods by introducing probabilistic P-RAM's in which each processor is equipped with a register for generating random bits.

Instead of producing random bits dynamically one could equivalently produce the required random bits in advance and include them as inputs to a deterministic calculation. In this way a sampling method is reduced to m decision problems, one for each binary degree of freedom. An example of such a decision problem is 'Does Ising spin s_j $(1 \leq j \leq m)$ have value $+1$ after M iterations of the

Monte Carlo procedure using random numbers x_i?' The m decision problems may be run in parallel with, in the worst case, a factor of m increase in the number of processors. *Therefore, the sampling algorithm has the same parallel time requirement up to a constant factor as the associated decision problem.*

In statistical physics, the problem size is conventionally identified with the system size; the number of bits, m required to specify a system configuration. This differs from complexity theory where it is the number of bits required to state the problem that is identified as the problem size. The following definition insures that the two notions of problem size are compatible. For a given sampling method with r random inputs, o ordinary inputs and m outputs, we define the associated natural decision problem as follows. The input is of length $m + o + r$. The first m bits represent the degrees of freedom of the system. Of these bits exactly one is a 1. The position of the 1 specifies which degree of freedom of the system (e.g. which Ising spin) is to be evaluated. Since the selected degree of freedom is expressed in *unary*, the decision problem size is at least as great as the system size. This helps insure that the problems considered are in **P** and that the number of processors used will be polynomial in the input size. The next o bits are the ordinary inputs to the problem expressed in a suitably compact form. These inputs might include the size of the lattice, the temperature, the number of iterations of an elementary Monte Carlo step and other relevant parameters expressed in binary notation. The final r bits are the random bits needed for the sampling method. So that the answer or other potentially useful information is not built into these bits, we require that they be interpreted as independent random variables that take the value 1 with probability $1/2$. We restrict our attention to 'reasonable' sampling methods where r is bounded by a polynomial in m. The decision problem for a sampling method can now be studied using conventional computational complexity theory.

3   Decision Problems for the Fractal Models

Each model considered below generates random *mass fractals*—sets of 'occupied' sites whose number scales as a noninteger power of the lattice size.

Mandelbrot percolation: This random fractal was first described by Mandelbrot [7]. Mandelbrot percolation is defined on a d-dimensional lattice. It is parameterized by a rational retention factor Q ($0 \leq Q < 1$), a positive integer rescaling factor N and iteration number k. System configurations are described by a bit at each lattice site. If the bit is a 1, we say the site is 'occupied.' For purposes of illustration, we consider the two dimensional version on an $N^k \times N^k$ square lattice. A configuration is generated in the following way: at the ith step ($0 \leq i \leq k - 1$) the lattice is completely divided into, $N^i \times N^i$ non-overlapping squares and each square is independently 'retained' with probability Q. If a square is retained, the site(s) in it are not changed. If a square is not retained then all of the site(s) in it are changed to unoccupied. After k steps unoccupied regions with a wide range of sizes are typically created. The resulting set of occupied sites is a random fractal with limiting Hausdorf dimension,

$D_H = 2 + (\log Q)/(\log N)$ if $D_H > 0$.

A natural decision problem associated with Mandelbrot percolation takes as input random numbers, x_i with $0 \le x_i < 1$. These numbers are used to generate 'retention bits' that are 1 if $x_i < Q$ and 0 otherwise. Each retention bits determines whether a particular square of a given size is retained.

Mandelbrot percolation (dimension d, scale factor N, precision b)
Given: A non-negative integer k, a designated lattice site s expressed in unary with $|s| = N^{dk}$, a retention factor Q ($0 \le Q < 1$) with Q represented by a b-bit binary number (Our method of producing random numbers via coin tossing suggests this coding choice. Such a scheme does not allow all possible rationals in the interval $[0,1)$ to be represented.) and a list of $(N^{dk} - 1)/(1 - N^{-d})$ random numbers x_i with $0 \le x_i < 1$ expressed as a b-bit number.
Problem: Is site s occupied by the Mandelbrot percolation process?

The instances of Mandelbrot percolation require that the dimension, scale factor and precision are all fixed inputs. In terms of the discussion of Section 2 relating decision and sampling problems, $|s| = m$, $\lceil \log_2 k \rceil + b = o$ and $b(N^{dk} - 1)/(1 - N^{-d}) = r$.

Diffusion limited aggregation: Diffusion limited aggregation [9] is a cluster growth model where new occupied sites are added to the growing cluster one at a time. Here we illustrate DLA for a two dimensional lattice with growth initiated along a line. A random walker is started at a random position along the top edge of an $L \times L$ square lattice. The walker moves until it is a nearest neighbor of an existing occupied site at which point it joins the cluster. Initially, the bottom edge of the lattice is considered occupied. If a walk fails to join the cluster, hits the top boundary of the lattice or is unable to move (goes off the lattice or encounters a site that is occupied in its first move), it is discarded. A new random walk is started as soon as the previous walk has joined the cluster or been discarded; the process continues until a cluster of the desired size is grown.

Diffusion limited aggregation (dimension d)
Given: Three positive integers L, M_1 and M_2, a designated site s expressed in unary with $|s| = L^d$ and a list of random bits specifying M_1 walk trajectories each of length M_2 defined by a starting point on the top edge of the lattice together with a list of directions of motion.
Problem: Is site s occupied by the aggregation process?

Metropolis dynamics for the Ising model: Configurations of the Ising model are defined by spin variables, σ_i, on a lattice where each spin may take the value -1 or $+1$. The conventional way to obtain equilibrium states of the Ising model is via the Metropolis Monte Carlo algorithm. At each step of the algorithm a site i is chosen at random and the energy change, ΔE_i, for flipping the spin at this site is computed. The energy change is given by $\Delta E_i = 2J\sigma_i \sum_{<i,j>} \sigma_j$, where the summation is over nearest neighbors of site i and J is the coupling energy. If $\Delta E_i \le 0$ the spin is 'flipped' ($\sigma_i \to -\sigma_i$), whereas if $\Delta E_i > 0$ the spin is flipped with probability $e^{-\Delta E_i/T}$, where T is the temperature. After this procedure has been iterated sufficiently many times, the resulting probability distribution for the spin configurations is close to the equilibrium state.

Metropolis dynamics is governed by a random list of sites and, for each site in the list, a random number x_i with $0 \leq x_i < 1$ such that the site is flipped if $x_i \leq e^{-\Delta E_i/T}$. (To save on space in the statement of decision problems, let IN(z) stand for "A positive integer L, an initial configuration of L^d spins $\{\sigma_i\}$ with $\sigma_i \in \{-1, +1\}$, a temperature variable $Q = e^{-zJ/T}$ where Q is expressed as a b-bit binary number, and a designated site s expressed in unary with $|s| = L^d$.")

Metropolis dynamics (dimension d)
Given: IN(4), a list of M sites and a list of M random numbers x_i with $0 \leq x_i < 1$ expressed as a db-bit number.
Problem: Is $\sigma_s = +1$ after running the Metropolis algorithm?

Given the random numbers x_i we can assign *flip variables*, $g_i \in \{0, \ldots, d\}$, to each site i. For example, in three dimensions the flip variables are defined by the inequalities $g_i = 0$, if $0 \leq x_i \leq Q^3$; $g_i = 1$ if $Q^3 < x_i \leq Q^2$; $g_i = 2$ if $Q^2 < x_i \leq Q$; and $g_i = 3$ if $Q < x_i < 1$. If a site k is chosen for a possible flip at step i and $\Delta E_k/4J \leq 3 - g_i$, then the flip is carried out; otherwise, the spin is not changed. In other words, a chosen spin i will flip at step j if it has g_i or more neighbors of the opposite sign. It is clear that the Metropolis decision problem can be **NC** reduced to a version in which the random input is expressed as a list of flip variables; it is this variant of the problem that we show is **P**-complete.

Cluster dynamics for the Ising model: Cluster flipping algorithms due to Wolff [10] and Swendsen and Wang [8] are very efficient methods for generating equilibrium states of the Ising model near criticality. We illustrate the Wolff algorithm on an $L \times L$ square lattice. The starting point is a configuration of spins, $\{\sigma_j\}$. Next the bonds of the lattice are independently occupied with probability p as in bond percolation. The occupation parameter is related to the temperature, T, according to $p = 1 - Q$ with $Q = e^{-2J/T}$ and J the coupling energy between neighboring spins. A site u on the lattice is chosen at random and a cluster is grown from this site. A site v is in the cluster grown from u if there is a path from u to v such that all the bonds along the path are occupied and all the spins along the path including σ_v are equal to σ_u. The cluster of spins defined in this way is 'flipped' ($\sigma \to -\sigma$ for each σ in the cluster) which yields a new spin configuration. The procedure is iterated M times. If the temperature T is chosen to be the critical temperature and if M is sufficiently large the final configuration of spins is close to the equilibrium Ising critical point. At the Ising critical temperature, the clusters defined by the algorithm are critical droplets [2] with Hausdorf dimension, $D_H = 15/8$.

Wolff dynamics (dimension d)
Given: IN(2), a list of M sites and dML^d random numbers x_{ij} with $0 \leq x_{ij} < 1$ expressed as a b-bit number.
Problem: Is $\sigma_s = +1$ after running the Wolff algorithm?

Given the random numbers x_{ij} we can assign *bond occupation variables* b_{ij} such that $b_{ij} = 0$ if $x_{ij} \leq Q$ and $b_{ij} = 1$ otherwise. Bonds are counted as occupied if $b_{ij} = 1$. It is clear that the Wolff decision problem can be **NC** reduced to a version in which the random input is given as the b_{ij} instead of the x_{ij}. This new version is proved **P**-complete.

The Swendsen-Wang algorithm is very similar to the Wolff algorithm except that in each step of the algorithm *all* connected clusters defined by the occupied bonds are identified. All sites of each cluster are assigned the same spin value. The spin values for each cluster are determined independently by a fair coin toss. For each iteration of the Wolff or Swendsen-Wang algorithm, every bond of the lattice is occupied with probability p equal to $1 - Q$. To implement this we utilize random numbers x_{ij} with $0 \le x_{ij} < 1$ for each nearest neighbor pair (ij). The bond (ij) is occupied if x_{ij} is greater than Q. At each time step a cluster is grown from the starting point according to the occupation variables and the current spin configuration as described above. This cluster is flipped and the procedure repeated M times. For the Swendsen-Wang algorithm the problem statement requires random 'bits,' c_i equal to ± 1, to be used to determine the spins in the clusters. Sites are given a conventional ordering. Connected clusters defined by Q and the variables x_{ij} are labeled by the lowest ordered site, l, in the cluster and all the spins in the cluster are assigned the value c_l.

Swendsen-Wang dynamics (dimension d)
Given: IN(2), a number of iterations M, a list of dML^d random numbers x_{ij} with $0 \le x_{ij} < 1$ expressed as a b-bit number and a list of ML^d random bits, c_i.
Problem: Is $\sigma_s = +1$ after running the Swendsen-Wang algorithm?

References

1. C. H. Bennett. How to define complexity in physics, and why. In W. H. Zurek, editor, *Complexity, Entropy and the Physics of Information*, page 137. SFI Studies in the Sciences of Complexity, Vol. 7, Addison-Wesley, 1990.
2. A. Coniglio and W. Klein. Clusters and Ising critical droplets: A renormalisation group approach. *J. Phys. A: Math. Gen.*, 13:2775, 1980.
3. R. Greenlaw, H. J. Hoover, and W. L. Ruzzo. *Limits to Parallel Computation: P-completeness Theory*. Oxford University Press, 1995.
4. J. Machta. The computational complexity of pattern formation. *J. Stat. Phys.*, 70:949, 1993.
5. J. Machta and R. Greenlaw. The parallel complexity of growth models. *J. Stat. Phys.*, 77:755, 1994.
6. J. Machta and R. Greenlaw. The computational complexity of generating random fractals. Technical Report 95-02, University of New Hampshire, 1995.
7. B. B. Mandelbrot. *The Fractal Geometry of Nature*. Freeman, San Francisco, 1983.
8. R. H. Swendsen and J.-S. Wang. Nonuniversal critical dynamics in Monte Carlo simulations. *Phys. Rev. Lett.*, 58:86, 1987.
9. T. A. Witten and L. M. Sander. Diffusion-limited aggregation, a kinetic critical phenomenon. *Phys. Rev. Lett.*, 47:1400, 1981.
10. U. Wolff. Collective Monte Carlo updating for spin systems. *Phys. Rev. Lett.*, 62:361, 1989.

Author Index

Andonov, R. 195
Arbab, F. 131
Aykanat, C. 75

Baden, S.B. 203
Banerjee, P. 147
Bik, A.J.C. 249
Biswas, R. 35
Botorog, G.H. 263

Castillo, S. 49
Çatalyürek, Ü.V. 75
Cela, J.M. 339
Chandy, J.A. 147
Christou, I.T. 89

Dearholt, W. 49
Deshpande,V. 63
Devesa, N. 327
Diderich, C.G. 229
de Dinechin, F. 195
Dorward, S.E. 105
Dürsteler, J.C. 339

Eğecioğlu, Ö. 119
Eswar, K. 237
Everaars, C.T.H. 131

Fink, S.J. 203

Gengler, M. 229
Gonzalez, T.F. 217
Greenlaw, R. 351
Grigni, M. 319
Grote, M.J. 63

Hänssgen, S.U. 313
Hagerup, T. 1
Hennigan, G. 49
Heun, V. 287
Higaki, M. 277
Hirabayashi, R. 277
Hunt, G.C. 171

Ibarra, O.H. 159

Kohn, S.R. 203
Konuru, R.B. 237
Kuchen, H. 263

Labarta, J. 339
Lamari, M. 307
Lecouffe, M.P. 327

Machta, J. 351
Manne, F. 319
Matheson, L.R. 105
Mayr, E.W. 287
Melab, N. 327
Messmer, P. 63
Meyer, R.R. 89
Moreira, J.E. 237

Naik, V.K. 237
Nelson, R.C. 171

Oliker, L. 35

Parkes, S. 147

Rajopadhye, S. 195

Reimer, N.H. 313
Rieffel, M. 299

Sawyer, W. 63
Schreiber, R. 285
Shinano, Y. 277
Simon, H.D. 87
Smith, T.R. 201
Sohn, A. 87
Srinivasan, A. 119
Strawn, R.C. 35

Tarjan, R.E. 105
Taylor, S. 299
Tichy, W.F. 313

Toursel, B. 327
Träff, J.L. 183

de la Vaga, W.F. 307

Watts, J. 299
Wijshoff, H.A.G. 249
Wilde, D.K. 195

Yang, T. 159
Yelick, K. 145
Yu, Y. 159

Zaroliagis, C.D. 183

Springer-Verlag
and the Environment

We at Springer-Verlag firmly believe that an international science publisher has a special obligation to the environment, and our corporate policies consistently reflect this conviction.

We also expect our business partners – paper mills, printers, packaging manufacturers, etc. – to commit themselves to using environmentally friendly materials and production processes.

The paper in this book is made from low- or no-chlorine pulp and is acid free, in conformance with international standards for paper permanency.

Lecture Notes in Computer Science

For information about Vols. 1–1050

please contact your bookseller or Springer-Verlag

Vol. 1051: M.-C. Gaudel, J. Woodcock (Eds.), FME'96: Industrial Benefit and Advances in Formal Methods. Proceedings, 1996. XII, 704 pages. 1996.

Vol. 1052: D. Hutchison, H. Christiansen, G. Coulson, A. Danthine (Eds.), Teleservices and Multimedia Communications. Proceedings, 1995. XII, 277 pages. 1996.

Vol. 1053: P. Graf, Term Indexing. XVI, 284 pages. 1996. (Subseries LNAI).

Vol. 1054: A. Ferreira, P. Pardalos (Eds.), Solving Combinatorial Optimization Problems in Parallel. VII, 274 pages. 1996.

Vol. 1055: T. Margaria, B. Steffen (Eds.), Tools and Algorithms for the Construction and Analysis of Systems. Proceedings, 1996. XI, 435 pages. 1996.

Vol. 1056: A. Haddadi, Communication and Cooperation in Agent Systems. XIII, 148 pages. 1996. (Subseries LNAI).

Vol. 1057: P. Apers, M. Bouzeghoub, G. Gardarin (Eds.), Advances in Database Technology — EDBT '96. Proceedings, 1996. XII, 636 pages. 1996.

Vol. 1058: H. R. Nielson (Ed.), Programming Languages and Systems – ESOP '96. Proceedings, 1996. X, 405 pages. 1996.

Vol. 1059: H. Kirchner (Ed.), Trees in Algebra and Programming – CAAP '96. Proceedings, 1996. VIII, 331 pages. 1996.

Vol. 1060: T. Gyimóthy (Ed.), Compiler Construction. Proceedings, 1996. X, 355 pages. 1996.

Vol. 1061: P. Ciancarini, C. Hankin (Eds.), Coordination Languages and Models. Proceedings, 1996. XI, 443 pages. 1996.

Vol. 1062: E. Sanchez, M. Tomassini (Eds.), Towards Evolvable Hardware. IX, 265 pages. 1996.

Vol. 1063: J.-M. Alliot, E. Lutton, E. Ronald, M. Schoenauer, D. Snyers (Eds.), Artificial Evolution. Proceedings, 1995. XIII, 396 pages. 1996.

Vol. 1064: B. Buxton, R. Cipolla (Eds.), Computer Vision – ECCV '96. Volume I. Proceedings, 1996. XXI, 725 pages. 1996.

Vol. 1065: B. Buxton, R. Cipolla (Eds.), Computer Vision – ECCV '96. Volume II. Proceedings, 1996. XXI, 723 pages. 1996.

Vol. 1066: R. Alur, T.A. Henzinger, E.D. Sontag (Eds.), Hybrid Systems III. IX, 618 pages. 1996.

Vol. 1067: H. Liddell, A. Colbrook, B. Hertzberger, P. Sloot (Eds.), High-Performance Computing and Networking. Proceedings, 1996. XXV, 1040 pages. 1996.

Vol. 1068: T. Ito, R.H. Halstead, Jr., C. Queinnec (Eds.), Parallel Symbolic Languages and Systems. Proceedings, 1995. X, 363 pages. 1996.

Vol. 1069: J.W. Perram, J.-P. Müller (Eds.), Distributed Software Agents and Applications. Proceedings, 1994. VIII, 219 pages. 1996. (Subseries LNAI).

Vol. 1070: U. Maurer (Ed.), Advances in Cryptology – EUROCRYPT '96. Proceedings, 1996. XII, 417 pages. 1996.

Vol. 1071: P. Miglioli, U. Moscato, D. Mundici, M. Ornaghi (Eds.), Theorem Proving with Analytic Tableaux and Related Methods. Proceedings, 1996. X, 330 pages. 1996. (Subseries LNAI).

Vol. 1072: R. Kasturi, K. Tombre (Eds.), Graphics Recognition. Proceedings, 1995. X, 308 pages. 1996.

Vol. 1073: J. Cuny, H. Ehrig, G. Engels, G. Rozenberg (Eds.), Graph Grammars and Their Application to Computer Science. Proceedings, 1994. X, 565 pages. 1996.

Vol. 1074: G. Dowek, J. Heering, K. Meinke, B. Möller (Eds.), Higher-Order Algebra, Logic, and Term Rewriting. Proceedings, 1995. VII, 287 pages. 1996.

Vol. 1075: D. Hirschberg, G. Myers (Eds.), Combinatorial Pattern Matching. Proceedings, 1996. VIII, 392 pages. 1996.

Vol. 1076: N. Shadbolt, K. O'Hara, G. Schreiber (Eds.), Advances in Knowledge Acquisition. Proceedings, 1996. XII, 371 pages. 1996. (Subseries LNAI).

Vol. 1077: P. Brusilovsky, P. Kommers, N. Streitz (Eds.), Mulimedia, Hypermedia, and Virtual Reality. Proceedings, 1994. IX, 311 pages. 1996.

Vol. 1078: D.A. Lamb (Ed.), Studies of Software Design. Proceedings, 1993. VI, 188 pages. 1996.

Vol. 1079: Z.W. Raś, M. Michalewicz (Eds.), Foundations of Intelligent Systems. Proceedings, 1996. XI, 664 pages. 1996. (Subseries LNAI).

Vol. 1080: P. Constantopoulos, J. Mylopoulos, Y. Vassiliou (Eds.), Advanced Information Systems Engineering. Proceedings, 1996. XI, 582 pages. 1996.

Vol. 1081: G. McCalla (Ed.), Advances in Artificial Intelligence. Proceedings, 1996. XII, 459 pages. 1996. (Subseries LNAI).

Vol. 1082: N.R. Adam, B.K. Bhargava, M. Halem, Y. Yesha (Eds.), Digital Libraries. Proceedings, 1995. Approx. 310 pages. 1996.

Vol. 1083: K. Sparck Jones, J.R. Galliers, Evaluating Natural Language Processing Systems. XV, 228 pages. 1996. (Subseries LNAI).

Vol. 1084: W.H. Cunningham, S.T. McCormick, M. Queyranne (Eds.), Integer Programming and Combinatorial Optimization. Proceedings, 1996. X, 505 pages. 1996.

Vol. 1085: D.M. Gabbay, H.J. Ohlbach (Eds.), Practical Reasoning. Proceedings, 1996. XV, 721 pages. 1996. (Subseries LNAI).

Vol. 1086: C. Frasson, G. Gauthier, A. Lesgold (Eds.), Intelligent Tutoring Systems. Proceedings, 1996. XVII, 688 pages. 1996.

Vol. 1087: C. Zhang, D. Lukose (Eds.), Distributed Artificial Intelliegence. Proceedings, 1995. VIII, 232 pages. 1996. (Subseries LNAI).

Vol. 1088: A. Strohmeier (Ed.), Reliable Software Technologies – Ada-Europe '96. Proceedings, 1996. XI, 513 pages. 1996.

Vol. 1089: G. Ramalingam, Bounded Incremental Computation. XI, 190 pages. 1996.

Vol. 1090: J.-Y. Cai, C.K. Wong (Eds.), Computing and Combinatorics. Proceedings, 1996. X, 421 pages. 1996.

Vol. 1091: J. Billington, W. Reisig (Eds.), Application and Theory of Petri Nets 1996. Proceedings, 1996. VIII, 549 pages. 1996.

Vol. 1092: H. Kleine Büning (Ed.), Computer Science Logic. Proceedings, 1995. VIII, 487 pages. 1996.

Vol. 1093: L. Dorst, M. van Lambalgen, F. Voorbraak (Eds.), Reasoning with Uncertainty in Robotics. Proceedings, 1995. VIII, 387 pages. 1996. (Subseries LNAI).

Vol. 1094: R. Morrison, J. Kennedy (Eds.), Advances in Databases. Proceedings, 1996. XI, 234 pages. 1996.

Vol. 1095: W. McCune, R. Padmanabhan, Automated Deduction in Equational Logic and Cubic Curves. X, 231 pages. 1996. (Subseries LNAI).

Vol. 1096: T. Schäl, Workflow Management Systems for Process Organisations. XII, 200 pages. 1996.

Vol. 1097: R. Karlsson, A. Lingas (Eds.), Algorithm Theory – SWAT '96. Proceedings, 1996. IX, 453 pages. 1996.

Vol. 1098: P. Cointe (Ed.), ECOOP '96 – Object-Oriented Programming. Proceedings, 1996. XI, 502 pages. 1996.

Vol. 1099: F. Meyer auf der Heide, B. Monien (Eds.), Automata, Languages and Programming. Proceedings, 1996. XII, 681 pages. 1996.

Vol. 1100: B. Pfitzmann, Digital Signature Schemes. XVI, 396 pages. 1996.

Vol. 1101: M. Wirsing, M. Nivat (Eds.), Algebraic Methodology and Software Technology. Proceedings, 1996. XII, 641 pages. 1996.

Vol. 1102: R. Alur, T.A. Henzinger (Eds.), Computer Aided Verification. Proceedings, 1996. XII, 472 pages. 1996.

Vol. 1103: H. Ganzinger (Ed.), Rewriting Techniques and Applications. Proceedings, 1996. XI, 437 pages. 1996.

Vol. 1104: M.A. McRobbie, J.K. Slaney (Eds.), Automated Deduction – CADE-13. Proceedings, 1996. XV, 764 pages. 1996. (Subseries LNAI).

Vol. 1105: T.I. Ören, G.J. Klir (Eds.), Computer Aided Systems Theory – CAST '94. Proceedings, 1994. IX, 439 pages. 1996.

Vol. 1106: M. Jampel, E. Freuder, M. Maher (Eds.), Over-Constrained Systems. X, 309 pages. 1996.

Vol. 1107: J.-P. Briot, J.-M. Geib, A. Yonezawa (Eds.), Object-Based Parallel and Distributed Computation. Proceedings, 1995. X, 349 pages. 1996.

Vol. 1108: A. Díaz de Ilarraza Sánchez, I. Fernández de Castro (Eds.), Computer Aided Learning and Instruction in Science and Engineering. Proceedings, 1996. XIV, 480 pages. 1996.

Vol. 1109: N. Koblitz (Ed.), Advances in Cryptology – Crypto '96. Proceedings, 1996. XII, 417 pages. 1996.

Vol. 1110: O. Danvy, R. Glück, P. Thiemann (Eds.), Partial Evaluation. Proceedings, 1996. XII, 514 pages. 1996.

Vol. 1111: J.J. Alferes, L. Moniz Pereira, Reasoning with Logic Programming. XXI, 326 pages. 1996. (Subseries LNAI).

Vol. 1112: C. von der Malsburg, W. von Seelen, J.C. Vorbrüggen, B. Sendhoff (Eds.), Artificial Neural Networks – ICANN 96. Proceedings, 1996. XXV, 922 pages. 1996.

Vol. 1113: W. Penczek, A. Szałas (Eds.), Mathematical Foundations of Computer Science 1996. Proceedings, 1996. X, 592 pages. 1996.

Vol. 1114: N. Foo, R. Goebel (Eds.), PRICAI'96: Topics in Artificial Intelligence. Proceedings, 1996. XXI, 658 pages. 1996. (Subseries LNAI).

Vol. 1115: P.W. Eklund, G. Ellis, G. Mann (Eds.), Conceptual Structures: Knowledge Representation as Interlingua. Proceedings, 1996. XIII, 321 pages. 1996. (Subseries LNAI).

Vol. 1016: J. Hall (Ed.), Management of Telecommunication Systems and Services. XXI, 229 pages. 1996.

Vol. 1117: A. Ferreira, J. Rolim, Y. Saad, T. Yang (Eds.), Parallel Algorithms for Irregularly Structured Problems. Proceedings, 1996. IX, 358 pages. 1996.

Vol. 1118: E.C. Freuder (Ed.), Principles and Practice of Constraint Programming - CP '96. Proceedings, 1996. XIX, 574 pages. 1996.

Vol. 1119: U. Montanari, V. Sassone (Eds.), CONCUR '96: Concurrency Theory. Proceedings, 1996. XII, 751 pages. 1996.

Vol. 1120: M. Deza. R. Euler, I. Manoussakis (Eds.), Combinatorics and Computer Science. Proceedings, 1995. IX, 415 pages. 1996.

Vol. 1121: P. Perner, P. Wang, A. Rosenfeld (Eds.), Advances in Structural and Syntactical Pattern Recognition. Proceedings, 1996. X, 393 pages. 1996.

Vol. 1122: H. Cohen (Ed.), Algorithmic Number Theory. Proceedings, 1996. IX, 405 pages. 1996.

Vol. 1125: J. von Wright, J. Grundy, J. Harrison (Eds.), Theorem Proving in Higher Order Logics. Proceedings, 1996. VIII, 447 pages. 1996.